SOVEREIGN
FICTIONS

THINKING LITERATURE
A series edited by Nan Z. Da and Anahid Nersessian

Sovereign Fictions

POETICS AND POLITICS
IN THE AGE OF
RUSSIAN REALISM

Ilya Kliger

The University of Chicago Press
Chicago and London

PUBLICATION OF THIS BOOK HAS BEEN AIDED BY A
GRANT FROM THE BEVINGTON FUND.

The University of Chicago Press, Chicago 60637
The University of Chicago Press, Ltd., London
© 2024 by The University of Chicago
All rights reserved. No part of this book may be used or reproduced
in any manner whatsoever without written permission, except
in the case of brief quotations in critical articles and reviews. For
more information, contact the University of Chicago Press, 1427
East 60th Street, Chicago, IL 60637.
Published 2024

33 32 31 30 29 28 27 26 25 24   1 2 3 4 5

ISBN-13: 978-0-226-83186-2 (cloth)
ISBN-13: 978-0-226-83187-9 (paper)
ISBN-13: 978-0-226-83188-6 (e-book)
DOI: https://doi.org/10.7208/chicago/9780226831886.001.0001

The University of Chicago Press gratefully acknowledges the
generous support of New York University toward the publication
of this book.

Library of Congress Cataloging-in-Publication Data

Names: Kliger, Ilya, author.
Title: Sovereign fictions : poetics and politics in the age of Russian
   realism / Ilya Kliger.
Other titles: Poetics and politics in the age of Russian realism
Description: Chicago ; London : The University of Chicago Press,
   2024. | Includes bibliographical references and index.
Identifiers: LCCN 2023032763 | ISBN 9780226831862 (cloth) |
   ISBN 9780226831879 (paperback) | ISBN 9780226831886 (ebook)
Subjects: LCSH: Russian literature—19th century—History
   and criticism. | Realism in literature. | Society in literature. |
   Sovereignty in literature. | Literature and society—Russia.
Classification: LCC PG3015.5.R4 K55 2023 | DDC 891.709/003—dc23/
   eng/20230807
LC record available at https://lccn.loc.gov/2023032763

Contents

NOTE ON TRANSLITERATION
AND TRANSLATION vii

INTRODUCTION 1

CHAPTER 1 · Russian Realism:
Another Social Imaginary 10

CHAPTER 2 · State: Other Reality Effects 54

CHAPTER 3 · Family: Other Domestic
Fictions 97

CHAPTER 4 · Nation: Other Imagined
Communities 146

CHAPTER 5 · Précis: Poetics and Politics in
Russian Realism 189

EPILOGUE · Making the State Visible 235

ACKNOWLEDGMENTS 239

NOTES 243

INDEX 277

On Transliteration and Translation

In transliterating from Russian to English, I have used the Library of Congress system, modifying it occasionally to conform to customary English spellings of names of people and places. Unless noted, all translations are mine. Existing translations are quoted with occasional changes in the interest of clarity and accuracy.

Introduction

This book sets out to trace the outlines of a social imaginary ascendant during what might loosely be termed "the age of Russian realism." By "social imaginary," I mean an implicit understanding of how members of a group fit with each other, of who belongs and who doesn't, of what responsibilities belonging entails, of what can and cannot be expected of others, of how an individual can be delimited and defined.[1] Taking as axiomatic Fredric Jameson's assertion that "all literature [can] be read as a symbolic meditation on the destiny of community,"[2] I construct a poetics of Russian realist sociality, showing how a distinctive logic of human togetherness underpins the images, predicaments, and personas prevalent in the narratives of a given place and time.

When it comes to "symbolic meditation on the destiny of community," what applies to all of literature applies more conspicuously to nineteenth-century fiction, whose preoccupation with the emergent experiences of living in "society" writ large has been exhaustively documented.[3] It is this attempt to grapple with the contemporary and local social predicament—in whatever form it most fundamentally manifests itself—that I designate as "realist." More often than not, the underlying impulse overlaps with a significant number of characteristics from the following list: "third-person narrators, probable scenarios, detailed descriptions, linear narratives, present-day settings, urban milieus, domestic interiors, ordinary psychologies, everyday language, marriage plots, naturalistic objects, free-indirect style, and a maturing protagonist."[4] To be sure, even an exhaustive overview of the corpus of nineteenth-century European fiction would yield very few (if any) texts that hold consistently to all of these specifications. On the other hand, any number of these features could be present in a text that we might not designate as realist. Beyond these devices and motifs, then, realism is here understood as a hermeneutic horizon, an assumption that it is impossible to know a person, to see the outlines of a situation, to grasp the dynamics of a relationship, or indeed to ascertain anything at all properly without appealing to the broad dynamics of social life, to specifically structured circumstances of togetherness. The specific manner in which such a social hermeneutic maps onto the more conventional ontological notion of reality (what is really there? what are the facts of the matter?) will in each case be different. Notions of the "realistic," realist fiction more or less openly tells us, are effects of social relations themselves.

While none of the texts treated in this book meet all the conditions for "realism" listed above (suffice it to recall the interior monologue of a dog in *Anna Karenina*), all of them operate with a robust sociological horizon. The precise purview of the term "society" (*obshchestvo*) itself shifts over time, expanding its range of meanings until it comes to include the population as a whole. But regardless of how narrowly or broadly it is conceived, regardless even of whether it is named as such, some notion of contemporary and local sociality is central to all of the works gathered here. Precisely what that notion is, or rather what is consistent throughout a number of such notions, is the proper subject matter of what follows.

The corpus of texts with which I deal below clusters around a temporal and a generic core. According to a more traditional classification, some of them (two historical novels, a novel in verse, a narrative poem, a comedy, a semiepistolary tale—most from the 1830s) might be characterized as "Romantic" or "Sentimentalist." Yet each was repeatedly taken up, reinterpreted, and assimilated at later stages in the development of the realist hermeneutic of city, domestic, or interior life, of gender dynamics, of social stratification and injustice. I thus read these texts as *protorealist*, or even as *urrealist*, insofar as they display some of the essential tendencies of the later period in skeletal and therefore more explicit form. Partially overlapping with this historical pattern, the generic makeup of the corpus clusters around literary fiction, and especially the novel. But verse, drama, and the long narrative tale, or *povest'* (which contemporaries often did not bother to distinguish from the novel, *roman*)—and, further out, as it were, on the margins of the literary field, critical essays, personal letters, journal entries, memoirs, and so on—all are in a sense *pararealist*, responding to, deploying, and feeding back into the same depository of scripts, figures, and motifs from which the more narrowly "literary" realism selected its core material.

The book draws its case studies of Russian realism from the literary output of eleven authors. Nine of them were born within the twenty-year span between 1809 and 1829, all were male members of the (serf-owning) gentry estate, and all, at one time or another, were employed in the service of the state. One of the wagers of this book is that despite the wide range of differences among their biographical trajectories and the shapes taken by their work, it is possible to detect a consistent set of preoccupations—we might call them social-imaginary dispositions—that affected the kinds of stories these authors tended to tell. Gentry and male, they were raised as members of the state service elite and came of age within the cultural field whose status as the state enlightenment project was being reasserted within the Nicholaevian social formation.[5]

An obvious danger in such a selection consists in assuming that a more or less canonical set of texts produced by more or less well-to-do members of the privileged estate and gender can be treated as a natural subject of analysis, exhausting, or at least in some sense "representing," the literary production of the period as a whole. The danger is all the more serious given the frequency with which such an assumption has historically been made. Inheriting that history, one is hard-pressed to declare one's total independence from it, but my explicit purpose here does run contrary to the methodological premise that the work of any person or social group can "stand for" the cultural production of the social whole. Rather, I assume that just as works by nineteenth-century Russian women and nongentry male authors gravitated toward social imaginaries responsive to the social positions they occupied, so, too, did the work of the generation of gentry writers who supply the literary material for my analysis here. As a service estate, embedded within a tangled history of political collaboration and antagonism, the male gentry was positioned to interpret the social world around it with reference to figurations of the autocratic state. This estate *habitus*—its "structuring structure," or a range of practical and representational dispositions acquired by virtue of being raised into belonging to a social group[6]—is then reinforced by the pronounced dependence of the cultural field on political authority, yielding a set of preoccupations distinctive of time, place, and social position and detectable in the lives and works of the authors here at issue. Provisionally, these preoccupations can be said to converge on a social imaginary that foregrounds the figure of the state as the site of deep-seated ambivalence: the locus of harmonious togetherness and universal belonging, on the one hand, the source of coercion and illegitimate power, on the other. On a case-by-case basis, this ambivalence could manifest in hostile withdrawal, in sympathetic critique, in protest, rebellion, or enthusiastic acclamation. Social position, in other words, did not determine a narrowly conceived specific ideology but delineated a field of intensified symbolic activity. Regardless of the attitude adopted toward it, the figure of the state remained the compelling horizon against which the realist social hermeneutic was pursued.

This did not mean, of course, that other dimensions of contemporary social life—and correspondingly, other realist devices and motifs (everyday language, marriage plots, believable psychology, the maturing individual)—fell altogether out of these authors' purview. Rather, just as the active involvement of political authority (censorship, journal closures, arrests of editors and contributors) repeatedly inflected the workings of the burgeoning literary market as well as the individual biographies of the cultural producers, so, too, the devices and motifs associated with the figure of the sovereign state (elevated rhetoric, ancestral interdictions, uncontainable affects, coercive pedagogy) transmuted and reorganized the more standard realist material.[7] At work, in short, is something akin to what Yuri Tynianov called "deformation": a redeployment of inherited forms, their reduction to the status of material, organized by a new principle of construction. This principle of construction, I am suggesting, *just is* the orientation of the Russian realist social imaginary toward the figure of the state.

But all of this needs to be argued at length. For now, I would like to make clear that in pointing to the distinctiveness of Russian realist poetics and in relating it to the specific social formation within which it arose and to which it contributed, I posit nothing like an absolutely unique and separate phenomenon, a *Sonderweg* in narrative poetics. At stake, instead, is a specific articulation—among other specific articulations—of a set of shared elements belonging to the institutional and experiential ensemble of European modernity. Each such articulation may be said to highlight elements left in the shadow by others. The Russian realist hermeneutic, in particular, adumbrates the prominent role of the state within the modern social formation, a role that is often disavowed, covered up by visions of ostensibly spontaneous social process conceived as an aggregate of individual actions. In adumbrating the agency of the state, and of sovereign power in particular, the Russian realist social imaginary may be said to mount a critique, to extend a promise, and to produce an obfuscation—all at once. As critique, it makes vivid the fact that social arrangements, regarded as both infinitely complex and unpremeditated, are in fact shaped from positions of political power and bulwarked by violence. As promise, it offers a vision of the state as the locus of the common good, of universal belonging, of harmonious coexistence. As obfuscation, it repeatedly reenacts and thus reproduces a fixation on charismatic authority, cleansing violence, and melancholy frailty.

Occupied with over twenty literary (and another dozen nonliterary) texts by eleven literary (and a half dozen paraliterary) authors, this book is an exercise in what might be called "medial reading." Such reading may be opposed to both its "distant" and "close" counterparts, as long as we understand the latter two in their paradigmatic manifestations. So, for example, the kind of analysis I pursue has little recourse to the presuppositions that usually ground practices of close reading. Neither the notion of a literary work as an autonomous organic whole nor a philosophy of language that posits its essence in an infinitely subversive play of signification is relevant here. Instead, I am interested in broad patterns across a large number of stylistically and thematically different works by an ideologically diverse group of authors across a relatively large span of time. This interest rests on the assumption that such broad patterns can help us delineate the social-imaginary *langue* of the period, to describe the repository of grammatical and semantic forms that one is compelled to draw upon when one sets out to grapple narratively with the socially real.

Such an attempt to outline the compelling presuppositions of the realist hermeneutic—to write a history of the period without generals[8]—may appear, then, to share affinities with "distant" structuralist or quantitative approaches. Yet the kind of analysis I pursue is too entangled in textual detail and on subtle cadences of salience to rely on algorithmic, digital "reading." Nor is the notion of structure adequate here as long as it is statically conceived. The patterns I hope to highlight are better understood in Russian Formalist terms as "dynamic forms." At issue, in other words, is an attempt to locate subtle distinctions between what in the text counts as a constructive principle and what counts as material upon which the principle performs its deformations. Such a distinction cannot be made without a bifocal analysis that pays attention as much to intratextual dynamics as to the positioning ("orientation") of the text in relation to its proximate, extraliterary domain.[9] This is, as I have already suggested, the domain of literature's social existence, and more specifically, of its exposure—both as a field and as concrete biographical individuals—to the authority of the state. What is necessary is to see how the constructive principle, the textual trace of the social situation in which the text is produced, operates upon the customary material of realist fiction.

The first chapter of the book, then, opens with an instance of such deformation at the moment when the notion of realism—literature's mission of confronting the social "actuality" of modern life—becomes articulated in Russia. In the course of approximately a year and a half, between 1839 and 1840, the critic who came to be associated most strongly with the origin of the Russian realist tradition—Vissarion Belinsky—discovers and attempts to deploy in the service of literary criticism the philosophy of G. W. F. Hegel. My reading of Belinsky's Hegelian articles traces a series of realignments that the German philosopher's terms and patterns of thought undergo at the hands of the Russian critic. More specifically, I show how Belinsky tends to leave out of his Hegelian account of modern "actuality." Hegel's groundbreaking deduction of the domain of civil society (*bürgerliche Gesellschaft*) within the modern state. As a result, the very conception of the state undergoes a permutation and, with it, so do the narrative frameworks appropriate for the representation of individuals in their social setting.

The claim of the chapter, and indeed of the book as a whole, is that this particular deformation of Hegelianism—its assimilation in the cultural context, oriented toward a different social imaginary—anticipated the trajectory taken by much realist fiction in Russia. In order to set up the contrast while avoiding overly general accounts of Western novelistic traditions, I discuss three case studies, reading Johann Wolfgang von Goethe's *Wilhelm Meisters Lehrjahre* (1795-96), Honoré de Balzac's *Père Goriot* (1835), and Charlotte Brontë's *Jane Eyre* (1847) alongside Hegel's deduction of civil society institutions in *Elements of the Philosophy of Right* (1821). As a result of this analysis, three distinct "sociotopes" come into focus, all taking the existence and legitimacy of independent, self-interested individuals as a starting point and tracing out principles of their coming together into coherent functioning groups. These sociotopes roughly correspond to the three "sites" of aggregation that we find in Hegel's account of civil society: the "system of needs" bringing persons together in the domain of marketlike exchange (Balzac); "actualized right" projecting a vision of self-governing subjects connected to each other through their sense of duty (Brontë); and "common interest" uniting individuals who have come to identify their private desires with the interests of a group (Goethe). Needless to say, these mechanisms of aggregation do not exhaust the imaginaries organizing Western European realist fiction; they serve here merely as signposts outlining the space of social-imaginary possibilities against which Russian realist practices can be read. The rest of the chapter, then, takes up some major strains within recent Europeanist literary criticism to show how it more or less explicitly grounds nineteenth-century fiction in the sociotopes of civil society. I suggest, finally, that the social conditions in which the Russian version of literary realism arose and flourished may demand that we look for its deepest social-imaginary roots in the diverse figurations of state authority instead.

With this comparative context in the background, the four chapters that follow focus on Russian material. Chapter 2 takes up a number of works— Alexander Pushkin's *The Bronze Horseman* (written 1833), Nikolai Gogol's *Government Inspector* (1835), Mikhail Lermontov's *A Hero of Our Time* (1840), Ivan Goncharov's *The Same Old Story* (1847), Ivan Turgenev's *Rudin* (1856), Aleksei Pisemsky's *One Thousand Souls* (1858), Vasily Sleptsov's

Hard Times (1865), and Fyodor Dostoevsky's *Demons* (1872)—in order to highlight a pattern according to which a formidable, magnetic figure of political authority intrudes into the disordered social sphere and supplants one or another sociotope of aggregation as the one genuine actuality, the force to be reckoned with. Redemptive and destructive at once, it is linked to traditional but varied figurations of sovereignty—exceptional, extrajudiciary exercise of power, the association of state and rational modernization, the paradoxes of legitimacy and pretendership, the motifs of rebellion and violent suppression, the entanglement between rational management and despotic whimsy—in the face of which social life as such, individuals encountering each other privately in private pursuits, appears weightless, ghostly, and unreal. Somewhat figuratively, we can say that these works set out in search of what is essential in contemporary social life and discover, in various guises and to various effects, the political authority of the state. Along the way, they discover, too, a vision of individuality as a puzzle, a problem, even a scandal, rather than a fundamental and unquestioned presupposition.

Chapter 3 turns to consider the fruitful representational nexus of the family and the state. What this nexus makes possible across a broad range of texts—Pushkin's *Eugene Onegin* (first complete edition 1833) and *A Captain's Daughter* (1836), Alexander Druzhinin's *Polinka Saks* (1847), Goncharov's *The Same Old Story*, Pisemsky's *Boyarshchina* (1858), Turgenev's *On the Eve* (1860) and *First Love* (1860), and Lev Tolstoy's *Anna Karenina* (1878)—is a determinate deformation within the paradigmatically realist material of what might be called the "socialization of the heart." Instead of an account of the conflict between authentic intimacy and social convention, instead of worries about social hierarchy and middle-class mobility, we find a starker script according to which the mutually reinforcing figures of authority—the patriarchal family and the state—stand between individuals and the realization of their wishes and desires. These figures appear in various guises: as brute violence, disciplinary regulation, internalized threat, binding guilt, and even magnanimous release. Regardless of the way in which it manifests itself, even at its most benevolent and mild, this power is tendentially lethal: it is the sovereign's power over life and death.

Focusing on another figural cluster of sovereignty, chapter 4 undertakes analyses of a set of texts—Dostoevsky's *Crime and Punishment* (1866) and *The Idiot* (1869), Turgenev's *Spring Torrents* (1872), Tolstoy's *War and Peace* (1869), and Goncharov's *Oblomov* (1859) and *The Precipice* (1869)—that combine images of political authority with those of national belonging. What we find here is a determinate reinflection of the novelistic material of the imagined community as it was classically described by Benedict Anderson. Instead of dissolving into homogeneous space, the center continues to haunt the periphery; instead of releasing progressive linear time, the past interrupts its movement. Instead of forward-directed integration into the national whole, the protagonist is retroactively reclaimed (doomed/redeemed) by an irresistible force that binds him or her to the substance of the nation. In Anderson's terms, we find here a hybrid social imaginary, part national and part imperial-dynastic. Within this hybrid, the latter element—the imaginary of central and sacral sovereignty—operates as the constructive principle, supplying the means for the deformation of traditional realist material.

The proliferation of generic hybridity becomes the focal point of the discussion in chapter 5. This culminating section represents an attempt at a poetics of Russian realism on the basis of the corpus of texts discussed in more detail in the preceding four chapters. The prominence within that corpus of motifs and narrative devices associated with the figure of the state suggests an affiliation with tragedy, which historically has tended to focus on the paradoxes of sovereign power. Again and again, we encounter sudden narrative reversal and recognition; entrenched, unmediated conflict; central and irreducible ambiguity; intense and rhetorically heightened affective states. Constructed out of all of these devices and motifs is a social imaginary that privileges visions of substantive belonging, which is to say, visions of the individual, whose separateness from the group is only provisional and transpires at a high cost to group and individual alike.

This, in brief, is what the book attempts to accomplish. Several words must also be said about what it does not set out, or is by conceit unable, to do. It is a familiar paradox that the more material one attempts to include, the more glaringly one leaves things out. This is, to be sure, only fair, insofar as my explicit ambition here is to give a sense of a major tendency within the Russian realist corpus as a whole. A number of authors and countless works remain outside the purview of the book, even if that purview is roughly limited to the generation of male and gentry authors who entered the literary scene during the reign of Nicholas I. What of Nekrasov, Grigorovich, Saltykov-Shchedrin? What of early Dostoevsky, later Pisemsky, shorter Turgenev, much of Tolstoy? Further case studies could have been included that in one way or another align themselves with—and thereby further delineate—the major hypothesis of the book. Perhaps as many would have run orthogonal to it. My hope, regardless, is not to argue that the social-imaginary pattern described here subsumes every Russian realist text, or that the corpus can be fully understood by reference exclusively to its social-imaginary orientation toward the authority of the state. Rather, my claim is simply that such an orientation manifestly traverses the corpus, allowing us to see familiar texts in new ways, to make sense of the specificity of the Russian realist tradition, and to expand our conceptual apparatus for grappling with nineteenth-century realism in general.

The book's focus on broader patterns leaves less room for detailed historical and literary-historical contextualization. This is all the more regrettable given the project's interest in the relationship between social subject position and literary form. At the same time, much excellent work in this vein has been done, work without which the analysis that follows would not have been possible.[10] The issue of context is further complicated by the fact that it is not something given in advance, a fact of the matter that needs only to be reconstructed. Just as every literary text, as it were, draws toward itself and organizes around itself the literary and extraliterary facts that become its context, so also—indeed, all the more so—a work of criticism or theory, which selects contexts commensurate with the questions it asks of its material. Fernand Braudel famously distinguished between the "almost changeless," *longue-durée* horizon of environmental history, the "gentle rhythms" of social history, and the stormy, short-term "history of events."[11] It is evidently the second of the three historical horizons that is most pertinent to what follows. The hope is that something may be not only lost but also gained by provisionally and partially withdrawing attention from the turbulent surface of "eventful" history, with its waves of reaction and reform, its cultural openings and closures, periods of economic stagnation and growth, and by focusing instead on the relationship between literary form and social formation.[12] It is to the analysis of this thought-provoking conjuncture—which might be designated "social realism under autocracy"—that this book is ultimately dedicated.

Russian Realism
Another Social Imaginary

[CHAPTER ONE]

What Is Actual: Hegelian Variations

It is impossible, of course, to date the origin of Russian realism with any meaningful precision. One episode stands out, however, as an emblematic conceptual origin, if not a literal, chronological one. The episode—a cause célèbre in its own right—involved Vissarion Belinsky, the leading literary critic of his generation, misinterpreting a sentence of German philosophy. Belinsky paid a heavy price for what he would soon come to regard as a passing derangement: prompt remorse and lasting regret, patronizing comments by his closest friends, strained relationships, and disdain for his lack of philosophical sophistication continuing to this day. The sentence Belinsky ostensibly misunderstood was the notorious speculative trap from the preface to G. W. F. Hegel's *Elements of the Philosophy of Right* (1821): "What is rational is actual; and what is actual is rational."[1] If Belinsky misconstrued the couplet, he was certainly not alone.[2]

In the course of approximately a year and a half, between 1839 and 1840, Belinsky published a number of articles that relied heavily on Hegelian terminology and called for "reconciliation with actuality" (*primirenie s deistvitel'nost'iu*). The period marked a sudden ultraconservative turn in his writing, reversing the central political and aesthetic orientations that had characterized his work until then. Contemporaries and later scholars have argued that Belinsky simply mistook Hegel's rather technical term "actuality" (*deistvitel'nost'* in Russian, *Wirklichkeit* in the original) to mean all that is the case, brute objectivity, the given.[3] This misunderstanding made his call to reconciliation sound passive, invoking the attitude of submissiveness to the reigning order of things. Meanwhile, in its original context, the term referred to social life as a product of conscious human action, human rationality actualizing itself in the world. In Hegel, a modern social order can be fully actual only if its members—free and rational agents—can recognize it as a product of their own collective activity (hence *ac*tuality, *Wirk*lichkeit, *deistv*itel'nost') and assent.

While not incorrect, this account of the difference between Hegel's notion of actuality and Belinsky's is, at least in one important respect, incomplete. What it leaves out is the precise social content of the sort of objectivity to which the two contrasting notions refer. For Hegel, contemporary *Wirklichkeit* manifests itself in a constitutional monarchy, supplemented by "many of the social and political policies and tendencies that we now recognize as part of the liberal tradition."[4] Belinsky's *deistvitel'nost'*, by contrast, connotes Russian autocracy at its most rarefied, embodied in "the regally sublime spirit of the Russian czar."[5] In his 1839 review of Vasily Zhukovsky's poem *The Borodino Anniversary*, he sidesteps the standard "liberal-nationalist" interpretation of Russia's victory over Napoleon as an accomplishment of the entire "people" and dwells instead on the leading role of the monarch. "For us Russians," he writes, "there are no national [*narodnykh*] events that don't spring forth from the living well of supreme power."[6] Without the presence of the czar—"on whose face [the people] read thunder, and grace, and royal valor"—even military triumph would amount to nothing but a "meaningless gathering of an idle crowd."[7] Explicitly resorting to Hegelian terminology, Belinsky concludes that in Russia, only absolute obedience to the will of the sovereign makes possible "free" and "conscious" participation in "rational actuality."[8] Or, succinctly: "in the czar consists our freedom."[9]

This last motto must have been especially offensive to the liberal-minded members of Belinsky's circle of friends. And to the many of them to whom the details of Hegel's philosophy were both familiar and precious, Belinsky's statement may have sounded less obviously wrong than parodic, disturbingly like and grotesquely unlike the original. After all, the identification of freedom with the modern state is Hegel's own, as is the notion that the modern state, precisely insofar as it recognizes the centrality of the individual, must delegate sovereignty to a single person, the monarch.[10] Belinsky's departure from Hegel is thus a subtle one, a shift in emphasis with regard precisely to the *kind* of monarchy—the precise modality of statehood—with which the subject must become reconciled. Hegel stressed the irreducibility of the monarch's individual decision *only* "in the last instance" without reducing the social formation as a whole to the person of the sovereign. By contrast, Belinsky personalizes the state, identifying it directly with the figure of the ruler. He conceives of society as a single body of "the people" made flesh, made visible and active in the sublime, valorous warrior-czar.

Not simply the czar, then, but ideally the czar at war—it is telling that

Belinsky begins his reconciliation campaign on the occasion of the unveiling of a new monument on the site of the Battle of Borodino. For Hegel, war reveals something fundamental about the state: its capacity to demand that, in time of emergency, everyday social life be suspended and the complex network of interlacing individual pursuits be reduced to a single entity, the polity as such, fighting for survival. In times of war, the state is condensed to its bare essence, a singularity in which all private interests, including even the interest in staying alive, must be abjured, and all that remains is political being as such. It is noteworthy, then, that Belinsky chose to be reconciled not with the Hegelian state in its normal functioning but with the Hegelian state as it appears in a moment of danger, at its most abbreviated and abstract. What he leaves out in the process are the multiple forms of life unfolding within the parameters of what Hegel designates as "civil society" (*bürgerliche Gesellschaft*), the very forms of life that constitute the social content of modern *Wirklichkeit*.

Within the overall schema of the *Philosophy of Right*, civil society occupies an intermediary and a unique position between the forms of life rooted in the family and the political state. *Intermediary*, because life in civil society facilitates the individual's transition from the small community of natural kinship to the great community of rational belonging, or citizenship. *Unique*, because unlike the family and the state, relations in civil society are aggregative and contractual: they begin with (the assumption of) separate individuals, who come together because they turn out to need each other for the satisfaction of their own needs. The family and the state, by contrast—and here Hegel departs from the adherents of social-contract theory—are "substantive" unities, social formations in which (the sense of) connectedness and interdependence prevails over the experience of one's own separateness and the drive for self-determination. Just as the family is a single entity, the members of which are mere accidents,[11] so, too, "it is only through being a member of the state that the individual has objectivity, truth and ethical life."[12] In this respect, the "first" moment of the family is isomorphic with the "third" moment of the state: the two share the basic social imaginary that prioritizes belonging and cohesion over the individualism that marks the "second," intermediary domain of civil society. According to Hegel, the state can be characterized as truly modern, rational, and free only if it makes room for the dynamism of individual interests playing out within civil society. Conversely, only the modern state tolerates, indeed relies on, the element of "negation" unleashed by the self-seeking activity of individuals.[13]

What the sections on civil society allow Hegel to do, then, is elaborate a social space—and corresponding social imaginaries—where individuals can encounter the political order without either side being threatened or undermined. As we shall soon see in more detail, he outlines three principles of socialization: the system of economic exchange, through which individual desires are both cultivated and satisfied; the system of law, through which individuals rise to the recognition of themselves and others as subjects of rights; and the system of collective organization, in which individuals learn to pursue the interests they have in common with others. These stages, for Hegel, constitute a kind of education for citizenship—a conjectural path taking the subject from the family, to alienated individualism of the market, to civil existence as a law-abiding person, to the citizen's concern for the common good, the good of the polity as a whole. This is, in Hegel, the proper domain of *Wirklichkeit*, the place where subject and object, activity and reality meet.

The term "civil society" (*grazhdanskoe obshchestvo*) appears rarely in Belinsky's reconciliation-period writing, and the sphere in which individuals pursue their personal desires and satisfy their needs is consistently characterized in dismissive tones as "unactual" and "ghostly" (*prizrachnyi*). But the questions that give rise to the concept of civil society in the Prussian theorist of the state trouble the Russian literary critic as well.[14] Inheriting much and eclectically from Hegel, referring directly to the infamous motto from the *Philosophy of Right*, Belinsky seems to find absolutely no use for the complex social machinery constructed in what are arguably that work's most innovative and consequential sections. Instead, in order to answer the question of how an individual becomes reconciled with the actuality of political life in common, he repeatedly resorts to stark scenarios of sacrifice and service to the collective welfare. One memorable example of such sacrifice is drawn, emblematically enough, from the history of the Russian state, the drama of Peter I and his polity threatened by his own closest kin.

In Belinsky's retelling of the well-known story, the "individual," or "particular" dimension of Peter's persona is linked to his deeply felt bonds with his family. A loving father and a loving brother, he is also a man of politics, however, wholly dedicated to the welfare of his people. And so, when his sister and his son rise up against him, he weeps for his sister but judges and punishes her, weeps for his son but judges and punishes him as well. At the culmination of the story, Belinsky exclaims:

The scales of justice are ready: on one side, the natural love of the parent, on the other—the fate of the people.... The people have triumphed—an awesome and solemn minute! [...] The objective world has defeated the subjective world, the universal has defeated the particular. Why is such a victory so great? [...] Because the rights of the subjective man are infinitely powerful in his soul and can be defeated only though self-sacrifice for the benefit of the universal.[15]

The passage performs two types of displacement vis-à-vis the Hegelian paradigm of the modern state. The first displacement involves a transposition of the dynamics that in Hegel play out in civil society onto the terrain of political crisis. Correspondingly, instead of negotiation between, and gradual ascension from, particular to universal interests, we find a stark confrontation between the two, a clash in which the former must be sacrificed to the latter. The second displacement likewise involves the occlusion of civil society dynamics in favor of the drama of confrontation between the immediacy of (particular) kinship-feeling and duty to the (universal) state. By contrast with Hegel, for whom the modern state's "invention" of civil society is called upon precisely to prevent such irreconcilable conflict, Belinsky's second displacement involves what would from Hegel's vantage point constitute an "archaization" of the relationship between the individual and the state. At stake in the conflict between kinship-feeling and the dictates of political order, in other words, is the sort of clash between the substantive unities of the family and the state that Hegel identifies as emblematic of classical Greece. Hegel's discussion of this clash can be found in the well-known passages of his *Phenomenology of Spirit* (1806), constituting an extended commentary on Sophocles's *Antigone*. Hegel reads the play as presenting a confrontation between two protagonists absolutely committed to opposing *substantive* social imaginary horizons: Antigone to the bonds of the family/oikos and Creon to laws of the city/polis.[16] In this account, the lethal dynamic of the tragedy consists in its staging of the logics of substantive belonging as absolute and therefore incapable of recognizing externality except as radically criminal: Antigone from the perspective of the laws of the city in the name of which Creon speaks and acts; Creon from the point of view of Antigone who ventriloquizes the divine laws governing relations within the family. What the play shows, according to Hegel, is precisely the one-sidedness of each of these principles and the need for reconciliation between them—the need for the particular individual, as particular, to become visible to the state, which would, in turn, be recognized by the individual as legitimate. This is, for Hegel, the singular achievement of modernity, one that is made possible with the emergence of the sphere of civil society as it is elaborated in the *Philosophy of Right*.[17] Civil society, in other words, presents us with the sort of social imaginaries through which tragic scenarios of absolute separation and belonging may be avoided. Meanwhile, as the passage on Peter I demonstrates, in thinking the relationship between the individual and the state, Belinsky gravitates precisely toward the tragic: with its stark either/or, its absolute, substantive scripts of belonging.

Images of total unity and total opposition proliferate in Belinsky's writings from the period. He who does not belong to the community, the individual in his particularity, appears as a "ghost," an ontological offender, transgressing not just against morality or the law, but against "substance" itself, against the imaginary locus at which a given form of human togetherness converges with the cosmic order.[18] And just as from the perspective of a community united by substantive bonds, those who are excluded appear in teratological colors, so, from the perspective of the excluded individual, the substantive whole takes on hostile shapes, appearing as an "invisible, hundred-armed giant" and "a colossal and hostile phantom." In personal correspondence, Belinsky echoes these images referring to actuality as "a fiend with iron claws and iron jaws," or, in terms still more resonant with our discussion, as "the *fatum* of the ancients."[19]

A distinctive social imaginary thus underpins Belinsky's engagement with Hegel's political philosophy. Within this imaginary, the individual is not, as in Hegel, tucked away in the interstices of multiple and more or less spontaneous social aggregations, but confronts substantive wholes—the family and the state with their absolute demands of belonging and threats of expulsion—*immediately and directly*. Instead of a series of mediations between individuality and the substance of the state, we have, in Belinsky's tragic and crisis-ridden account, the alternatives of total unity on the one hand and implacable hostility on the other. What is the proper subject matter for Greek tragedy in Hegel, in Belinsky becomes the proper subject matter for modern "poetry of actuality," insofar as it is called upon to grapple with the most serious problems of contemporary life.

This notion that proper literary reckoning with actuality (what was not yet, but would soon be explicitly called "realism")[20] paradigmatically contains a tragic dimension, is indeed what we find in Belinsky's criticism from the time. This is somewhat complicated by the fact that, as Belinsky himself recognizes and welcomes, the current literary-historical conjuncture gave pride of place to prose. What thus emerges as the proper genre of actuality is a hybrid construction, descriptive and, though to a lesser extent, prescriptive both: works of narrative fiction containing a tragic kernel, sharing with tragedy a basic social imaginary cathected on patterns of conflicted separateness and belonging. Belinsky mentions several examples: Walter Scott's *Bride of Lammermoor*—"a tragedy in the form of a novel"; James Fenimore Cooper's *Pathfinder*—"a Shakespearean drama in the form of a novel."[21] As late as 1844, in an essay on Pushkin, he argues that "in the modern world even the novel—this world's [...] true epic poem—is the more successful the more it has been imbued with the dramatic element."[22]

One of Belinsky's essays from the time contains an extensive, and for our purposes illuminating, discussion of yet another instance of "poetry of actuality," Gogol's historical novella (*povest'*) *Taras Bulba* (1835), telling the tale of the eponymous seventeenth-century Southern Ukrainian Cossack and his two sons in an uprising against Polish rule. Belinsky describes Bulba as "a tragic figure,"[23] "a hero, representative of an entire people, an entire political society at a certain point in its existence."[24] This society, says Belinsky, "possesses a single common character, tightly cohesive and linked by some strong cement."[25] The language here is unmistakably that of "substance," the image of a kind of archaic, undifferentiated polity in which all are united by a common purpose. The central intrigue of the story unfolds against this social background and depends on it. Bulba's younger son, Andriy, falls in love with a Polish woman and switches sides in order to defend her and her city from his own people. Bulba then seeks out his son during a battle and executes him. Belinsky comments: a human being exists in two spheres, the subjective, where he belongs only to himself, and the objective, where he depends on external connections with others and to which he is "linked by the unbreakable bonds of blood and spirit."[26] As long as the two domains exist in harmony with each other, the person has nothing to fear. But if his personal inclinations pull him in one direction, while his substantive connections pull him in another, a "tragic collision"[27] emerges, and then, regardless of how he acts, success and happiness are beyond his reach: "he has been overtaken by fate."[28]

In Belinsky's reading, the central element of the plot thus functions according to the principle of *substantive belonging*. We are dealing, in other words, with a far-reaching connectedness between the individual and the body politic, signified through references to tribal solidarity, familial kinship, and political unity, rendered more urgent in times of war. The link between the individual and this undifferentiated polity is staged through the sequence of rupture and violent reintegration. In Andriy's case, this is the scenario of treason and death at the hands of his father. The more intensely the individual's act of separation from the substance is dramatized and felt, Belinsky suggests, the more vivid and violent the final "reconciliation," the sacrificial affirmation of belonging. The heavy price Andriy has to pay for his transgression, death at the hands of his own father, is an index of the depth of his substantive roots. And conversely, Andriy's falling out of the community is not merely individual alienation but a heavy blow to the polity itself, a substantive wound. This is why he must be killed by none other than the person who will feel his loss most keenly, his own coreligionist, comrade, and kin.

Belinsky's attempt to define the proper generic form for the representation of contemporary actuality thus leads him into what is, from a strictly Hegelian perspective, an incongruous conclusion: a mixing of genres and a historical conflation to boot, applying the form most characteristic of Greek antiquity to contemporary social conditions.²⁹ This incongruity, in turn, parallels the slippage that occurs in Belinsky's engagement with Hegel's political philosophy. We may formulate the correspondence between the transpositions as follows: *where the imagination of human togetherness is dominated by the figure of substantive sociality, there realist narrative will undergo the warping effects of tragic drama.*

Hegel's own observations on the modern novel as the vehicle for the representation of contemporary actuality differ in telling ways from those of his Russian follower. Where Belinsky's narratives of actuality follow the logic of fate, assuming that human self-assertion provokes the (social) world to recoil in a hostile manner against it, Hegel's vision of the encounter of the individual with contemporary life unfolds according to providential principles. For Hegel, fate is an "outdated," "archaic" category, appropriate for the world that has not come to terms with the legitimacy of individual self-assertion. In modernity, the "*fatum* of the ancients" is superseded by the providential script, according to which a person acting in a self-willed, erring, even transgressive fashion contributes to the dynamism and richness of the social world.³⁰ Correspondingly, it is providence, rather than fate, that organizes the paradigmatic narrative of the modern novel. Here, the individual's quest to realize his desires and ideals spurs him into activity in the social world, which, through this activity, "realizes itself rather than [his] ideals."³¹ The hero may *subjectively* oppose the world, regard it as an obstacle to his self-realization, but *objectively*, he contributes to its complexity and richness. This co-optative dynamic ensures, in turn, that things ultimately go well for the individual: "However much he may have quarreled with the world or been pushed about in it, in most cases at last he gets his girl and some sort of position, marries her, and becomes as good a Philistine as others."³²

Civil Society Narratology

To sum up: a consideration of Belinsky's brief but passionate engagement with Hegel—just at the moment when the Russian critic was formulating the first fully fledged theory of Russian realism—yields three parallel divergences. Hegel links contemporary actuality with the modern social formation as a whole, including the family, the state, and most significantly, civil society; he considers the novel of social apprenticeship as this actuality's proper literary representation; and he conceives of the relationship between the individual and the social whole in providential terms. Belinsky tends to omit from his account of contemporary actuality its most contemporary domain, civil society; he posits tragedy (or the tragic novel) as this actuality's proper genre and emplots the relationship between the individual and the social whole as fate. The inner coherence of Belinsky's Hegelian misprisions suggests that we are not dealing simply with lack of philosophical sophistication on the part of the critic, or his poor command of German, or the game of "telephone" involved in consulting his friends and acquaintances on the details of Hegelian philosophy. Rather, in viewing contemporary Russian life and literature through the prism of Hegel's conceptual apparatus, Belinsky encounters the resistance of local lifeworlds and the social imaginaries shaping them. In the resulting give-and-take, Hegel's philosophy (political and aesthetic) comes out transformed in symptomatic ways. As the following chapters of the book will show, Belinsky's reconciliation-period "misreadings" turn out to be highly prescient in capturing the basic lineaments of deformation that realist fiction undergoes under the influence of substantively oriented social imaginaries.

In order to prepare the ground for the discussion that follows, I would like now to look more closely at what it is that Belinsky's texts are unable or unwilling to accommodate. This will mean delving into Hegel's discussion of civil society in his *Philosophy of Right* to draw out a number of institutional *loci*—what I will call "sociotopes"—grounding specific social imaginaries that prove operative in Western realist fiction more broadly. I will thus read Hegel's text as a depository of rudimentary narratives, in different ways telling the story of self-interested individuals aggregating into more or less cohesive groups. Like realist fiction itself, Hegel's notion of civil society represents a response to the historical predicament of the emergence, at the end of the eighteenth century and the beginning of the nineteenth, of an extensive domain of commodity exchange, ostensibly detached from the system of political rule. "This development," writes Jürgen Habermas, "has put too great a strain upon the classical doctrine of politics. Since the end of the eighteenth century, it has split apart into a social theory grounded in political economy on the one hand and a theory of the state inspired by modern natural right on the other."[33] In his analysis of the relationship between civil society and the state, Hegel attempts to produce a philosophical account of their convergence, folding the disjointed, chaotic activity of private individuals into an ordered life of a polity. Thus, at the start of his discussion of civil society, he both alerts and reassures us: "the whole [of civil society] is the sphere [*Boden*] of mediation in which all individual characteristics [*Einzelheiten*], all aptitudes, and all accidents of birth and fortune are liberated, and where the waves of all passions surge forth, governed only by the reason which shines through them."[34] To show how variegated individual activity is "governed" immanently—this is the task that Hegel's discussion of civil society as the constitutive dimension of the modern state shares with much nineteenth-century realist fiction.

The section on civil society is divided into three subsections, each treating a basic principle of aggregation. These principles operate simultaneously and interdependently, but Hegel examines them one by one in the order of increasing complexity and heightening self-consciousness on the part of the aggregated persons. At the "lowest" level, we have individuals organized by what Hegel calls "the system of needs," a network of relationships into which individuals enter insofar as their real or socially symbolic needs cannot be satisfied without the participation of others. This is the market, or, more broadly, the economic domain of labor and consumption, within which we encounter others as means to our own ends. Despite the apparent arbitrariness and contingency of such encounters, their course is organized by a kind of necessity, a set of quasi-natural laws, discovered by political economy, that detects the workings of a providential "invisible hand" guiding individuals' self-interested behavior into a system of interdependence. Within this system, the individual undergoes a multipronged education, learns to be more discriminating and discerning about his desires (his natural needs become diversified, refined, and imbued with social affects through interaction with others), learns the discipline of occupation, and, most importantly, comes to experience—in a way that is not yet fully conscious—his dependence on others.[35]

At the next level of aggregation, Hegel considers the principle of *actualized right*, a legal system that validates and secures the person and property of individuals in civil society. Within the sociotope of *actualized right*, individuals come together as more than self-seeking particulars, but as persons, formally identical and equal.[36] While the system of needs alone, devoid of the guarantees of justice and right, would in principle permit all sorts of infractions against persons and property, within the sociotope of actualized right such infractions become crimes, transgressions against the law as the objective, institutional expression of universality. Here, persons are conceived as capable of abstracting from their desires in favor of obedience to the law as the precondition for the life of a collective made up of discrete individuals.[37] Within the system of actualized right, we learn to recognize others as their own ends, subjects of need and seekers of satisfaction like ourselves, but also, like ourselves, capable of abstracting from those needs in order to conceive of themselves as members of a community of (formally) free and (formally) equal persons.

The third and final moment of aggregation within civil society is the principle that Hegel formulates as "care for the particular interest as a *common* interest."³⁸ This is achieved through the institutions of "the Police" and "the Corporation." The former, in Hegel's contemporary use of the term *Polizei*, designates a range of agencies whose role was to regulate production and distribution, the provision of utilities, prevention of fraud, inspection of goods, public health, relief of poverty, and so on—all to anticipate and forestall the inevitably contingent outcomes of interactions within the economic domain of the system of needs. By "corporations," in turn, Hegel means groupings based on common occupational or other social interests: trade guilds, religious associations, educational societies, and so on. The aggregative principle underlying both of these institutions involves the recognition of interest held in common with others. Within this sociotope, larger social groups pursue the welfare of individuals who belong to them, not as abstract subjects of right (whose life and property is protected by law), but as particular persons with their concrete desires and needs.³⁹ Conversely, individuals undergo yet another kind of education, learning to identify and become active as members of groups. "We saw earlier," writes Hegel, "that, in providing for himself, the individual in civil society is also acting for others. But this unconscious necessity is not enough; only in the corporation does it become a knowing and thinking [part of] ethical life."⁴⁰

This is, in brief, Hegel's deduction of the most significant and innovative feature of the modern state, the aggregative logic whereby individuals are both asserted in their independence and integrated into a polity. For the most part, to most of its members, the state appears as nothing other than civil society itself—a more or less complex network of interactions between private persons. Seen from this point of view, from the perspective of everyday normalcy, the state in its capacity to set the parameters within which private interactions unfold, vanishes, remains hidden in plain sight. We feel ourselves free, without realizing that the conditions of this freedom presuppose membership in a well-ordered state.⁴¹ This subtle occlusion of political sovereignty is, in turn, complemented by the ostensibly noncoercive, educational function of civil society sociotopes. Plainly put, we have here an implicit narrative in which the individual, having begun as a self-interested bearer of needs, "naturally," "spontaneously" rises to the recognition of his profound and beneficial entanglement with the needs and interests of others. The institutions of civil society make up the objective conditions for the possibility of such an education.⁴²

Hegel's repeated emphasis on education in these sections echoes his comments on the novel. The two discussions can in fact be viewed as complementary: sociotopes of civil society that enrich the brief account of fictional apprenticeship to the modern world with specific, recognizably novelistic themes and narrative shapes. Desire, duty, quest for a calling;

discovery of dependence; acquisition of respect for universal principles; achievement of social belonging—these motifs and plots, embedded in civil society's sociotopic imaginary, thoroughly pervade European realist fiction. Or put another way, European realist fiction construes social relations on the basis of the same aggregative sociotopes that emerge from Hegel's discussion of civil society. Hegel anticipates a poetics of novelistic sociality; realist fiction endows the conceptual skeleton of Hegel's sociology with narrative-mimetic flesh. Both grapple at the level of social imaginaries with the modern predicament of the rise of the figure of the individual to ideological prominence and the emergence of the social as a sphere of supposedly depoliticized private relations.[43] In the rest of this section, then, I would like to discuss briefly three novelistic examples, which will, in turn, serve as occasional points of reference throughout the book: Balzac's *Père Goriot* (1835), Brontë's *Jane Eyre* (1847), and Goethe's *Wilhelm Meister's Apprenticeship* (subsequently *Wilhelm Meisters Lehrjahre*; 1795-96). Each of these novels can be seen as relying on (and promoting) a wide range of civil society imaginaries while privileging one dominant sociotope with particular insistence: *the system of needs* in Balzac, *actualized right* in Brontë and *common interest* in Goethe.

György Lukács was, as far as I know, the first to characterize Balzac's fiction in Hegelian categories, specifically with reference to the workings of the capitalist market: "The vast scale of Balzac's work," writes Lukács, "constitutes a gigantic fresco on which the 'animal kingdom of the spirit' of capitalism is depicted in all its monstrosity."[44] *Père Goriot* illuminates this domain with particular insistence by locating the social world of the novel quite precisely between the substantive poles of the family and the state. Toward the end of the novel, in deathbed delirium, old Goriot (this "Christ of paternity") calls upon the institutions of the state to correct the dire predicament in which children abandon their fathers as soon as they have nothing left to gain from the fulfillment of their filial duties. He calls upon the police to bring his daughters to him and demands that laws be introduced forbidding marriage. Peter Brooks comments on the latter appeal: "Marriage is accursed because it destroys the vertical, genetic relationship of father and child, creator and creature, to substitute for it a horizontal social relationship which, the novel has amply demonstrated, is a denatured contract, a barter, commerce, institutional prostitution."[45] We confront an alternative, then: the moral and political absolutism of the Old Regime modeled on paternal authority, or the world made up of self-interested and therefore at least tendentially predatory individuals. Drawing on standard monarchist ideologemes, the novel imagines life without paternal/sovereign authority as sheer animalistic struggle to the death for the satisfaction of desires and needs. Goriot's deathbed cries express the yearning for the supreme power that would establish a normatively coherent order based on substantive principles of natural kinship and divinely sanctioned political authority. But the supreme power does not come; the world is given over in its entirety to the destructive play of interests and wills.

Still—and this qualification measures the realist novel's social-imaginary distance from the Hobbesian "state of nature" and, in turn, its proximity to Hegel's civil society—the utter unruliness of the self-seeking individual is only apparent. In reality, the sphere of its activity is quite structured; and it is precisely to the description of this structure that the novel is explicitly dedicated. Rastignac's life in Paris begins with a kind of "aesthetic education," in the course of which he learns what to desire, comparing himself with others, measuring the countryside against the standards of the city. Luxury, sensual pleasure, social status—these are the socially supplied needs he will pursue: "if, in the beginning, [the young man in Paris] is dazzled by the covered carriages trotting down the Avenue Champs-Élysées on a fine day, he learns soon enough to want one of his own."[46] This *social wanting* is what drives the hero through the novel, leading him right up to the moment when love, ambition, and desire for luxury melt together, constituting a single undifferentiated, socially constructed object of pursuit.[47]

Rastignac's second lesson consists in the realization that diverse regions of social life, distinctions of status and estate, are actually connected in an all-embracing system of exchange from which nothing, not even filial affection or romantic passion, is exempt. And when it comes to this system of socially produced and indefinitely exchangeable needs, there are no universals or absolutes. In his mentor Vautrin's succinct words: "There are no principles, just things that happen; there are no laws, either, just circumstances."[48] Vautrin goes on to criticize the contemporary French criminal code, "every sentence [of which] shines with absurdities."[49] From the point of view limited strictly to the system of exchange among self-interested agents, the universality of the law is indeed a difficult concept to grasp. This despite the fact that such universality (basic property and civil rights) must be presupposed as a basic condition for the possibility of a stable and functioning system of needs.[50]

The universality of the law, in turn, lies at the core of the social imaginary organizing the protagonist's trajectory in *Jane Eyre* (1847). The stakes of Jane's maturation are evident from the start, beginning with the sequence of her first rebellion against mistreatment by her adoptive family and especially by the villainous young man John Reed. "Wicked and cruel boy!" Jane cries during the opening scene. "You are like a murderer—you are like a slave-driver—you are like the Roman emperors!"[51] In her own description, she behaves like a "rebellious slave" and is treated accordingly: physically restrained and locked up. Then we read this: "I could not answer the ceaseless inward question—*why* I thus suffered; now, at the distance of—I will not say how many years, I see it clearly."52 What becomes visible here is the gap between the empirical and the transcendental subjects of this fictional autobiography, the heroine and the narrator Jane. The former is caught up in her immediate feelings; the latter hovers above them, and her actual explanation of the family's dislike for little Jane is less consequential than her ability to rise above the limited perspective of the child and gain insight, however approximate, into the minds of others.

Jane's path from particularity to universality—to the recognition of herself and of others as subject to the same psychological mechanisms and moral principles—begins with the assertion of freedom and equality. When shamed by the maid for having struck "young master," Jane exclaims: "Master! How is he my master? Am I a servant?" The assertion of equality is reiterated later in the novel in her shocking offer of marriage to her acknowledged "Master," Mr. Rochester, at whose estate she is employed as a governess: "I am not talking to you through the medium of custom, conventionalities, nor even of mortal flesh—it is my spirit that addresses your spirit; just as if both had passed through the grave, and we stood at God's feet, equal—as we are!"53 The rhetoric of equality here depends on the consistent rejection of all external determinations, first social (customs and conventions) and then natural (the mortal flesh). To meet with others on an equal footing, to overcome status, economic, and gender differences, both individuals must "pass through the grave," shed everything but their spiritual selves, in the universality of which they are brought together.

The sublime character of universality implied by the notion of actualized right emerges with greatest vividness in the scenes that follow Jane's discovery of Rochester's marriage to the mad Bertha Mason. Continuing to feel irresistible attraction to him and subjected to pressure on his part bordering on violence, Jane still refuses to stay with him as his second wife/lover. Faced with the double danger arising from her own passion and from Rochester's overweening insistence on possessing her, Jane resists the temptation and the fear alike by privileging the voice of "intolerable duty."54 Preparing to flee the Rochester estate, to lose not only her dearly beloved, but also the means of sustenance, endangering her very survival, she reasons thus:

> I care for myself. The more solitary, the more friendless, the more unsustained I am, the more I will respect myself. I will keep the law given by God; sanctioned by man. [...] Laws and principles are not for the times

when there is no temptation: they are for such moments as this, when body and soul rise in mutiny against their rigor; stringent they are, inviolate they shall be.[55]

Jane's "care of the self" here is of a peculiar sort. If in Balzac caring for oneself means seeking to satisfy one's natural and social needs, in Brontë, it is a matter of the heroine's concern for her human dignity, for the universal in herself. This, in turn, implies precisely the ability to overcome need, to rise above it in the service of a stable social order. The willingness to sacrifice everything, all particular determinations (desires, comforts, life itself) to the implacable divine/human law—this is the lesson of universality Jane must learn, and only upon this willingness can her claim to equality be securely grounded.

It is important to observe how the conception of passion itself switches registers from the opening scene of the novel to this moment of renunciation. Passion is the agent of rebellion against violence and oppression first; then it is a tyrant, aligned with the threat of physical violence coming from the imperious Rochester himself. The shift is indicative: unless the passions are reined in, we are trapped in the ill-fated alternative between tyranny and rebellion. Genuine equality transpires only among self-governing individuals, individuals with a firm foothold in the universal. Jane proves exemplary in this regard, just as her double, Rochester's animal-like wife, Bertha Mason, serves as the exemplar of self-government's total collapse.[56]

The universalist principle of actualized right in *Jane Eyre* highlights the ambiguous nature of this form of aggregation as both social and antisocial in the extreme: social because it alone ensures an orderly community of self-governing subjects who require no external government and therefore need not fear tyranny, antisocial because it requires that all human bonds be subject to the standard of the law and sacrificed instantaneously if they don't meet it. Thus, what gives Jane most difficulty as she leaves Rochester's estate in the middle of the night is the realization that her escape will cause her beloved much pain, may even serve as his undoing. Still, she feels she has no choice but to go. The ruthlessness of the law consists in its demand that particular bonds be sacrificed to the only proper relationship, the relationship between universals.

Such ruthlessness has no longer any function at Hegel's third level of aggregation, the level of common interest, illustrated here through a brief consideration of Goethe's paradigm-setting bildungsroman, *Wilhelm Meisters Lehrjahre*.[57] Here, the apparently disconnected adventures of young Wilhelm with a traveling theater troupe, filled with detours, errors, and broken promises, turn out to have contributed to a benevolent providential pattern that is in the end revealed to the protagonist himself. "How strange," he is finally compelled to exclaim. "Can there be some pattern in chance events?"[58] This recoding of the hero's blind movement under the guidance of little more than his desires into the language of providential order—this operation of the "invisible hand"—suggests to Joseph Vogl that (despite Wilhelm's refusal to work in his father's trading company) we have before us a prototypical instantiation of "economic man," the *Homo oeconomicus*, whose self-seeking activity "produces—unintentionally and unconsciously—harmonious social relations."[59] If this were the case, however, we would have little more than an optimistic—for both Balzac and Hegel, indeed, naive—version of the system-of-needs sociotope. As it happens, the situation is complicated by uncertainty precisely about the source of the providential order into which Wilhelm is at last integrated: does it arise spontaneously on its own, or is it facilitated by the efforts of the members of the mysterious Society of the Tower, who turn out to be not only witnesses but also active participants in Wilhelm's education, leading him to social usefulness and personal fulfillment?

The novel casts the Society of the Tower as a kind of corporation in Hegel's sense, embracing representatives of different classes and professions, both men and women who are convinced that rational cooperation and pursuit of common interest will tend to converge with the interests of concrete individuals, as well. As one of the leaders of the Society observes concerning the reforms he hopes to implement at his estates: "it is clear to me that certain dispositions, though advantageous to me, are not absolutely essential, and some of them could be changed for the benefit of my workers. One doesn't always lose by giving up."[60] If we take into account the constant, purposeful, albeit gentle guidance of the numerous educators of the society, who possess a deep understanding of social interdependence and mutuality of interests, then the "invisible hand" turns out to be quite visible, and the system of needs comes to double as a kind of voluntary association dedicated to the pursuit of common needs as personal and of personal needs as common. From the "higher" point of view of this sociotope, the competition of interests characteristic of the system of needs reappears as the domain of madness and chaos. Here is how Wilhelm himself describes the inner workings of his theater troupe to one of the Society's primary educators, Jarno:

> Every one of them wants to be first and foremost and exclude all the others. None of them understands that by this means he and the others cannot achieve much. They think they are absolutely unique, but in fact they are totally unable to do anything that is not mere routine, though they are always restless and clamoring for something new. They work strenuously

against each other, and yet a modicum of self-interest and self-love would suffice to bring them together again.[61]

In response, Wilhelm's mentor bursts out laughing: "Don't you realize that you have been describing the whole world, not just the theater? I could provide you with characters and actions from all classes of society for your savage brushstrokes."[62] We see here the difficulty involved in translating across social imaginaries: just as the attitudes associated with actualized right and common interest may appear abstruse and even delusional from the perspective of the system of needs, so the standpoint of common interest disdains the ethos of the competitive marketplace, regarding it as not much of a "system" at all.

Goethe's Society of the Tower figures the point of intersection between civil society as an aggregate of individual wills and the state as the power that holds those wills together in a coherent whole. Here a form of togetherness appears in which there is almost no conflict between the two tendencies: the aggregative and the substantive, individual freedom and the common good. "Almost" is a crucial qualification, however, since the novel contains moments of fleeting anxiety about the possibility of harmonizing these tendencies.[63] Quickly resolved, these moments of tension nevertheless serve as reminders of the potential difficulty involved in suturing together freedom and belonging. In Hegel's own account of the modern state, this very tension is evident at two points in particular: in the circular logic that construes civil society and the modern state as each other's conditions of possibility, and correspondingly, in the ambiguity with which "the state" is used to designate both "the whole of a civilly and politically well-organized society" and more narrowly, government or the "political state."[64]

Distributions of the Social

In his *Critique of Hegel's "Philosophy of Right"* (1843), the young Karl Marx zeroes in precisely on this tension. Marx credits his erstwhile master with astutely registering the separation between civil society and political authority characterizing the contemporary social formation. Less convincing to Marx is Hegel's attempt to "dissolve" the tension between them, to reunify the two domains through a gradualist account of the private person's heightening consciousness of citizenship. This dissolution proves to be nothing but a *semblance*, a concealment and mystification of the real state of affairs.[65] The real state of affairs, meanwhile, consists in the fact that once we posit such an entity as an unpolitical, private person, the political domain—the domain of the common good—will always remain occulted and unreachable as such. What results is a mystifying dualism, according to which human beings, political in their very essence, are broken up into "worldly," egoistic individuals, interested only in their own wellbeing and "otherworldly" virtuous citizens concerned with the common good. The former exist in actuality, the latter only in the imagination, or at extremely rare moments in their lives—say, when voting. As Marx puts it contemporaneously in *On the Jewish Question* (1843): "Man as he really is, is seen only in the form of *egoistic* man, and man in his *true* [political] nature only in the form of the *abstract citizen*."[66]

This dualism results in the further complication that even when we do have access to the occulted polity, we have it as "civil" persons pursuing our private interests. As a result, the political sphere of the common good is both lifted up, separated from particular interests, and at the same time profaned, subjected to the influence of those very interests. It is in this sense that Marx writes of Hegel's conception of the political state that it is "an abstraction of civil society."[67] As an abstraction, it both stands apart from the aggregate of self-interested individuals and, at various levels, incorporates these egoistic dynamics. Indulging in Hegelian terminological play, we might suggest that instead of a concrete universal (immanent and just), the modern state transpires as an abstract particular (occulted and biased). Or in the words of Shlomo Avineri, "What began as an experiment in conflict resolution ends with the total domination of the individual by the political state, while the political state can never detach itself from its civil society background."[68] Marx's point is that instead of resolving the contradictions that arise in bourgeois society between the domains of private egoism and political citizenship, Hegel conceals them. This concealment is, in turn, mimetic in nature; Hegel's concept of the modern state simply imitates and thus reasserts the occlusions that are already present in contemporary society itself.

These contradictions in Hegel's account of modern society are taken up—consequentially for later discussions of bourgeois cultural forms and of realist fiction in particular—in the work of Antonio Gramsci. Following Hegel, Gramsci views civil society as the sphere of education to citizenship, a set of institutions, practices, and imaginaries, whose task consists in the legitimation of the social order. Meanwhile, the state, or "political society" in the narrow sense, maintains the function of exercising coercive force when the work of these mediating institutions breaks down. In Gramsci's formula: "State = political society + civil society, in other words, hegemony, protected by the armour of coercion."[69] The critical, Marxian element of Gramsci's engagement with Hegel comes through most clearly in his dismissal of the modern state's pretensions to true universality and realized freedom. Gramsci accounts for Hegel's misprision of the current state of affairs in a characteristically historicist manner, pointing out that "Hegel's conception belongs to a period in which the spreading of the bourgeoisie could seem limitless, so that its [...] universality could be asserted: all mankind will be bourgeois."[70] The bourgeoisie's claims to universality is based on its position as the first ruling class in history that is *in principle* infinitely inclusive, posing as "an organism in continuous movement, capable of absorbing the entire society, assimilating it to its cultural and economic level."[71] Thus, the bourgeois state as a whole—the "integral state" that includes both civil society and the political state apparatus—functions by obtaining the individuals' consent and collaboration, by "turning necessity and coercion into 'freedom.'"[72] This turning of coercion into "freedom" is precisely the role of what Gramsci calls "hegemony," a subtle, often altogether unnoticeable "collective pressure [...] in the form of customs, ways of thinking and acting, morality, etc.," dispersed through everyday social interactions within civil society.[73] While all forms of domination, according to Gramsci, combine elements of coercion and hegemony, the bourgeois state skews the ratio between the two heavily toward the latter. What we have instead of the reign of universal, freely and rationally socialized humanity, then, is the whole of society organized in the interests of a particular class, which proves uniquely capable of occluding the very fact of its domination and presenting its reign as the reign of rational freedom for all.

In this light, realist narratives of ostensibly spontaneous social aggregation appear as media for purveying a hegemonic vision of reality, educating its readers into the acceptance of the normative authority of the "way of the world." Franco Moretti, for example, leans on the Hegel-Marx-Gramsci line of political theory to characterize the realist novel's role in articulating the hegemonic version of the real. In Moretti's view, the novel gravitates to civil society mimesis, occluding the coercive workings of the state:

> The State embodies a "mechanical" and "abstract" form of social cohesion, intrinsically remote and foreign to the countless articulations of everyday life: this is why its exercise of power appears of necessity to be an outside coercion, a force inclined by its very nature to be arbitrary, violent. Civil society appears instead to be the sphere of "spontaneous" and concrete bonds. Its authority merges with everyday activities and relationships, exercising itself in ways that are natural and unnoticeable: strictly speaking, within civil society it is improper to speak of the "exercise of authority" as something distinct from the normal course of things.[74]

In a similar vein, Fredric Jameson comments on the realist novel's role in establishing bourgeois cultural hegemony through the production of "the newly quantifiable space of extension and market equivalence, the new rhythms of measurable time, the new secular and 'disenchanted' object world of the commodity system, with its post-traditional daily life and its bewilderingly empirical, 'meaningless,' and contingent *Umwelt*."[75] Following Lukács and Lucien Goldmann, Jameson asserts here a deep-seated alliance between the form of the realist novel and the commodity form, an alliance understood as a hegemonic reality principle: a claim about how things "really" and "naturally" are. Really, naturally—and therefore *noncoercively*; what hegemonic dominance strategically leaves out is the fact of dominance itself: the existence of the locus from which violence would flow if the "natural" order of things were ever in need of protection; the existence, too, of the locus from which decisions on how to sustain such an order are ceaselessly being made. The realist device of ostensibly naturalistic, non-miraculous plotting, the optical illusion of the story omnisciently telling itself, lines up with bourgeois hegemony not through projections of secularization and disenchantment alone, but also, and perhaps fundamentally, through the vision of social life as spontaneous, self-organizing, uncoerced.

One fundamental category naturalized within the realist paradigm is the category of the self, the bourgeois subject who, in Louis Althusser's rearticulation of the Gramscian notion of hegemony,[76] internalizes not only particular behavioral norms and beliefs, but also deep-seated imaginaries of what it means to be an individual: a "centered," self-sufficient, autonomous entity that must regard itself in this way in order to participate in the reproduction of subsisting commodity relations (to make contracts, sell labor, own property, etc.). This is the "uncoerced" self of civil society, the self whose illusory freedom transpires as both the condition and the ideological concealment of real domination. Althusser comments: "The individual *is interpellated as a (free) subject in order that he shall submit freely to the commandments of the Subject, i.e. in order that he shall (freely) accept his subjection*, i.e. in order that he shall make the gestures and actions of his subjection 'all by himself.'"[77] This outsourcing of subjection to the individual eliminates the need for direct coercion, except where interpellation fails and the repressive state apparatus must take upon itself the pacification of subjects unwilling or unable to assume proper interiorities and social roles.

The link between the modern novel and the figure of the autonomous individual emerges in the earliest attempts to grasp the historical significance of the genre. According to these accounts, the novel gives voice to the hopes and anxieties of ascendent individualism. Althusser's concept of interpellation invites us to formulate the relationship differently. Here (realist) subjectivity would have to be grasped as the effect of internalized domination. Instead of assuming that realist texts "express" something about the modern individual, the critic would strive to give an account of what sorts of individuating effects they produce and how.[78] We encounter such an approach, for example, in Jameson's analysis of the emergent devices of literary perspective, which participate in the bourgeois cultural revolution by producing in readers the experience of subjective centeredness.[79] We may likewise recall Catherine Gallagher's account of the rise of modern fictionality (the practice of producing and experiencing the effect of plausibility), training the subject in the practice of flexible mental operations (speculation, assessment of credit and risk, etc.) advantageous to proper orientation in the emerging market economy.[80] Here, too, belongs Mary Poovey's discussion of the way in which debates on poverty in midcentury Victorian Britain underwent a deformation within contemporary novelistic discourse, producing *individuals* (out of political-economic aggregates) and with them, interiorities, genders, psyches—all underwriting "the normalization of emotional and sexual behaviors increasingly conceptualized as 'private.'"[81] Or, to bring up one final example, we can register, with Nancy Armstrong, the mechanisms by which the interpellated individual appears as an effect of an entire character system, articulated to the opposition between "good" (normal, virtuous, well-behaved) and "bad" (deviant, overweening, criminal) subjects. "Between the subject who freely accepts his or her subjections and the criminal or heretic," Armstrong writes, "the novel introduced a whole world of possibilities without which, I believe, a modern secular state ruled chiefly by ideology could not have emerged when and how it did."[82] From such a more or less explicitly Althusserian perspective, realist fiction appears as in part a technology for the production of a subject—epistemically centered, economically speculative, sexually gendered, psychologically norm-bound, politically neutralized—consonant with the hegemonic dynamics of civil society aggregation.

    The emergence of Western realism within the social formation marked by the disavowal of coercive state power is a topic still more frequently raised in connection with the work of Michel Foucault. Especially relevant in this connection are Foucault's genealogies of modern disciplinary and governmental power that emerged in the eighteenth and nineteenth centuries to supplement and, up to a point, supplant the traditional power of the sovereign. At stake here—and this may account for the enthusiasm with which Foucault's work has been recruited for literary analysis—are a set of explicitly articulated social imaginaries, carrying with them figurative, chronotopic, narratological, and even literary-generic associations.

Thus, the exercise of sovereign power relies on the centrality and visibility of the monarch, whose authority is most clearly intuited in ritually scripted, spectacular displays of overwhelming force (e.g., public torture and execution, rituals of acclamation). By contrast with the highly theatrical manifestations of sovereignty, "discipline" names a set of subtle, ideally altogether invisible techniques of surveillance, classification, normalization, and training associated with the modern institutions of the prison, the school, the factory, the hospital, and the army. In the emblematic figure of Bentham's panopticon, we have the all-seeing but impersonal agent of internalized discipline whose centrality organizes the space around it as homogenous and infinitely divisible. Here, power is no longer concentrated at the charismatic center, but evenly and efficiently distributed in space and time to produce knowable, useful, and docile subjects, highly adept at internalizing rules. Lastly, "governmentality," or "biopower," construes the subject as a *Homo oeconomicus*, endowed with needs, desires, interests, and drives. Governmentality manages and reproduces individuals as members of a population, "a living mass" made up of chaotically but also, through statistics, predictably striving selves.

From the perspective of the disciplinary regime, sovereign power is highly inefficient, irrational, crude, easy to elude and to resist, and vulnerable to accusations of despotism and illegitimacy. Disciplinarity juxtaposes to these "traditional, ritual, costly, violent forms of power" its own "subtle, calculated technology of subjection."[83] In turn, the challenge that the figure of the *Homo oeconomicus* presents to the sovereign consists in the claim that the intractable complexity of socioeconomic life renders the state's active intervention (e.g., in the mercantilist system under the ancien régime) useless and even harmful.[84] Instead of an intrusive, meddling political apparatus, what is needed to contend with this newly emerging vital-economic sphere of activity is "an omnipresent government [...] that manages civil society, the nation, society, the social."[85]

Endowed with figurative personae (the sovereign, the panopticon, *Homo oeconomicus*), paradigmatic actions (the taking and granting of life; surveillance and training; stimulus and regulation), chronotopes (the charismatic center and the eternal now; the Cartesian grid and calendrical time; the growing organism), and narrative shapes (scripted performance, stories of normalization, tales of spontaneous development)—Foucault's accounts of these regimes of power can themselves be grasped as paraliterary texts.[86] His genealogies of discipline and governmentality, in particular, have proven fruitful for discussions of European realism. According to D. A. Miller's by now classic analysis, for example, the nineteenth-century "police novel" performs a complicated maneuver of expressing explicit distaste for the police as a tool of state coercion, while internalizing at the level of form the very power it thematically disavows. Like the police it mocks and demonizes, the novel renders subjects most knowable precisely where they constitute the greatest threat to the social order; it promotes the virtues of prudence and caution; and it actuates the process by which expressions of undisciplined desire subject the individual only more thoroughly to (narrative) control.[87] Here, Lukács's "problematic" hero—the existentially and socially alienated, the criminal, the mad, and so on—is less the focal point than the pretext that sets in motion the complex novelistic machinery of classification, normalization, and control: in short, "a hidden and devious discipline, […] defined in terms of the spatial extension of its networks and the temporal deployment of its intrigues."[88]

More recently, Lauren Goodlad has mounted a polemic against this "panopticist" line of inquiry into nineteenth-century British fiction in particular. Goodlad argues that Victorian social imaginaries lend themselves more readily to the kind of analysis that Foucault developed in the course of his research into the history of governmentality. "Throughout the [nineteenth] century," she writes, "Britain's ruling classes strove to govern indirectly: to implement parliamentary power in ways that encouraged self-help, philanthropy, voluntarism, and local government."[89] Goodlad quotes the Victorian journalist Walter Bagehot's essay "The Character of Sir Robert Peele" on the difficulty and, indeed, harmfulness of forceful rule over

> a complicated network of ramified relations, interlacing and passing hither and thither, old and new—some of fine city weaving, others of gross agricultural construction. You are never sure what effect any force or any change may produce on a framework so exquisite and so involved. Govern it as you may, it will be a work of great difficulty, labour, and responsibility; and no man who is thus occupied ought ever to go to bed without reflecting that from the difficulty of his employment he may, probably enough, have that day done more evil than good.[90]

What emerges here as well as elsewhere in Victorian discourse on the social is a vision of thorough entanglement between the instances of civil society and the state. Within the governmental regime, the minimally intrusive, regulatory state is dissolved—vast and invisible—in the network of interacting individuals, all with their civil liberties and property rights. Once again, Bagehot: "though liberal governments take so much less in proportion upon them, yet the scale of operations is so much enlarged by the continuing exercise of civil liberty, that the real work is ultimately perhaps as immense [as in the case of a despotic government]."[91] This governmental terrain is where, according to Goodlad, Victorian social imaginaries play out, often taking the form of a tension between too little governance and too much. Dickens serves as the paradigmatic example here, with his desire for order that would be reliable but not coercive: "rational but unbureaucratic, omnipresent but personal, authoritative but liberatory, efficient but English."[92]

On this new social-imaginary terrain, a new question arises, occupying a prominent strain within Victorian fiction: how does belief in material and spiritual improvability square with suspicion of bureaucratic expansion of the state apparatus? Who will supply education and economic opportunity? According to Goodlad, this role is assigned to the social bond itself, a mechanism by which virtuous members of the middle class and gentry—recognizing the seriousness of their social obligation to the less fortunate—enable the spiritual and material improvement of those who know how to benefit from their aid. Thus conceived, society itself is the individual's Providence.[93]

Goodlad notes that such a solution remains problematic as long as the egalitarian assumption of "the limitless improvability of all human beings regardless of class, race, and, to a certain extent, sex/gender" coexists with vast inequalities in education, wealth, and power.[94] Moreover, such governmentally (or "pastorally") inclined fiction keeps confronting an excess population of unpastored and ungoverned characters, symptoms of the ostensibly "natural" processes of immiseration on a vast scale. As Emily Steinlight argues, the inherent failure of governmental techniques to be inclusive in their empowering mission made up subject matter that Victorian fiction eagerly accommodated, exposing the flaws of the socioeconomic system and gesturing with hope toward "a social state prepared to serve unmet human demands."[95] For Steinlight, the image of population in excess of the social order marks the limit of the dominant theoretical paradigm, which views the novel as a medium for playing out scripts of enfranchising socialization. Yet this limit is also a condition of possibility, since in fact the two scripts—of the benevolent integration of the desiring individual and of the exclusion of one or another kind of human detritus and excess—presuppose each other. The mad, the racially tainted, the criminal, the saintly, the sexually deviant, the incorrigibly poor, and the facelessly unindividuated—all mark the boundary of the social order. As members of the population minimally regulated within the regime of governmentality, they are allowed "naturally" to go extinct. Thus, outside the dominant narratives of discipline and social enfranchisement congealing around the protagonists, we find the problem of population management instantiated in the disastrous destinies of the immiserated supporting cast.

What literary scholars working within the Foucauldian paradigm tend to leave out—understandably, when it comes to European realist fiction—is the allegedly outdated, premodern regime of sovereignty: too rhetorically sublime, too naively overweening for the prosaic world of contemporary everyday life. To be sure, motifs of sovereign power do appear at the margins of the realist canvas. And whenever sovereignty is briefly glimpsed, it comes accompanied with customary associations: a valorized but no longer viable vision of sacred and omnipotent paternity (the ravings of the dying father in Balzac), or the archaic authority of the husband and feudal lord (Mr. Rochester's gothic inclinations), or a kind of Mercantilist meddling with the private lives of individuals (Goethe's Society of the Tower). Yet in each case, the imaginary of sovereign power marks not the focus but the limits of what is narratively compelling.

Hannah Arendt describes the novel as "the only entirely social art form."[96] By "the social" Arendt means the newly preponderant and specifically modern sphere of human togetherness in which private, interested, life-reproducing activity acquires public prominence. Here, individuals come together in pursuit of their self-interest, the interest in maximizing their worldly flourishing. Accompanying and legitimating this development, there arise the modern disciplines of economics, statistics, and behavioral science, all assuming that, in aggregate, social beings will follow predictable patterns of behavior. What results, according to Arendt, is a vast domain of human equality and conformity, akin, paradoxically, to the equality of "household members before the despotic power of the household head, except that in society, where the natural strength of one common interest and one unanimous opinion is tremendously enforced by sheer number, actual rule exerted by one man, representing the common interest and the right opinion, could eventually be dispensed with."[97] The rise of the social, then, coincides with the familiar double movement by which despotic coercion is both internalized, absorbed into the minutiae of the everyday, and at the same time disavowed.

Arendt does not discuss the modern novel at length, but in linking it to the increasing imbrication—continuity, conflation, confusion—between civil society and state power, she gives voice to something like a literary-critical common sense: that the shapes of sociality organizing the material of European realist fiction traverse and articulate the new social-imaginary terrain of the hegemonic "integral state." First articulated in Hegel, critiqued and supplemented by Marx, and taken up by social theorists most influential for the theoretical study of European realism, this "state ruled chiefly by ideology" can be characterized by the progressive emptying out of traditional status categories, the emergence into public prominence of private life and self-interested activity, the dispersal of coercion, the preponderance of ideological and hegemonic over direct and repressive forms of authority, and the occlusion of politics and of sovereign power as its most condensed and dramatic instantiation. The resulting realist "distributions of the social," as they have been delineated within the critical tradition with which I have briefly engaged above, include the coordination of individuals through desire, competition, and exchange; the staging of upward mobility through socialization, self-discipline, and versions of *Bildung*; the delineation of the domestic sphere—apolitical, authentic, intimate, rigidly gendered—as society's "moral core"; the staging of providential interconnectedness among apparently unconnected individuals, highlighting the unity of social and national life and the coordinating work of the "invisible hand"; and the production of constitutive exclusions, not only of the mad, the deviant, the racially marked, the insufficiently individuated (the rabble, the mob, the excess population), but also of the brashly aristocratic, the archaically paternalist, and the charismatically majestic.

Dominance without Hegemony

Meanwhile in Russia, as Gramsci memorably asserts: "the State was everything, civil society was primordial and gelatinous."[98] Gramsci gives expression here to what was by the time of his writing a truism: that Russian autocracy had feared and successfully resisted the formation of a semiautonomous civil society as a medium for its rule. With important qualifications, latter-day historians have tended to gravitate toward similar conclusions.[99] One, modulated version of Gramsci's thesis emerges in Marc Raeff's comparative study of the well-ordered police state (*Polizeistaat*) as it emerged in the German lands and in Russia during the eighteenth century and into the nineteenth. Raeff points out that wherever it was conceived and implemented, the project of augmenting the resources of the state through the mobilization of its subjects' quest for prosperity was haunted by a basic tension. By emphasizing the individual's direct relationship to the state, the project tended to undermine group solidarities and to spur on the emergence of self-interested, competitive subjects. Yet this in turn required that the state function as an intermediary to keep conflicting egoisms at bay.[100] It is here—at the level of the reaggregation of newly atomized individuals into groups—that the divergences between Western and Central Europe, on the one hand, and Russia, on the other, became most evident. While other polities could (and had to) rely on a preexisting social matrix of guilds, estates, parishes, and so on, the Russian state, beginning with Peter I, "remained in command and retained the initiative until the end of the nineteenth century, for there was no comprehensively structured society either to deter or to challenge it."[101]

This last point directs our attention at the other side of the state-society equation, where we seem indeed to have a great deal of fluidity, porousness, and atomization, with "gelatinously" defined estates and "primordial" group solidarities.[102] This lack of stable social stratification meant, on the one hand, greater variety and dynamism of discourses within the public sphere (at least once such a sphere began to develop in earnest), but on the other hand, a corresponding diffusion of the moral authority that, at least up to a point, continued to be rooted in the traditional institutions of the state.[103] Additionally, the porousness of social categories and commitments, as well as the emphasis on the unifying function of the state, tended to blur boundaries among what in Western societies were increasingly differentiated domains: the public and the private; state and church; the market, functioning according to its own "laws"; art existing for its own sake, and so on.[104]

To many nineteenth-century commentators, the inchoate nature of modern Russian society manifested itself as a chronically insufficient internalization of social norms. Unless directly coerced to do so, one simply refused to "behave," became unpredictable, irresponsible, insufficiently disciplined, a "bad subject" overall. As Viktor Zhivov has shown, the modern state's "civilizing mission" appears to have taken a peculiar path in Russia, where it could not rely on a preexisting set of religious practices of individuation through confession, self-examination, peccatorial calculation, and penance. Within Russian Orthodox soteriology, salvation tended to depend less on individual behavior and intentions than on divine mercy, which was largely uncontrollable and unpredictable. This meant that the subjective-cultural soil for the modern (Petrine) state's project of imposing discipline (confessional and other) on its population was in certain respects unprepared. While in the West such disciplinary institutions of religious life as confessional self-accounting tended to bring to life—make accessible for governance—the free, responsible, private, self-enclosed individual, the Orthodox tradition tended to leave intact the more spontaneous, less tractable visions of salvation (including its communal, rather than individual, character).[105] Thus, individuation itself—the emergence of the modern, self-governing, self-standing subject—unfolded directly within the sphere of the civilizing state. During the reign of Peter, salvation could be recast as achievable through disciplined service to the common good, instantiated in the state.[106] And though it did not penetrate deeply into the population as a whole, this notion of secular salvation through the state became highly consequential for the elites.

The dynamic of vigorous imposition, from above, of the sacralized-disciplinary notion of the "common good" can likewise be traced at the level of the history of Russian political concepts. Oleg Kharkhordin's account of the vicissitudes of the term *gosudarstvo*, for example, culminates with the formulation of what seems at first glance to be a paradox. In the context of both Russian and Western European absolutism, there eventually developed a notion of the "fatherland," res publica, "commonwealth"—in short, the domain of the common good separate from the person of the ruler himself or herself. The peculiarity of this concept's emergence in Russia consisted in the fact that rather than being introduced by republican thinkers who were in one way or another opposed to absolutism, it was imposed from above by the autocrat himself. According to Kharkhordin, what explains this peculiar situation when "monarchs [use] their considerable power to impose from above the conception of *respublica* on a recalcitrant populace" is an urgent need to control and regulate the population with greater efficiency and less effort. "In Russia, the increase in control had to happen faster and in a very limited period of time—since the czars had to catch up with the rest of Europe, which had moved farther along the road of technical progress and population management."[107] This geopolitical predicament of belatedness, as well as a population unprepared to cooperate with its own disciplinary remolding, accounted—at the beginning of the eighteenth century—for the state's peculiar monopoly not only on violence but on the notion of the common good. By comparison with Western Europe, where the discourse of res publica tended to emerge "from below," in the context of the emerging, albeit elite, "society" and frequently in opposition to the government, the Russian state's near-exclusive custodianship of the "common good" emerges as distinctive. In Yanni Kotsonis's words, the imperial state becomes the privileged "locus of mass integration," which "tended over time to encompass other possible planes of universal belonging—society, nation, and economy in particular."[108]

The Russian imperial state's function, both symbolic and practical, as the site of universal belonging converges with a long-standing native tradition of identifying the state with the sacralized figure of the ruler. Michael Cherniavsky calls attention to the fact that while medieval European princes were placed both above and below the law simultaneously (which is to say they were expected both to make the law and to observe it), the Russian conception of the saintly prince positioned him unambiguously *above* the law, his personal piety serving as the guarantee of wise and righteous rule. As the state became secularized toward the end of the seventeenth century and the standard of piety retreated, the ruler's personal will came simply to be identified with the law: "Law in Russia did not serve as a middle term between the tsar and the people, but, identified with the *person* of the Tsar, served to emphasize the identity of the ruler and the State."[109] Zhivov puts this even more forcefully:

The European concept of the monarch as the disposer of the common good leads in Russia to an unprecedented sacralization of the czar, originating during the time of [Czar] Alexei Mikhailovich and characterizing the entire imperial period of Russian history. In the Russian version of the mythology of the state, the monarch acted as the earthly God and the earthly savior, connected by a mysterious charismatic link with the heavenly God and the Savior-Christ, and at the same time as the Apostle leading his state along the path to salvation.[110]

In this context, secular, post-Petrine Russian culture acquired mythopoetic features, working to spread enlightenment that, precisely because it flowed from the charismatic top, could be expected magically to transform society as a whole. Zhivov suggests that by the end of the eighteenth century, as cultural production gained relative independence from the state, the myth-making, form-giving and order-creating functions previously attributed to the monarch were transferred to culture itself, eventually leading to the sacralization of the figure of the poet.[111] Such sacralization may have indeed been a latent phenomenon in Romantic and post-Romantic Russian culture, periodically crystallizing messianic or prophetic expectations around this or that cultural producer (Pushkin, Gogol, Dostoevsky, Tolstoy, etc.). Yet strictly speaking, we are not dealing here with a case of *transfer*—since by Zhivov's own admission the monarch and the state retained sacred attributes throughout the entire imperial period—but rather with something like *contagion*. Under this vision, the state and culture come to inhabit together—sometimes harmoniously and sometimes not—a kind of charismatic center, the locus of symbolic value, meaning, and social order. On this charismatic terrain—defined by Clifford Geertz as "an arena in which the events that most vitally affect [the community] take place"—state and culture confront each other as collaborators, competitors, or agonists. Geertz again: "It is involvement, even oppositional involvement, with such arenas and with the momentous events that occur in them that confers charisma. It is a sign [...] of being near the heart of things."[112]

"The heart of things," then—the arena of serious decisions, important events, and weighty acts—is how reconciliation-era Belinsky conceives of the state as the ultimate substance and true actuality, opposed to the ghostly world of private interests and occupations. Throughout the nineteenth century, in different microhistorical contexts spanning the "age of realism," representatives of diverse ideological orientations drew and commented on the position of the Russian state as the uniquely charismatic locus of both coercive power and meaningful togetherness. Several examples will allow us provisionally to highlight elements of the imaginary arising from and fertilizing the soil of this social formation.

At the beginning of 1836, the poet, translator, and educator of the crown prince, Vasily Zhukovsky, makes the following entry in his journal on the occasion of a fire in a popular St. Petersburg circus (*balagan*):

> It is possible to say that in Russia only one person, in accordance with his position, becomes deeply involved both in general happiness and in general disaster, and His Majesty was indeed the most active participant in this tragedy. He almost ran into the fire himself, turned pale when he heard about it, returning home terribly upset. But even in this there is something terrifying: in all general misfortunes, His Majesty must lead with his charisma [*pleniat' soboiu*]; and how long can he go on in this manner? Yet everything rests on him. [...] It is possible to say that these unfortunates perished from the same causes from which those who have collapsed from heat or lie half-frozen in the snow or wounded on the road die in our country so often. People fail to help them from fear of trouble with the police. Astonishing indifference bursts into the souls of passersby. And so, when the circus [*balagan*] caught fire, it occurred to no one to rush to the rescue; people waited for the police, and when the police arrived, there was no one left to rescue. [...] Here is another remarkable feature, insulting to our character. Three hours after this general disaster, almost near the place where the burnt bodies of 300 Russians were still smoldering, where the relatives of the dead wailed, their access to the dead denied by the police, the magnificent Engel'gardt house lit up, carriages streamed toward it, filled with the best Petersburg nobility, which represents in our country the entire Russian European intelligentsia; it occurred to no one (with some exceptions) that the misfortune is general; they danced and laughed and reveled till three o'clock and drove away as if nothing had happened. [...] Our people is made up of separate persons, not bound by any common union stemming from firm morals, duty. [...] Upon this universal lack of solidarity [*beschuvstvii*], autocracy now stands—stands for now. The consciousness of itself is awakening in it, but this consciousness is private, individual; there is something dangerous about this, and it can easily issue in violent rampage [*buistvo*]. Our people is made up of a multitude of animals, each chained separately in a cage. They sit there by themselves, oblivious to their fellowship; they are all in the same circus [*balagan*], and they seem to make up a society [*obshchestvo*], but everyone is separate and even seems ready to tear at his fellow; unchain them, and they will rip apart their master and chew each other up.[113]

Noted for the first use of the word "intelligentsia" in Russian, the entry describes a moment of crisis, a calamity that instantaneously distributes the social into "the many," who remain passive and indifferent to each other's troubles, and the charismatic "one," visibly affected by the common plight and working heroically to intervene. The abhorrence with which the diarist regards the indifference of the crowd is affectively balanced out in the image of the sublime sovereign's readiness to sacrifice his life for his subjects. As for the indifference itself, its roots are twofold: it is inherent in "our people" but also an acquired trait, learned through encounters with the arbitrarily acting police. The police—this other, profane, agent of autocracy—deepens the passivity of the people, making it both possible and necessary to regard the sovereign as the sole source of unity and salvation. The figures of the police and the emperor, in other words, function both in opposition to and in concert with each other: the police separates (in reality); the monarch unites (in the imagination). Had the police not separated, the people might not need the monarch to unite them. The resulting state of affairs enables atrocities such as the ball at the Engel'gardt house, where the nation's supposed leaders come together to enjoy themselves while the dead bodies of their fellow Russians still smolder nearby. The people gathered at the ball, the educated elite, the intelligentsia, would have been natural candidates for what Nancy Armstrong has called "the moral core" in the Victorian context.[114] Yet they prove to be the most abject and thoughtless of all, morally bankrupt precisely in their inability to leverage their privileges for the common good. By the end of the entry, we are prepared then to encounter the striking image of the Russian people made up of chained and caged animals that would tear their master and each other apart if allowed to roam free. Here we have the Hobbesian projection of lupine enmity of all against all, justifying the sovereign's absolute monopoly on violence. Resorting to ambivalent figuration once again, the diarist asserts that Russian autocracy "stands upon" the lack of social solidarity. Autocracy draws its legitimacy from the exclusively self-seeking predilections of its subjects, and yet it, too, is always in danger of succumbing to "rampage," itself becoming like the uncaged animals it is called upon to tame. Sovereignty, this ambiguous figure of the heart of things, the site of both common good and sheer violence, is the only thing that "stands," remains actual and substantive amid the chaos of social fragmentation—stands *for now*.

Confronting the traumatic event of the fire, Zhukovsky resorts to the scenario of "dominance without hegemony," in which an excess of coercion and charisma, force and meaning, comes to compensate for the absence of shared values, norms, and institutions.[115] Missing here are precisely the aggregative workings of civil society, the individuals' coming together more or less spontaneously into groups in which private and common interests mix in various proportions. Instead, we are left with a vision of isolated, undisciplined subjects, connected by no hegemonic culture, animalistic and predatory in their self-centered indifference to the common. Autocracy then emerges as the only actor on stage: frightening and sublime, despotic and benevolent, arbitrary and universal.

Almost twenty years later, in an article written in 1855 with the purpose of formulating the most urgent tasks for the new reign, the young Russian jurist and Hegelian philosopher Boris Chicherin offers a historical overview of the relationship between society and the state in Russia. Chicherin writes: "there is no nation [*narod*] in Europe whose social spirit is as little developed as [Russia's]; everybody lives separately, and common needs and interests are nobody's business."[116] The origin story of the Russian state, the invitation of the Varangians to rule over the Slavic tribes, testifies to the "the inability of separate persons to come together into a union grounded in their own powers and their own activity."[117] The state could not be formed organically from within but had to be imported from the outside, and much of Russian history since then has deepened this original failure. Following Hegel, Chicherin sees the proper function of the state as harmonizing the varied and often conflicting demands that exist in society and thus giving all a stake in the preservation of the lawful order. "Only such conciliatory activity endows government with true strength, for then it finds support everywhere. Every social interest, having become lawful, thereby becomes attached to the general lawful order and joins itself to the government."[118] Instead, what Chicherin finds in contemporary Russia is an omnipresent state, a sprawling bureaucratic apparatus that makes it "impossible to take a step without running into some government official, without encountering a superior, an administrator, a warden."[119] Rather than stimulating, satisfying, and harmonizing individual aspirations, the state obtrudes into every impulse, obstructs every initiative. And echoing Zhukovsky: "We know that the government is everything and we are nothing, and we don't see any way out of this predicament. [...] Hence the general indifference toward the social cause [*obshchestvennomu delu*]. Everyone sees that he can't do anything useful for the fatherland, and this is why everyone concentrates on his private life and cares only for his personal interests."[120] As the coercive state apparatus expands, individuals retreat deeper into the private sphere, from within which they confront the authority of the state in a direct, unmediated way, as the prevailing principle of common life.

Thus the Westernizer Chicherin on the occasion of the imperial succession. Several years later, in the aftermath of the sovereign decree on the emancipation of serfs, the second-generation Slavophile Ivan Aksakov voices a similar complaint. In the sixth article of the series, titled "On the Mutual Relationship of the People [*narod*], the State, and Society" (1862), Aksakov diagnoses a perverse and perilous distribution of activity among the three elements of the contemporary Russian social formation mentioned in the title. In Aksakov's view, the state occupies too prominent a role within the triadic relationship, serving as the sole source of dynamism, the only agent of change; society and the common people retreat into passivity, lose their independence, and languish:

> In a word, the czar's decree and the czar's patronage begin to penetrate everywhere and throughout—and soon upon the idle expanse of the Land [*Zemlia*], filling the void created by the absence of any social environment and social activity, there remains only—and exclusively—autocratic initiative. Activity belongs only to the government; it alone imparts vitality and motion, creates and institutes; everything else is plunged into inaction and, little by little, into lethargy. Evidently, life and movement descending downward from the government do not light up the fire of real life and are themselves effective only until the heavy hand of power lets go.[121]

According to Aksakov, the reigns of Ivan IV and Peter I set the tone for the rest of Russian history, in which the organic social expression of the people's life remains underdeveloped, while the external forms of state power predominate. Thus: "the excessive, overflowing activity of the government, overtaking the domains of private and social activity, deadens life, paralyzes the national [*narodnyi*] organism, muffles the spiritual powers of the people [*naroda*]."[122] At the time when the state has just once again displayed itself as the agent of dynamism, transforming society from above with its decree ending serfdom, Aksakov's observations were not destined to contribute to the hypotrophied life of social opinion in Russia. As if to dramatize Aksakov's diagnosis, Emperor Alexander II himself overruled the censor's attempts to make the text of this final article of the series acceptable and forbade its publication altogether.[123]

Both Chicherin and Aksakov bemoan the imbalance in the relationship between society and the state, tacitly anxious that, unless remedied, it will make the country vulnerable to revolutionary upheaval. Others welcomed aspects of this predicament, emphasizing in particular the benefits of poorly developed civil society institutions. To them, the current situation in Russia left open the possibility of a more holistic, harmonious, and just society to come. In an unpublished article, quoted by Dostoevsky in his *Writer's Diary* (March 1876), the social activist Nikolai Peterson argues that "associations, corporations, cooperatives, trade and other partnerships" cannot be regarded as instances of authentic human togetherness:

> History indeed testifies that all these unions originated out of fraternal enmity and were based not on the need for social intercourse […] but on the

feeling of fear for one's survival or on the wish for gain, profit, or benefit, even at the expense of one's neighbor. When we examine the structure of all these progeny of utilitarianism, we see that their main concern is to organize firm control of everyone over all and of all over everyone—to put it simply, wholesale espionage arising from the fear that one person may cheat another.[124]

According to Peterson, the fact that these institutions have not taken root in Russia can be viewed as a promising sign for the coming universal reconciliation. Associations within civil society continue and even intensify the struggle of all against all, while genuine human association will bring together the people as a whole, freeing it from all internal divisions. Thus: "the feeling of unity, without which human societies cannot exist, is still effective among us, even though it acts unconsciously on people and leads them not only to great deeds but also, very often, to great vices."[125]

Noteworthy in Peterson's text is the link between the emergence of associations and the spread of disciplinary surveillance and control. If individuals come together not from genuine recognition of interdependence or with the purpose of combining their efforts toward the realization of a common task, but rather out of mutual fear and enmity, then it is no wonder that they would seek the means of taming each other's predatory impulses. Echoing Marx and anticipating Foucault, Peterson (as well as, it appears, Dostoevsky) understands civil society as little more than an amplification of egoism, on the one hand, and compensatory disciplinary surveillance, on the other. An early follower of Nikolai Fedorov's teachings, Peterson places greater trust in the community of "mutual love" or "universal unification," which would avoid both the fragmentation of interests and the complementary discipline of generalized "espionage."[126]

The motif of civil society underdevelopment is prominent in Alexander Herzen's essay "On the Development of Revolutionary Ideas in Russia" (1851). Like the eschatological mystic Peterson (and his tentative sympathizer Dostoevsky), the émigré socialist Herzen views the weakness of Western-style civil society in a positive light, insofar as it leaves open more space for radical, emancipatory change. Unconstrained by respect for private property or the law, Herzen's compatriots bow before the reigning order only because—and for as long as—they feel directly coerced by it:

> In Russia, behind the visible state, there is no invisible state, one that would represent the apotheosis, the transfiguration of the reigning order of things, there is no unreachable ideal that never coincides with reality even if it keeps promising to do so. There is nothing behind these fences where a force exceeding our own keeps us besieged. The question of the

possibility of the revolution in Russia comes down to material force. This is why [...] this country becomes the soil best prepared for a social regeneration.[127]

By "invisible state" Herzen means the internalized, idealized, and therefore, in the minds of its subjects, legitimate polity, inspiring obedience not under threat of coercion but out of deep-seated, habitual respect for the social order, in the preservation of which the subjects of the state have a personal stake. The task of the Russian revolutionary, then, is more straightforward: it is easier to scale a fence than to navigate a vast labyrinth of barriers and ditches, some of which—in the form of diverse disciplines, hegemonic practices, and ideological interpellations—pass through one's own self.

Whether it is positively or negatively assessed, to whatever historical genealogy it is attributed, the motif of state "dominance without hegemony" pervades sociopolitical writings of the time. It should not come as a surprise, then, that similar considerations make their way into contemporary attempts to makes sense of the national literary trends as well. Eloquent in this respect is Pavel Annenkov's review of Alexey Pisemsky's 1858 novel, *One Thousand Souls*. The article begins with a kind of preamble in which the critic uses the novel under review as a pretext for comparative reflections on recent trends in European and Russian socially-minded fiction. Contemporary European novelists, Annenkov claims, tend to explore the workings of the human heart in everyday private interactions and relationships, steering clear of broader political concerns. These latter may occasionally intrude into the lives of characters but never come to occupy center stage. Even the creators of the so-called social novel (*sotsial'nyi roman*) in Europe—the critic singles out George Sand and Charles Dickens—made sure that "administrative and political issues" remain marginal in their work.[128] In Annenkov's description, such novels center on the conflict between the "real and valid [*deistvitel'nykh*] human needs," on the one hand, and the "abstract demands of society," on the other. This conflict, however, is mediated through the introduction of certain characters "abounding with dignity and in possession of a remarkable power of moral influence." Through their intercession, the errors, demands, and excesses of private persons are moderated and the punishing forces ("raw violence and bloody vengeance") disarmed.[129]

Prominent in this account is the figure of mediation, a "moral influence" that can reconcile individual strivings with the demands of social order, prevent desiring individuals from turning into "bad subjects," and preclude societal norms from hardening into sovereign injunctions. This type of mediation is, in Annenkov's view, insufficiently practiced in Russian realist fiction. Here, especially with the recent fashion for fictionalized exposure of bureaucratic abuse (encouraged by the newly crowned, reform-minded Alexander II), administrative, rather than personal, matters come to the foreground. The novel under review, too, though artistically superior to other instances of the "exposure" genre, falls into this category. Hence, the title of the review essay: "Delovoi roman v nashei literature" ("The Administrative Novel in Our Literature").

Why, then, does Russian fiction assume a different shape? With requisite wariness of the censors, Annenkov suggests:

> Perhaps [our private, civil life] retreats too soon at the sight of every expression of right, however arbitrary and even impotent it may be? [...] Do we see many examples when, with its own moral means, through a noble, honest and lawful struggle, [society] reformed a human being, without waiting for the saving hand from the outside, which alone is, in our country, tasked with the hard work of making people and unmaking them [*delat' i razdelyvat' liudei*], as it were, without the participation of public opinion.[130]

And further: "Given the absence of [moral convictions guiding our social relations], and so given the immaturity of our private life, deprived of strength and true self-sufficiency, it is natural that the official side of society acquires unusual importance. Sooner or later it will try to overshadow all the other sides nudged forth into God's world and will be alone responsible for the entirety of life."[131]

Because the sphere of social interactions fails to yield a meaningful shape immanently, from within, the state works to fashion it directly, "making and unmaking" people from without. Annenkov then wonders whether the history of European art offers any analogies for the current disposition of the literary field in Russia. What comes to mind, somewhat unexpectedly at first glance, is classical antiquity:

> After all, there was an epoch when indeed a particular person and the history of a people walked together in an amicable embrace, where the thoughts of the former constituted the content of the latter, where the latter only said what the former said, an epic era that left us samples of its impeccable works. Why not try to resurrect it? Of course, to achieve this kindred unity and indistinction between a private person and official life we should first of all greatly simplify our entire circumstances of living [*byt*], which, it seems, cannot be expected, but why despair?[132]

Setting aside the question of whether Annenkov believes such a change to be desirable (the sense one gets from the essay is that he emphatically does not), we may ask what such a simplification of "our entire circumstances of living" would look like. At play here is something akin to the "two liberties" thesis, prominent in nineteenth-century liberal thought. As formulated by Benjamin Constant in his lecture "On the Liberty of the Moderns as Compared with That of the Ancients" (1819), the difference between these two conceptions of liberty hinges on the imagined expansiveness and elaboration of social space. The "ancients" saw themselves as direct participants in the government of their polities; self-government was the sphere of the most consequential exercise of their freedom to act. By contrast, the "moderns" treasure freedom as the space in which they can pursue their own goals without interference from political authority. The reason such interference appears oppressive to the moderns has everything to do with the fact that they live in larger, more complicated, commercial societies in which their sense of belonging to the political unit as a whole fades out, appears distant and abstract by comparison with their everyday preoccupations. "The bigger a country is, the smaller is the political importance allotted to each individual. The most obscure republican of Sparta or Rome had power. The same is not true of the simple citizen of Britain or of the United States. His personal influence is an invisibly small part of the social will that gives the government its direction."[133]

Constant's two conceptions of liberty imply two social-imaginary purviews: one in which the individual is directly and vividly—substantively—linked to the state, and the other in which he or she is caught up in a complex network of—aggregative—private relationships and concerns. Correspondingly at stake are two distinct dynamics of individuation: one in which the self is expressed in a direct confrontation with political power (both in its exercise and in being subject to its exercise), and the other in which the self is expressed through commerce (both literal and figurative) with other selves, while questions of political power, foundation, and belonging are relegated to the margins of experience, if not altogether beyond. Something like this dichotomy underpins Annenkov's notion of social simplification and marks the ambiguous position of contemporary Russian fiction between two nonoverlapping social imaginaries. Annenkov's critical intuition here, like Belinsky's before him, bespeaks a disturbance of asynchronous transplantation, a hybrid distribution of the social, combining awareness of complex "modern" intercourse with the "archaic" sense of intimate immediacy in relation to the charismatic center of power and meaning. It is this immediacy that excites reconciliation-era Belinsky with its heroic scenarios of sublime self-sacrifice and disturbs Reform-Era Annenkov with its illiberal, amoral, and unmodern air.[134]

Another Realist Fiction

When Belinsky speaks of "substance" or Annenkov of "simplification," they name among other things a predicament—the warping of elaborate social arrangements by scenarios of confrontation with the state—that forcefully shapes the lifeworlds of cultural producers in the age of Russian realism. Throughout the eighteenth century, elite culture and the monarchy maintain a relationship of intense mutual interdependence, supplementarity, and occasional contestation.[135] The state-culture knot loosens somewhat during the early decades of the nineteenth century as the literary field gradually gains autonomy from the system of patronage and dependence on the royal court.[136] Yet the emerging literary market within which realist fiction rises to prominence remains heavily inflected by state intervention of varying types: from censorship and journal closures to sponsorship of official organs and recruitment of individual authors. The authors themselves continue to be tempted by the ideal of service to the state while also feeling that their lives and livelihoods rest precariously at its mercy.

Retrospectively assessing the condition of the mid-nineteenth-century Russian literary field, the writer and literary critic Nikolai Engel'gardt observes: "In Russia, the censorship authority arose before literature and the press. This explains why it had the opportunity to analyze each line, each verse. [...] Literature and the press were so insignificant that the monarch himself had time to read everything and to note the disrespect of some author of feuilletons [...] for the St. Petersburg police and cabmen."[137] And further: "Censorship was merciless only because literature—above all when it came to the number of organs, capital, and quantity—was weak and insignificant. [...] There was no moral connection between the reader and the writer. The reader did not consider it obligatory to protect the writer, was not at all in solidarity with him, while in the West every [literary] organ [had] a party backing it up."[138]

Engel'gardt's analysis recapitulates a familiar motif: the weakness of social bonds leaves much room for, indeed solicits, heavy-handed state interference. And the reverse: state interference accounts for the literary field's financial fragility and lack of self-sufficiency. The relationship between the state and the market in the literary domain comes through vividly in the distinctive history of Russian copyright regulations, which placed matters of intellectual property within the jurisdiction of censorship authority. Ekaterina Pravilova comments on the unusual character of this arrangement in comparative perspective: "The 'police' character of the copyright system was unique to Russia: unlike other European legislation, Russian laws on copyright formed a part of the censorship regulation, and only in 1887 finally entered the Civil Code."[139] The establishment of literary ownership rights—an important factor in the emergence of a literary market—remained closely linked to the institutions of direct state prohibition and control.

The state's peculiar proximity to and close supervision over cultural work introduced far-reaching ambiguities into the political dynamics of literary production. At first glance, such supervision strives to neutralize literature's antagonistic potential. Not only does it make impossible (barring an anomalous lapse) to publish works directly critical of the state, but it also balks at the introduction of topics touching on broad social concerns. To recall one telling example, Turgenev's short story *Mumu* (1854), which contains not even an oblique mention of politics, nevertheless endured several contentious encounters with censorship on the grounds that its readers might be led to criticize the institution of serfdom, which "as one of our state institutions, cannot be subject to the censure of a private person."[140] The impulse to protect the regime from the written word at times found grotesque manifestations; thus, writing for Herzen and Nikolai Ogarev's London-based *Golosa iz Rossii*, Nikolai Mel'gunov tells of the excision of the ominous compound "*Kaiserschnitt*" (cesarean section) from a medical treatise.[141] Apocryphal or not, the episode bespeaks a social imaginary urgently attuned to the figure of the czar (along with his requisite regicides).

Of course, censorship practices were neither uniform nor even consistent in their character. In addition to periodic changes at the top of the hierarchy, individual censors often found ways to mediate between writers (frequently their own colleagues and friends) and the government, enabling certain works to appear by drafting skillful, tension-diffusing reports. Thus, for example, Ivan Goncharov (who served as a censor from the end of the 1850s until well into the 1860s) shrewdly intervened on behalf of the publication of *Mumu* in a separate volume of Turgenev's tales, arguing that to exclude it now, after it had already been published in a journal, would only call undesirable attention to the story, whereas published alongside others, it will no longer be able to have the impact it had upon its first appearance.[142]

Goncharov's argument in this case gestures at a more general consideration, highlighting the paradoxical capacity of censorship to broaden and sharpen, rather than neutralize, the political import of literary texts. A congenial line of thinking appears to motivate the authors of the 1862 *Draft Statute on Publishing* (*Proekt ustava o knigopechatanii*), commissioned by Alexander II. Among other provisions, the authors of the draft insist that the practice of issuing censorship ordinances in the name of the sovereign himself is unique to Russia and brings with it a two-pronged complication: it does not leave literature sufficient autonomy from politics and at the same time endows it with inflated political significance. The draft refers to the view of an earlier commission that direct subordination of literature to the word of the sovereign can expose the person of the monarch himself to the displeasure of his subjects.[143]

The authors of the report seek to depoliticize literature by rethinking it as an autonomous domain to be regulated by an appropriate agency, but not directly in the name of the czar. The difference between the monarch (whose word is law) and the "private" minister (whose ordinance may function as a temporary regulation) might appear subtle at first glance, but it is urgent for the commission, whose members insist that the monarch and the subject must not encounter each other—not to mention clash— face to face on the terrain of literature. Let journalistic disagreements resolve themselves; the correct view can defeat the misguided one by means of persuasion. By weighing in on one side of the debate, the sovereign draws through the literary field a clear line of demarcation between obedience and rebellion, making it more politically consequential than it needs to be. To allow literature greater autonomy, in other words, is to neutralize it, to place it further from "the heart of things" and back where it "belongs": in the ideological labyrinths of social intercourse. To keep a strict watch over it, conversely, is to "simplify" its social horizon, to reduce it to an encounter with sovereign power and thus to charge it with politically explosive potential. The eventual censorship reform of 1865 largely failed to achieve this outcome, eliminating prepublication reviews for all periodicals in Moscow and St. Petersburg, but preserving post-factum punitive authority, empowering the Ministry of the Interior to prosecute a wide range of transgressions. Central among them was failure to "protect the inviolability of the Supreme Authority and its attributes" or to show "respect for members of the reigning house."[144]

To be sure, the assertion of state control over the work of nineteenth-century writers was not limited to censorship practices and official regulations. These were in fact the most workaday forms of encounter in the field of sovereign power. More dramatic scripts took the shape of imprisonment, exile, penal servitude, ban on publication, perlustration of personal correspondence, estate searches, fatherly admonitions by the monarch, and so on. "By placing themselves close to the seat of autocratic power," writes Gareth Jones, "writers inevitably encouraged the Russian autocrats to seek to control their production and their lives."[145] William Todd describes the situation similarly: "The government did live in fear of what the Emperor Alexander II in a pre-Foucauldian moment called 'the dangers which are the result of the ungovernability and excesses of the printed word.' But it also lived in hope that the printed word could serve its ends, propagating the official policy of 'Orthodoxy, Autocracy, and Nationality.'"[146]

Alexander Pushkin's brief life is exemplary as a depository of scripts played out between the poet and the czar. Here we have the punishment of exile (twice), the dubious privilege of the sovereign's personal oversight, state commissions, police perlustration of intimate correspondence, paralyzing indebtedness to the treasury, and painful prohibition of foreign travel. Even on the poet's deathbed, the czar remains a privileged interlocutor: Pushkin sends a note requesting that Nicholas not abandon his family after his death, and the emperor replies with the promise. Less variegated, but not less remarkable, is Dostoevsky's trajectory from the site of execution for political crimes at the end of the 1840s to invitations to dine with the grand dukes, children of Alexander II, during the late 1870s. A similarly paradoxical fate befell Herzen and Ogarev's journal *The Bell* (*Kolokol*), published in London, banned in Russia, yet routinely read by Alexander II's ministers and the emperor himself. The point to emphasize here is not so much the dynamic of opposition and persecution or collaboration and reward, but rather a fundamental *intimacy* between literature and the state, intimacy that could with comparable probability break a life or endow it with high meaning (sometimes both in the same gesture).[147]

The paradoxes and dramatic reversals organizing the lives of cultural producers owe their urgency not only to the state's ambivalent project of interdiction and co-optation but just as much to the long-standing and powerful ethos of service informing the social imaginaries of the writers themselves. Emerging as part of the state's "civilizing" project, members of the cultural elite continued to owe their property, privileges, status, and vocation to the post-Petrine state.[148] And as the state accumulated sacred status, service itself acquired numinous, soteriological implications.[149] It was through service to the state, understood as the universal locus of meaningful togetherness, that individuals gained not only sustenance and status but also normative identity and value.[150] Directly exposed to the power of the state, members of the elite were often willing to embrace the exposure in exchange for proximity to the symbolic center in relation to which their lives attained an aura of higher purpose and substantive significance.

Well into the nineteenth century and more than occasionally, writers conceived of their own literary work as a form of service to the state.[151] An excerpt from Gogol's *An Author's Confession* (1847; published 1855) is telling in this regard:

> I saw clearly that I could no longer write without a plan that was completely definitive and clear, that the purpose of my work, its essential usefulness

and necessity should be well understood, as a result of which the author himself would conceive a true and strong love for his labor, [the love] that gives life to everything and without which work stands still. In a word, so that the author himself feels and is convinced that, by creating his creation, he fulfills that very duty for which he has been called to the earth, for which he was given abilities and strength, and that, while fulfilling it, he also serves his state, as if he really was in public service. The thought of service never vanished from my mind.[152]

The passage registers a moment of synthesis in Gogol's account of his biography between his persistent striving for social usefulness and his literary gifts. Only when he comes to realize that it is possible to use the latter in the service of the former does he acquire the proper frame of mind for undertaking the culminating literary project of his life in earnest. Literature as service, then: both to God and to the state, to God and to the state simultaneously and jointly.

To be sure, the monarchy's official position on service obligations for the nobility as well as cultural (and of course individual) perceptions of those who served varied throughout the eighteenth and nineteenth centuries. Over time, the nobility, and the Westernized intelligentsia more broadly, created and confronted other worthwhile objects of service: the fatherland, the people, the nation, and so on. The state could be perceived as having fallen away from the ideal of enlightened and civilizing service or as standing in direct opposition to it. But even struggle—since it was struggle over the same "sacred" terrain of the common good—furthered the codependent relationship between culture and the state, so that moments of cathartic convergence remained possible even in cases of extreme enmity. Thus, the political émigrés Herzen and Ogarev greet Alexander II's statements of intention to end serfdom with a triumphant "You have conquered, O Galilean!" followed by the assertion that "he [the czar] works with us—for the sake of a great future!"[153] Far from exceptional, such moments of conversion are typified at the conclusion of Turgenev's 1874 tale *Punin and Baburin*, whose protagonist, the lifelong republican and political exile Baburin, exclaims upon reading the Emancipation Manifesto "God save the czar!"[154] Within the service-oriented social imaginary guiding the elite's relationship to the state, the option of rushing to the side of the sovereign (as soon as it became remotely possible to do so) remained open even in cases of radical opposition.

Early in Herzen's epic memoir *My Past and Thoughts*, we find a passage that enacts this dynamic of conflicted symbiosis with emblematic precision. Herzen speaks there of his youthful love of Friedrich Schiller, singling out in particular the tragedy *Don Karlos* (1787). The play, and especially the plotline associated with the marquis of Posa, appeals to him as a script for political struggle. Yet the struggle takes a peculiar form. At the culmination of the play, the rebellious, freedom-loving Posa momentarily becomes the tyrannical Phillip II's closest adviser and only friend. Posa attempts to convince the Spanish emperor to renounce his power and grant his subjects religious and political freedoms, but the mission eventually fails, and he is killed. Herzen comments, "I imagined in a hundred variations how I would speak to Nicholas, and how afterwards, he would send me to the mines or the scaffold."[155] True friend of the tyrant and conspirator against him, adviser and victim, loyal collaborator and implacable enemy, Posa stimulates Herzen's political imagination, capturing something fundamental about the conflicted attitude of the Russian gentry intellectual toward the monarchy: even in opposing it, one cannot altogether be rid of its charismatic allure. Not merely a psychological trait, such ambivalence is embedded in a social formation within which the panmodern process of gradual autonomization of the literary field—its disentanglement from the patronage of the court and its alignment with the market—takes on a distinctive shape under the pressure of counteracting tendencies: strict political censorship; frequent and dramatic intrusion of sovereign power into the lives, livelihoods, and lifeworlds of writers; and the resilient tradition of locating higher meaning in the state as the sole and sacred locus of universal belonging.

From the soil of this distinctive institutional and existential orientation, the characteristic social imaginaries of Russian realist fiction arise and mix in various proportions and to varied effects with the realist problematics of the pacification and accommodation of individuals within civil society. The texts to which we are about to turn treat most of the same themes and unfold along many of the same plotlines as contemporary Western European fiction. Here, too, various narrative patterns and character types gather around the realist problematic of self-fulfillment in society: an individual—naive, idealistic, passionate, alienated, often socially underdetermined, often of middling or poor means, sometimes from the provinces, sometimes from abroad—appears in various social settings, all more or less complexly delineated, more or less stifling of the protagonist's individuality, more or less artificial, conventional, stagnantly antiquated, oppressively modern, and so on. Standard realist motifs are everywhere: introduction to modernity and social life; a path of development, or *Bildung*; choice of mentors; courtship and marriage; career possibilities; financial difficulties; marital infidelity; intergenerational conflict within the family; and more. And yet, here we also confront a set of orthogonal concerns: sovereign power, its majesty and its abuses; substantive belonging and separation; imaginaries of coercion and service, obedience and rebellion, overweening power and sacrifice; and an urgent preoccupation with the dilemmas and dramas involved in the basic constitution of human groupings as such. Put another way, Russian realist fiction is compelled to reckon with the emergence to the foreground of literary form of the private person in the context in which it is not civil society but the state that appears as the robust and serious model of togetherness and belonging.

These latter engagements with sovereignty are not simply added on to the standard realist motifs associated with civil society configurations. They operate rather as "dominant," form-giving elements, reshaping the transplanted social-imaginary material of Western realism under the influence of the local, state-oriented "literary environment." To deform here does not mean to depart from some ostensibly "normal," "shapely" realism, but rather to rearrange the inherited thematic and formal material within the forcefield of local social horizons. We have already glimpsed the workings of such deformation in Belinsky's encounter with Hegel. The encounter provides us with our first case study in the distinctive orientation of Russian realist social imaginaries toward the absolute logics of the state substantively construed. To recognize such an orientation means here to shift our analytic perspective, placing at the center of our inquiry what in European realism is altogether excluded or relegated to the margins, at best. Instead of focusing on the dynamics of social aggregation, we are compelled to confront the conditions for the possibility of a depicted social life, the behind-the-scenes articulation of social space by political authority, that establishes the parameters of what is socially possible. This requires that we elaborate a set of principles, a poetics, for a social imaginary grounded in a vision of human collectivity as *substantive*: absolute, pervasive, primordial, both coercive and meaning-giving. It requires, in other words, that we read Russian realist fiction—the fiction of *deistvitel'nost'*—as the fiction of substantive community. The next four chapters are dedicated to this task.

State

[CHAPTER TWO]

Other Reality Effects

Making Substance Visible

Belinsky's analysis of *Taras Bulba* highlights the substantive bond at the dramatic center of the historical novella with the following words: "He conflated national enmity with personal hatred."[1] The formula captures the logic organizing the kernel sequence of the tale: Andriy's treasonous love for the Polish girl and his death at the hands of his own father in the midst of a battle. Within the horizon of national enmity, private acts come to bear substantive consequences. The situation of existential peril for the community overrides both Andriy's love for the beautiful Pole and Bulba's love for his son, recasting the intimate reciprocities of private desire and affection into the substantive models of political belonging. War is the pretext for the conversion of *private* feelings into *political* confrontation.

In the review of Fyodor Glinka's *Sketches*, Belinsky describes the substantive consolidation triggered by war as follows:

> Everything in [the social body] is asleep in a kind of slumbering calm, everything is so normal and mundane: the judge goes to the court in order to get his pay and live off of it; the warrior carries out his responsibilities as a matter of duty, which makes up the conditions for his sustenance; the merchant thinks of his profits; in a word, everything is occupied with itself, and everyone is an Ivan or a Peter, a Sidor or a Luka. But suddenly a storm of foreign invasion sweeps by the sleeping multitude [*narod*] and breaks out in thunder and lightning over its carefree head—and there are no more individuals [*liudei*]: there appears a [unified] people [*narod*], there are no more personal and private interests: all cares [*dumy*] are given to the fatherland; the motley crowds have merged into a general mass, at the head of which appears the czar.[2]

Belinsky's narrative about the conversion of a multitude of self-seeking Ivans and Peters into a single body with the sovereign at its head functions as the answer to an implicit question: Given that individual lives unfold most proximately amid an elaborate network of social aggregations, how, if at all, can their fundamental, substantive togetherness be made visible? Or in the critic Pavel Annenkov's terms: Under what conditions does everyday social life become radically "simplified" so that there is no longer any difference between the private and political domains? The answer is a long-standing one: What makes the state in its purity available to experience is war. In war, the state is manifested not as a mere composite of civil society linkages but as a substantive unity that subtends these links and makes them possible in the first place. Hegel, on whom Belinsky more or less directly draws here, puts it as follows: "It is a grave miscalculation if the state, when it requires this sacrifice [of all individual interests during a war] is simply equated with civil society, and if its ultimate end is seen merely as the *security of life and property* of individuals [*Individuen*]. For this security cannot be achieved by the sacrifice of what is supposed to be *secured*."[3] War is not a struggle for individual life and property, since these are often sacrificed for the preservation of what serves as the condition for the possibility of, and the principle of organization for, life and property as such.

Later in the article, Belinsky invokes another situation in which the substantive unity of the state occupies center stage, the interregnum:

> The Blessed [Alexander I] has died. Why is it that in the first-throned city [Moscow], from the tollgates to the walls of the holy Kremlin, thick crowds of countless people stretch on both sides, barely kept in order by the double formation of soldiers […] ? Who called them here? No one; even those who have the right to convene people are more concerned that their numbers will not cause them harm. Why are the faces of all bright and joyful, alien to all everyday care, all self-seeking thoughts? Why are the eyes of all turned in one direction with yearning and trembling expectation? Why does the air shake suddenly from a moaning "hurray" as if coming from a single breast and a single mouth, accompanied by the regal ringing of bells and thunder of cannons? The new czar enters ancient Moscow to be anointed for his reign.[4]

Here, the image of spontaneous unity, of the multitude gathering into a single body, fills in the gap between the reigns of Alexander I and Nicholas I, preserving the czar's "body politic" in the momentary absence of the "body natural."[5] The death of the monarch presents a moment of peril for the polity; indeed, Belinsky's scene of acclamation covers up a wound delivered to the reigning order by the Decembrist uprising in St. Petersburg. The crisis of the interregnum makes itself felt in the emphasis on the "one body," purged of all fragmenting egoisms, looking with one set of eyes, breathing with one breast, acclaiming in unison. Barely noticed in the festive environment is the double formation of the soldiers, keeping the crowd "in order." The state manifests itself as love and force.

War, interregnum, rebellion—Carl Schmitt has referred to these crises as "states of exception," making visible the foundations of human community on which the individuals' private and social lives depend. The state of exception is "a case of extreme peril, a danger to the existence of the state," but exactly what circumstances amount to such a case of peril cannot be foreseen or circumscribed by law.[6] Rather, the state of exception is a matter of decision, and this decision belongs to the sovereign, an agent positioned above the law insofar as he or she can suspend it in order to protect or restore public order and security. Ultimate power must lie in the hands of a single individual, who, in an emergency, can put an end to the otherwise potentially endless deliberations on the question of what constitutes the public good. The sovereign's decision on the exception transpires as a radical reduction of the entire range of human relationships to those of friend and enemy, some who belong to the "intense association" of the given political grouping and others who don't: traitors, rebels, hostile powers, and so on.[7] Everything private and personal is stripped down to reveal a basic structure of belonging, a structure that functions as the condition for the possibility of social life as such.

Schmitt's diagnosis of the contemporary social formation roughly coincides with the assessments of the theorists who have supplied much of the conceptual apparatus for recent scholarship on European realism: state and society are entwined in such a way that only individuals and their ostensibly spontaneous aggregations remain visible. "What had been [...] affairs of state," Schmitt writes, "become [...] social matters, and vice versa, what had been purely social matters become affairs of the state—as must necessarily occur in a democratically organized unit."[8] To various degrees, Gramsci, Althusser, and Foucault recognize that behind the subtle and insinuating disciplinary, hegemonic, and ideological apparatuses lurks (the possibility of) sheer sovereign violence. It is this inevitable surplus of absolute power that Schmitt repeatedly highlights as the insuperable precondition of political community as such. Drawing on a wide range of philosophers of European absolutism such as Jean Bodin, Thomas Hobbes, Samuel Pufendorf, Joseph de Maistre, and others, he thus supplies something like a starting point for a poetics of realism nurtured in the soil of a state-centered social imaginary. This is to say that the "state of exception" can be understood as the horizon against which the traditional realist concern with individuation is taken up in Russia. One comes of age, loves, desires, dreams of domestic bliss, seeks a position in society—all against a more or less explicitly articulated sense of danger to the fundamental order of things. One's apparently private pursuits acquire political weight, confront sovereign prohibition, imperil substantive community, and position the acting individual as an outsider vis-à-vis the "intense association" of the tribe.

We have already seen how the state of exception recodes Gogol's Andriy from lover to traitor, from *Homo oeconomicus* of sorts, a man of private impulses, into a *Homo politicus*, a man who imperils the integrity of the political grouping. Subjectively, even in battle, Andriy remains a private person, a man of the boudoir; all he can see is his beloved ("tresses, long tresses were all that he saw, and a breast like a river swan").[9] But objectively, he has become an enemy, has transgressed against the polity, which now confronts him in the figure of his "terrifying father," to whose execution he submits without as much as a word of protest.[10] Bulba insists that he, and he alone, must be the one to kill his son (not, to be sure, kill in battle, but set aside and execute). Bulba's famous formula for the occasion—"I begot you, and now I shall kill you!"—expresses the manner in which substance is personified in the figure of the sovereign-father who wields power over life and death.

Two more texts from the 1830s—both central to the formation of realist poetics in Russia—trace the dynamics of individuation against the social-imaginary horizon of the state of exception. Pushkin's "Petersburg tale" in verse, *The Bronze Horseman* (composed in 1833), unfolds on two ontological planes, the political and the private, each marked by a distinctive stylistic register. The political is lexically, metrically, and thematically indexed to the eighteenth-century odic tradition, while the private is narrated in a kind of belletristic verse, tending toward the everyday prosaic language of the 1830s.[11] The political plane of the tale presents the scene of Peter I's foundation of Russia's imperial capital and, with it, of a new imperial order. This expression of sovereign power is heightened and legitimized through the image of mythical creation of order from chaos, a heroic imposition of civilization onto recalcitrant nature. The lower stylistic register of the tale treats an emergent realist theme, an anecdote about a young civil servant whose dreams of modest domestic happiness are dashed when his beloved perishes in a flood.

The event of the flood refers us back to the divinized ruler's foundation of the polity, allegorizing, in this natural catastrophe, chaos's threat to the painstakingly ordered political cosmos. Scholars have detected evident allusions in the text both to eighteenth-century popular rebellion and to the more recent Decembrist uprising, which nearly coincides with the year of the historical flood. The figure of the flood, in other words, encapsulates the state of exception as the condition of urgent political peril.[12] It is in the imaginary space opened up by this condition that what was once private—the poor civil servant Eugene dreaming about a wife, a job, and a household—becomes political: a wild, mad, rebellious figure challenging the Imperial Horseman. Driven mad by his grief, Eugene wanders the streets of the capital, and one night, walking past the equestrian statue of Peter, he raises his fist at the demiurge with the reckless words: "Hey, Architect of marvels, beware of me!" The Horseman comes alive and chases Eugene through the night, its gallop echoing through the empty, moonlit streets. Presented in something like free-indirect discourse, the scene of the chasing unfolds on the border between the subjective and the objective domains: in Eugene's mind, clouded by grief and rage, and in the streets of the city created by Peter's fatelike will.[13] There is a sense, in other words, that the disturbance in the poor civil servant's mind reverberates through the objective order itself, reaching all the way to that order's founder and symbolic guarantor. Eugene's madness disturbs the Immovable Mover, stirs him into motion. Or perhaps it is the other way around, and the deity's founding, nature-defying madness reverberates through the centuries, sweeping up in its movement Eugene's destiny and his mind.

What matters more than resolving this ambiguity is the entanglement itself between the political order and private life—the direct encounter between the sovereign and the subject—transpiring in the space opened up by the emergency of the flood. This state of exception, in turn, mirrors the paradoxical structure of sovereignty itself: Does the flood function as an allegory of sovereign power, whose overwhelming violence confirms the incommensurability between the ruler and the subject, or does it operate as a threat to the order of things presided over by the ruler? Does the Horseman tower over the waters of the flood as the protector of the city and subduer of the elements, or as the deity of the elements themselves, the dark demiurge of disorder?[14] In other words, the "prosaic," "realist" anecdote about "poor Eugene," framed by the imperial creation story, highlights not only the customarily noted motif of the individual succumbing to the superior force of history and the state but also the paradox structuring sovereignty as such: the convergence within it of law and violence. Commenting on this paradox as it is conceived by theorists of sovereignty from Hobbes to Schmitt, Giorgio Agamben writes: "Insofar as it is sovereign, the *nomos* [the law] is necessarily connected to the state of nature and the state of exception. The state of exception (with its necessary indistinction between [violence and justice]) is not external to the *nomos* but rather, even in its clear delimitation, included in the *nomos* as a moment that is in every sense fundamental."¹⁵ This indistinction between law and violence in the figure of the sovereign is what Pushkin's Peter finally signifies: in subduing the elements, he has internalized them.

The flood, as the catastrophic event that suspends the normal order of things, sets in motion a sequence of narrative and symbolic operations disclosing the inner workings of sovereignty. This state of exception precipitates the crossing of a boundary between the private and the political; in confronting the Horseman, "poor Eugene" challenges the reigning order, subjects himself to judgment in terms of the substantive standards of "intense association," is found lacking, and cast out. But at the same time, the challenge prompts the political entity par excellence to reveal its "private," untamed essence, the violence concealed beyond the appearance of order at the core of civilizing modernity—boiling rage. This split within the figure of the sovereign mirrors the split within the state of exception itself, which is both a real condition (of siege, natural disaster, rebellion, etc.) and a sovereign decision that a given condition warrants the status of exception and the suspension of the law. Like violence, which is both the cause and the effect of sovereignty, lawlessness is both the cause and the effect of the state of exception.

This final point is vividly illustrated in Gogol's 1836 comedy *Government Inspector*. The play stages the intrusion of the state into the private lives of a town's officials, reminding them that their lives—which have indeed been conducted as private—have belonged to the state all along. The constructive principle of the play is the by now familiar one of "simplification," placing individuals directly under the substantive jurisdiction of political authority. Gogol adduces several dramatic postscripts to the play in which he envisions a series of discussions following its performance. One participant in such a discussion comments on the frequency with which Russian plays introduce the figure of the government "like the inevitable *fatum* in the tragedies of the ancients." "We all belong to the government," the person says, "almost all of us [are state servants]; the interests of all of us are more or less connected to the government."¹⁶ Yet another participant adds: "A certain mysterious faith in the government is locked within our [i.e., Russian] breast [...]. God grant it that the government always and everywhere heed its calling as a representative of providence on earth and that we believe in it as the ancients believed in the fate that punishes transgressions."¹⁷ Finally, in passing, we get the reaction of a commoner: "The voivodes were nimble [*prytkie*] to be sure but still turned pale when the czar's reckoning [*rasprava*] came."¹⁸

The state, or the government, or the czar's reckoning—this is evidently the key to the play. Yet its representation turns out to be quite a tangled affair. Political authority appears in the play twice: first in the guise of the unwitting impostor Khlestakov and last in the form of the ostensibly genuine Inspector from St. Petersburg. The first, spectral appearance—occupying the body of the play itself—functions as the locus for the aggregation of the self-seeking impulses of the officials, rendered literal in the form of more than one thousand rubles in bribes accumulating in Khlestakov's hands. At this level, social life appears as a single continuous and all-embracing network of self-interested interactions; represented by the impostor Khlestakov, the government is no different from the unruly subjects whose behavior it purports to regulate. Indeed, the officials act in the presence of political authority as if this authority belonged to them. And the play's concluding dramatic reversal catches up to them just as this co-optation of authority appears to triumph with the celebration of the betrothal between Khlestakov and the Mayor's daughter; the Mayor believes himself to be marrying into the government—extending the principle of privacy into the domain of the "universal locus." In other words, the effect of the play hinges on the anxiety that there is, in the end, really no such thing as the state, that private "nimbleness" is all. Then the czar's reckoning will never come, or worse, the czar himself is nothing other than an impostor.[19]

The final, cathartic announcement of the True Inspector at the end appears to reassert the existence and effectiveness of public authority. This second acclamation substitutes the social imaginary of substantive belonging for that of self-interested aggregation with the decisiveness and irreversibility of an ending. The True Inspector never appears as such but marks the limit beyond which the play refuses to go. In thus rendering state authority transcendent and sparing it all but the most rarefied representation, the play testifies to a persistent anxiety: What if this authority, too, turns out to be corruptible? What if it is in the end impossible to tell the difference between legitimate rule and its earthly versions, prone to earthly frailties and passions?[20] This anxiety in turn underpins the dual schema of the state of exception, in which universal law both opposes and entails private lawlessness. The play is thus positioned as the point of intersection and conflation between private and political domains: Here, once again, the individual officials are shown forcefully to belong to the implacable, fatelike polity. They turn out never to have existed apart from the state and therefore to have committed countless transgressions against it. Meanwhile, the state itself balances messianically on the verge of arriving and, in the meantime, remains "fallen," as it were, privately owned.

Briefly, then, what we find in these three protorealist texts from the 1830s (a historical novella, a "Petersburg tale" in verse, and a "comedy that ends in tragedy")[21] are projections of sociality unfolding against the horizon of the state of exception: war, natural disaster, the scandal of merely private pursuits—all provoking the exercise of sovereign power (of the tribal Father, the Imperial Horseman, the impersonal State) that itself proves warlike, disastrous, and scandalously private ("patrimonial"). By bringing together and conflating the dimensions of the private and the political, the state of exception inscribes the substantive order of the polity directly in the destinies of the protagonists. Andriy's love becomes/is treason; Eugene's grief becomes/is rebellion; the officials' private affairs become/are crimes and blasphemies against the state. Conversely, the polity is personified, both in the sense of being embodied in specific figures and in the sense of being or threatening to become those figures' private patrimonies: Bulba as father and Bulba as executioner, the giver and taker of life; Peter as the immortal, immovable founder of the modern Russian state and as the enraged deity of chaos he had worked to suppress; the Inspector called upon to restore order and justice and the Inspector as the puerile impostor, profaning justice and profiting from its (non)exercise. These scenarios foreshadow in highly explicit terms what in the fully fledged realist texts will have to be more painstakingly brought out.

Pedagogy of the Police (The Same Old Story)

Ivan Goncharov's *The Same Old Story* (1846), one of the earliest realist novels in Russia, tells of a young man newly arrived in St. Petersburg from a distant estate, his head crammed with "outdated," bookish ideas and hopes, bound for debunking and frustration. Young Alexander Aduev's career in the imperial capital consists mainly of amorous and creative failures, demonstrating, on his part, a lack of practical instinct, an inability to moderate impulses, to calculate the outcomes of his actions in advance. This rather standard bildungsroman framework, however, is supplemented and to an extent supplanted by a series of extended conversations between Alexander and his uncle Pyotr Aduev, a government official of high rank. The elder Aduev serves as a mentor for his obstinately naive nephew, using his failures and disillusionments as object lessons in modern ways of the world. During such conversations, Pyotr lists the ways in which his nephew has misconstrued a given situation, lectures him on the proper means of rational discipline, links apparently accidental events into causal chains, and often predicts the future. The values that he attempts to instill in his pupil are those of exhaustively rationalized modernity: self-control, instrumental practicality, and calculating order.

One of the most distinctive characteristics of Goncharov's bildungsroman is the absolute centrality to it of the relationship between the protagonist and the mentor. At various points in the European novels discussed in the previous chapter, Wilhelm, Eugène, and Jane also come under the influence of more experienced characters and eventually face the need to synthesize their lessons or to choose among them. These mentors are spokespeople for principles that organize these novels' prevalent modes of social aggregation. The criminals' banker Vautrin, the high-society lady Madame de Beauséant, the status-seeking baroness Delphine de Nucingen—all speak on behalf of the system of needs, albeit with different intonations and ethico-semantic nuances. Miss Temple, Helen Burns, St. John Rivers, as well as, increasingly, Jane herself ("Listen, then, Jane Eyre, to your sentence…")[22] extol duty and self-discipline demanded by the principles of actualized right. At various points in Goethe's novel, Wilhelm learns from a religious figure (the Abbé), a military man (Jarno), an enlightened landowner (Lothario), and, more indirectly, a devout Canoness ("The Beautiful Soul")—all associated with the Society of the Tower, seeking to harmonize personal and common interest.[23] The dispersed structure of mentorship in these novels correlates with an unmistakable emphasis on mobilizing and guiding individual desire as a basic building block of social aggregation; novelistic sociality is conceived as an aggregate (sometimes harmonious, other times not) of individual dispositions and drives.

In *The Same Old Story*, the situation is in some sense "simplified." Here, the dyadic schema of mentorship completely subsumes the skeletally represented social world, forestalling the possibility that other mentors might arise out of spontaneous encounters within it. Accordingly, this mentor—the oldest man in the family, a high-ranking government official, and the namesake of the Imperial Horseman—speaks not for this or that element of society but for all of it at once, for the entire enlightened, state-ushered "modern age." The text stresses the entanglement between modernity and the state in the image of the uncle's factory, which, rather than signifying entrepreneurial, economic activity, conjures up the rational organization of the bureaucratic apparatus: "And day after day, hour after hour, today and tomorrow, the bureaucratic mill grinds on without a hitch, uninterrupted, never resting, as if people don't exist—nothing but wheels and springs."[24]

The wider social world, then, appears in reduced, schematic form, as a series of episodic involvements for use as object lessons in extended discussions between the young man and his all-knowing uncle. All storylines converge in Pyotr Aduev's office, or, occasionally, in the living room of his young wife, Lizaveta Alexandrovna. Such a rigid organization of the narrative leaves no room for constructing an immanent social totality, a complex interweaving of characters and events that relies on the assumption of a providential harmony among the diverse individual desires.[25] Alexander's several loves fall by the wayside and disappear as soon as he has learned his lesson; his uncle uses them as examples but cannot remember their names. An unexpected meeting with a close childhood friend, unhappiness in love, an artistic endeavor—everything is but a pretext for the elder Aduev's admonitions and exhortations. Instead of an account of the hero's integration into contemporary social life, the text repeatedly stages infantilizing regression—back to the family, attending to his uncle's teachings, accepting the consolations of the aunt. In short, Alexander's development unfolds not so much in society proper, but under the auspices of the three-term metaphor of the sovereign, especially relevant during the reign of Nicholas I: state-father-teacher.[26]

The elder Aduev's pedagogical techniques are peculiar. So, in the course of an early "lesson," he reads Alexander's letter addressed to a childhood friend, forbids him to send it, and dictates an alternative letter instead: "You want me to dictate the truth?" he asks, and Alexander immediately assents: "Please do!" (51; 1:216). A little later on, assent turns into obedience: "Forgive me, uncle. I am ready to obey you" (54; 1:219). Next, Pyotr burns his nephew's letter to his beloved (as if by accident), under false pretenses confiscates Alexander's poems for use around the house as insulation, and throws his sentimental keepsakes out the window. When Alexander can no longer stand the abuse, he demands to know how his uncle himself would characterize his actions. Pyotr unflappably replies: "Throwing out of the window into the canal a bunch of immaterial tokens and any other kind of useless rubbish cluttering up the room" (48; 1:213). The entire sequence is given here in a comic register, recalling Petrine models of carnivalized ruthlessness committed in the name of modernity, rationalization, and efficient control. In addition to the slapstick character of the abuse, the comic effect relies on the mechanistic obsessiveness with which actions are categorized and classified; hence the absurd nominalization in the uncle's reply.

Another telling episode depicts the uncle's attempt to cool off the raging feelings of the young man in love. In the course of the scene, the elder Aduev displays almost supernatural insight into the intimate goings on between the lovers, and, twice, Alexander expresses the suspicion that his uncle has been spying on him (75, 76; 1:238, 239). Pyotr Aduev's explanation is simpler: all people are more or less the same, and all such stories unfold in approximately the same way everywhere and always. Two codes are brought together in a kind of mutually contaminating metaphor: Pyotr Aduev's calculus of human behavior converges with the language of state surveillance; the outcomes of administrative rationality and the employment of salaried spies lead to the same result—only the former functions more efficiently. Together with the earlier allusion to the common contemporary police practice of perlustration, this exchange can be helpfully contrasted with the dynamic of realist disciplinarity as D. A. Miller describes it in *The Novel and the Police*. The central emphasis in Miller's account of nineteenth-century British and French fiction is on the double gesture whereby these narratives assert their distaste for power and the powerful (most prominently emblematized in the figure of the police) and at the same time exercise policing power in subtle, seemingly noncoercive ways. Compelling and influential as this model has been, it seems to fit poorly with Goncharov's novel, whose preoccupation precisely with coercive pedagogical techniques is undeniable. Here we encounter for the first time what might be called "surplus sovereignty," which in one way or another leaves its mark on the Russian realist tradition. Instead of explicitly dismissing and tacitly internalizing the operations of coercion, the text dwells on the civilizing workings of force. Instead of turning itself into an invisible agent of disciplinary power, Goncharov's novel turns that power into an object of oblique but unmistakable fascination. Thus, Pyotr Aduev good-humoredly complains that he cannot give Alexander a flogging the way he has his factory workers flogged when they misbehave (283; 1:425). Alexander, in turn, experiences his uncle's mentorship as profoundly oppressive. "Good God! When would he be able to free himself from his uncle's irresistible influence? Would his life never be free to take its own independent and unexpected course, but forever be determined by Pyotr Ivanovich's predictions?" (211; 1:359).

Pyotr Aduev's position as a representative of the state, a factory owner, the male head of the family, sole mentor to his nephew, and, all in all, custodian of enlightened modernity figures the intersection and entwinement of several kinds of mutually reinforcing authority that may, in its essential manifestations, be characterized as the authority of the "well-ordered police state" (Raeff). The shape assumed by Alexander's "development," and accordingly the basic trajectory of this bildungsroman, transpire not against the horizon of civil society aggregation, but within the representational parameters of a personified raison d'état. This version of the bildungsroman represents the movement whereby *the private becomes political* by falling under the jurisdiction of the state, which, in its struggle against ("archaic," "elemental") disorder—the elder Aduev repeatedly refers to his nephew as "wild" (*dikii*)[27]—mobilizes educational techniques that are more unequivocal and direct by comparison with those operating through the "spontaneous bonds" (Moretti) of civil society. Here, the narrative of development/socialization results not in an increased capacity for accommodation and self-realization but in a stark alternative of utter dejection and lifelessness (Alexander at the end of the main part of the novel) and total identity with his mentor (Alexander in the epilogue). This alternative testifies to the violence underpinning Pyotr Aduev's educational methods and correspondingly to the perception of spontaneous impulse, unregulated desire, and expressive behavior as explicit threats to the order he represents.

The political stakes of the confrontation between uncle and nephew come to light in an early scene, during which the newly arrived young provincial happens upon the monument to Peter I, the Bronze Horseman, and like Pushkin's "poor Eugene," is transfixed by the sublime sight (40; 1:206).[28] This emblematic encounter bares the basic structure of the substantive, "simplified" confrontation at the core of Goncharov's bildungsroman. Like Pushkin's Eugene by the statue of the imperial demigod, Alexander, too, is dwarfed by a Pyotr, implacable spokesman for the new world order, which he imposes on his nephew with the unceremoniousness of his beard-shaving forebear—until at last, in the epilogue, the hero is absorbed into the substance without a remainder.

To be sure, *The Same Old Story* makes the state visible in a distinctly lower, properly realist-novelistic register, and the state of exception, so starkly dramatized in Pushkin's poem, operates here as a perpetual undercurrent, the sense that the inappropriately desiring individual poses a threat to the subsisting order and must be disciplined urgently and at all costs. The nature of the threat posed by Alexander is manifold. He is, at the level of literary and cultural history, the bearer of an antiquated worldview, suffused with the impractical romantic idealism, associated with provincial backwardness.[29] At the level of personal psychology, he possesses an inherently naive and impulsive disposition, a tendency to yield to the feelings of the moment wholly, to be carried on the waves of emotion. But these are all standard characteristics of a nineteenth-century *Bildungsheld*. What distinguishes Alexander has less to do with his personal traits than with the nature of the relationship between the contents of his inner life and the image of objectivity with which they ultimately clash.

That objectivity—voiced by Poytr Aduev and enacted by the novel's plot—refuses to treat what it finds in the subject as something that can be remolded, adapted, or "effectuated" but sets out simply to root it out. The operative model of socialization here is akin to the absolute state's civilizing project of taming the impulsive, overweening, and inefficient feudal aristocracy. It is here that the novel's convergence with Pushkin's "Petersburg Tale" can be most clearly located. As many scholars have observed, behind the appearance of a low-ranked nineteenth-century civil servant, Pushkin's Eugene carries within him an archaic core that links him at once to the feudal nobility of old and to the mutinous Decembrists, whose uprising so fatefully inaugurated the exacting reign of Nicholas I.[30] Odd as it may sound at first glance, something like this can be said of Alexander as well.

Against such a historico-political horizon, certain elements of the text emerge in a new light. Worth noting, to begin with, are the many instances of Alexander's "Asiatic" wildness: his passionate impulses, his inability to calculate, his impulsive gesticulation, terrifying his uncle and at one point in the novel shattering the bust of an ancient tragedian. Notable in this context, too, are his mother's prescient attempts to prevent his departure for the capital. "Here, you alone are the master," she says, pointing at the fields, the woods, the lake that make up his vast domain, "but there [in St. Petersburg] maybe everyone will be bossing you around" (8; 1:178). Notable, too, is the characteristically aristocratic notion that disputes are settled in battle: the practice of dueling in defense of one's honor asserts the nobleman's independence from the state, which in turn struggles to abolish it. In connection with his wish to fight a duel with a romantic rival, Alexander receives a major scolding from his uncle: "You want to compete with a club in your hands! We are not in the steppes of Kyrgyzstan. In the civilized world we have other weapons" (144; 1:300). These other weapons are the subtler ones of instrumental rationality, enabling Alexander to outmaneuver his rival and remain his beloved's preferred choice.

The elder Aduev's lecture anticipates Norbert Elias's description of the new courtly habitus imposed upon the aristocracy within the parameters of the absolutist state:

> But even if the use of physical violence now recedes from human intercourse, if even dueling is now forbidden, people now exert pressure and force on each other in a wide variety of ways. […] If the sword no longer plays so great a role as the means of decision, it is replaced by intrigue, conflicts in which careers and social success are contested with words. […] Continuous reflection, foresight, and calculation, self-control, precise and articulate regulation of one's own affects, knowledge of the whole terrain, human and non-human, in which one acts, become more and more indispensable preconditions of social success.[31]

Pyotr Aduev, spokesman for the well-regulated state, evidently operates with a similar historical schema in mind: from feudal (provincial, "romantic") anarchy to absolutist (urban, "realist") order. His civilizing mission vis-à-vis his nephew-pupil bares the novel's basic social imaginary, testifying to the prominence at its core of the image of *raison d'état* whose survival and persistence must be safeguarded at all costs against the hydra-headed threat: archaic past, elemental nature, untamed affect, and the obstinately "uncivilized" masters of their own domains. Deep down, underneath layers of realist irony, Alexander stands, much like his predecessor Eugene, for the elements of disorder (nature, passion, the untamed aristocracy, the past), which is to say he embodies what is to be excluded and what will inevitably return. As such, his trajectory makes visible not the workings of society but the constitutional presuppositions of the modern state.³²

Alexander's inevitable "return" takes place in the novel's epilogue, which demands that we reread the novel against the grain of its own humorously dismissive treatment of the protagonist. Alexander's literal return from his estate, where he had retreated in despair at the end of the main body of the novel, coincides with his total and final capitulation to his uncle's precepts—just at the moment when the latter is no longer sure of them himself. Here we see Pyotr Ivanovich's complete triumph over the elemental forces driving his unruly nephew; Alexander's "education" is complete, and he comes to resemble his uncle in word and deed. The novel emblematizes the perfect merging of mentor and pupil by concluding with the two in an embrace. Yet all of this is given to us in light of another development, which changes—indeed, reverses—the meaning of the statesman's triumph.

It turns out that Pyotr's wife, Lizaveta Alexandrovna, is suffering from some ill-defined, but dangerous affliction, an apathy so powerful it threatens to become deadly.³³ An exchange with the doctor leaves the elder Aduev with the realization that the technology of rational control has backfired: "How treacherous fate can be, Doctor! Wasn't I ever so solicitous of her? [...] I have always weighed every step, it seems [...] but somewhere along the way one gets knocked down. And when? In the midst of so much success, such a career!" (318; 1:455). Just as the uncle triumphs over his nephew, Lizaveta's dire condition retrospectively highlights the validity and vitality of the very stance Alexander has now abandoned. His former clinging to passion and impulse is revealed as a power recoiling against the order that suppressed it, and the reluctant, slow-witted student reappears as a tragic nemesis as well.

Indeed, a strong tragic undercurrent runs just beneath the generic surface of this first Russian realist bildungsroman.³⁴ Instead of tracing the path of an individual's pacification, of his aggregative ascent to the order of things, the novel exposes a fundamental antagonism. And Alexander, in his separation from the substantive order ventriloquized by the uncle, turns out to have carried within him principles capable of shaking that order to its foundations. In turn, the power of this recoil and the damage it does retrospectively accounts for the uncle's own implacable attitude toward these opposing principles. The young man's seemingly comical protests are registered as having all along been something more than frivolous balking at actuality, as something, rather, that goes to the very core of that actuality itself and exposes its coerciveness as the source and symptom of its instability.

Toward the end of his first sojourn in St. Petersburg, defeated but not yet reconciled, Alexander encounters a young woman he inwardly calls "Antigone." The girl is a naive, earnest person who reminds Alexander of his own younger self. Though stylistically the novel never presents Alexander in an elevated register, the invocation of the tragic heroine points to surprising structural resemblances between the novel and the play. We might say, following Hegel's influential interpretation widely circulating at the time, that both texts stage a confrontation between two equally powerful but one-sided principles, each of which is in the course of the confrontation undone through the other. Like Antigone, Alexander—the young, vibrant, still living Alexander of the main body of the novel—is annihilated by the relentless "lessons" of his uncle voicing the substantive truth of the modern state. Like Creon, Pyotr Aduev is undone—through his wife's illness—by his own single-minded pursuit of all that rises up against the "civilizing process": unpredictable acts, unmanageable affects, purely private desires, unruly enmities and affections. Broken, utterly taken up into the universal in the epilogue, Alexander comes unwittingly to defend the very principles that have smothered his uncle's wife. Conversely, in having resisted absorption into the substance of the well-ordered state, he has acted in the grip of forces the eventual defeat of which proves self-defeating.

Much like Pushkin's narrative poem, then, Goncharov's comic bildungsroman is structured around a tragic kernel that interrogates the price of establishing and maintaining a certain ostensibly normal order of things. This making visible of the state is achieved through the staging of a fundamental entanglement between the individual who is deemed hostile to the desired order and the order itself, whose representative descends, at the turning point of the narrative, to the level of the hostile individual. The antagonism constitutive of the political field can be elaborated as a pair of related reversals: in standing apart from the substantive order as its negation, the individual becomes urgently important to it, and in pursuing the individual as hostile, the order becomes enmeshed in individuality. Just as Alexander must shed his idiosyncrasies to merge with the civilizing-sacred state, so Pyotr—the omniscient and unmovable statesman, patriarch, and mentor—is compelled to step down from the pedestal, unmasked as limited and private. The final lines of the novel present us with an emblem of this double movement: the embrace in which the Aduevs (figuratively, the individual and the state) become one—and switch places.

"The (Im)partial Idea of the State" (*One Thousand Souls*)

In his discussion of the emergence of governmental techniques and theories of the absolute state from the discourses of religiously motivated rule for the spiritual benefit of "the flock," Foucault defines raison d'état as "that which is necessary and sufficient for the republic to preserve its integrity."[35] The notion of "reason" suggested by raison d'état contains at once an objective and a subjective dimension. Reason denotes the essence of the state, its fundamental workings, as well as the ruler's (or subject's) capacity to grasp this essence and to act in accordance with it. By contrast with Christian pastoralism, this new formula of government is entirely self-referential: the reason, or purpose, of the state is not the salvation of its subjects but the state itself, its perfection, its strength, its flourishing (ideally indexed to the flourishing of its population). No longer rooted in the order of nature or the divine, the state has its reason and its purpose in itself.

Both of these features pervade the dynamics of *Bildung* in *The Same Old Story*. Collaborating with Pyotr Aduev's mentorship practices, the overall plot of the novel relentlessly redirects Alexander's energies to the efficient, rational pursuit of his own worldly flourishing in compliance with the essential workings of the civilizing state. When the protagonist fails to do so, the narrative punishes him and the mentor chastises him. At the same time, no meaning or purpose is posited beyond the idea of proper, state-sponsored, and state-enhancing quest for "career and fortune." Toward the end of the novel, Lizaveta Alexandrovna interrogates her husband on behalf of their dejected nephew: "So we're all bound to follow the dictates of this modern age of yours [...] all of which are sacred and true?" To which Pyotr eventually replies with the weighty statement: "Yes, it's sacred because it's rational" (280–81; 1:422). This elevation of rationality to the status of the sacred renders the realm of transcendent meaning immanent to the workings of the secular state, upon which rests the only salvation there is.

In Foucault's account, the notion of raison d'état relies more or less explicitly on what looks like its opposite: the sudden, violent suspension of the political order, or coup d'état in its seventeenth-century denotation. The coup d'état is the violent manifestation of the state itself, its appearance at the moment of crisis. This manifestation in turn only discloses what is the case to begin with, the immanent externality of the figure of the sovereign—who stands above the law, creates and guarantees it—vis-à-vis the state itself. "When necessity demands it," writes Foucault, "*raison d'État* becomes *coup d'État*, and then it is violent."[36] Goncharov's novel reveals this surplus sovereignty throughout the narrative, but it becomes especially glaring at the end, when the statesman-mentor-husband is compelled to see himself as the purveyor of "cold and skillful tyranny," responsible for his wife's dire condition (323; 1:459). This last transformation recalls the movement of *The Bronze Horseman*, which begins with a glorification of the order and reason of Peter's flourishing state, and ends with the display of the savage force that has bulwarked that order all along.

Étienne Falconet's monument appears as an emblem of a kind of order and rule in another realist novel about a young man's sojourn in the capital, Alexey Pisemsky's *One Thousand Souls* (1858). Like Goncharov's Alexander Aduev, Pisemsky's Yakov Kalinovich confronts the statue on the day of his arrival in the city. In both cases, the encounter provokes intense feelings: a sudden lifting of spirits in Alexander and an intense gloomy anxiety in Kalinovich. The tableaux by the monument indicate that the *Bildung* of each protagonist will unfold in the substantive shadow of the sovereign-founder and will thus take on a dualistic, confrontational shape, challenging the distinction between the private and the political. Proleptically, these encounters with the Imperial Horseman mark the two positions available to the protagonists throughout the text: either "poor Eugene," small and powerless against the forces of civilizing modernity, or "Architect of marvels"—if not the sovereign himself, then at least fully identifying with his project. Both protagonists come to occupy both of these positions sequentially. By the end of the main part of *The Same Old Story*, Alexander is utterly defeated and dejected, while in the epilogue he reappears as a robust reincarnation of the hostile power that had haunted him throughout. Kalinovich is morally and physically crushed by his experiences in St. Petersburg, until in the final sections of the novel, he reappears as the crushing power himself.

One Thousand Souls tells the story of a young man who feels that his natural endowments and ambitions entitle him to greater wealth and higher social status than he possesses at the start. Having graduated from Moscow University, Kalinovich is appointed to the position of a school inspector in a backwater provincial town of Ensk, where he meets the family of the retired inspector Godnev, his brother, "the Captain," and his daughter Nasten'ka. Kalinovich is drawn to this family of modest means and generous hearts but feels painfully superior to his environment. Spurred on by intense ambition and by his Mephistophelian mentor Prince Ivan, he eventually rejects quiet domestic happiness, seduces, deceives, and leaves Nasten'ka, departing for St. Petersburg. There, he experiences failure after failure, realizing that a young man cannot make a career and earn a fortune without plentiful means or high connections. He falls gravely ill and writes a desperate letter to Nasten'ka, who, in an act of (self-)sacrifice, abandons her dying father to join him in St. Petersburg. As Kalinovich's health improves, ambition returns. He begins to feel restless and, tempted once again by Prince Ivan, abandons Nasten'ka for the second time in order to marry a fabulously wealthy middle-aged woman (Prince Ivan's former mistress), for whom he feels nothing but aversion. As a result of the marriage, Kalinovich acquires enormous wealth and, with its help, begins quickly to ascend the ranks of the civil service. With this, the third and penultimate part of the novel ends.

The first three-quarters of the novel, then, project a scale model of the social world, resembling those of its recent Western European predecessors and contemporaries. This world is organized around the two basic poles of *domesticity* (honest, traditional, lower gentry, provincial) and *socialization* (unscrupulous, modern-nihilistic, aristocratic, metropolitan), and set into motion as a trajectory whereby the bonds of substantive family kinship dissolve under the pressure of intercourse within the system of needs. Balzac in particular comes to mind once we recognize a set of parallels between Kalinovich's mentor, Prince Ivan, and Balzac's charismatic villain, Vautrin, as he appears in *Père Goriot*. Both mentors draw a sharp contrast between ordinary people and those who are marked out by talent and ambition. Both assert that, given society as it is, only great wealth can facilitate the achievement of an ambitious young man's desires, that an honest career will get one nowhere. Both insist, further, that the boundary between honesty and dishonesty itself cannot be drawn with any assurance and that it would therefore be best to dispense with sentimental inhibitions. Both offer the young man a path to fabulous wealth through marriage on the condition that they pay off their mentors (sixty thousand rubles in one case; two hundred thousand francs in the other). Both older men end up under arrest, highlighting the corruption and criminality of the social life into which they have so much insight. In both novels the relationship between the protagonist and the mentor is contractual in nature. The mentor turns out to be nothing but a more experienced economic man than the pupil; no fundamental, qualitative boundary can be drawn between them. The social world is made up of desiring, "interested" individuals, whose liberation from the constraints of traditional family relations is presented in both novels as the betrayal of fathers and the decline of fatherhood. Broken by paralysis and abandoned by his daughter, old Godnev dies, and old Goriot, dying and delirious, appeals to the authorities to outlaw marriage, the exemplary contract of the modern novel.[37]

Against the background of such thoroughgoing similarities, the differences between the novels stand out all the more starkly. Though he learns much from the worldly criminal, Rastignac rejects the bargain and finds an alternative path to success: a way to lead a compromised life, but without yielding to crime and corruption entirely. No such alternative path is available to Kalinovich, whose options bifurcate into a stark alternative: either keep failing or follow the prince's prescriptions to the end. The absence of the third, synthetic option signals the abeyance of a model of mutual accommodation between individual desire and social constraints. Similarly unavailable in *One Thousand Souls* is the option of reconstituting the domestic sphere as an emotional refuge from the ruthless self-seeking of social life. What turns out to be possible, however, is to step beyond the dichotomy of virtuous domesticity and marketlike sociality altogether—and into the representational domain less readily available to Pisemsky's Western predecessors and counterparts: the domain of the authority of the state, dramatized as the revelation of force (the coup d'état) called upon to reckon with social disorder. Here, the supreme power to which Goriot appeals in vain actually does come, and it comes in the guise of the protagonist himself.

By the start of the novel's part 4 the narrative of ambition gives way to the drama of the rise and fall of a political man.[38] The Faustian bargain with Prince Ivan endows the protagonist with world-making powers, placing him above the distasteful workings of the social domain into a position from which that domain itself can, at least in principle, be remade. This is accompanied by a striking change in the protagonist's characterization. No longer a resentful, hapless man of ambition, he emerges before us endowed with an aura of a statesman bent on punishing the very vices in which he used to indulge and the very people with whom he had conspired. In his capacity as the vice-governor and later governor of the same province where he once began as a lowly school inspector, Kalinovich is nearly omnipotent, utterly honest, and implacable in the service of the well-ordered police state. With apparent dispassion, he pursues his former mentor Prince Ivan and imprisons him for forgery. This particular twist in the plot is especially noteworthy, encapsulating the principle according to which the state is called upon coercively to impose order upon the social world incapable of ordering itself immanently from within.

Marking the pivot between parts 3 and 4—and correspondingly between two versions of the protagonist—is the scene during which, on his wedding night, Kalinovich slips out of his conjugal bed and appears at the site of a fire to save a woman from a burning house. Reminiscent of His Majesty from Zhukovsky's journal, Kalinovich appears at the scene of a public crisis, accomplishes a heroic feat and, and, acclaimed with shouts of "hurrah" and "bravo," disappears. Thus, in a quasi-mythological scene of rebirth in the fire, the ambitious hero dies and the heroic statesman is born. Shortly afterward, with three-quarters of the novel done, the narrator feels the need to reintroduce his protagonist:

> Throughout my novel the reader has seen that I have never flattered my hero, but, on the contrary, I tried to present all his moral flaws in an in-

tensely vivid way, but in this case I cannot afford to pass over in silence that in his chosen official activity he appears as a remarkably active and perhaps even useful person [...]. The young vice-governor, still on the university benches, by the arrangement of his own heart, always felt a great sympathy for the pursuit of the impartial idea of the state.[39]

Thus, the story of the subject of interests culminates with a drama about the rise, exploits, and fall of a representative of political power who tries to remake the social world around him. Here the question of how to succeed in society is replaced by the problem of its radical "correction," and the hero turns from an economic man in search of status and comfort into a kind of *polis ex machina*, seeking to enforce the law and restore justice. In this context, we may recall the observation from Gogol's dialogues on *Government Inspector* that without the government, no Russian drama can be resolved. Here, as in Gogol's comedy, the government plot proves necessary as a principle of narrative closure. Without it, the chain of the hero's social misadventures is potentially endless.[40]

The suturing of part 4 to the first three parts of the novel results in a whole series of glaring inconsistencies. While still in St. Petersburg, Kalinovich has repeated encounters with the intelligent and gentlemanly Belavin, whose company he prefers to any other. Throughout, the older man embodies the standard of sober, ethically palatable, normatively stable comportment, to which neither the rest of society nor the young protagonist himself can live up. In part 4, the statesman Kalinovich is reunited with Nasten'ka, who, in retrospect, revises our understanding of Belavin. He now appears as a lukewarm type, whose decency can be attributed to lack of genuine feeling. Kalinovich's vices, by contrast, are understood as stemming from passion and strength, now finally put to proper use in the service of the state (447–48; 3:443). A similarly unexpected evolution occurs in Nastenka's uncle, who, earlier in the novel, suspects that Kalinovich had seduced his niece without serious intentions and considers himself the young man's mortal enemy. Having reappeared in these final sections of the novel, now with the full knowledge that his suspicions had been correct, he nevertheless smiles radiantly at the newly appointed governor and serves him tea. Even Nasten'ka herself at one point appears to ask Kalinovich for forgiveness—as if she had wronged and abandoned him and not the other way around.

In the process of the hero's rehabilitation, the whole system of characters undergoes a corresponding change, and many of those who stood ethically above Kalinovich the careerist, end up ontologically below Kalinovich the statesman. And the point, of course, is not that his sins are now forgiven, that he has repented or reformed. Rather, a special aura accrues to the protagonist as he begins to act on behalf of the state. "Kalinovich" simply switches social-imaginary codes and is now judged against a different set of standards. It is with this transition that the sudden increase in the hero's charisma and the corresponding elevation in the stylistic register of the narrative as a whole are associated. Also linked with this shift is the displacement of the central conflict of the novel: from the confrontation between conscience and ambition, self-realization and social barriers, we face a naked opposition between corrupt society and a state that enforces justice. Kalinovich himself formulates the nature of this conflict in a maxim worthy of *Leviathan*: "There are many of them, but I am only one/alone [*odin*]" (455; 3:451).

This formula designates a situation in which the state is forced to intervene in response to society's inability to regulate itself. As vice-governor and then governor of the province, Kalinovich acts to contain the corrupting influence of willful individuality, but he does so precisely as a willful individual standing above the constraints of the law. He thus instantiates the drama of the coup d'état, staging the workings of the coercive state apparatus, itself as an extralegal entity anchoring the legal order. The drama is here played out within the biography of a single individual, whose old and new instantiations—the self-seeking and unscrupulous man of ambition in the first three parts of the novel and the formidable statesman in part 4—cancel each other out in a paradoxical concord. Their disjunctive identity captures the dualism inherent in the figure of sovereignty itself: the dualism between the sovereign as the guarantor of law and justice for all, on the one hand, and as the source of despotic violence, on the other.

It is fitting, then, that *One Thousand Souls* became the pretext for Pavel Annenkov's meditation on the differences between European and Russian realism and on the roots of these differences in divergent imaginaries of social relations. Annenkov reads the novel as a symptom of the "gelatinous" nature of civil society in Russia, of its members' failure to become self-governing, disciplined participants in a hegemonic normative culture. Here again, only the sovereign acts for the common good, and his actions necessarily take on an ambiguous, sinister form. Annenkov comments on the figure of Kalinovich in part 4:

> He uses the law as an alibi but acts out of personal urges [his distaste for Prince Ivan, his desire for personal vengeance], taking them for the only measure of justice and usefulness. The fate of society is thus put on the line and indeed Kalinovich ends up uprooting abuses through new abuses and uprooting vices by replacing them with vices of another kind

[...]. Thus, his brute [punitive] activity [akin to the activity of the grand viziers of Turkey carrying back to the capital bags filled with the heads of criminals] appears to society as something like an extraordinary natural event [*neobyknovennyi fenomen*], which cannot be foreseen and from which there is no protection. He comes to pass like an earthquake, a rain of stone, a flood, a destructive storm, etc.; his existence among the people does not bring with it the premonition of [...] a luminous social ideal, capable of conquering hearts, and so it is only natural that people turn away from him, leaving him prey to his enemies and to his own ever-growing spite, which happens to have accidentally found the honorable stately seat [*chinovnich'e lozhe*] for its manifestation.[41]

Annenkov stresses here that notwithstanding the rhetoric of the common good, Kalinovich's actions reveal precisely the private, patrimonial nature of his rule. Missing altogether is the hegemonic capacity to "conquer hearts." But as the critic himself suggests by treating the novel as symptomatic, *One Thousand Souls* does not merely condemn the governmental methods of a hypocritical egoist. Instead, it highlights the logic by which the actions of the statesman begin to resemble the actions of those he works to prosecute. As in Agamben's gloss on Schmitt and Foucault, the sovereign exception at the root of all legitimate political power marks the locus in which the private and the political become one; law and violence come to share a single source, embodied in the ambiguous figure of the sovereign.

Returning to the novel in his later, obituary recollections of Pisemsky, Annenkov describes Kalinovich as "a kind of Peter the Great" and adds a curious twist to the earlier interpretation: "One quality washes away his shortcomings: Kalinovich rises in the midst of the drama as a person who could, on occasion, hold high the banner of state authority if the latter were in danger, and for this one quality assumed in him, his rights to the title of an honorary hero of the novel are restored and the sympathies of readers are called to him."[42] Here, Kalinovich appears to be in possession of precisely those characteristics that are necessary for the preservation of the polity during a state of emergency. Written soon after the assassination of Alexander II and the execution of the members of the "People's Will," Annenkov's comments on the timeliness of the Kalinovich figure for the situation when state authority is in danger ring with special poignancy.

In an 1859 review of a series of contemporary works gathered under the umbrella term, *oblichitel'naia literatura* ("literature of exposure"), the young literary critic Nikolai Dobroliubov points out that authors working within that paradigm focus their criticism on low and mid-level functionaries while ignoring fundamental, systemic problems (most prominent but unnameable: autocracy and serfdom) and keeping higher-level officials safe from reproach. Dobroliubov writes:

> If bearers of governors' ranks are touched at all, the incrimination goes according to the following scenario: the noblest governor, benefactor of the province, champion of legality and the public sphere is depicted; two or three well-meaning officials gather around him; and all together they occupy themselves by punishing abuses. Sometimes, the governor does not appear on stage at all, but his existence is assumed behind the curtains, as the bulwark of virtue, like the *fatum* of the ancients. As for other authorities, they come less and less under attack as they approach the rank of governor.[43]

The association of the figure of the governor—the microcosm of supreme authority—with the "*fatum* of the ancients" echoes Belinsky on the fateful character of substantive "actuality" and, still more closely, Gogol on the role of the government in the denouements of Russian dramas. There is little doubt that the formula also applies to Kalinovich, who appears at the end of the novel as a manifestation of the coup d'état, called upon to realize the deathbed yearnings of old Goriot: to bring meaningful, righteous, substantive order into the anomic world of universalized self-interest—through coercive acts. The impersonal and "impartial idea of the state" proves to be personal and partial after all. For Annenkov, the paradox would not arise in the first place if Russian social life had been more robust, if it had developed from within itself regulative norms and values, hegemonic forms of collective coexistence. In the end, the liberal critic would rather keep the state out of society and the representation of its dramas out of fiction. But since in his view the conditions for the realization of such a social and aesthetic ideal are not in place, Pisemsky's novel (like much Russian realist fiction) refuses to oblige.

Political Theology (*Demons*)

Early in Dostoevsky's *Brothers Karamazov* (1880), one of the brothers, the freethinking theomachist Ivan, expresses a view enthusiastically embraced by a group of learned monks. At stake is the question of whether the institutions of the church should be relegated to a determinate and thus limited position within the state or should instead permeate the whole of the state in such a way that the two would become indistinguishable. Ivan's vision, converging with the vision of the monks, is that "every earthly state must eventually be wholly transformed into the Church and become nothing else but the Church, rejecting whichever of its aims are incompatible with those of the Church. And all of this will in no way demean it, will take away neither its honor nor its glory as a great state, nor the glory of its rulers."[44]

According to Ivan, the institutions of the church should belong not in the politically neutral space of civil society but at the core of the state itself, bulwarking, glorifying, and taming it at once. He proposes, in other words, a kind of political theology, a way of thinking about politics and religion in mutually reinforcing, complementary terms. Ivan clarifies the specific character of this imaginary with the help of the figure of the criminal. Under the system in which state and church, legal and religious-moral authority remain separate, sanctions against a person who has broken the law are limited to external punishment.[45] Such punishment leaves intact within the individual a kind of inner reserve of normative independence, with the help of which the criminal can remain convinced of his moral innocence even when he has transgressed. Once state and religious authority become one, the individual, too, is unified; both the transgression and the punishment become absolute, and as such, truly fearsome. Instead of legal violation, ontological monstrosity; instead of punishment, excommunication: not a relative or partial but a total expulsion of the offender from the political community. The binary script of total inclusion/exclusion testifies to the substantive character of the polity thus construed.

The rest of the novel explores both utopian and distopian versions of such political theology: through Alyosha's "[monastic] obedience in the world" issuing in the creation of a reconciled community-church of schoolchildren as well as, at the other side of the spectrum, in the Grand Inquisitor's theocratic rule. More broadly, however, the novel's refusal to take for granted the division between the moral order of private life and the legal order of the state has deep roots in the imperial "myth" of a sacralized state responsible for both the earthly flourishing and the spiritual salvation of its subjects. The state-culture-soteriology alliance may have broken up by the end of the eighteenth century, when culture began to claim sacral-civilizing status for itself, provoking a more repressive stance on the part of political authority.[46] Yet even as literature cast off its predominantly affirmative stance toward the state, it had by then thoroughly internalized a number of political-theological motifs, recasting them now in an ambivalent light and with keen awareness of the ironies and paradoxes inherent in them.

Unrealist as they might appear to be, figurations of political theology in fact pervade a large number of prominent nineteenth-century Russian texts. We have already glimpsed them in the figure of the godlike, "fateful" Horseman in Pushkin and the deus ex machina–like True Inspector in

Gogol. The motif of the statesman as a superhuman avenger reappears in Pisemsky's novel, endowing naked force with salvific/demonic charisma. Goncharov's text reckons with the divinization of state-civilizing reason, expressed in Pyotr Aduev's maxim: "sacred because rational." It also contains a telling political-theological joke, a deliberate conflation of two senses of the word "cross" (*krest*). Toward the end of the main part of the novel, the dejected protagonist is comforted by his young aunt, who tells him to "bear his cross" patiently. Just then, the elder Aduev appears, and either having misheard or pretending to mishear, wonders whether Alexander has received "a cross" in the sense of a medal for distinguished state service.[47] The slippage comically emphasizes the discursive shift from the elevated register the aunt and nephew adopt with each other to the resolutely prosaic language and thought of the uncle. Yet beneath the humorous veneer, serious content lurks: an image of the state servant as the long-suffering savior, ready to die for our sins.

Still, no major Russian realist is as consistently preoccupied with political-theological motifs as Dostoevsky, whose late novelistic work presents us with a number of elaborate imaginaries linking political power to religious transcendence, dramatized in the apocalyptic paradoxes of legitimacy and pretendership.[48] In addition to the already mentioned elements of *The Brothers Karamazov*, we may also note testimonies on the projected continuation of Alyosha's biography in which the people-loving monk turns into a political terrorist, possibly even a regicide.[49] As an early passage in the novel suggests, such a (counter)conversion would take place as a function of a basic homology between religiously and politically inflected desire for universal brotherhood. Secondhand testimony in this regard is supported by the general consistency of this (counter)conversional plot line with the master narrative sketched out in Dostoevsky's notes toward a projected epic novel, *The Life of a Great Sinner*.[50] Here, too, we find hints for a trajectory of a monk who leaves the monastery, becomes a great criminal, and subsequently returns to pious life. Guided in both holiness and sin by a kind of "elemental strength," the protagonist temporarily yields to the temptation of power (*vlast'*) and "limitless dominion" (*bezgranichnoe vladychestvo*) and reaches the nadir of his spiritual journey with the assertion "I myself am God."[51] The notes invoke two historical prototypes for the protagonist, placing side by side the seventeenth-century leader of a Cossack rebellion, Stepan Razin, and the seventeenth-century founder of a religious sect and self-proclaimed incarnation of God-Sabaoth, Danila Philippovich. Together, the God of military might and the mighty leader of Cossack hosts make up the Great Sinner's political-theological profile, invested as much by the fear of violence and pretendership as by messianic faith in such a person's capacity for radical, world-saving good. We find elements of such characterization already in *Crime and Punishment*, whose protagonist—associated with Peter I and Napoleon, on the one hand, and on the other with Christ—weaves together the codes of sovereignty and martyrdom.[52] Similarly, the Christlike hero of *The Idiot* is associated with the figure of the deposed pretender to the Russian throne Ivan VI, who appears in Dostoevsky's unrealized plans for a piece titled "The Emperor."[53]

It is *Demons* (1872), however, that displays the most elaborate network of political-theological motifs, linked to the image of messianic kingship. Introducing its protagonist Nikolai Stavrogin into the narrative present, the novel draws on the final scene of *Government Inspector*. The novel's entire provincial "society," high and low, is gathered in the drawing room of Stavrogin's mother when the servant solemnly announces the arrival of the hero, not expected until a month or so later. Everyone in the room freezes in stupefaction.[54] The intensity of hope and dread associated with this appearance suggests once again the pattern according to which meaningful order arrives—whether in the form of punishment or redemption or, perhaps paradigmatically, both—from elsewhere than the represented social life itself.[55] What both Gogol and Dostoevsky make explicit, however, is that such external and often violent intrusion from outside the given social world carries with it an anxiety of imposture—an ambiguity highlighted by the appearance in the room, in place of the real thing, of Stavrogin's double, the decidedly Khlestakov-like figure of the clownish and sinister intriguer Pyotr Verkhovensky (Petrusha).

Petrusha's momentary supplanting of Stavrogin, who appears in the room quietly only a few minutes later, sets up the two characters as a kind of tandem. The ultimate meaning of their entanglement becomes clear during a later conversation in which Petrusha outlines to his "idol" his plan to smash the flimsy social order and crown Stavrogin Russia's true czar. "And the earth will groan with a great groan: 'A new, just law is coming,' and the sea will boil up, and the whole circus (*balagan*) will collapse, and then we'll see how to build up an edifice of stone" (422; 10:326). The narrative into which Petrusha emplots Stavrogin is apocalyptic, messianic, and political: as the country's ruler, he is to be the bearer of the "new, just law." Conflating the scripts of martyrdom and the prerogatives of the sovereign, Petrusha exclaims: "It's nothing for you to sacrifice a life, your own or someone else's." And further: "You are a leader, you are a sun, and I am your worm" (419; 10:324). Before us is a rather remarkable premise—with hardly a precedent in European realism—according to which the central intrigue of a novel hinges on whether its protagonist will agree to be installed as the monarch, once the "circus" (*balagan*) of contemporary social life has collapsed.[56]

Petrusha is not the only character in the novel whose high hopes are invested in the magnetic protagonist. Earlier in the text, the ardent nationalist Shatov exhorts him, "you, you alone could raise this banner [of Russia's national regeneration as a God-bearing people]" (253; 10:201). To the lame madwoman Marya Lebiadkina, to whom Stavrogin is secretly married, he appears now as her fairytale redeemer-prince, now as the prince's killer; one moment a regal "falcon" and the next, the seventeenth-century pretender to the throne, Grigoriy Otrep'ev ("False Dmitry"). The aura of associations surrounding the protagonist is made up of many further instances, all gravitating toward politics and religion both. Here we have the legendary "Decembrist L——n" (Mikhail Lunin, whose earlier regicidal plans served as a pretext, in 1825, for the verdict of life in penal servitude); the already mentioned Stepan Razin and Danila Filippovich; Shakespeare's Prince Harry, the future great King Henry V; the legendary figure of the "Hidden One," the true prince who has miraculously escaped the courtiers' attempt to assassinate him and will soon reveal himself as the people's ruler and redeemer; and the folkloric counterpart of this last, Ivan Tsarevich. Stavrogin's name is derived from the Greek "stavros" for "cross," while his designation as a "wise serpent" hints at an apostolic mission.[57]

This kaleidoscope of diverse associations—invoking the "higher" registers of tragedy, legend, chronicle, ode, and hagiography—does not fix Stavrogin within a specific political or theological tradition, but rather presents him against the horizon of anxious anticipation, frustration, reverence, doubt, and dread associated with projections of messianic sovereignty and/as apocalyptic imposture. It is not surprising, then, that scenes of Stavrogin's acclamation take the shape of (sometimes ambivalent) expression or denial of faith. The roots of such political fideism can be traced back to the conflation between spiritual and secular authority in the seventeenth and eighteenth centuries. As the figures of God (or Christ) and sovereign drew closer together, it became more difficult to distinguish between righteous and sinful rule.[58] Unlike the question of the czar's justice, the problem of authenticity could not be resolved with reference to a preexisting independent standard (e.g., adherence to tradition or to divine commandments) but became a matter of sheer faith. This logic is borne out, for example, in the language of Peter I's admonition to his son, Alexey, which leans heavily on the Pauline doctrine of justification by faith.[59] Such faith is the more in demand the more political power is conceived in charismatic terms, since the accrual of charisma to the monarch allows rulers to project even (especially!) their excesses as confirmation of their superhuman status. Their acts had to be conceived as originating in an occult realm that could not be made sense of from a this-worldly ethical perspective.[60]

Repeated expressions of faith (or disappointed faith) in Stavrogin's political-messianic mission signal the prominence in the novel of the problematic of sovereign "election," adding to the list of already familiar literary figurations of the state. To the foundational (*The Bronze Horseman*), the civilizing-pedagogical (*The Same Old Story*), and the avenging (*Government Inspector, One Thousand Souls*), Dostoevsky's novel adds yet another variant: the eschatological figure of the (pretender-)ruler-redeemer whose appearance in the world is marked by mystery, scandal, and exception, whose excessive acts overstep the norm and thereby constitute the sanctity of the actor, and whose identity is established through faith. This figure of the sovereign redeemer gives flesh to a veritable yearning for the (messianic) state, which can be said to lie at the affective foundation of all the other state-centered imaginaries here at issue: the conviction that this is the *only* locus of universal belonging, the very "heart of things," the "solar plexus" of action and meaning.

Conceived within the paradigm of political theology, the hero proves poorly suited for standard realist narratives of socialization. Members of the older generation—Stavrogin's mother, his former tutor, and others—continue to hope that he will come to his senses, marry a beautiful heiress, settle down, and become a respectable member of good society. But these "social" hopes, together with the generic horizon of the bildungsroman they assume, prove petty by comparison with the novel's more authentic preoccupations. Still, the question remains: How do such preoccupations find a place within realist narrative? Or what comes to the same thing: How is realist narrative "deformed" in accommodating political theology as the work's dominant, constructive principle of characterization?

Central in addressing this question is the Schmittian notion of "decision," or "exception," which structures Dostoevsky's narrative throughout, especially when it comes to the protagonist. For Schmitt, the authority to "decide on the exception," to suspend the reigning legal order, defines the figure of the sovereign: "The exception is that which cannot be subsumed; it defies general codification, but it simultaneously reveals a specifically juristic element—the decision in absolute purity."[61] Schmitt further argues that the modern political concepts of sovereignty and exception should be understood as secularized versions of the theological concepts of God and the miracle.[62] Just as God legislates prior (both logically and chronologically) to the order of creation, the sovereign is authorized to suspend and reconstitute the legal order. Just as the miracle constitutes a break in the order of nature, completely unprepared by that order itself, the decision interrupts the order of things in a way and at a time that cannot be scripted in advance. In representational terms, frustrated expectations and broken rules can thus be seen as fruitful soil for the staging of sovereignty effects. In this context, the hero's transgression of social norms does not unfold against the horizon of ultimate accommodation. Instead, transgression is here itself the telos of the norm; the norm is there to be transgressed, directing our attention to the mystery of the hero: Who is this man who is set up again and again as the exception to the rule?

The novel introduces Stavrogin through a series of scandalous actions, which simultaneously expose the rottenness of social norms and point to the occult interiority of the one person apparently not subject to them. His excesses begin with three incidents in the course of which he flamboyantly offends proper provincial society. The first incident takes place at a club, whose most respected member has the habit of pointlessly adding to everything he says, "No sir, they won't lead me by the nose!" During one of the gatherings at the club, Stavrogin hears him utter these words, seizes him by the nose, and pulls him several steps across the room. The clownish townsman Liputin, excited by rumors of the scandalous scene at the club, invites Stavrogin to his own house, where the latter sparks further scandal by kissing Liputin's wife on the lips. Finally, the elderly provincial governor himself chides Stavrogin for his "unbridled acts, so beyond all convention and measure," and asks him to explain. Stavrogin leans toward him, as if to speak in a whisper, and when the governor moves closer—"he was an extremely curious man"—the hero bites hard into his ear. Realist causality is reestablished when we discover that at the time of these incidents Stavrogin was beginning to succumb to a serious illness. But a surplus of scandalous charisma remains, preparing the revelation of the still more profound affront to social conventions: Stavrogin's secret marriage to Marya Lebyadkina.

Like Gogol's ambiguous Inspector (Khlestakov and/or the Real One), the tandem of Stavrogin and Petrusha exposes contemporary Russia in a state of emergency, threatened by collapse. The frivolousness, vanity, and hypocrisy of the older generation breed chaos and madness in the young. The "circus," according to Petrusha's predictions, is about to crumble, with or without his help. Hence arises the need for the ruler-hero, who would rebuild it all anew, upon new foundations. And so the novel nudges aside standard realist sociotopes of aggregation, foregrounding instead the political drama of messianic leadership and imposture. This drama depends on and "deforms" the realist terrain of everyday social interactions with their aggregative principles of need, right, and common interest. Desires (for money, pleasure, status) flow and interlace into a network of relationships but converge on the figure of a protagonist who inspires needs but needs nothing from anyone. Images of common interest appear (especially in connection with the nationalist Shatov) but turn out to depend on one person alone—Stavrogin and his mission.

The figure of actualized right, with its demand for self-mastery, flashes up in Kirillov and Stavrogin himself, but in neither case is that figure linked with sociable living. Through suicide, Kirillov overpowers the last remaining master he has, fear of death, and thus hopes to bring about the emancipation of humanity from its supreme Master. Stavrogin's capacity for self-control, meanwhile, functions as perhaps the most vivid demonstration we have of his "calling"—or better, his "election"—for sovereign rule. In his final epistolary confession to Darya Shatova, he writes: "I've tested my strength everywhere. [...] This testing for myself and for show proved it to be boundless. [...] In front of your very eyes, I endured a slap from your brother; I acknowledged my marriage publicly" (675; 10:514). At first glance, such self-mastery might be understood within the paradigm of actualized right as precisely what is needed for stable social life. Marriage must be something publicly recognized; escalation of physical violence is to be avoided. Yet a closer look at the first of the two episodes mentioned in Stavrogin's letter will reveal something else altogether at stake.

To begin with, we should observe how the motif of "testing one's strength," blends here with the added emphasis on the dimension of publicity: the for-show. Stavrogin tests his strength repeatedly and directly in public, "posing riddles" that solicit the almost mystical fascination of everyone around him. What is "for show" here is the very capacity to spurn the opinions of those to whom this capacity is being shown. Put another way, what the public witnesses is the power that rises above the public and constitutes an exception in its midst. At issue more specifically is the scene during which Stavrogin withstands a public blow in the face from Shatov without responding. What follows in the dilation of the dramatic moment after the blow is a kind of odic exemplum, a digression describing a precedent for the hero being acclaimed. Here we have an extended character portrait of the heroic Decembrist Mikhail Lunin, focusing on his love of danger as a test of self and an exercise in overcoming fear. The first-person narrator concludes the digression as follows:

> I repeat once more: I considered [Stavrogin] then and consider him still [...] to be precisely the sort of man who, if he received a blow in the face or some equivalent offence, would immediately kill his adversary, right there on the spot, and without any challenge to a duel.
>
> And yet, in the present case, something different and wondrous occurred. (205; 10:165)

The wondrous exception consists precisely in Stavrogin's refusal to act violently. The hero proves not only to possess supreme power (to take someone's life) but also to be capable of mastering that power. The narrator dwells on the scene of self-mastery, in particular:

> It seems to me that if there were such a man, for example, as would seize a red-hot bar of iron and clutch it in his hand, with the purpose of measuring his strength of mind, and in the course of ten seconds would be overcoming the intolerable pain and would finally overcome it, this man, it seems to me, would endure something like what was experienced now, in these ten seconds, by [Stavrogin]. (205; 10:166)

The motif of self-mastery in *Demons*, then, displays once again the dynamic in which the sociotope of self-regulation (here, the notion that sociable living requires individuals to master their passions) is transposed from the domain of aggregative socialization into the field of substantive sovereignty and thus appears in an altogether different guise. No longer are we dealing with mastery over one's passions but rather with self-mastery as a public display of infinite power, infinite insofar as it loops back on itself in the hero's act of self-possession. At an early point in the novel, Stavrogin's former tutor, Stepan Trofimovich, suggests that his scandalous actions "were merely the first stormy impulses of an overabundant constitution, that the sea would grow calm, and that it all resembled Shakespeare's description of the youth of Prince Harry, carousing with Falstaff, Poins, and Mistress Quickly" (42; 10:36).

The invocation of the Henriad alerts us to the fact that behind the question of how and whether a wild, willful youth can become a responsible statesman stands the question of how legitimacy can arise from lawless usurpation. Prince Harry's drunken revelry with lowlifes and vagabonds appears in Shakespeare as part of his father's comeuppance for the illegitimate assumption of royal power and (indirect) ordering of the murder of the Richard II. Prince Hal's "biography," his turning into the valorous Henry V, encapsulates the unity and duality of sovereign power: just as Henry IV's lawless act of usurpation is both opposed to and united with his lawful rule, Hal's wildness is opposed to and united with his future decisiveness and valor. Shakespeare's trajectory is redemptive: legitimacy is in the end established through virtuous rule and glorious victories, while past usurpation only occasionally haunts it as vague anxiety. *Demons*, on the other hand, seizes and dwells on the anxiety itself. Stavrogin never passes from Prince Hal to Henry V; his infinite power remains unrestrained by an "ideal" or a "burden" and instead expresses itself in excessive arbitrary acts, including the arbitrary act par excellence—once again, an exception, given the expectations of everyone present—of mastering one's own impulse. He thus presents us with an image of occult power (sovereignty as secularized divinity), displaying itself in excess and exception, grounded in nothing but transcendent power itself and forever haunted by the suspicion of pretendership.

The *Deistvitel'nost'* Effect (*Hero of Our Time, Rudin, Hard Times*)

Figurations of the state of exception—war, natural disaster, government corruption, normative confusion, and social disorder—constitute the horizon of sociality against which the texts we have considered so far repeatedly unfold. These texts "deform" the standard realist concern with the vicissitudes of socialization into a setting for the enactment of diverse scripts of sovereignty: foundational, pedagogical, justice-dispensing, messianic. These scripts play a form-giving, organizing role in relation to the rest of the represented social material. The imaginary of the state is installed not only as a substitute for civil-social dynamics but also as their organizing principle and basic frame. In these ways, the texts perform a kind of *hypostatization of the political*: treating what would seem to be "external" and "abstract"[63]—what is only occasionally gestured at in our European examples—as its proper subject matter, intrinsic and concrete. The state is made visible—as the constitutive violence of foundation or the civilizing pedagogy of the raison d'état, or the preemptive defensiveness of the coup d'état, or the political theology of (impostor) redemption—and this visibility constitutes one of Russian realism's peculiar and essential signifiers of what is really real in the domain of social life. In what follows, then, I would like to discuss briefly three shorter texts—early, middle, and late—with a steadier eye on the workings of Russian realist "reality effects," in their variety and consistency alike.[64]

When it comes to visions of a derealized society confronting a hyperreal representative of the state, Lermontov's *A Hero of Our Time* (1840) offers a particularly intriguing case. Often placed at the origin of Russian "psychological realism," the novel focuses relentlessly on the figure of the protagonist.[65] His inner life during his adventures on the periphery of the empire (primarily in the Caucasus)—his mysterious motivations, contradictory actions, changing feelings—is the center of gravity around which the far-flung episodes of the novel rotate. The novel gestures at "the truth" about Pechorin in two basic ways: it supplies pairs of paradoxically combined attributes, and it attempts interpretation from external signs to inner characteristics. An air of enigmatic superiority surrounds him throughout. In the words of a woman who loves him, Pechorin possesses something that other men don't have, "something proud and mysterious," some "irresistible power."⁶⁶ He is supremely worthy of our attention.

The motif of power is central to the psychological portrait of the protagonist, anticipating the psychopolitical problematics of *Demons*. It is perhaps most clearly articulated in his own reflections on his character:

> My ambition [*chestoliubie*] is stifled by circumstances, but it has manifested itself in another way, for ambition is nothing other than a thirst for power, and my best pleasure is to subject everyone around me to my will, to arouse feelings of love, devotion and fear—is this not the first sign and the greatest triumph of power? (109–10; 6:294)

In his 1840 review of the novel, Belinsky quotes this passage verbatim.⁶⁷ So, more or less, does the conservative critic, scholar, and poet Stepan Shevyrev.⁶⁸ In the literary-journalistic language of the time, the word "circumstances" frequently served as code for various forms of political coercion. It was common, for example, to refer to omissions made on account of censorship as having been made "due to circumstances beyond the editors' control." Exactly which "circumstances" stifled Pechorin's capacity to pursue his ambition and exactly in what this ambition consisted is left unclear. Boris Eikhenbaum has argued that, as in the case of Lermontov's own (first) sojourn in the Caucasus, at issue is punishment for some type of political dissent.⁶⁹

Yet the irony of the situation consists in the fact that by placing the hero on the periphery of the empire, the punishment recasts him as an agent of the expanding imperial state. It is in this latter capacity that Pechorin embarks on a surveillance mission in "Taman'," uncovering and in the end displacing a group of contraband smugglers.⁷⁰ In the same capacity, he has the daughter of a Circassian chieftain kidnapped in "Bela." In both cases, sheer personal whim functions as the pretext for the action: curiosity in the first case, sexual desire in the second. What makes these acts unfold the way they do, however, is a function of Pechorin's position as a representative of the empire's military might. Here we have a familiar conflation between personal and political power, the power of an individual to impose his will upon others, woven into the political authority of the state.

The complications that arise from this blend become particularly evident during an exchange in which Pechorin's superior, Maksim Maksimych, reprimands him for abducting Bela. Walking into Pechorin's quarters, Maksim Maksimych suspends their previous friendly relations and attempts to reestablish military hierarchy. But Pechorin continues to assert his will, eventually forcing his commander to relent. "What else could

I do?" Maksim Maksimych muses in retrospect. "There are people with whom one must absolutely agree" (23; 6:219).[71] Pechorin's superior is unable to discipline him because he shares with the culprit an imaginary according to which the "primitive" life of the Caucasian tribes is simply there to be claimed by the "civilizing" forces of the empire. Thus, the figure of sheer possessive, destructive whim emerges as the obverse side (or inner sanctum) of civilizing conquest.[72] Pechorin's actions blur the boundary between the imperial and the wild, the political and the private, reprising the familiar paradox structuring the state of exception: in the figure of the sovereign (universal) law and (private) violence are one.

This conflation, in turn, manifests itself in the peculiar way in which the novel invokes fate, suggesting a double bind in which the hero finds himself as both fateful and fated, a melancholy agent of others' demise. "Can it be that my single purpose on this earth is to destroy the hopes of others?" Pechorin wonders. "Since I have been living and breathing, fate has somehow always led me into the dramatic climaxes of others' lives, as if without me no one would be able to die, or to come to despair! I have been the necessary character of the fifth act" (117; 6:301). The "fifth act," the act without which the drama remains incomplete, adds a narratological dimension to the psychic paradoxes of sovereignty associated with Pechorin. Once again, Gogol's formula of political "finalization" comes to mind. This script is evident throughout the journal sections of the novel, beginning with "Taman'," where fate is said to have thrown him "like a stone into the peaceful circle of honest smugglers" (71: 6:206), and ending with "The Fatalist," in which Pechorin proves mysteriously attuned to the death-bearing destiny of the reckless Serbian officer Vulich.

Most dramatically of all, however, such finalization structures the kernel tale of the novel, "Princess Mary." The tale's uniqueness and its centrality in the work as a whole consists in its focus on Russian, rather than peripheral, society. Made up of members of the gentry gathered at the Caucasus resort town of Pyatigorsk, this society contrasts sharply with the breathtaking scenery surrounding it. Among the features that make this society unworthy of serious treatment is its own preoccupation with appearances. Everyone frantically produces and reads signs of their own and each other's respective position: social status, military rank, wealth, cut of uniform or dress, sophistication of wit, and so on. The social scene appears to Pechorin as an elaborate theater of banality, without real consequence or meaning. Everything here is a scene, a stage, a stance, an enactment.[73] This society is thoroughly unactual, ghostly, appearing to the hero as an "optical illusion, a meaningless flickering of Chinese shadows."[74]

It is upon this ghostly social life—which is at the same time the product of his derealizing gaze—that Pechorin descends: not only as the bearer of fate but also as the scripter of the overall plot, indeed, as its spectator, playwright, director, and lead actor all in one. Pechorin manipulates members of this society for his own entertainment, plotting and counterplotting with such mastery that the world, true to its ontology as unactual, appears to offer no resistance. His power proves its superiority again and again, and he proceeds, in his journal, to dwell on its mystery and its uses. The case of Pechorin discloses, more clearly perhaps even than that of Kalinovich, the circular reciprocity of the relationship between the overweening hero and the social world. Because that world is unreal, Pechorin has unlimited power over it. Yet that unreality itself is produced as a function of Pechorin's power. The hero's charisma grows at the expense of the world's derealization: the less real the world, the more masterful, the more frightening and fascinating, the hero.

What is really real here, showing through the ghostly veil of social pantomime, is an interiority—lying at the ostensible origin of Russian psychological realism—whose paradoxical lineaments mirror quite precisely the ambiguities of sovereign power. Here, the sense of unlimited force and the destructive drive that both creates and exposes the unreality of social relations is combined with contemplative melancholy and passivity, a condition in which the self, too, with all of its impulses and passions, recedes into ghostly existence. What the novel stages instead—and at the expense—of social aggregation is the figure of the violent and suffering man of unlimited power: a man both fateful and fated, rebel and bearer of imperial might, brutal civilizer and uncivilized himself.[75]

In *A Hero of Our Time*, as elsewhere in the texts we have discussed, the social as the unreal takes shape under the influence of something external to it. This other domain, associated with (political) charisma, violence, exception, and finalizing fate, remains external vis-à-vis the represented social world, descending upon it now and then as a moment of truth, as what is actual or real. Ivan Turgenev's first novel, *Rudin* (1856), stages this dynamic in yet another way. Here, the distinction between the domains of the real and the unactual is drawn in a "Scandinavian legend," told by the eponymous protagonist to a gathering at a noblewoman's salon. In the legend, a king and his warriors are sitting around a fire in a barn when a bird flits in through the open door on one side and leaves through the other. The king understands this as an allegory of the brevity of human life: we, too, come from darkness and return to it, and our sojourn in the world is fleeting. But the oldest of the king's warriors raises an objection: "even in the dark the bird is not lost but finds her nest." Rudin comments: "Even so our life is short and [pitiful]; but all that is great is accomplished through men. The consciousness of being the instrument of these higher powers ought to outweigh all other joys for man; even in death he finds his life, his nest."[76] The king's mistake consists in taking sheltered, intimate, enclosed human life for the only life there is. The old warrior points to the existence of another life enveloping the life around the fire: it looks like darkness from inside the barn, but it is in fact the bird's true abode, and ours.

The spatial-symbolic arrangement of the legend corresponds to the structure of the novel as a whole. Its main plotline opens with Rudin's introduction into a set of established relationships within the circle of cultured gentry at Darya Lasunskaya's estate. This well-lit, comfortable inner chamber of social interactions, however, is no more than an evanescent haven for the protagonist, whose brief stay is framed by the wide-open spaces of groping, issueless journeying "in the dark." In the course of his stay, Rudin conquers the heart of Lasunskaya's daughter Natalya with fiery monologues about the high calling of humanity to strive for the betterment of the common lot. During one of their secret meetings, Natalya tells Rudin that her mother had forbidden their marriage (on account of his lower social standing) but that she was willing to elope with him nevertheless. Rudin, however, proves unable to reciprocate Natalya's courage. Her mother's prohibition makes him conclude that they must resign to their fate. We thus face the possibility that it has all been "mere words" with Rudin. Mikhail Lezhnev, Rudin's erstwhile university friend turned implacable critic, confirms this suspicion. In Lezhnev's view, Rudin is little more than a poseur, "an actor," even a "coquette," constantly playing a role and showing off (123; 6:318).

Yet Rudin's journey does not end with his awkward departure from Lasunskaya's estate. Several "epilogues" reframe the central episode of the novel, reinterpreting, rehabilitating, and rhetorically elevating the protagonist. To begin with, two years after the end of Rudin's sojourn in the town, in the middle of a more or less spontaneous gathering of many familiar figures, the same Lezhnev proposes a spirited toast in his honor. In the toast and the conversation that leads up to it, Rudin's flaws are recast as a matter of "a cruel and unhappy fate," a fate indexed as specifically political: "It would take us too far if we tried to trace why Rudins spring up among us" (158; 6:349).

Next, after another break of several years, Rudin and Lezhnev accidentally meet on the road and renew their former friendship. Both are traveling, in a sense, on state business. Lezhnev is brought to town on account of military recruitment, while Rudin is being punitively confined at his small far-away estate. In his capacity as a political exile for having attempted to introduce "radical reforms" at a gymnasium where he was employed as a teacher, Rudin merits not only Lezhnev's renewed friendship but direct acclamation: "It is not a worm, not a spirit of idle restlessness—it is the fire of the love of truth that burns in you, and clearly, in spite of your failings; it burns in you more hotly than in many who do not consider themselves egoists and dare to call you a humbug perhaps" (185; 6:366). And soon afterward: "But how do you know,—perhaps it was right for you to be ever wandering, perhaps in that way you are fulfilling a higher calling than you know" (187; 6:367).[77] Once again, Lezhnev summons the motif of empty words, or mere speechifying, only to dismiss it as no longer relevant: Rudin's own body, upon which life has inscribed true and unmistakable suffering, now backs up his words, endowing them, even if only retrospectively, with a substance, a visible "fate." Familiar key words—mystery and excessive strength—reappear during the discussion. "You were always a mystery to me," says Lezhnev. "You have so much strength in you and such tireless striving toward the ideal" (176; 6:364).

The incongruity between the central episode of the novel and its interpretative frame increases to the end. So in the 1860 edition of the novel, Turgenev adds yet another "epilogue," depicting Rudin's heroic death in June 1848 on a Parisian barricade as he tries to raise the spirits of the defeated workers. The scene adds still more weight to the novel's second, political code. Rudin speechifies, flirts, strikes poses in the salon, but he dies heroically—in political struggle. He is doubly emplotted within two distinct social imaginaries. One, the private, is the world of unreality; the other, the political, is the real world. The introduction of this second social imaginary rescues Rudin from theatrical vacuity, revealing the "superaddressee" of his heightened speech and dramatic gestures, the dimension of politics in which his ghostliness in relation to the (itself ghostly) social world reappears as substantive actuality in relation to the state.

Early reviewers of the novel noticed the inconsistency between these two versions of Turgenev's protagonist. Some hinted at the well-known fact that Rudin's real-life prototype was none other than the revolutionary Mikhail Bakunin, imprisoned by the Russian state at the time of the novel's composition.[78] In view of this fact, the novel finds itself in a complicated, even compromising, position—one that is nevertheless symptomatic of the predicament of Russian realist fiction. The inconsistencies in Turgenev's first novel register the difficulty of giving an adequate account of a generation of the gentry intelligentsia without taking into consideration their relationship to the state. This latter problematic, in turn, proves difficult to foreground due to a kind of double censorship: the censorship of the form habitually preoccupied with private individuals and their social relationships and the censorship of the state that takes literary matters to heart. Registering these constraints, Turgenev's friend and early reviewer of the novel, Alexander Druzhinin, suggests that the "Rudin type" could not express itself fully within the confines of the novel's central episode, in the context of a gentry salon. In order to render someone like Rudin fully comprehensible to the reader, Druzhinin argues, one would have to present a more detailed account of his attempts to bring his ideals to realization.[79] It is perhaps in response to advice such as this—given earlier in person—that Turgenev introduces the later figure of Rudin as a political exile. And it is perhaps in response to reviews such as this, sensing that he had not gone far enough, that he adds the scene of Rudin's death on the barricades several years later.[80]

The complex history of the text's production aside, it is possible to detect in its compositional awkwardness marks of laboring under the pressure of contradictory demands: the traditional novelistic motifs of courtship deformed and rendered unreal by the social imaginary that construes the (gentry) individual directly in relation to the state. Confined to the salon, the hero suffers sociopsychological shipwreck, appears as a poseur, a coquette, is superfluous, is expelled. But in the domain of political struggle, he reappears in a different guise: rhetorically elevated and sacrificed to the common cause. And this takes us back to the Scandianavian legend, with its delineation of two differently imagined lifeworlds. One—inside the barn, in the light and warmth of the fire—is private, domestic, particular. Here one lives and perhaps flourishes, but one is always already (almost) dead. As the king says, this life is fleeting and unreal. The other lifeworld—which, to the sensibility softened by domestic comforts, appears cold and dark—is the substantive life of humanity, the public life of the common good. This life is actual and—because it is transindividual—eternal. Here, one gives one's life for others, serves higher ends, and through this giving and serving acquires true actuality and lives on. Moving from the salon into exile or to the barricades, the hero crosses social-imaginary fields: from the (aggregative) realm of the private to the (substantive) realm of the political. In the process, he sheds his spectral, theatrical aspect and, in accumulating traces of actual suffering, becomes real.

The dynamic of the real and the apparent, though differently thematized, likewise organizes the narrative of Vasily Sleptsov's *Hard Times* (*Trudnoe vremia*, 1865). The novel (or *povest'*) opens with the arrival to a country estate of the radical writer-activist Riazanov, fleeing poor health and the onset of political reaction in the aftermath of the St. Petersburg fires, peasant unrest, and the Polish uprising of 1863. Riazanov is visiting his old university friend Shchetinin, a liberal landowner working to establish mutually beneficial relationships with the newly emancipated peasants. Much of the narrative is focalized through the perspective of the outsider Riazanov, and one of the earliest descriptions we get presents us with a transparent political allegory, constructed around the image of Shchetinin's manor house. Everything about the recently "reformed" building, Riazanov concludes, "clearly indicated that one could burn down old houses of this sort, but they could never be remodeled."[81]

The choice between burning down and remodeling marks the divergence in the approaches between the two friends.[82] Shchetinin is caught up in the daily work of postemancipation landowning. He struggles to establish a new way of life with his peasants, to whom in moments of increasingly frequent frustration he refers as "crude reality" and "raw material" (31; 230). According to Shchetinin, peasants must be educated out of their servile habits and made to understand the mutually beneficial nature of contractual relationships; they must be turned into law-abiding, self-governing citizens who understand that their own interests can and must be harmoniously aggregated with the interests of others. One telling early episode involves Shchetinin's conversation with a peasant who appears to have let his heifer wander onto the nobleman's land. "You must understand that I don't need your money; it won't make me rich," Shchetinin says. "I am fining you for your own good. [...] You'll even thank me for teaching you some good sense" (32; 231). At another point in the text, we find an indigent peasant household instructed on the benefits of cleanliness. Deference before social superiors—the requirement that a peasant take off his hat—is referred to as "politeness" (129; 301). Literacy and reading are recommended to keep peasants from getting drunk at a tavern (123; 297).[83] Throughout, the text calls attention to the difference between preemancipation and postemancipation conditions. Ostensibly, harsher punishments have been supplanted by subtler disciplinary methods: instruction from social superiors on proper behavior, literacy efforts, fines, enforced prayer, solitary confinement barns, and so on. But the boundary between the disciplinary and the coercive proves highly unstable. The text repeatedly plays on the ambiguity in the word "to instruct" (*uchit'*) which could mean both to educate and to inflict a beating. And in fact, scenes of brutal punishment are plenty and pivotal in the text.

From Riazanov's point of view, his friend's project of turning peasants into law-abiding citizens is hopeless, because it fundamentally mistakes the nature of their relationship. We are in the presence here of sheer dominance, attempting to mask itself as hegemony. An early exchange between the two friends goes a long way toward clarifying this logic. The czar's recent emancipation manifesto granted peasants personal freedom and at the same time subjected them to dire economic dependence on their former masters. Shchetinin complains that the peasants, failing to grasp what is in their own interest, refuse to accept the terms of their emancipation. Riazanov ironically wonders if the army had to be called upon to compel the peasants to accept Shchetnin's "gift" of land (18; 221). A firm, coercive framework shows too clearly through the legal-contractual order within which Shchetinin hopes to operate in good conscience. The complex postemancipation social relations are perpetually in danger of being "simplified" (for example, by the military), of being reduced to the exercise of brute, coercive force. Coercion emerges as the truth of lawful, mutually beneficial relations, while these latter are repeatedly exposed as a sham.

At a turning point in the narrative, we witness the outbreak of violence that constitutes the "really real" of the hegemonic order Shchetinin attempts to bring about. In this scene, Riazanov and Shchetinin's wife, Marya Nikolaevna, witness the whipping of a peasant (160; 324). When Shchetinin finds out about the incident, he is upset and blames his friend for exposing his wife to such horror. Riazanov replies with his customary feigned naivete: "You made a mistake when you didn't instruct her earlier that it was inappropriate for a proper lady to look at peasants when they are being flogged" (162; 326). Marya Nikolaevna's own glimpse of this brutal truth constitutes a breaking point in her already fraying relationship with her husband. Earlier in the text, Marya Nikolaevna accuses Shchetinin of trying to turn her into a "domestic woman." Here is how she recounts the history of their life at the estate: "You'd said to me, a long time ago: 'Masha, please keep the house!' Well, so I did. Then some sick peasants came and you said to me, 'Masha, you should go and see what's wrong with them.' So I started treating them" (77; 264). Having married Shchetinin in order to undertake work together with him for the "common cause," Marya Nikolaevna finds herself confined to the traditional tasks of a virtuous landowner's wife. Insofar as this does nothing to undermine the status quo and in fact perpetuates it, insofar as this life is broadly "domestic," Shchetinina cannot bring herself to regard it as real life.

Turning for recommendation and advice to Riazanov, she expresses her shock at the state of affairs in which her well-meaning husband works to make a profit off his starving former serfs. Riazanov himself refuses either to be surprised or to judge. He says: "Everything depends on the conditions in which a person is placed: under some conditions, he'll strangle and rob a close relative; under others, he'll take off and give away the shirt on his back. The visible results are always natural and normal, once the cause is known; but the power doesn't lie in them" (173; 334). To her question in what does such power lie, Riazanov replies: "In what you and I don't see and don't know. There is a certain 'x,' an unknown quantity; everything hinges on that; as for all this, it's not worth a dime" (173; 334). The statement characterizes manifest reality—the specific shape of social relations on Shchetinin's estate and elsewhere—as a mere appearance, a manifestation of the mysterious "x," which remains, as it were, outside the field of vision and yet determines its shape.

Riazanov's "x" refers to the constitutive function of the political order as such, the decision, instantiated in the relevant contemporary context of the monarch's emancipation decree of 1861. The decree instantaneously suspended the reigning social order and reconstituted it within a new framework. Within this framework, the difficulties encountered by Shchetinin, as well as the much worse difficulties experienced by his workers, were natural and inescapable. This is why, for Riazanov, Shchetinin's constant, compromised fussing is "not worth a dime," ghostly activity in a ghostly world. The real thing is elsewhere, concealed just underneath the veneer of contractual relations. The "x" is the political decision itself and, of course, the underlying power to enforce it: through beatings, floggings, and, in the last resort, military intervention.

Hard Times is thus constructed along a set of asymmetrically organized oppositions: between social relations and political power, contract and violence, appearance and truth, linked to the antagonists Shchetinin and Riazanov, respectively. The asymmetry results from the fact that while Shchetinin's efforts and views constitute the focal point of the text and its basic material, Riazanov's perpetually ironic gaze accounts for its "form," for the mode in which the material is presented. Shchetinin anchors the novel's manifest social reality, while Riazanov, with his deeper truths, stands passively outside it: futile and misguided activity, on the one hand, all-knowing but impotent irony, on the other. The latter stance has given contemporary critics reason to characterize the protagonist as a despairing skeptic, a Byronic alienated man.[84] Indeed, Riazanov seems incapable of becoming seriously preoccupied with any aspect of life on Shchetinin's estate. Like the Romantic ironist who keeps gesturing toward the unavailable Absolute, something to which irony would no longer apply, the radical gestures toward a new social organization that would be worthy of serious activity after all. In both cases, we find that there is no path that can lead the protagonist from the given world he rejects to the desired world that is not given. "'It follows that one must conceive, invent a new life,' Ryazanov explains to Shchetinina, and until then...' He waved his arm contemptuously" (176; 336).

Sleptsov's text gives us a way to make sense of this convergence between the ironist and the radical by invoking a concrete historical situation, one of extreme reaction setting in by the time of the novel's events. Already on arrival, Riazanov appears to us carrying upon his body and psyche traces of oppression. Early in the novel, he glances at himself in the mirror and is dismayed by what he sees: "a gaunt figure with an emaciated face and an immobile gaze" (10; 216). He speaks—in minimally Aesopian language—of the death, imprisonment, and exile of all the best representatives of the revolutionary movement (178; 338). At one point, he is shown reacting with disgust to what we are meant to understand is a heavily censored version of his article in the new issue of a journal. Elsewhere, he sardonically mentions the bad sealing wax on a recently received letter, evidently implying perlustration (147; 315). Thus, while for Shchetinina naked violence functions as reality's traumatic unveiling, Riazanov's own attunement to its presence everywhere stems from his direct exposure to state coercion. He inhabits a simplified world, reduced to a reckoning with sovereign rule and bypassing the ghostly delusions of legal order and civility.

The paradoxical inner world of the charismatic agent of imperial conquest in *A Hero of Our Time*, the dark night in Rudin's Scandinavian legend, and the hidden "x" in Sleptsov's novella—all figure the realm of the really real, the space of *deistvitel'nost'* as such. They make the state visible as overbearing power and as the socially reductive script of direct and conflicted substantive belonging. Fateful and fated, imperial and "wild," the figure of Pechorin transpires at the line of demarcation between the political and the private. This substantive conflict reveals the deep tension between the state's "reason" and its "blow," its "body politic" and "body natural"—a revelation achieved against the background, and at the expense, of social unreality, its permeability to supreme power. The added scene of Rudin's death on the barricades is from this perspective nothing other than the most explicit articulation of the principle of belonging whereby the protagonist is extracted from the domain of unactual setting of the salon (where all speech and action are mere posing) and placed into the domain of political confrontation (the absolute reality of which is sealed in death). The state of exception, paradigmatically encapsulated in *A Hero of Our Time* by imperial conquest and in *Rudin* by revolution, appears dispersed everywhere throughout *Hard Times*, in scenes and invocations of violence without which it is impossible to sustain the order of contractual relations and civic obligations. A similar distribution of the real and the apparent organizes the other texts we have analyzed in this chapter. The ghostly world of private pursuits in *Government Inspector* is haunted by the reality of the State, whose arrival in the end reasserts the persistence of the actual. Poor Eugene's dreams of personal happiness dissolve upon his awakening (the "unclouding" of his mind) in the confrontation with the imperial founder and guarantor, Peter I. The cardboard social world of *The Same Old Story* does little more than exemplify the "sacred" rationality of the statesman. The statesman's vengeance in *One Thousand Souls* unmasks the universe of social climbing. And phantasies of the hero's social success in *Demons* prove irrelevant and petty by comparison with the novel's true stakes: the real drama of sovereign power in which messianic hopes are ambiguously invested. This realism's "real" is the other, the converse of manifest sociality: the exception that gives form, is traumatically unveiled, allows the narrative to conclude.

Family [CHAPTER THREE]
Other Domestic Fictions

Sovereign Mediations

Accounts of the rise of the novel in Britain and France frequently allude to the legacy of local debates on patriarchalism. Paradigmatic in the British context is Robert Filmer's posthumously published *Patriarcha, or the Natural Power of Kings* (1680; written before the English civil wars of 1642–50), which posits a strict continuity—both conceptual and historical—between paternal and political power. Refuting the increasingly current notion that sovereign authority stems from a contract among a "multitude" of "by nature" free persons, Filmer argues, first, that God had granted fathers the absolute authority of life and death over their progeny and, second, that the biblical patriarchs were in fact also the first kings.[1] Filmer's aim is not to set up a mere analogy but to trace a direct line of inherited authority from God to humankind's first father (Adam), to the patriarchs, to kings.

Among a series of works written in opposition to Filmer's ultraroyalist work, John Locke's *Two Treatises of Government* (1689) was probably the most influential. Locke introduces a rigorous distinction between familial and political subjection, famously arguing that while parents do "have a sort of rule and jurisdiction over [their children] when they come into the world, and for some time after,"[2] political rule is established by means of a "compact" through which people in the purported state of nature "agree together mutually to enter into one community, and make one body politic."[3] Locke's contractual imaginary extends to his understanding of the family as well: when children grow up and lose their natural dependence on their parents, fathers and sons become equals. Likewise, the unity between husband and wife is based on a "compact" into which the two enter consensually, while preserving the right to separate.[4] Locke's language of compact and consent desubstantializes both polity and family, realigning them with the emergent emphasis on individual agency and natural rights.[5] The underlying social imaginary according to which individuals ontologically precede the "intense association" of the group, which is formed only through their consent and with the aim of fulfilling their innate, prepolitical, prefamilial purposes—this we can recognize as the fundamental assumption of what I have here called "aggregative" construals of social life.

Eighteenth-century European fiction—British predominantly, but French and German as well—intervenes in the debate in two interrelated ways: first, in treating the domain of intimate relations as autonomous from the concerns of the larger polity and aristocratic alliance, and second, in advocating for the organization of that domain along consensual (affectionate), rather than patriarchal lines, or at least for finding a compromise between the two. Ian Watt comments on Richardson and Defoe: "They themselves are strongly on the traditional side as regards the authority of the father and the vital importance of the family group as a moral and religious entity; on the other hand, the tendency of their novels seems to be towards the assertion of individual freedom from family ties."[6]

A similar tendency to undermine sovereign authority, conceived as an "intertwining of despotic royal and despotic familial power," emerges in Lynn Hunt's discussion of the figure of the "good father" in prerevolutionary France.[7] The eighteenth-century novel, with its interest in the family as the site for the upbringing of autonomous selves, allied itself with the task of making the father "good," which is to say tolerant, caring, permissive. Hunt locates one symbolic shift toward such a vision of paternal authority in a sequence of events from Jean-Jacques Rousseau's *Julie, ou la nouvelle Héloïse* (1761), in which Julie's father comes to recognize that explicit severity is a less effective way to recruit his daughter's consent than "a soft touch."[8] By the time we get to Bernardin de Saint-Pierre's wildly successful *Paul et Virginie* (1788), published on the eve of the Revolution, the fathers are altogether absent, and the children are represented from their own perspective as wholly autonomous beings. Highlighting the family-state analogy, Hunt concludes with the provocative claim that the emergence of the ideal of the "good father" in literature and, subsequently, the total effacement of the paternal figure in the years before the Revolution may have not only foreshadowed but actually brought about the real king's eventual beheading.[9]

Tony Tanner finds a similar—though in many ways less radical—development in the history of the European adultery novel, showing among other things how paternal authority recedes throughout the eighteenth century. In Tanner's account, we begin with the father whose role is to "to prohibit or command—never to inquire into his daughter's preferences or needs" in Samuel Richardson's *Clarissa* (1747),[10] move on to the father who separates in Rousseau's *Julie,* and lastly to the arrangement, most evident in Goethe's *Wahlverwandtschaften* (1809), where paternal authority vanishes from the domestic sphere but is relegated to the aesthetic-mythical realm through a series of images, "archetypes of male power, the power of the father in its most generic sense."[11] These authoritative ancestral figures constitute the mythological background against which the adulterous "elective affinities" are allowed to play out (in the absence of directly embodied authority) but are fatefully punished all the same. By the middle of the nineteenth century, as Nancy Armstrong and Margaret Cohen among others observe, the dominant strains of British and French fiction consign figures of (tyrannical) paternal authority to the margins of their social imaginaries and distribute individuals along the continuum between the two nonpolitical figures of the domestic woman and the economic man.

The European novels I have chosen for illustrating the narrative patterns of civil society aggregation highlight the recession of authoritative paternity with more or less detail and emphasis. All three feature fathers who die: before the narrative begins (*Jane Eyre*), in the middle of the narrative (*Lehrjahre*), or at the end (*Père Goriot*). We have seen that Balzac's text generates a robust paternal metaphor, positing the decline of the father's authority as the correlate of the emergence to dominance of the contemporary sociotope made up entirely of "economic men." Worse, though the tableau of the dying father strains to allegorize the loss of absolute authority associated with the Old Regime, the father himself has been all along compromised by the very system of needs above which he is assumed to tower at the end: his own authority, after all, is derived from the wealth he had accumulated through shady speculations during the early days of the Revolution that had put an end to the Old Regime in the first place. In Goethe's novel, the father is first disobeyed, then deceived, without any serious consequences for the prodigal son, and then dies "off-screen," leaving Wilhelm free to pursue his own purposes outside the constraints of his guild. In the end, paternal authority passes to the Society of the Tower, whose forms of exercising it are more subtle, more diffuse and, most importantly, better aligned with Wilhelm's own impulses. Jane Eyre's father is dead before the novel begins, but an early encounter with patriarchal authority highlights its ambiguous status in her life. Punished for a rebellious outburst, little Jane is imprisoned in the red room at dusk and, still in the grips of her rage, summons the image of her dead uncle who would protect her from such persecution. But the image gets out of hand as Jane begins to feel, with paralyzing terror, that the room is actually haunted by her protector's ghost. The dynamic by which the authoritative male elder functions as both protector and threat is repeated several times throughout the novel, but Jane succeeds in neutralizing the fearsome, tyrannical aspects of patriarchal authority through the language of self-government and faithfulness to the governing self.[12]

All three novels, then, grapple with figurations of patriarchal authority, staging its threat as well as its defeat, displacement, or neutralization. To be sure, overweening fathers and husbands continue to appear within the Victorian tradition in particular, starkly exemplified by Mr. Dombey's violent treatment of his second wife and his daughter in *Dombey and Son* (1848), or, in *Middlemarch* (1872), by Edward Casaubon's demand that, even after his death, his wife "avoid doing what I should deprecate, and apply [herself] to do what I should desire."[13] But the tyrannical Dombey is tamed and "domesticated" by the novel's end, while Dorothea Brooke simply renounces Casaubon's will and the fortune conditioned on her obedience and follows her own path—without, in the end, any serious repercussions. The less fortunate outcome of Flaubert's *Madame Bovary* (1856) has little to do with the authority of the hapless husband, and much with Emma's consumerist entanglement in the "system of needs." Ultimately, these texts transpose the sovereign authority of the father/husband (figure) onto one or another social-imaginary paradigm of civil society aggregation, whose "Lockean" parameters (the emphasis on the pursuit of self-selected purposes by free, self-governing individuals) deprive symbols of parental authority of their legitimacy and force. None of this means, of course, that together with the patriarchalist paradigm, the problem of power as such has been obviated. Rather, power now reappears in subtler and less visible forms, in hegemonic construals of class-based virtue, sexual difference, domesticity, interiority, and so on.

The Russian realist tradition confronts patriarchal models of political power in ways that are indexed to its distinctive conjuncture of literary history and social formation, mediated through a set of imaginaries that foreground the persistence of stark, force-bearing authority. Rather than stage a gradual domestication of the sovereign patriarch or operate on the premise of this figure's historical supersession, Russian texts repeatedly bring figurations of spectacular patriarchal authority to light, explore its multiple manifestations, dramatize its paradoxes, and reflect upon its psychic and bodily effects. Before considering a wider range of such fictional (and parafictional) explorations, I suggest we look briefly at several passages that mark out the relevant social-imaginary terrain with special clarity.

The first of these chronologically is Nikolai Karamzin's anticonstitutionalist "Memoir on Ancient and Modern Russia," presented to Emperor Alexander I in 1811. "In the Russian monarch," Karamzin writes, "all authorities are united: our rule is fatherly, patriarchal. The father of the family judges and punishes without a protocol, so the monarch in certain cases must act according to conscience alone."[14] Karamzin deploys the paternal metaphor against the expanding bureaucratic-legalistic model of governance, inherited from the Western model of the well-regulated state, whose Russian emulation produces diverse excessive and vacuous rules and promotes corruption. By contrast, the patriarchal metaphor implies the sovereign's absolute, irrevocable transcendence of the bureaucratic apparatus and the law, his direct and unmediated proximity to the lives and vital interests of the empire's subjects, whose multitude is rhetorically reduced to the size of a family. The power of the sovereign is (like) that of the paterfamilias insofar as it pierces the intermediary fields of normative social intercourse and state regulations, and reaches its subjects directly. The very act of presenting the "Memoir" to the monarch—through the mediation of the emperor's sister, the Grand Duchess Ekaterina Pavlovna—functions as an exemplary case of such direct, extralegal, and nonbureaucratic contact between the sovereign and his subject.[15]

Another example of patriarchalist political language can be found in one of Belinsky's reconciliation-period articles:

History cannot depict the development of the idea of the father into the idea of the czar; history does not remember this, because it is a primordial [*dovremennoe*] phenomenon. But it is all the clearer that the one [God] who inspired in the human being the feeling of mystical, religious respect for the cause of his days, consecrated the dignity and title of his father, he [also] consecrated the dignity and title of the czar, exalted his head above all mortals and made his earthly destiny independent of the arbitrary will of the people, having made his person sacred and inviolable.[16]

In his polemic against contractarian theories of the state and of sovereign power in particular, Belinsky converges with Hegel but far overshoots any specifically Hegelian meanings of the analogy between the two substances of the family and the state.[17] Rather, we are here confronted by an explicitly sacralized, politico-theological version of absolutism, the convergence of familial and political authority at the vanishing point of primordial times, a vision of human connectedness that is itself not human-made. The person of the monarch is as sacred and inviolable as the person of the father, to whom mystical respect is due simply for being, like God, the "cause of our days." The distance between this vision and the fatherless, revolutionary idyll of *Paul et Virginie* is, needless to say, immeasurable.

A passage from Gogol's *Selected Passages from a Correspondence with Friends* (1847) supplies a complementary perspective on the state-family parallelism by recasting the very notion of contract in terms not of consent but of blood sacrifice:

> Consider by what marvelous means, even before the full meaning of this power had been explained either to the sovereign or to his subjects, the seeds of a mutual love were sown in [Russian] hearts! No royal house began as extraordinarily as the house of the Romanovs began. Its beginnings were already a feat of love. The last and humblest subject of the empire yielded up his life to give us a Czar, and the purity of his sacrifice has inseparably bound the sovereign to his subjects ever since. Love has entered into our blood; it has bound us in a blood relationship with the Czar.[18]

Gogol speaks here of the original ascent to the Moscow throne of Mikhail Fyodorvich Romanov, elected by the Assembly of the Land (*Zemsky Sobor*) at the end of a prolonged and bloody crisis of power and foreign invasion. The contract between the Russian people and the Russian czars is here construed not as a matter of consent by self-interested individuals but, on the contrary, as a function of the wartime sacrifice of self-interest. Sanctified by sacrifice, the unity between the ruler and his subjects is now a familial bond of blood kinship. This event, once again, is imagined as primordial, in the sense both that it stands at the very origins of history and that it escapes rational comprehension.

Gogol's conjectural account of the "contract" of self-sacrifice—by explicit contrast with the European natural law tradition—alludes to an episode of Russian history that had become central to its state mythology since at least the Patriotic War of 1812. Mikhail Glinka's 1836 opera *A Life for the Czar* makes up perhaps the single most important contribution to that mythology. The opera (libretto composed primarily by the poet Egor Rosen but closely overseen by the emperor himself) tells the story of the peasant Ivan Susanin's heroic sacrifice of life for the newly elected Mikhail Romanov. In the first act, Susanin's daughter Antonida waits for the return of her betrothed, Sobinin, from battle. Sobinin returns with news of victory: Moscow has been saved. The conversation then turns to the impending marriage, eagerly awaited by the young, but Susanin refuses to allow it until the day when God gives Russia a czar. Without a czar, our common "birth father" (*otets rodnoi*), Russia is declared an orphan. The paternal metaphor operates here in the familiar way: political authority is linked to the authority of the father both analogically and metonymically in the sense that within his household, the father speaks in the name of the czar. More interestingly still, in the opera, the father gives voice to the czar's absence, extends the generalized state of exception into the private domain and thus deprivatizes it, annulling the principle according to which individuals are imagined to be free to lead their lives as they wish. The father, who will soon sacrifice his life for the czar (sealing the bond of blood kinship between the monarch and the people) for now fills in for him—with a prohibition.[19]

The patriarchalist paradigm was far from universally endorsed during the early—let alone later—decades of the nineteenth century. Karamzin's memorandum may have displeased the emperor himself, who at the time entertained a more reformist vision of autocracy. We have already touched on the uproar Belinsky's reconciliation-period articles caused in literary circles. The repentant critic himself would several years later pen a passionate retort to Gogol's *Selections*—a text that would inspire at least a generation of Russian radicals. At times, the patriarchal code is invoked specifically with the purpose of demonstrating its perniciousness. A striking example in this regard is Nikolai Kostomarov's novella *The Son* (1865), which is, like *A Life for the Czar*, a historical narrative with an explicit ideological message for its current moment. Where Glinka's opera presents an ultraloyalist defense of Nicholas I's dynastic reign in the aftermath of the suppression of the 1830 Polish rebellion, Kostomarov's narrative voices a national-democratic protest against the dynastic pretensions of the postemancipation empire.

The Son tells the story of a young man, Osip, who, upon returning home from heroic service during the Russo-Polish War, finds his mother laid out in a coffin, with a visible wound on her head. It soon comes to light that her murderer was Osip's father, Kapiton. Since the crime is being covered up at home, Osip decides that he must seek "justice in the name of the czar and his truth."[20] The motif of the czar's (and God's) "truth-justice" (*pravda*) sounds repeatedly throughout the text, which in the end shows that no such thing can be found. Osip sets out for the city of Saransk, the seat of the voivode, the czar's representative in the region. It turns out, however, that the voivode is on friendly terms with Osip's father, who regularly sends the official lavish gifts. Instead of investigating the claim, the voivode sends for Kapiton. Kapiton arrives with another sizable bribe, and the two older men—the representative of state power and the father in a paradigmatic tandem—conjure higher authority still, informing Osip that the Law Code (of 1649) forbids sons to petition against their fathers. The two men then preside over Osip's whipping, a punishment for having "raised his hand" against his father. Recovering from his wounds, Osip flees Saransk and joins the Cossack rebels stationed nearby. In their ranks, as one of their leaders, he zealously pursues the rebellion's democratic and redistributive practices. He takes part in the sacking of Saransk and, though not unhesitatingly, executes the treacherous voivode. In further pursuit of his father, whom he now intends to kill himself, Osip enters his own estate, gives away his family's property to the communal treasury (the *duvan*) and sets his own home on fire. Continuing on the tracks of his father, who had escaped in time, Osip is finally captured, tortured until he takes back his accusation, and executed. As the novella concludes, all is once again quiet in Moscovy; with the help of the state treasury, newly remarried Kapiton is flourishing once again on the rebuilt estate. In the final scene, a toast is raised to "to the health of his Royal Majesty, the great Sovereign Czar and Grand Duke Alexei Mikhailovich, Autocrat of the Great, and Small, and White Russias." The toast is followed by Kapiton's own decree that his son's name be relegated to oblivion: "May his memory perish from the land of the living!" The priest seals the decree with the novella's final word: "Amen!"[21]

The narrative speaks plainly. Once again, familial and political authority allegorize and bulwark each other. The father and the sovereign, on the one hand, patricide and rebellion, on the other, define the terms of the patriarchal metaphor organizing the narrative's semantic space, characterized as the space of exception. Kostomarov's text clearly militates against patriarchalism, but it also testifies to its generative power for nineteenth-century Russian political imagination more broadly: a matter of deep conviction for some, a utopian hope for others, an object of polemic for others still, and an insistent thematic and figurative temptation for most. Given the intimate entanglement between the monarchy and the educated elites, and given that the monarchy itself aggressively promoted familial figurations of its own power—it is hard to see how cultural production could avoid frequent and multifaceted reckonings with patriarchalist topoi and motifs.

Glinka's historical opera and Kostomarov's historical novella both make explicit the dynamic by which the paternal prohibition transmits the political state of exception directly into the domain of personal relations. I will call this intrusion of substantive social imaginaries into the field of private affairs—*sovereign mediation of intimate life*. For two peasants to marry, Russia must have a czar: from the perspective of aggregative sociality, with its "methodological individualism" and its postulate of the autonomy of the private domain, the two dimensions conjugated in the opera's premise are incommensurable. Sovereign mediation of intimate life dramatizes the interruption of such privatized aggregative scripts, replacing stories of *individuals* with dramas of *individuation*. Such dramas unfold according to a pattern in which one separates from the "intense association" of the familial/political bond only to be fatefully reclaimed by it. This reclaiming, or reining in, of the provisionally and precariously individuated subject is brought about, or channeled, by authoritative male figures—fathers and husbands as a rule, but also their displaced figurations—endowed with an aura of political power variously evaluated and conceived.

The proliferation and prominence of such figures, in turn, signals a difference in continuity between Russian realist representations of domestic and intimate life and their Western European counterparts. The shared figurative background linking the head of household to political rule allows for gradational and functional differences to stand out. While in Western realist fiction the power of fathers and husbands is gradually disassociated from that of the state, accorded an increasingly marginal place, and, if threatening at all, successfully neutralized, Russian texts compulsively conflate these domains and elevate the authoritative male figure to dramatic centrality.[22] The rest of this chapter explores several scenarios according to which such centrality becomes manifested: *interdiction* as the most explicit enactment of the sovereign "no" to individual desire; *government* as a series of forms of patriarchal control over the (female) subject; *refuge* as an attempt to recast domestic intimacy as a politylike community of affect, placing absolute demands on its members; and *displacement* as a mode of deferred and occulted punishment for familial transgression.

1. Interdiction

In his essay "The Statue in Pushkin's Mythology," Roman Jakobson isolates a narrative invariant for three of Pushkin's poetic works involving a statue as the driver of the action: *The Bronze Horseman*, *The Stone Guest* (1830), and the fairy tale of *The Golden Cockerel* (1834). In Jakobson's account, the invariant plot opens with the situation in which a certain "man is weary, he settles down, he longs for rest, and this motif is intertwined with desire for a woman." However, "the statue, more precisely, the being which is inseparably connected with the statue, has supernatural, unfathomable power over this desired woman." Finally, "after a vain resistance the man perishes through the intervention of the statue, which has miraculously set itself into motion, while the woman vanishes."[23] Jakobson suggests that Pushkin's "statue myth" represents the poet's response to the experience of personal capitulation to Nicholas I, a complex affective amalgam of resignation and impotent rage. The poet's relationship to the monarch is thus redoubled as a narrative of sovereign prohibition; the desired object turns out to have always been forbidden because it belongs to Another. An attempt to be united with her is cast as transgressive and punished by death.

The three statue narratives—much like *Taras Bulba* and *A Life for the Czar*—position intimate encounters within the force field of the state of exception. A natural disaster puts in question sovereign authority in *The Bronze Horseman* and at the same time folds the protagonist's private life into the myth of political foundation and imperial order. Eugene's beloved

Parasha turns out to belong to the myth as much as, if not more than, she belongs to the romance. The "little tragedy" of *The Stone Guest* revolves around Don Guan's challenge of the grave statue of the Commander, whom he had earlier killed and whose widow he now passionately desires. The text frames pursuit of the desired object as a blasphemous transgression against the authority of the husband and the dead, a familial disturbance coded as a disturbance in the ontological order, soliciting the deadly intrusion of the statue-husband into the world that had appeared to belong wholly to living, desiring individuals. Meanwhile, erotic pursuit in *The Golden Cockerel* is traversed by the problematics of territorial integrity and the interregnum as the ruler becomes weary of having to defend his borders against multiple enemies and outsources those responsibilities to the magic amalgam of the magus-cockerel. The latter then assumes the position of the sovereign and comes to claim the object necessary to complete the retired and thus "privatized" czar's domestic bliss.

There are two other texts by Pushkin that Jakobson does not discuss but that at certain points in the narrative also resort to the structure of sovereign triangulation. Jakobson does not mention them for the obvious reason that they do not, at least explicitly, feature statues. Yet they are important for our purposes as works of novelistic fiction central to the subsequent realist tradition. The first of these texts, in the order of explicitness with which the pattern of sovereign triangulation structures it, is *The Captain's Daughter* (1836), a historical novel from the age of the eighteenth-century peasant uprising led by Emelian Pugachev (pretender-czar Peter III). The novel explores the problematic of paternal-sovereign power through a series of substitutions that begin when the young protagonist, Pyotr Grinev, has a dream about a fierce-looking, bearded peasant on his deathbed, posing as his father. Grinev's mother tries to convince him to approach the peasant, kiss his hand, and receive his blessing, explaining to the puzzled young man that this is in fact his "proxy father" (*posazhenny otets*: the respected man who fulfills the role of the father at a wedding). When Grinev refuses, the peasant jumps up from his bed and begins to wield an axe wildly, filling the room with dead bodies.

The dream foreshadows Grinev's encounter with Pugachev himself, first in the role of a guide through the snowy steppe and later as the leader of the formidable uprising. This latter encounter issues in an episode in which Pugachev helps the hero rescue his beloved Masha Mironova from the persecutions of a villain. Having reunited the lovers, Pugachev suggests that they marry immediately and offers himself as a Grinev's "proxy father." Curiously, earlier in the text, Grinev had written to his father to ask permission to marry Masha and received a categorical prohibition. A tight link is thus established between the figures of the father and the

Pretender, resulting in a hybrid patriarchalist figure, which triangulates (forbidding/enabling) the lovers' unity in marriage. The same pattern organizes the novel's ending, but now with the legitimate sovereign, the Empress Catherine II, interceding between the lovers: first separating them by sending Grinev into exile for treason, then yielding to Masha's pleas, accepting her explanations, and pardoning him.

Thus, sovereign power over life, death, and conjugal union—instantiated in the agonistic imperial couple (Catherine and her murdered husband, Peter III, come back as nemesis-impostor)—traverses the field of intimate relations between private individuals. The union is ultimately permitted, but the principle of triangulation remains.[24] Love and marriage lose their narrowly domestic purview and instead delineate spaces for the dramatic intrusion of substantive forces into the personal domain. The intrusion consists not merely in the act in which the sovereign/father intercedes against or on behalf of the lovers but also, more fundamentally, in the fact that the story of their intimate relations crosses over into the field of foundational political power where each is placed under mortal threat.

A subtler triangulation of a similar kind, but now detached from the problematics of the state of exception, structures the culminating scene of *Eugene Onegin* (1823–1831). The scene stages an encounter between star-crossed lovers, interrupted by the metallic clinking of the spurs, which announces the arrival of a nameless General, the husband who separates. As the scene begins, we walk in on a classic sentimental tableau: Tatyana is in her drawing room, a letter from Onegin in her hands, tears in her eyes. Commenting on the function of the tableau in French sentimental fiction, Margaret Cohen writes: "When the novel's underwriting conflict [usually, between love and duty] reaches such a level of intensity that it threatens to explode, the narration loses access to the protagonist's interiority, as if overcome by the tension it represents. Instead of following the movements of the soul, the narration offers a picture. It describes the protagonist staging the crisis with her own body."[25] Pushkin's narrator invites us to read Tatyana's appearance for signs of authentic inner disturbance: "In that brief instant then, who couldn't/Have read her tortured heart at last!"[26] She is torn between her feelings for Onegin and the reality that she has been "given to another." In Cohen's account, the French sentimental tableau staged for its readers the moment of the heroine's sacrifice of her happiness for the sake of collective welfare (represented by the bonds of matrimony); traditionally, witnessing the heroine's suffering, the enamored hero, too, would be compelled to sacrifice the fulfillment of his desire, to restrain "the natural impulse to act on his love."[27] In Pushkin's version, one element is subtracted and one added to the French model. Onegin is abandoned before we get to witness his own internalization of sacrifice—its necessity remains external and coercive, a blow of fate rather than an individual decision. This externality is in turn reinforced by the appearance of the daunting figure of the horseman-husband, the enforcer of the sacrifice, the agent of separation, whose arrival puts an abrupt end to the novel's plot.

At least one early reader of this concluding episode, decoding it perhaps through this same sentimental lens, detected a political allegory. Pushkin's school friend, the poet Wilhelm Küchelbecker, exiled in connection with the Decembrist uprising, records in his Siberian prison diary from 1832 the following cryptic reaction: "To someone like me, his lyceum friend, the person who grew up with him and knows him by heart, the feeling that fills him is everywhere noticeable, even though, like his Tatyana, he doesn't want the world [or high society—*svet*] to know it."[28] In his commentary on the novel, Vladimir Nabokov glosses Küchelbecker's carefully phrased statement as follows: "Pushkin is very like the Tatyana of Chapter Eight: he is full of feelings (liberal ideas) that he does not want the world to know, but he is given to another (Tsar Nicholas)."[29] In other words, the final scene presents us with a confrontation, and ultimately a prohibition, that is coded not only in familial but also in political terms. Accordingly, in close parallel with Jakobson's statue plot invariant, the action of the novel concludes with Tatyana's disappearance (she tells Onegin she loves him, will never be his, and leaves), the appearance instead of her husband, and Onegin's narrative death:

> She left him then. Eugene, forsaken,
> Stood seared, as if by heaven's fire.
> How deep his stricken heart is shaken!
> With what a tempest of desire!
> A sudden clink of spurs rings loudly,
> As Tanya's husband enters proudly—
> And here... at this unhappy turn
> For my poor hero, we'll adjourn
> And leave him, reader, at his station...
> For long... forever."[30]

Thus, the "little tragedy," the fairy tale, the "Petersburg tale," the historical novel, and the novel in verse all converge on the pattern of triangulation, in which the transcendent figure of sovereign interdiction intrudes into the sphere of erotic/intimate relationships and mediates (mostly bars) the hero's access to his beloved. Unlike the French sentimentalist material analyzed by Cohen, the Russian version of the pattern—at least as far as we can tell from the small corpus of texts discussed so far—highlights not the liberal subject's internalized conflict between negative and positive rights but external prohibition, operating within the imaginary of power that in various proportions combines figures of familial authority with those of political majesty and supernatural might.

That political allegorization of intimate life would go on to constitute a major element of Russian realist fiction is evident from Nikolai Chernyshevsky's classic diagnostic essay from 1858 titled "The Russian at the Rendezvous." The essay is written on the occasion of the appearance of Ivan Turgenev's novella *Asya*, but it ranges widely to raise the question: Why does the Russian narrative tradition abound in stories of well-educated and high-minded young men failing to fathom, express, let alone act on, their true feelings when facing a woman who reciprocates their love? In addition to *Asya*, Chernyshevsky brings up Turgenev's own *Rudin* and *Faust*, Mikhail Lermontov's *A Hero of Our Time*, Nikolai Nekrasov's *Sasha*, and Alexander Herzen's *Who Is to Blame?* Had Goncharov's *Oblomov* (1859) already appeared, it would have doubtless been also included, as it was, together with the earlier *Eugene Onegin*, in the updated list from Nikolai Dobrolyubov's kindred essay of a year later, "What Is Oblomovitis?" Confronted by such a pattern—reappearing in works authored across generations, ideological positions, and aesthetic orientations—Chernyshevsky asks a question that in its basic structure resembles Annenkov's query about the Russian "social novel": Why do narratives of courtship take such a peculiar shape in Russia by comparison with Western models, where successful unions between lovers turn out to be possible even across class and status boundaries and in defiance of familial opposition? Why does "the Russian" strike such a pathetic figure at the rendezvous?

At its core, Chernyshevsky's answer consists in this: that the protagonist's inability to act decisively at the right moment is a symptom of his exclusion from political activity. According to the critic, if a man develops without being able to lead the life dedicated to the pursuit of the common good, he becomes enmeshed in narrow, merely private preoccupations, concerned only with his own well-being. Such a small-minded person is unprepared for decisive action in any domain of life; his will is infected with passivity that makes it impossible to behave in any but the most conventional way. In order to be able to act decisively under extraordinary circumstances, confronted by something as "great and living" as another's love, one must have developed the capacity for action at the level of what is essential and for taking responsibility for the consequences of such actions. This kind of education, Chernyshevsky suggests, cannot be gained through socialization as such—social life, accepted as it is, teaches only to conform. Excluded from civic decision-making, contemporary Russians are comfortable enough in the world made up of ordinary events but feel completely out of their element when confronting an exceptional situation. Then, says the critic, they are like a sailor who has spent all his life navigating the shallows between St. Petersburg and Kronstadt and is suddenly asked to find his way in the wide-open spaces of the ocean.[31]

The "ocean" is Chernyshevsky's metaphor here for the twin extraordinary situations of passionate love and decisive political action. This last horizon, though guiding his analysis throughout, emerges with absolute clarity only at the end, where the critic calls upon these "best men of ours," the well-meaning, liberal-minded, but weak-willed and indecisive members of educated elite, to recognize the revolutionary moment that is upon them.[32] To back down at the rendezvous is to back down before the sovereign, to fail to wrest from him the right to self-rule. Put somewhat flatly, in Chernyshevsy's reading of this pattern, there are not two but three persons at the rendezvous: the hero, the heroine, and the sovereign standing between them. What the specific shape taken by the rendezvous reveals is the fate-bearing presence of this (now invisible) "third," the triangular nature of the encounter.

Chernyshevsky's reading of the "Russian at the rendezvous" plot pattern establishes a continuity between the explicit accounts of sovereign mediation we find in the 1830s and their psychologized reenactments from the 1840s and 1850s. In the process, it produces what might be called a psychopolitical interpretation of early Russian psychological realism, a way of understanding the psychic complexions of its protagonists as a function of specific kinds of entanglement with political power. These entanglements, in turn, arise with greater likelihood from the experience of being raised in the circumstances and traditions of the service elite. It is not by chance, then, that the essay selects for its critique the work of a paradigmatic representative of that estate, Ivan Turgenev. What is more surprising perhaps is that Turgenev himself would soon produce a strikingly similar psychopolitical genealogy of the very type whose behavior at the rendezvous had caught the attention of the critic.

The novella *First Love* (1860), published approximately two years after Chernyshevsky's article on *Asya*, is, at least at first glance, a purely intimate tale of a sixteen-year-old boy infatuated with a young woman who turns out to be having an affair with his father. This loosely Oedipal triangle, however, anchors a pervasive political allegory, most explicitly hinted at in the story's epilogue, appearing in the French and German translations of the tale, but not in the Russian original. In this postscript, two listeners of the story narrated by the middle-aged Vladimir Petrovich respond to what they have just heard. After an awkward exchange followed by still more awkward silence, the conversation zeroes in on the essential. One of the listeners begins:

> "We were unnerved by your simple and artless tale... not because it struck us with its immorality—there is something deeper and darker than simple immorality here. You yourself are not to blame for anything, but one can feel some general, national guilt, something like crime."
> "What an exaggeration!" observed Vladimir Petrovich.
> "Maybe. But I repeat the words from *Hamlet*: 'something is rotten in the state of Denmark.'"[33]

The story takes place at a dacha on the edge of Moscow, where young Volodya spends his last summer before enrolling at the university. Its plot centers on Volodya's beautiful neighbor, Zinaida Zasyekina, who gathers around herself a small crowd of adoring suitors: a poet eager to sing her praises, a hussar bodyguard, a doctor doubling as master of ceremonies, a retired captain, occasionally serving as a physical prop, and a Polish count in the role of a villainous intriguer. Young Volodya, newly arrived with his family and quickly in love with the beautiful older girl, is soon admitted to the circle in the role of a "pageboy."

This final designation highlights a metaphorical link between Zinaida's salon and the royal court. The link is made explicit in a kind of poetic improvisation during which she casts herself as a queen, surrounded by handsome and clever men all madly in love with her. The queen "possesses," or "rules over" (*vladeet*) them but doesn't love them. The man she loves, the man who, in turn, "possesses," or "rules over" (*vladeet*) her, waits outside the illuminated palace, in the dark garden, by the fountain.[34] The enigmatic lover, ruler, and possessor in the garden is Volodya's father, Pyotr Vasilievich, whom Volodya describes as remarkably handsome, self-assured, and "authoritative" (*samovlastnyi*). This last term, in particular, carries with it obvious political connotations. The primary meaning of *samovlastie* refers to autocratic state rule. Only secondarily and metaphorically is it extended to personal temperament or behavior.

Pyotr Vasilievich is further endowed with two Roman prototypes: Caesar and Anthony (with Zinaida casting herself as Cleopatra) (157; 9:22 and 174; 9:42).[35] Expressions such as "*otkloniaiushchaia ruka*" (which can be literally translated as "rejecting hand," with the sense of rejecting a petition or a plea) and "*ne dopuskal menia do sebia*" (once again, literally: "did not admit me into his presence") both resonate with the sense of distance that accrues to sovereign majesty. In fact, the only extended conversation between Volodya and his father pertains directly to politics. The exchange begins when "in the capacity of a young democrat," Volodya broaches the topic of freedom. His father is dismissive. Real freedom, he says, consists in "the will [*volia*], your own will and the power [*vlast'*] it can give, which is better than freedom. Learn how to express your will [*umei khotet'*]—and you will be free, and you will be in command [*komandovat' budesh'*—or, in a crossed-out variant: *vlastvovat' budesh'* (you will reign)]" (164; 9:31; 9:352). In other words, to the broadly liberal conception of freedom as the capacity to pursue one's goals without being infringed upon and without infringing upon the similar pursuits of others, the father opposes a notion of *volia-vlast'*, best defined as the ability to dominate others. The only way not to be subjected to rule is to rule absolutely.

The story's most arresting literalization of such power unfolds before us some months after the family's return to Moscow. Following his father on a horse ride through the city one day, Volodya witnesses from a distance a barely comprehensible scene—all cryptic scraps of speech and expressive gestures—between the lovers from the previous summer. The scene ends with Volodya's father striking Zinaida on the arm with his riding crop. To Volodya's astonishment, Zinaida raises her arm to her lips and kisses the appearing welt. The lovers rush passionately into each other's arms and are concealed from Volodya's view (198–99; 9:71). This fearsome scene is followed immediately by another. Readers will have learned earlier that Pyotr Vasilievich is an unequaled rider and tamer of horses. Now we find out he "had a splendid English chestnut roan with a long slender neck and long legs. The mare was restless and vicious. Her name was Electric. No one could ride her save my father" (197; 9:31). When Pyotr Vasilievich returns from his violent rendezvous with Zinaida and gets back on the horse, she rears up and balances on her hind legs. Missing his riding crop, which he has just used on Zinaida and flung aside, Pyotr Vasilievich masters the horse by driving his spurs into her sides and striking her on the neck with a fist (199; 9:71).

The tableau of the grandly violent father on the rearing mare presents us once again with a double, politico-libidinal metaphor that establishes the rather commonplace link between a desired woman and a horse and, in the same gesture, overwrites it with the iconic imperial figure of the Horseman, where the animal is identified with the body politic and the rider with the ruler. The list of precedents is long, beginning with portrayals of Alexander the Great, who, like the master of Electric, is said to have been the only man able to ride his horse, Bucephalus, and ending with what is certainly the most direct and relevant prototype for the image of a reared-up horse, suspended on its hind legs, yet precariously contained: the Bronze Horseman himself. The reining in of a rearing horse by the horseman named Pyotr, coming directly after the similar taming of

Zinaida, thus serves as a point of convergence among images of political, religious, and brute physical authority: beasts, humans, and polities alike submit to the ruler's preternatural will.[36]

On the face of it, then, *First Love* is a story of a young man on the verge of manhood pursuing an object of his affections in competition with other men. At this level, we are confronted by a sequence of social encounters: salon games, sociable storytelling, witty banter, courtship ordeals, the emotional ups and downs that come with perceived progress to a goal or setbacks. The affair behind the scenes, however, warps the standard domestic problematic of courtship by adding to it a foreign element, a center of narrative gravity positioned outside (and in some ways above) the directly represented social world. Whatever transpires within Zinaida's "court," the entire sociopsychological complex at the center of the realist text turns out to have the status of mere appearance. Zinaida's riddles, her mood swings, her orders and requests, her entire relationship with Volodya are all secretly oriented to an absent cause and take shape in response to the hidden movements of an extrinsic factor. There is nothing Volodya can do to affect the situation. His rival turns out to have been an impossible one, retrospectively recasting his desire itself—at first merely private and perfectly legitimate—as a political and ontological transgression, threatening the paradigmatic double crime of incest and patricide. The paternal/sovereign interdiction bars the protagonist's access to the desired object as well as, more generally, to mature social existence.

The principle of familial-political or substantive triangulation is perhaps at its most vivid when one night, driven by an insuperable fit of jealousy, Volodya keeps watch in the garden, waiting with a ready penknife for his rival to appear. He expects it to be one of the men who frequent Zinaida's "salon." He hears steps and draws the knife, getting ready to attack: "The footsteps were coming directly towards me. I bent down and was ready to spring up to him... a man came into view... My God, it was my father!" (190; 9:61). This encounter affords the young man an insight so blinding that he is unable to process it for some time afterward. When he finally comprehends the true nature of the situation, he is crushed: "all the flowers of my dreams had been torn up in one instant and lay around me, scattered and trampled on" (194; 9:65). We have here a peculiar loss of innocence, a coming of age through the experience of the denial of genuine experience, its alienation to the figure of the sovereign-father, for whom the boy's admiration only grows as a result: "let psychologists explain this contradiction as best they can" (196; 9:67).[37]

Like Chernyshevsky's article, then, and with the greater concreteness and figurative force afforded by the medium, *First Love* makes evident the work of sovereign mediation in the intimate life of "the Russian at the rendezvous" and thus follows and reanimates the tradition of triangulating lovers with czars. The triangulation consists in the paradoxical move of simultaneously exiling the protagonist from the domain of the essential (political activity/love) and establishing the state of exception (the always threatening revolution, the threat of incest and patricide), within which private life becomes absorbed into the political. The text transposes the hero's amorous predicament from the codes of aggregative socialization to those of substantive confrontation, which is to say once again that his rendezvous with the beloved turns out to be also, and foremost, a rendezvous with the bearer of sovereignty effects.[38]

This way of putting things invites comparison with René Girard's well-known account of desire and triangulation in the modern novel. For Girard, novels at their best afford us a special insight into the true nature of individual wanting. The insight—anticipated incidentally by Hegel in his discussion of the system of needs—consists in the fact that despite appearances, our desires are not immediately our own but are, in one way or another, mediated by others. We learn (what and how) to want through imitation, which can take a number of forms, distributed along the continuum between the poles of "external" and "internal" mediation. External mediation presupposes an insuperable "spiritual" distance, a strict and unshakable hierarchy between the subject of desire and the Mediator. The relationship between the subject and the Mediator is, in this case, one of recognition and veneration: it is explicitly desire "according to Another." Thus Don Quixote desires and knows that he desires "according to" Amadis. Alternatively, the distance between the subject of desire and the Mediator may be reduced to the point at which the two operate within the same field of possibilities; the Mediator is just another person like us, located on the same ontological plane on which we find ourselves. This is, according to Girard, the modern, secular predicament: "Denial of God does not eliminate transcendency but diverts it from the *au-delà* to the *en-deçà*. The imitation of Christ becomes the imitation of one's neighbor."[39] The prevalence of such "internal mediation" allows for the possibility—or rather, ensures the likelihood—that the one who has been selected as the model for desire is also a rival. This fact in turn underpins a complex social psychology, rife with competition, identification, resentment, admiration—all tangled together into a rich fabric of affects characteristic of the modern novel. Meanwhile, for texts that privilege external mediation, such rivalry is ruled out, since the Mediator is placed safely out of reach beyond an ontological divide.

Girard's take on the modern novel, then, would seem to compel the view of "sovereign mediation" as an incongruous hybrid: a situation of rivalry and ontological difference both. The first time Volodya sees Zinaida, she is surrounded—framed as desirable—by a group of desiring men. Insofar as he expects one of them to appear that fateful night in the garden, his desire remains in the grips of "internal mediation": rivalry with those who taught him (what) to desire in the first place. But when his father appears instead, the regimes of mediation switch, and we are suddenly confronted with a case of rivalry with what is incommensurable. *Rivalry with the incommensurable*—the political-theological hinge that constitutes the blind spot of Girard's model precisely because he occludes the point of intersection between the *au-delà* and *en-deçà*: the father-statue-sovereign—is another way to describe the sort of substantive mediation of intimate life that accounts for the plot pattern anchored in the figure of "the Russian at the rendezvous."

2. Government

The pattern of sovereign interdiction relies on the representational structure of transcendence. The charismatic figure—enraged father, living statue, rearing horseman, ominous General, mysterious pretender, majestic empress, or, in Chernyshevsky's at once most abstract and most precise formulation, the political arrangement as such—transcends the prevailing field of representation, appears from behind, materializes in the dark, emerges from the occult spaces of phantasm and vision, to mediate between the protagonist and the object of his desire. The field of relations among private individuals striving for personal fulfillment in intimate relationships is traversed by the political unconscious of sovereign power—the power to subsume personal life within the state of exception.

In this section, I examine three texts that reorient the triangle to the perspective of the woman and thus illuminate the mechanisms of sovereign mediation from new angles: Pisemsky's early novel *Boyarshchina* (written between 1844 and 1846, but kept from publication by the censors until 1858), the already familiar *Same Old Story* by Goncharov, and Alexander Druzhinin's celebrated epistolary novella *Polinka Saks* (1847). Their dramatizations of familial-qua-political authority span a broad range of scripts, both corresponding to and in important ways departing from Foucault's genealogical classification of modern regimes of power: from spectacular displays of sovereign violence in *Boyarshchina*, to the prominence of disciplinary mechanisms in *The Same Old Story*, to pastoral regulation in *Polinka Saks*.

In placing the dramas of power and violence squarely at the center of domestic relations, these texts display their congeniality with the "second-generation" French sentimental novel, the "sentimental social novel" as Cohen designates it, because they view the female predicament within the family through the prism of broader social oppression. The work of the towering practitioner of this genre, George Sand, provides an especially illuminating reference point for the three texts at issue in this section. Two of her novels, in particular, both enthusiastically received in Russia, will be relevant here: Sand's first novel, *Indiana* (1832; first Russian translation 1833), evidently supplies the character and event network for *Boyarshchina*, while *Jacques* (1834; first Russian translation 1844) constitutes a major and well-known subtext for *Polinka Saks*. *The Same Old Story* more subtly alludes to both of these texts, balancing precariously between the two models of familial authority embedded in them.

Boyarshchina, named after the fictional provincial town in which the events take place and invoking despotic feudal rule (from *boyarin*—"lord"), narrates the fate of a young woman, Anna Pavlovna Zador-Manovskaya, married off by her father to a brutish landowner. The triangle emerges when Anna Pavlovna ("kind, sensitive, and terribly dreamy"[40]) meets young Elchaninov, whose passionate declarations she is unable to resist in the face of her husband's harsh treatment. In a fit of jealousy, Zador-Manovsky strikes her unconscious and orders that she be thrown out of the house. The honest, poor landowner Saveliy, himself secretly in love with Anna Pavlovna, brings her to her lover's quarters but advises that they leave the area, warning Elchaninov of the likelihood that the husband will appeal to Anna Pavlovna's father or to the government. "At the last words Elchaninov [turns] pale," registering the dread associated with the appearance of the triple-headed figure of authority: husband-father-state (1:136).

Both the father and the state are indeed soon drawn into the family affair. Informed of his daughter's escape, the father dies of grief. Zador-Manovsky passes the news of his death to Anna Pavlovna as a means of psychological punishment; the punishment is successful, as Anna Pavlovna's already fragile health begins to deteriorate. Next, Manovsky demands that the marshal of the nobility investigate the affair, issue a certificate of misconduct, and facilitate a divorce, which would render Anna Pavlovna a social outcast, unable to remarry. The police search Elchaninov's apartment for clues of Anna Pavlovna's presence, forcing her to hide out in the fields. Meanwhile, the fabulously wealthy old Count Sapega, lusting after Anna Pavlovna, presents himself as her father's old friend and thus her surrogate father and protector. Hoping to clear the field for himself, Sapega tempts Elchaninov by the promise of a dazzling state service career in St. Petersburg and thus removes the lover from the scene. By appealing to the provincial governor, Sapega neutralizes the husband as well, and has Anna Pavlovna's nearly lifeless body transported to his estate. There, protected from Sapega's unwanted advances only by the destitute and powerless Saveliy, the heroine goes mad and dies.

As we can see from this brief summary, images of patriarchal authority (spousal and paternal alike) are here commingled with plot devices linked to the workings of the state apparatus. At the end, we are confronted with the situation in which the punishing husband (Manovsky) and the monstrous father/ravisher figure (Sapega) compete for access to state power in the hopes that it would facilitate their capacity to control, punish, or sexually possess a young woman. Emblematically, the heroine of this piece of "domestic fiction" has no home to protect her. Her husband's house only exposes her more starkly to his abuse. Elchaninov's quarters prove highly permeable to both the husband and the police. In the fields, she is exposed to the elements. And on Sapega's estate, both danger and vulnerability peak. Homeless throughout, she is rendered directly vulnerable to the intrusions of men, whose power over her is bulwarked by the authority of the state.

Pisemsky's novel shares its basic cast of characters with George Sand's celebrated *Indiana*.[41] In both novels, three men surround the heroine: a brutish, narrowly practical husband (M. Delmare = Manovsky); a charming, ambitious young man who treats her as an object of his vanity and pleasure (de Ramière = Elchaninov); and a noble, self-sacrificing "guardian angel," who loves her silently and deeply (Sir Ralph = Saveliy). Situational echoes abound, as well. Both Delmare and Manovsky strike their wives in a fit of jealousy; both husbands are, in turn, felled by a stroke and die; both women mentally and physically languish with their husbands and temporarily regain their vitality with their lovers; both come to open rebellion; both put high-minded trust in their lovers; and both are bitterly disappointed. Both fathers vanish from the scene, but not before passing their daughters into the hands of husbands, unsympathetic and unloved. In both novels, the figurative language of political tyranny and enslavement abounds.

This last is especially evident in *Indiana*. The heroine's father, we are told, is a harsh plantation owner in the colonies, and in marrying Delmare, she discovers little more than another master, another prison, another solitude.[42] From the beginning, she resolves to keep quiet and save her love for the one who will liberate her.[43] By comparison with the older sentimental paradigm, constraint is externalized, appearing less as an inner sense of duty to collective welfare than as external oppression, which, as a woman, she shares with other oppressed members of society. Corresponding to this externalization of authority, desire for happiness/freedom/love manifests itself as open rebellion of "the heart." When M. Delmare questions Indiana about her whereabouts during the night she spends at de Ramière's, she admits that the law has made him her "master," but denies that he can have power over her will.[44]

Building on the basic plot line of *Indiana*, Pisemsky's text transforms it in telling ways. Instead of the wealthy Sir Ralph, whose powers of shielding the heroine from harm are nearly miraculous, we find the desperately poor Saveliy, the weakest of all male figures in the novel, unable to spirit his beloved away into a mountainous idyll (as Ralph does at the end of *Indiana*) or even to shelter her from harm in his meager quarters. He stays by her side when she is ill, guarding her against Count Sapega's undesirable advances, hides her from the police in the rye fields, takes her from husband to lover—each rescue only prolonging her anguish. There is no escape route for the heroine, and no alternative proves imaginable. As if to highlight this fact, *Boyarshchina* introduces the "terminal" figure of Count Sapega, whose unwelcome hospitality marks the fatal and distinctly unidyllic end point of the heroine's journey and whose participation in the veritable hunt for her body clarifies the basic stakes of the novel.

Thus, we are dealing here with the confrontation not between the "noble heart" and conventional society but rather between the recourseless, subjected female body and the brute force of total patriarchal domination. Rather than "heart" versus "code," as in Sand, at stake in Boyarshchina is body versus force. Even the ostensible moment of liberation—less an escape than an expulsion from her husband's house—is met with the lover's "You are forever mine and must belong to me like property." To which the heroine replies: "I don't have anyone but you. I want to and must belong to you!"[45] In a corresponding scene, Indiana resists de Ramière's sexual advances, refusing to succumb out of weakness.[46] The difference between the layered, "stoical" subjectivity of Sand's heroine and the reduced, minimal selfhood of Pisemsky's counterpart corresponds to the difference in the modalities of power to which the two sentimental heroines are subjected. Indiana's ordeal is the outcome of her "stoic" struggle to remain true to herself in the face of social corruption embedded in the institution of the family and in broader social life. Anna Pavlovna suffers because such is her fateful, creaturely predicament. She does not struggle; her movement through the plot is not propelled by insurgent agency; instead, she passes on from man to man: from the father who "urges," to the husband who tyrannizes and beats, to the lover who possesses and discards, and finally to the impostor-father who holds her captive and poses a constant threat of rape.

Two distinct types of political allegory, then, structure the two texts. In *Indiana*, the central male characters represent three distinct political orientations as well as three different social paradigms framing the heroine: familial oppression (the Napoleonic officer Delmare), aristocratic corruption (the Restoration-era socialite de Ramière), and republican virtue/idyll (Sir Ralph). Beyond the novel's obvious preference for the latter position, what matters is the existence of difference itself: the copresence of diverse ideological and existential stances among which the heroine is compelled to find her way. When it comes to *Boyarshchina*, we confront instead a monolithic vision of domination, staging, with numbing repetitiveness, sheer masculine-state power elicited by and trained upon the body of the heroine. The excess of mental and physical pain brought upon the entirely passive subject invokes Foucault's description of the asymmetrical power displayed by the sovereign in the course of an elaborately scripted public execution:

> The punishment is carried out in such a way as to give a spectacle not of measure, but of imbalance and excess; in this liturgy of punishment, there must be an emphatic affirmation of power and of its intrinsic superiority. And this superiority is not simply that of right, but that of physical strength of the sovereign beating down upon the body of his adversary and mastering it. [...] It is the prince—or at least those to whom he has delegated his force—who seizes upon the body of the condemned man and displays it marked, beaten, broken.[47]

What we have in *Boyarshchina*, then—and this becomes all the more evident in juxtaposition with its Sandian prototype—is sovereign power at its most naked and direct, flowing freely from one male figure to another, manifesting itself as the reality or the threat of physical brutalization, possessive domination, and sexual violence, bolstered throughout by the authority of the state. The heroine's only task is to serve as the site of its application and the scene of its spectacular exercise.

Druzhinin's wildly influential *Polinka Saks* projects a different scenario of sovereign mediation, modeled on another Sandian prototype. At the center here is the figure of Polinka's husband, Konstantin Saks, who strives to raise his much younger wife out of her profound immaturity and worldly ignorance in the hopes of turning her from a charming "toy" into a mature woman and a genuine "helper." These pedagogical efforts appear side by side with his work as a government inspector bent on rooting out corruption in the bureaucracy.[48] Polinka's immaturity, her blindness to the common lot and indifference to the common good, sets up an analogy with the fecklessness of the corrupt administration that Saks works to reform.

The plot highlights and deepens the entanglement between the activities of educating the wife and reforming the state when Saks departs on a new mission, leaving Polinka exposed to the advances of the young and handsome rake Prince Galitsky. As it turns out, the person Saks is called upon to prosecute for embezzlement, an official named Pisarenko, used to manage the estate of Galitsky's father. Galitsky writes to Pisarenko, promising compensation for his losses if the latter can keep Saks away by confusing matters indefinitely. With Saks stuck in the provincial town, Galitsky passionately assails Polinka, who begins to return his feelings. At least for a time, Saks loses control over both the affairs of the state and his own marital affairs. Tellingly, he gets out of both predicaments through two parallel acts of magnanimity. By promising to educate and promote Pisarenko's children, Saks gets the official not only to cease his obfuscations and confess his crimes but also to inform him of Galitsky's scheme. This magnanimous act channels the benefits the protagonist grants to another back to the protagonist himself. Thus understood, the sequence anticipates the kernel event of the novella as a whole: Saks's granting Polinka her freedom and receiving her eternal love in return. But of this more soon.

For now, I would like to mention another thematic thread in *Polinka Saks*. This is the topic of estate management, crystallizing around the figure of Saks's correspondent, Zaleshin. Zaleshin is a benevolent hedonist unable to enjoy life on his estate until he has made his serfs prosperous, healthy, and fat. "A happy man," he explains to his friend, "is like a gas lamp; he throws out a circle of light all around for a certain distance" (34; 15). At the end of the novella, having granted Polinka a divorce, Saks plans to travel abroad and asks Zaleshin to take over the management of his estates. He instructs his friend to lighten the burden of the serfs, to help them prosper, and even to release some of them in accordance with the 1842 decree on "obligated peasants." Thus, the text sets two images of emancipation side by side: domestic and political.

On closer examination, however, we notice a fundamental disagreement between the two friends on the question of government. As Saks makes clear to Zaleshin, to govern is to do more than spread one's own happiness to one's inferiors; it means actively to intervene—in fact, to struggle. And Saks's privileged name for his opponent in this struggle is "society," "obshchestvo." *Obshchestvo* brings forth corrupt officials such as Pisarenko and at the same time deliberately retards the development of promising young women such as Polinka. As we have seen, his two battles—against corruption and for Polinka's soul—converge at the level of plot. The struggle for Polinka culminates in the confrontation between Saks and Galitsky, the man of society, as corrupt (recall his link to the embezzler Pisarenko) as he is elegant and charming. It is this confrontation—and in particular the scene of its resolution through the husband's act of magnanimous release—that constitutes the dramatic core of the novella.

The scene is carefully prepared and then narrated in two letters written by the lovers to their respective correspondents. In these letters, the figure of Saks undergoes a distinct heightening, transformed from an enamored husband, honest statesman, and decent man into a mysterious, charismatic figure, inspiring mystical dread. From the lovers' severely limited perspectives, we witness his opaque manipulations behind the scenes, arousing in them premonitions of approaching doom. The lovers are held in terrified ignorance by the person whom they recognize as the master of their destinies.

At last they are brought together in a highly ritualized encounter in an old house, "beautiful but gloomy" (98; 50), depicted in a gothic manner, endowed with a majestic aura of the reign of Catherine II, and located in the vicinity of the infamous political prison of Schlisselburg. Having thus held the lovers in terrified suspense, Saks nevertheless berates them for their fear: "Are we living in Mexico or under a feudal regime?" he asks rhetorically and hands the divorce papers to Galitsky (100; 52). The question frames the divorce as a granting of political freedom. His insistence on the prevailing (evidently "European") enlightenment, accompanied by the act of releasing the lovers to their desire, is nevertheless belied by the bleak, ominous setting, the suspense created by his behind-the-scenes machinations to obtain the divorce, as well as the elevation of his own person to the position of a greathearted sovereign, whom Galitsky acclaims thrice in the course of his epistolary description of the scene: "Praise be to Saks, eternal praise to this great man!" (100; 51) "Where could one possibly find the gratitude worthy of this magnanimous man!" (100; 52) "If only—not now, but five years from now—I could die for this man!" (102; 53).

The culminating scene—following the script of sovereign mediation—is indeed a single continuous display of power in which the heightened figure of Saks concentrates in itself the authority of the statesman, the husband, and the father. Saks must rely heavily on his access to the machinery of the state in order to obtain the divorce. As a husband, he wields power over his wife: the very generosity of his granting of freedom depends on his capacity to constrain. Finally, in giving away Polinka to Galitsky, he claims the status of her father and promises to watch over her wherever she is taken and to punish the lover as soon as he causes her to shed a single tear: "Remember, no matter what you do, two eyes will be watching you, wherever you are, I will follow you step by step. You are taking my child, not a woman. Woe to you, if my child is unhappy" (101; 52).

Druzhinin does not hide—and his first readers quickly recognized— the novella's roots in Sandian poetics, particularly in her epistolary novel *Jacques*.[49] A number of conspicuous features betray the connection: Saks's educational undertaking vis-à-vis his much younger wife; his transformation, at the decisive turning point, from a fearsome, jealous husband into a loving, forgiving, and releasing "good father"; his "enlightened" position on love, marriage, and female infidelity; his readiness to sacrifice everything to the happiness of his beloved; the idealization of the hero;

the extolment of his greatness by everyone involved. What clearly unites the texts, contrasting them sharply to both *Boyarshchina* and *Indiana*, is the readiness of the husbands to renounce patriarchal authority, to abstain from vengeance or punishment for infidelity, and to allow their actions to be guided by the heroine's pursuit of self-realization. Still, as husbands and elder men with significantly greater social, political, and economic capital, they maintain positions of superiority, providentially overseeing their wives' journeys, acting less (if at all) directly on them than on their environments.

At the level of the social imaginary, then, *Jacques* and *Polinka Saks* share the logic of what Foucault has called "governmental reason," a passive, merely supervisory principle of government acting on habitats and environments, rather than directly on individuals, and oriented toward the maximization of the welfare of a society or a population. This form of "government according to the rationality of the governed themselves"[50] is limited not on the basis of right (By what right does the sovereign exercise his power? How far does his power rightfully extend vis-à-vis his subjects?) but rather on the basis of utility (Where and how can the sovereign intervene effectively to promote the worldly flourishing of the population?). In accordance with governmental reason, sovereign intervention must be kept to a minimum, because processes that unfold at the level of whole populations are too complex for the ruler to grasp, and the effects of directly acting upon such a network are impossible to anticipate. In his capacity as a sworn custodian of his wife's happiness, Jacques is aware of his limitations and renounces his authority over his future wife from the start, preserving no more than the role of protector. His hope is to shield her from all the false ideas and habits that society imposes on women so that she can remain true to her uncorrupted nature.[51] His method consists in holding back, maneuvering around her feelings in such a way as to encourage some and discourage others. He does not teach her anything directly, hoping only that her natural proclivities, her capacity for genuine happiness and trusting love, will break through the thin crust of an imperfect upbringing. In fact, Jacques goes still further in his pastoral zeal: realizing that his wife now loves another and is happy with him, he frees her by committing suicide, carefully plotting it to appear as an accident so as to forestall her feeling guilt. At the moment when it is no longer useful to the subject, the source of authority eliminates itself—a remarkably apt enactment of governmental reason's foundational fantasy.

It is at the level at which both texts partake of this social-imaginary schema that differences between them emerge most vividly. Simply put, the mutation that the motif of the permissive husband undergoes in

Druzhinin's text produces a curious hybrid structure in which elements of governmentality coexist with and are ultimately absorbed into the overarching diagram of sovereign power. Most telling in this regard is Saks's method of release. Rather than arrange for his wife's happiness behind the scenes and disappear, Saks provokes near mystical dread as the young couple awaits his decision for a month, then stages an elaborate ritual of liberation that triggers passionate acclamation and paralyzing gratitude, and in the end, produces the opposite effect from the one ostensibly desired. Happiness itself now reappears as an edict, a command, whose nonfulfillment is punishable in dreadful ways ("woe to you, if..."). Not only does Saks continue to stand between the lovers as it were psychologically, but he keeps his promise by following them literally everywhere they go.[52]

At this point, the narrative transgresses most forcefully against verisimilitude. In one episode, toward the end of the novella, Saks appears before Polinka like an apparition in her house in Florence and questions her about her state of mind. This appearance, proof itself of perpetual surveillance, recapitulates his earlier behind-the-scenes maneuverings for obtaining the divorce. The act of liberation and the act of subsequent haunting stand in a relationship of paradoxical equivalence and are further linked to Polinka's death. At the moment of the visit/ation, Polinka realizes that she in fact loves—and has always loved—her former husband alone. Her already poor health turns sharply for the worse, and in a matter of months, she dies. Among her parting words to her correspondent is the following fervent acclamation: "May God bless this man, who, in parting, gives life, resurrects, finishes the education he has started" (106; 55).

We might say, then, that while *Jacques* unfolds within a broadly consistent regime of governmental "laissez-faire," *Polinka Saks* overwrites it with a prominent scenario of sovereign magnanimity. Here the heroine is not only released but also reclaimed; released and reclaimed at the very same moment, in fact, since Polinka comes to understand and begins truly to love her husband only at the moment of the release. *Jacques* places sovereignty "under erasure," with the figure of the self-eliminating husband marking a constitutive evacuation (a veritable *kenosis*) of authority vis-à-vis the individual in pursuit of happiness. Druzhinin's version gives us the authoritative husband's failure to eliminate himself; an attempt to do so only endows his power with a nimbus of saintliness, an enhanced capacity to inspire death-dealing love, and a supernatural reach into the life of the ostensibly emancipated subject.

We thus begin to glimpse a pattern, in which Russian rewritings of French sentimental fiction, and of Sand's novels in particular, pull the original texts toward more robust and spectacular displays of substantive belonging—a different principle of individuation against the horizon of familial authority conceived as a form of sovereign mediation of intimate life. *Boyarshchina* transposes *Indiana* from the plane of struggle against illegitimate authority to the plane of sheer asymmetrical brutality, marking the body of the woman with the brand of the many-headed sovereign. *Polinka Saks*, *Boyarshchina*'s ostensibly emancipatory obverse, bent on charting a noncoercive path for its young heroine à la *Jacques*, finds itself rerouted into a story of the statesman-husband's far-reaching, death-dealing hold over the wife he has released. Both texts thus anticipate the ruthless motto we will find in Aleksandr Ostrovsky's 1863 drama *Sin and Sorrow Are Common to All*: "from the husband—only into the coffin; nowhere else!"[53]

Such, too, surprisingly enough, is the quiet verdict of *The Same Old Story*. To be sure, at no point does Lizaveta Alexandrovna attempt to leave her statesman-husband; nor is she brutalized to death like Anna Pavlovna or, like Polinka, consumptive from love for her selfless husband. She does pine away, however, and the concluding image of a languishing woman, framed by two men, may alert us to the presence of a sentimental pattern underneath the realist problematic of male "career and fortune." Indeed, once the novel is reoriented with Lizaveta Alexandrovna in focus, we find hints everywhere of a dormant yet discernible sentimental triangle, complete with an older, emotionless, hyperrational, authoritative, and publicly oriented husband; a significantly younger woman of tender heart and developed sensibility whose capacity for strong romantic feeling remains unrealized within her marriage; and a like-minded, though not quite deserving, young man, well versed in the language of the heart. Encounters between Lizaveta and Alexander are frequently depicted in eroticized language. She appears to him (and to the reader for the first time in the novel) as "beautiful women in a peignoir," who wipes the young man's tears and kisses him on the forehead (154, 1:309–10). One of Alexander's lovers, Julie, conceives a violent jealousy toward his "young and pretty" aunt (222; 1:370–71). Occasionally they speak to each other as passionate lovers might. "I cannot run away from you," Alexander says to Lizaveta, "I have not the strength [...]. What have you done to me?" In short, the text repeatedly models interpretations for its readers, evoking the suspicion of more than familial affection between Alexander and his uncle's wife. It is no wonder, then, that some early reviewers of the novel noticed this undercurrent of a quasi-incestuous sentimental drama (1:724).

Yet the drama stays dormant. Its incestuous implications surely account for this fact. But incest needs to be viewed here in concert with—and as a correlate of—other forms of authoritative prohibition. Aduev describes eloquently and at length his methods of familial control:

You have to mould a woman out of the girl according to a well-designed plan—a method, if you like—of your own, so that she understands and plays the role she has been assigned. [...] Accord her freedom of action within her sphere, as long as you monitor vigilantly her every movement, every sigh and every action, so that each and every momentary mood change, outburst, the first sign of any feeling, always meets with the apparent equanimity, but ever-watchful eye of her husband. You have to maintain constant vigilance without tyranny [...] and it must be done subtly and without her noticing; and in this way you will lead her in the desired direction. (146–47; 1:303)

Aduev gives voice here to yet another principle of rule, one that relies neither on direct coercion (which he disdainfully deems "Asiatic") nor on governmental laissez-faire (which, one senses, is not sufficiently secure for him) but on a technology of vigilant surveillance, invisible confinement, and subtle subordination of the will, resonant with Foucault's conception of disciplinarity. Discipline, we recall, is a way of organizing human multiplicities by dissolving them into individual bodies that can be contained, trained to play appropriate functions, observed, and if necessary, chastised. One animating metaphor for this technique is the organization of a populous realm along the lines of a convent, where individuals are strictly distributed throughout units of time and space with an eye to increasing the productive force and efficiency of the population.[54] From this point of view, as we have seen, Alexander's "wild," "uncivilized" gestures and impulses cannot be tolerated. He must be disciplined—body and soul—before he can be of use in the service of the well-regulated state.

The same goes for Lizaveta Alexandrovna within the familial domain. And just as with the nephew, so with the wife—the uncle's disciplinary techniques produce the unforeseen and undesired effects of profound dejection, an ebbing of energy, a melancholy indifference to the world. These symptoms confront us in the epilogue in the tableau of the fading heroine, pale, with "lustreless eyes, her blouse hanging loosely and evenly about her narrow shoulders and flat chest, her movements slow, almost sluggish" (319; 1:455). This "new Tatyana," whose beauty is not rosy-cheeked but of "another, higher form," appears before us in a parody of a sentimental pose: bent not over her beloved's letter but over her husband's household accounts. Troubled by the doctor's unsettling warnings about her health, Pyotr Aduev now seeks to elicit from her a spark of spontaneous impulse or desire: "Are you trying to go against your true nature, suppress your true instincts? ... That's wrong! I've never tried to coerce you [...]. I allow you total freedom." To which, Lizaveta Alexandrovna, baring the political allegory, replies: "My God! What do I need freedom for? [...]

What would I do with it? You have always been so good at arranging everything for both of us that I've got out of the habit of thinking for myself—so just keep on doing what you've always done, and I won't have any need for freedom" (321; 1:457).

A paradigmatic outcome of discipline, then: a "docile body" without excessive impulses or whims and a soul desiring only to be of use. When it dawns on her that her husband may have decided to retire for her sake, she is terrified and wishes that God take her life, so she would not stand in the way of her husband's career advancement (325; 1:462). Her grief-stricken exclamations articulate an inversion of the governmental script operative in *Jacques* and (up to a point) in *Polinka Saks*: instead of the self-elimination of authority for the sake of the freedom of the subject, we have the image of the self-elimination of the subject who has ceased to be useful to authority. And all this with the common understanding that no coercion had been involved and no freedom restrained.

When D. A. Miller and others speak of disciplinarity in the European novel, they tend to focus on surveillance and docility, containment and the distribution of roles, as the price for flourishing in the disenchanted world of realist prose. Desire is thus not so much suppressed as rechanneled into appropriate functions. The novels' complicity with the vast project of creating a disciplinary society is marked, among other ways, by the fact that such rechanneling carries with it and often fulfills the "promise of happiness."[55] Meanwhile, sentimental novels foreground the tragic outcomes of resistance to discipline, moments when desire refuses to flow into the appropriate openings or, to use Pyotr Aduev's favorite metaphor of the steam engine, when the steam builds up inside and blows up (or at least threatens to blow up) the machine.

In the quiescent triangle anchored by Lizaveta Alexandrovna, then, we can detect a subtle tension between disciplinary and sentimental codes. To be sure, discipline triumphs—the potential "lovers" never quite encounter each other as such; the threat of incest gives figural flesh to the prohibition imposed by the demand that everyone play their proper roles: the young woman as a wife, the young man as the pursuer of "career and fortune." Yet the sentimental code strains to have the last word. In terms of this code, what gets suppressed is not access to the object of desire but access to desire itself (318; 1:455). Thus, the text rewrites docility and usefulness, containment and the proper performance of roles, as "cold tyranny" and deadly disease. Even as discipline suspends fully fledged sentimental drama, surplus sentimentality allows us to glimpse sovereign mediation of intimate life behind the ostensibly neutral, matter-of-fact "realism" of a thoroughly disciplined world.

Linked closely to French sentimental fiction—and, at least in the cases of Pisemsky and Druzhinin, directly influenced by George Sand—the three texts discussed in this section display a profound consistency across equally profound variation. Their debt to sentimentality consists in staging a confrontation between the female heroine's desire and a robust, authoritative figure of the husband, reinforced to various degrees by links to paternity, mentorship, and the state. Two of the three husbands are explicitly cast as statesmen who carry their administrative habitus into their homes, while in Pisemsky, the state functions as the final instance of appeal for the power to dispose of the body of the heroine. By invoking Foucault's classification of modern power in connection with these texts, I have tried to make two things clear. First, that they stage on the site of domestic relations a wide range of scripts pertaining to modern technologies of governmental control. And second, that even in those narratives (*Polinka Saks*, *Same Old Story*) that avert their eyes from the spectacular exercise of asymmetrical power over the female body, projections of sovereignty nevertheless continue to haunt them, manifesting themselves through moments of charismatic heightening and acclamation, in episodes of transcendent (behind-the-scenes) plotting, in persistent metaphorical politization of the intimate, but most powerfully in the heroines' precipitous fading unto death.[56]

3. Refuge

Also published in the mid-1840s, sharing a set of similar preoccupations, and similarly in dialogue with Sand, Alexander Herzen's *Who Is to Blame?* (1846) departs from the three texts analyzed above in several important respects. The central and most obvious difference lies in the fact that in staging the domestic drama, Herzen's novel leaves out the figure of the formidable spouse standing in the way of the heroine's fulfillment. In doing so, however, the text preserves the prohibition itself, now tied to the more abstract dynamics of substantive order that renders individuation catastrophic. With Herzen's narrative in mind, it becomes possible to understand the figure of the husband in the scenarios of sovereignty we have just discussed as a hypostatization of the more general logic, according to which social groupings can appear in principle indissoluble.

Who Is to Blame? can be divided into three parts. The first presents a satirical panorama of contemporary Russian society; the second briefly tells the coming-of-age story of the novel's protagonist, Vladimir Beltov; the third locates Beltov as one member of the triangular relationship that initially complicates and in the end destroys a happy marriage. Early in the novel, the narrative focuses on the country estate of a provincial landowner, Aleksey Abramovich Negrov, spreading out to include sketches of aristocratic life in Moscow, the circumstances of a poor small-town doctor, local elections in the country, and the plight of a poor governess in St. Petersburg. The organization of this section is highly digressive, its social world aggregated through a series of brief biographical accounts. Society is presented as a chaotic, centrifugal force of sheer disembedding, redoubled in the meandering form of the narrative itself.[57]

The first section of the novel culminates in a marriage between Negrov's illegitimate daughter Lyuba and his son's tutor, Dmitry Krutsifersky. Noteworthy here is the social-symbolic import of the newly formed union in Herzen's novel. Marriage in this instance signals a rejection of broader social life, cast as a series of abusive and/or farcical encounters among irremediably disconnected persons. Herzen's analytic, garrulous narrator makes this explicit: in the midst of an insufficiently elaborated and vapid social space—"in the middle of the steppe"—marriage is the fruit of protest and the means of escape into the genuinely humane world of immediate sympathetic understanding (192; 4:125). Intimacy, sympathy, domestic bliss—in short, a kind of middle-class domesticity based on "the three elements of voluntariness, community of love and cultivation"[58]—will characterize the Krutsifersky household when we see it again in part 2 of the novel. In the meantime, the narrative leaves them aside to turn to its second thematic section: the biography of its protagonist, Vladimir Beltov.

Beltov's upbringing and early life are given to us in the shape of a brief bildungsroman: a young man with an excellent education and high ideals confronting contemporary Russian actuality in an attempt to a find a proper place for himself there. Beltov is educated by the peripatetic citizen of Geneva M. Joseph, man of virtue, adept of Jean-Jacques Rousseau, and passionate republican in word and deed. Inspired by his mentor's passion for the common good, young Beltov chooses for himself a career in the civil service. The consistency and even inevitability of such a choice testifies to the position of the state (within the local cultural imaginary) as the privileged site of universal belonging and the common good. Yet the choice is at the same time utterly absurd, since nothing could be further from M. Joseph's republican ideal than the bureaucratic obfuscations and intrigues with which Beltov is forced to contend in his position as a civil servant.

And so, three months after beginning his service, Beltov resigns. He goes on to study medicine and dabble in painting; he travels and eventually returns to his estate. The failure of a political career yields an indecisive, meandering protagonist:

> More than anything, [Beltov] was troubled by his former dreams of a career in the civil service or in government. Nothing in the world is so entic-

ing to an ardent nature as a role in current affairs, history-in-the-making. Anyone who has once harbored such dreams within his breast has spoiled himself for all other activities. (168–69; 4:106)

A political man, Beltov cannot be satisfied with anything less than work for the common good. Noteworthy for our purposes is the sentimental-political language of "love" accompanying this preoccupation. In the last letter to his pupil, M. Joseph writes: "Love of your fellow man and love of the common good [*blago*] must be [your] ends. If love should dry up within your soul, then you will never accomplish anything; you will be merely deceiving yourself" (159; 4:98). Later in the novel, when pupil and teacher meet again in Geneva, M. Joseph exhorts Beltov not to lose heart: "beware of embracing too sober a view of life. It can chill your heart and destroy all the love within it" (239; 4:165–66). It is not by chance, then, that Beltov's first—still oblique but public—declaration of love for Lyuba follows directly upon his relation of this encounter (242; 4:168) At stake here is something like a social-imaginary equivalence between the intimate and the political domains, an equivalence that in some respects recapitulates the familiar substantive parallelism between the family and the state.

This entanglement of love with politics is a common feature of democratic sentimentalism, whose most consequential representative, for Herzen as for many others of his generation, was once again George Sand. The closest relevant parallel here is with *Jacques*, whose protagonist confesses at the end that his true calling has always been "to act for the good of the masses" and that his turn to love—his attempt to benefit/liberate a single person instead—was a function of a kind of historical interregnum during which he could find no outlet for his urge to contribute to the flourishing of all. Jacques compares history to a great machine that at certain times stops working, rendering certain people—precisely those who could be the most powerful wheels in that machine— "superfluous" ("hommes inutile").[59] On the verge of confessing his love for Lyuba, Beltov draws a similar parallel between a *Homo politicus* excluded from participation in the historical life of the community and laborers condemned to unemployment and hunger from unavailability of work (241; 4:168).

It should come as no surprise, then, that the family drama precipitated by Beltov's appearance as a frequent guest at the Krutsiferskys carries with it strong political overtones. Before Beltov's arrival, the Krutsifersky household (including Lyuba, Dmitry, their infant son, and their older family friend, Dr. Krupov) appears to us as a blissful island of middle-class domesticity: "a pocket of affectionate bonding," the "moral core" of sentiment and personal cultivation, heeding as little to the demands of aristocratic alliance as to the instrumental requirements of practical life.[60] With the appearance of the protagonist bearing unrealized political aspirations, however, the household is transformed into a site for a more ambitious project with a twofold thrust: to free human relationships from external, institutional constraints and to rearrange them on other, more authentic, principles, suited to those who have been thoroughly emancipated. Domestic intimacy would thus be purified of possessive individualism and its concomitant mechanisms of domination, and expanded beyond the confines of the narrowly familial sphere. In the words of Martin Malia, for such admirers of Sand as Belinsky and Herzen, "liberation in personal relationships was inextricably interwoven with liberty in general, especially from the state."[61] We might add that such liberty was not meant to issue in purely individual pursuits but in a more adequate community of the genuinely free, prefiguring the full-scale transformation of society, the inauguration of what one might call the "affective" or even "affectionate" state.

Beltov's first (near) declaration of love for Lyuba is made in the presence of her husband and Dr. Krupov. Lyuba understands and is startled; Krupov turns it into a joke; we are not made privy to Krutsifersky's reaction. Declaring his love again, this time alone during a walk in the park, Beltov laments the secrecy in which they have kept their feelings. He exclaims, "Could it be that there is something hidden deep within my soul or within yours that we should be ashamed of, that we should conceal from others?" When Lyuba objects that she "belongs to another man and [...] loves him with all her heart," Beltov replies with a still more radical inquiry: "But tell me this. Must you absolutely reject one attachment for another, as if you had only a limited quantity of love to dispense?" (249; 4:174). Lyuba initially recoils from the idea but comes to entertain it later: "How splendidly we would organize our lives and our little circle [*kruzhok*] of four. We share mutual trust, love, friendship—yet we make compromises, sacrifices, and hesitate to speak our minds" (259; 4:183).

The fateful conversation in the park, culminating with a kiss, opens with an exchange on the standard sentimental opposition between society and nature. For the most part, says Beltov, people who have grown up in society treat each other with suspicion, seek to outwit each other, to appear to others in a favorable light. By contrast, "people neither fear nature, nor compete with it." Lyuba picks up the sentimental thread: "But I think that there is, or at least there could be, an affinity between people such that all external barriers to understanding would disappear and nothing would ever come between them" (247; 4:171-72). This is the project of a sentimental community, not mere domestic refuge from the contractarian egoism and mimetic vanity of social life but a substantive, natural bond of intimates as an *alternative* to it.

The two-step emancipation underway here—*from* the bonds of coercive institutions and *into* an alternative affective community—clearly does not amount to having an affair in secret or even to leaving the husband for the lover.⁶² Rather, it involves the recognition that natural, authentic, and genuine feelings of affection can serve as a kind of sentimental communal substance or, better perhaps, as the basis for a substantive community. Telling from this perspective is the conflation of familial categories in Lyuba's diary: Krutsifersky as husband, Beltov as lover-brother, Krupov as father figure and friend—all must coexist, not in a society in which aggressive and competitive instincts are regulated by contracts but in an authentic community of sentiment. The makeup of such a "circle"—in which, evidently, not all relationships have to be sexual—would embrace a range of social estates (Beltov and Lyuba are half-peasant, half-noble by birth, while Krutsifersky and Krupov are *raznochintsy*), with a special emphasis on the marginalized (Krutsifersky), the illegitimate (Lyuba), and the socially miscegenated (Beltov and Lyuba).

To grasp the specific political stakes of this "intense association" based on affectionate bonds, it is helpful to recognize that the heroine's inner struggle is here neither against external authority nor even against an inner sense of duty. Her inability to accept Beltov as a lover has nothing to do with what she somewhat dismissively refers to as "the sacred obligations of motherhood" (264; 4:188). On the other hand, her unwillingness to leave or betray Dmitry is due not to obligation or duty, but to love itself: "Could he [Dmitry] possibly suspect that I have fallen out of love with him and that I am in love with someone else? Good Lord! How can I explain it to him? It's not that I love someone else; I love him *and* I love [Beltov]" (261; 4:185). The conflict is not between duty and happiness or between external oppression and courage—here, Cohen's classification of French sentimental fiction turns out to be insufficient. What we have instead is a third kind of sentimental narrative rooted in the social imaginary of a substantive bond within which all exclusivity and individuation (associated with possessiveness and obfuscating interiority) must issue in tragic dissolution.

In his study of the role of ideas and practices of feeling in shaping the course of the French Revolution between 1789 and 1815, William Reddy describes something like a sentimentalist political ethos, corresponding quite precisely to the social-imaginary substratum upon which the concluding drama of Herzen's novel unfolds.⁶³ The underlying principle of this substratum consists in the belief that our natural sentiments, uncorrupted by social hierarchies and self-interest, would invariably guide us into "benevolent and affectionate bonds" with our fellows.⁶⁴ The role of sincerity is central: "Because feelings were deemed natural, they united people rather than isolating them; they were shared by all, a public resource. Public expression of intense feeling, rather than causing embarrassment, was a badge of generous sincerity and of social connectedness."[65] Within such a sentimentalist paradigm, lack of openness and sincerity with one's fellow intimates/citizens constitutes the gravest threat of all. Such lack testifies simultaneously to self-interest (to the act of mentally separating oneself from the community) and to deference for conventional proprieties, by definition unnatural and corrupt.

According to Reddy, such a sentimentalist approach to politics was based on an essentially incorrect theory of emotions and was bound to culminate in something like the Jacobin Terror. Where citizens are expected not only to practice citizenly behavior but also to have citizenly feelings, generalized paranoia is bound to set in. Some such social imaginary underpins the tragic bind at the conclusion of Herzen's novel. The central problem confronting the members of the fateful triangle is not transgression but transparency. The problem is not the kiss that Beltov and Lyuba exchange in the park but the subsequent withdrawal of all three members of the love triangle into the space of opacity, their reactionary retreat into self-enclosed privacy, their individuation. What turns out to be missing is precisely the absolute prerequisite of openness, authenticity, and sincerity without which a true sentimental community will inevitably tear itself apart. The narrator highlights this mechanism of breakdown by commenting on a kind of *mise en abyme* at the core of the novel's social imaginary: "It is vexing to make the comparison, but I have no choice. Beltov and Lyuba unwittingly found themselves in the same situation as Lyuba and Dmitry once had in the Negrov household, where they realized they understood each other even before they had managed to exchange a single word" (233; 4:160). Lyuba and Dmitry found the Negrovs unbearable and formed an unspoken alliance against, or rather simply outside, their domain. Now the same thing happens to the much smaller and more select circle of the Krutsifersky gatherings. Beltov and Lyuba understand each other better; their inner lives turn out to be more closely bound; so, unwittingly, they separate themselves from the rest. This, in turn, produces a cascade of further separations until nothing remains but isolated individuals—individuals, in other words, of whom the much maligned "society" had consisted to begin with.

Herzen's novel is structured by two separations, conceived within—and evaluated from the perspective of—two distinct social imaginaries. The first consists in Lyuba and Dmitry's escape from the dysfunctional social world into the domain of domestic bliss based on a bond of sensibilities. Though the marriage plot works here to reject, rather than legitimize, the social order, that order remains unperturbed, is even better off, more tranquil now that the two misfits have left. This is because the connections within that world are unserious, ghostly: they can be formed and broken more or less arbitrarily. Nasty though it is, this world does not bother to forbid or punish the formation, in its interstices, of the realm of personal, merely domestic happiness. The second rupture, however, takes place within an altogether different social imaginary, one in which connections are meant to be true, inherent, substantive. Within this social imaginary, all separation proves fatal. Here, intimacy is either shared by all or given to none. Thus, the formation of the Beltov-Lyuba dyad leads to the breakdown of the whole. Realizing that he can do nothing but further harm the people he loves, Beltov leaves; Dmitry sinks into drunken self-pity; Lyuba wastes away from consumption. "Our modern tragedies," comments the narrator, "do not end [as] drastically [as Shakespeare's]" (266; 4:190). No blood is spilled, but the community is destroyed and with it, to a greater or lesser extent, its individual members.

We are now ready to specify the nature of sovereign mediation in Herzen's novel. It consists in this: that with the help of the sentimentalist analogy between politics and love, a man endowed with a calling for the affairs of the state, where the state is understood as the locus of universal belonging and the common good, introduces the political impetus into the domestic sphere, turning it into a site for an ambitious social-imaginary experiment. This political impetus appears not as an interdiction proper or as a specific principle of rule (coercive, disciplinary, or governmental), but as a kind of substantive contagion, precipitating the conversion of familial affection into the broader affective bond, the prefigurative intense association of a sentimental-political community in relation to which all individuation constitutes a threat and solicits substantive retribution. In this context, Beltov serves as a kind of hinge for the shift in the underlying social imaginary from the domestic-private to the substantive-political. What is sovereign here in other words—what forbids and punishes—is substance itself, the logic of sociality, according to which belonging takes ontological precedence over separateness. This sovereign substance is made visible in the by now familiar cross-pollination of the figures of the family and the state, redoubled as a sentimental politics of the affective bond, a polisophilia of sorts.

4. Displacement

During a discussion of the *tableaux vivants* put together by the characters in Goethe's *Wahlverwandtschaften,* Tony Tanner comments on the novel's tendency to contain the image of the authoritative father within an aesthetic, painterly frame. The consequences of this move for the characters' destinies are ambiguous: fatherless, they give themselves over to the vicissitudes of desire; haunted by prohibitions of the forefathers, they end up paying a heavy price for freedom: "The idea of the seated dead silently waiting the inevitable arrival of the living offers a vivid image of the authority of the past passively preempting life in the present."[66]

In the early 1840s, the *Wahlverwandtschaften* became an important reference point for Herzen's attempt to think through the collision between the residual "formalism" of marriage and the sentimentalist political call for the emancipation of feelings. During the impassioned exchange with Lyuba in the park, Beltov exclaims: "How can one surrender completely [to one's genuine feelings], when one sees all sorts of phantoms [*privideniia*] that threaten and berate?" (248; 4:172). Here, too, the fathers are illegitimate, negligible, or dead; still, they haunt the lives of their children. Thus occulted, power acquires paradoxical features: it is absent, impossible to locate, but it is also everywhere and impossible to resist. An 1842 entry in Herzen's journal contains a passage exploring this dynamic in an elaborate political allegory:

> The pinnacle of Russian painting is certainly [Karl Bryullov's] "The Last Day of Pompeii." Strange that its subject matter transcends the boundaries of the tragic; the very struggle is [here] impossible. Wild, untamed Naturgewalt [force of nature], on the one hand, and ineluctably tragic perdition for all who stand before it [on the other]. Moreover, the imagination amplifies [what is there on the painting] and sees the same perdition beyond the painting's frame. What can the black-haired Pliny do against this force? Or a Christian? Why did such a subject inspire a Russian painter?
>
> By contrast. The pediment of the St. Isaac Cathedral will have a bas-relief, representing Isaac of Dalmatia proudly refusing to submit to the emperor, who rages and scolds him. It stands to reason that censorship will not permit this bas-relief.[67]

The diverse associations and strands of this rich passage converge on the focal question: "Why did such a subject inspire a Russian painter?" Invoking the painting some years later, no longer restrained by fear of further arrest and exile, Herzen supplies a helpful gloss: "Such is the inspiration drawn from the Petersburg atmosphere."[68] What is it about the Petersburg atmosphere that inspires images of violent natural forces wreaking chaos and destruction on helpless persons without recourse? A hint can be found in the second paragraph, establishing an analogy between the devastating eruption of the volcano and the violence of sovereign rage. The power of the state and elemental force enter into a relationship of supplementarity. More precisely, the state is occulted in the figure of elemental force. St. Petersburg, understood as the seat of imperial power, can reappear not only in the image of the Roman emperor Valens but, more impressively, as erupting Vesuvius. Of the two metaphors, Herzen suggests, the authorities would prefer the latter. The relationship between Emperor Valens and Isaac of Dalmatia is one of direct confrontation: the distribution of power between them is asymmetrical but not to the extent that renders resistance futile. This is why Herzen thinks that the bas-relief will be censored off the cathedral. Conversely, Bryullov's painting depicts inexorable destruction, destruction without struggle, where resistance is not only impossible but inconceivable. One may flee the eruption; one may bewail one's fate, or, given sufficient distance or an uncommonly stoic disposition, one may meditate on the futility of human endeavors. But one cannot struggle. As sheer force of nature, the source of political power is both absented and invested with overwhelming force, instilling in the subject the sense of creaturely vulnerability and in this way rerouting scenarios of legitimacy-challenging resistance into those of overwhelming violence on one side and helpless passivity on the other.

We have already encountered the scenario of displaced sovereign mediation: in Pushkin's statuary sovereigns and husbands, dead yet still living, supernatural; in several texts that associate the state with the "*fatum* of the ancients"; in Annenkov's identification of Kalinovich with a natural cataclysm; in young Volodya's encounter with proliferating figurations of death and destruction displacing the appearance of his father in the site of the expected rival (of which more in chapter 5). I would like now to consider in some detail two further (this time, "high realist") texts whose plots rely on mechanisms of displacement, whereby occulted figurations of an inexorable and invisible force supersede—conceal, bulwark, and fulfill the function of—sovereign mediation in the familial domain.

The first such example, Turgenev's 1859 novel *On the Eve*, weaves tightly together the motifs of familial and political emancipation from patriarchal and imperial despotism. The novel tells the story of Elena Stakhova's self-willed clandestine marriage to the Bulgarian revolutionary Dmitry Insarov and the couple's subsequent departure for Bulgaria in order to join the national uprising against the Ottoman Empire. The figure of the *political man* Insarov stands out through contrast with two young Russian men, the budding artist Shubin and the promising historian Bersenev—both his rivals for Elena's love.[69] Elena's choice of Insarov has everything to do with his exceptional status as a revolutionary, his evident willingness to sacrifice his own interests and even his life to a certain conception of the common good, here envisioned as national liberation. The novel opens with an exchange between Shubin and Bersenev, touching among other things on the value of personal happiness. Bersenev wonders: "Well, for example, you and I, as you say, are young; we are good people perhaps; each of us desires happiness for himself. [...] But is 'happiness' the sort of word that could unite us, could inspire us both, compel us to join hands? I mean, is it not a selfish word, not a word that keeps people apart?"[70]

It is worth pausing briefly with this question. The suspicion that the pursuit of personal happiness by "good people" separates them from each other and fragments the social fabric articulates a major anxiety, which a significant strain within European realist fiction attempts to assuage though its scenarios of aggregation. Each of these scenarios elaborates its own distinct conception of individual happiness. Within the Balzacian "system of needs," happiness means enjoyment and success, luxury and status. Within the aggregation of "actualized right," happiness is a kind of servitude of the heart—as *Jane Eyre* amply demonstrates, neither servitude (duty) nor heart (passion) alone is enough. Finally, when it comes to the aggregation of "common interest," happiness transpires when one's natural inclinations blend with an enlightened social project. Personal happiness and social cohesion are inseparable in Goethe; in Brontë, they come together in the figure of the individual who learns to be happy in a lawful way; in Balzac, the hero's pursuit of happiness contributes not to social cohesion as such but to a cohesive vision of the inchoate social whole, whose totality as a "system of needs" is given only in strife.

How, then, is happiness configured in *On the Eve*? For Elena and Insarov, it aligns with familial and political emancipation, emancipation from despotic rule. The despotisms of the family and the state are rhetorically entwined. Enraged by his daughter's insubordination—earlier in the novel, he calls her a "rapturous republican" ("vostorzhennaia respublikanka") (53; 8:32)—her father exclaims:

> There was a time [...] when daughters did not permit themselves to disdain their parents, when rebellious children trembled at paternal power [vlast']; that time is passed unfortunately—at least many people think it is; but believe me, there still exist laws which do not permit, which do not permit...in short there exist laws. Pray take notice of that: there exist laws! (191; 8:137)

Having invoked the law, the father threatens his daughter with God's wrath, asserts his ability to send her to a nunnery and to get Insarov sentenced to hard labor in Siberia (192–94; 8:138–39). Yet the father's patriarchal rhetoric is here infused with bitter irony. He is a weak man, a bungling adulterer, who financially depends on his wife. Just before this menacing diatribe, Shubin pointedly mocks him in his face, inquiring whether he fancies himself "a statesman" (187; 8:134). What's more, none of his threats comes to be realized. The family reconciles with Elena and Insarov before their departure for Bulgaria, sending them off with a toast. In short, we may say that the figure of the family appears here as a profaned substance, a ghostly authority at best. This is true as a matter both of external majesty and capacity for coercion and of the heroine's inner consciousness of belonging. Elena never feels at home in her father's house.

Still, the house maintains an enigmatic claim on her: enigmatic precisely because it seems so utterly groundless. Having declared her love to Insarov and agreed to leave with him, Elena returns home, which now appears to her as a phantom burden, weightless and heavy at once: "The things and people about her no longer seemed kind and affectionate [...]: they weighed on her persistently, like some ghastly, nightmarish burden; they seemed to reproach her, to upbraid her, to be unwilling to understand her... 'You still belong to us,' they seemed to say" (146; 8:102). The family's claim on Elena persists beyond the point at which its legitimacy is debunked. We witness here a mystification of the familial substance, its becoming ghostly and distending in space and time. Even Insarov is attuned to this process in some way. "God punish me if I am doing wrong!" he exclaims at the moment he decides to accept Elena's offer of marriage (159; 8:112).

As we learn soon, punishment does arrive, or at least misfortune and untimely death. On the way to Bulgaria, in Venice, Insarov dies of consumption; grieving Elena completes the journey and vanishes from sight, carrying on his struggle. As her husband lies dying, Elena struggles to understand the fate that has befallen them. She feels blameless and yet settles on the notion of guilt. Her thoughts once again turn to her family: "and your poor, forsaken mother, what of her sorrow?" (217; 8:157). As she dozes off, her dreams bring together images of the storm at sea, of her father, of a monastery and a prison. Motifs of elemental, familial, and political authority converge into a three-headed monstrous threat. We are left with a puzzle: the novel works to undo familial and political authority both, and yet they vengefully haunt the fugitive freedom-fighters to the end.

From the beginning, Elena is not looking for personal happiness. She is drawn to Insarov, because he is the only person in her circle who is fanatically dedicated to a common cause. Trying to pinpoint the nature of Insarov's charisma, what distinguishes him from her other admirers, Elena formulates it thus: "I believe the reason that [Insarov] is always so calm is because he gives himself up utterly to something... utterly—he doesn't need to worry, for he no longer has to answer for anything. Then, it's not what he wants, but what the cause demands" (120; 8:83). Literally: "It is not *I* that wants; *it* wants." Consistent with his attunement to the "*it* wants," Insarov attempts to flee Elena as soon as he realizes that he is falling in love. He feels unable even to visit one last time and say goodbye.

Elena bravely ventures out on her own to find her beloved before he leaves and declare her love. On her way, she is caught in a violent storm and seeks shelter under the roof of a decrepit chapel. There, she encounters an old beggar woman and, for lack of money to give her, offers a handkerchief. The woman divines the reasons of Elena's distress and, identifying herself as a fortune teller, promises to carry her sadness away together with her handkerchief. As the rain subsides, the old woman leaves, and Elena sees Insarov walking past her. The two confess their love for each other and pronounce themselves married "before people and God."

I have dwelled on this sequence of events in some detail to highlight the familiar motif of the rendezvous, which is here free of the psychically internalized prohibition that Chernyshevsky attributes to earlier literary protagonists in love. Still, the rendezvous is not entirely unmediated, shadowed as it is by the forces of accident, thunderstorm, and magic spell. And though here, these impersonal factors play an enabling role, bringing the lovers together rather than separating them, their sinister character begins to emerge soon enough. So, in an attempt to procure a forged travel passport for Elena, Insarov gets drenched in another thunderstorm, falls gravely ill, and never fully recovers. The lovers begin to think of the illness as a punishment—once again, it is unclear for what. The figure of the storm follows Bazarov from the moment he yields to the temptation of personal happiness. Even beyond his death, the storm pursues the ship that carries his coffined body to Dalmatia, and, in one version of the story at least, delivers the body to the raging sea. The rage that befalls them is not that of the Father, nor that of the Ruler, but that of a transcendent force, a kind of *Naturgewalt*, that treats them neither as dependents nor as subjects but as creatures of mortal flesh. As Insarov lies dying, Elena feels guilty not because she regrets their union or their political commitments, but because "happiness has to be paid for," or, even more grandly: "by virtue of the fact alone of being alive" (227; 8:164).[71]

In short, the novel dramatizes yet another pattern of sovereign mediation, in which the trajectories of the two insurgents—one against the authority of the family, the other against the authority of the state—converge at the point at which they fall under the jurisdiction of a fate-bearing force that takes over the responsibility for their pacification. This is precisely the point of the rendezvous, which founds their personal happiness and in the very same gesture consigns them to the way of all flesh. In the case of Elena, the introduction of occult punitive forces may be understood as the resolution for the following dilemma: How is substantive belonging to be staged, how is the individuation of a young woman to be problematized, how is liberation from familial constraints to be posited as transgressive—given that the authority of the family has been undermined and can no longer support the weight of substance? Insarov's subjection to occult punishment and the corresponding "descent" to creaturely status can be understood as a solution to a similar problem. In his review of *On the Eve*, Nikolai Dobroliubov observes that in the figure of Insarov the novel presents us an epic hero deprived of an epic. It is as if out of the entire *Iliad* and *Odyssey*, the author limits himself to narrating Odysseus's stay with Calypso.[72] All Insarov actually does in the novel is love, and by the time love must give way to "civic action," the novel ends. Insarov, then, is a political hero who has undergone a stark privitization.[73] And just as Elena falls under the jurisdiction of punitive fate as soon as she is free from her family and happy in that freedom, so Insarov becomes subject to the same occult mediator for as long as he remains within the private domain. Invoking Herzen's political analysis of sovereign *Naturgewalt* in his journal, we might say that *On the Eve*, too, projects an analogy: creaturely annihilation is to the private person what state violence is to the political insurgent and the rage of the father to the disobedient daughter. As for happiness, the question is evidently not—as it is in the Western texts we have explored—whether and to what extent one individual's pursuits can be reconciled with the cohesion of a society consisting of similarly driven individuals. Rather, in *On the Eve* happiness, this "selfish word," the word that fails to unite, transpires as a substantive wound and, as such, appears analogous to political insurgency and filial disobedience. Akin to transgressive hubris, it brings upon itself the disfavor of the gods, just as insurgency solicits state violence, while filial disobedience risks paternal anger. Personal happiness is placed in a stark collision with an occulted substance, made subject to the mediation of the ultimate sovereign "no," of death itself, the crowning allegory of the novel: "Death is like a fisherman who has netted a fish and keeps it in the water for a while; the fish is still swimming, but it is enmeshed, and the fisherman will haul it out when he pleases" (229–30; 8:166).

The mechanism of occult displacement of sovereign mediation manifests itself with great precision and succinctness in what is probably the most notorious epigraph in the history of Russian realism, *Anna Karenina*'s "Vengeances is mine. I shall repay." With sources in *Deuteronomy*, St. Paul's *Letter to the Romans*, and Arthur Schopenhauer's *World as Will and Representation*, and endowed with numerous echoes throughout the novel, the biblical verse invests the first-person pronoun with a basic ambiguity: who is this I who will repay? The genre memory of the sentimental triangle points in the direction of the husband-statesman; the verse suggests God; the shape of the plot signifies a fated course of events.[74] Provisionally, the three possibilities can be arranged as follows: the vengeance that by right belongs to the husband is outsourced to the "psychological-realist" unfolding of the plot and throughout associated with a quasi-divine, impersonal punitive force. An early scene in which for the first time Anna viscerally learns her husband's power over her highlights the workings of displacement. Having confessed her affair and too frightened of her husband's cold rage to wait for his decision on how to proceed, she considers fleeing. She runs out of the house onto the terrace: "She stopped and looked at the tops of the aspens swaying in the wind, their washed leaves glistening brightly in the cold sun, and she understood that they would not forgive, that everything and everyone would be merciless to her now, like this sky, like this greenery."[75] Cold, indifferent nature, the collective, all-embracing "everything and everyone," substitutes for and enforces the husband's punitive blow, guards her in his absence.

The triangle made up of Alexey Karenin, Anna, and Alexey Vronsky is by now a familiar one: a coldly overbearing, unemotional husband; a passionate, sincere, uncompromising woman whose vital forces remain dormant within the confines of her marriage; and a lover capable of awakening her passion but unable to live up to its absolute demands. Once again, the figures of the family and the oppressive, bureaucratic state converge. The convergence is most visible in the figure of the husband, who, much like Pyotr Aduev, takes his administrative habits into the intimate domain. A distinguished government minister, Karenin confronts the possibility of his wife's infidelity in a statesmanlike manner; he classifies, calculates, and decrees: "Thinking over what he would say, he regretted that he had to put his time and mental powers to such inconspicuous domestic use; but, in spite of that, the form and sequence of the imminent speech took shape in his head clearly and distinctly, like a report" (144; 18:152). The parallelism between the domestic sphere and the affairs of the state persists throughout the early confrontations between Anna and Karenin as the latter moves directly from one preoccupation to another. Having just penned a letter to his wife refusing to break "the bonds by which a higher power has united us," Karenin sits down in front of a book and drifts off in thought: "He was not thinking about his wife but about a certain complication that has recently emerged in his state activity, which at that time constituted the main interest of his work" (283–84; 18:299–300). The drafts of the novel contain explicit parallels between the family and the state, as sundry socialites quip at the Karenins' expense that just as nations have the governments they deserve, so with wives and husbands.[76]

Karenin conceives of himself as "head of the family" whose responsibility it is to use his power (*vlast'*) in order to stop his wife from entering into an illicit relationship with another man (144; 18:152). But unlike Pyotr Aduev, he scorns the technology of disciplinary control that would enable him to "forestall" and neutralize his wife's desire. Rather than subtly "educating" her into certain ways of thinking and feeling, he insists on her socially defined duties: "I have no right to enter into all the details of your feelings, and generally I consider it useless and even harmful. [...] Your feelings are a matter of your conscience; but it is my duty to you, to myself, and to God to point out your duties to you" (147; 18:155). The principles of government to which Karenin resorts may be designated as absolutist, presupposing an indifferent/tolerant neglect of Anna's feelings (which are viewed as "the business of her conscience and belong to religion") and an exclusive focus on her social role, to which certain duties accrue. Only transgression against codes of civility and failure to discharge certain duties will bring about punishment. This is the antisentimental governmental principle of the Old Regime, an attitude that permits one to "have whatever feelings one [has] as long as one remain[s] in relative control of one's publicly visible behavior."[77]

Tolstoy's narrator establishes distance vis-à-vis this approach by repeatedly drawing on the sentimental codes of sincerity, authenticity, and interiority. Just as in *On the Eve*, though for different reasons, patriarchal control over the heroine is shown as illegitimately oppressive. While Elena finds her family ideologically and ethically reprehensible as well as infuriatingly unheroic, Anna feels Karenin's authority unconsciously and viscerally, like the wife of the other statesman in our corpus, Lizaveta Alexandrovna. Being married to Karenin means keeping her vitality at bay, and this effort is precisely what the reader encounters when Anna is first introduced: "It was as if a surplus of something so overflowed her being that it expressed itself beyond her will, now in the brightness of her glance, now in her smile. She deliberately extinguished the light in her eyes, but it shone against her will in a barely noticeable smile" (61; 18:66). The dynamic is one of struggle or tension between animation and constraint, and the articulation of that struggle to the figure of her husband becomes explicit during a later scene where Anna prepares to go to bed with Karenin, and "not only was that animation which had simply burst from her eyes and smile when she was in Moscow gone from her face: on the contrary, the fire now seemed extinguished in her or hidden somewhere far away" (112; 18:119).

Karenin's haughty neglect of subtle disciplinary methods, his faith in the solidity of the order in which all have their proper roles to play and duties to fulfill, correlate with Anna's almost effortless initial escape. Unlike Lizaveta Adueva, who languishes under her husband's tutelage to the end and whose only available lover is an impossible one (her nephew), Anna falls in love quickly and passionately. Anna's affair with Vronsky is framed in terms that recapitulate Reddy's trajectory from absolutist honor codes of civility to the revolutionary language of emotional refuge, with its emphasis on sincerity, genuine affective bonds, natural, unconstrained impulses, and so on. By associating the Karenin family with the state, the novel opens the way to treating Anna's adultery as an act of emancipation, not unlike Elena Stakhova's escape from the dreary confinement of her own domestic sphere. Like Elena's too, Anna's liberation incurs a heavy price, and the punishment arrives not so much from the offended party—Karenin at one point relents, promises her a divorce, and even lets her keep her son—but from some more distant, occult, and relentless authority in whose name the epigraph to the novel speaks.

Whatever it is that unleashes the overwhelming power of physical destruction homes in on the body, or more precisely on the subject reduced to bodily existence. Noteworthy in this respect is the language of the scene following her first sexual encounter with Vronsky, in which she is depicted as having undergone a kind of social death. Hence the invocation of her "spiritual nakedness" as well as her failure, throughout the scene, to resist the power of gravity: her head droops, her body slides to the floor (149–50; 18:157). By aligning herself with her vitality, with her "nature," Anna loses her place in the symbolic order. She is, in the revealing words of her sister-in-law, "nobody's wife" (394; 18:415). Her social predicament crystallizes during the scene at the opera, where she is openly insulted from the neighboring box; the narrator compares her situation to that of a person being pilloried, her immobilized body exposed to public abuse (547; 19:119).[78]

Particularly curious here is the convergence between the predicament of symbolic abjection and the peculiar sociality of "sentimental refuge" in which Anna finds herself vis-à-vis her lover. Her husband's emphasis on role playing and civility are replaced by an insatiable demand for the authentic, the sincere, the expressively natural, to the exclusion of all conventional forms of behavior. Hence one of Anna's maxims: "Respect was invented to cover the empty place where love should be" (744; 19:323). As we have already seen in the case of *Who Is to Blame?*, the script of affective refuge produces an insatiable but self-defeating need for explicitness—something Anna fails to receive in large part because this stance treats all externalized signs of affection with suspicion. The salient point here is that Anna's rejection of the symbolic domain in her relationship with her lover in favor of sheer authenticity coincides with her expulsion from that domain for social transgression; sentimental "nature" and creaturely "nature" turn out here to be one and the same.

And so we come full circle to the epigraph. Boris Eikhenbaum has famously argued that the verse constitutes a tacit response to a recent pamphlet by Alexandre Dumas *fils* in which the French author recommends that the husband of an unregenerate adulterous woman kill her. Read in this context, the epigraph launches a polemic: it is not up to people to avenge wrongdoing; rather, punishment should be left to God. What the epigraph does not deny, in the meantime, is that some form of punishment is deserved and, indeed, in the course of the novel, received. Only the agent of punishment is now attributed to a higher authority, basically coincident with the unfolding of the plot. Eikhenbaum further observes that the higher authority in question here is not the biblical God, whether in Hebrew or Christian inflection, but something closer to Arthur Schopenhauer's impersonal and all-pervasive Will. On the basis of the epigraph's initial wording in one of the early drafts of the novel ("Otmshchenie moe"—which the critic reads as a literal translation of the German "Mein ist die Rache"), Eikhenbaum argues that its most direct source is Arthur Schopenhauer's *World as Will and Representation* (1844), a much beloved text with Tolstoy, to which he repeatedly returned.[79]

Schopenhauer reads the biblical verse in an idiosyncratic way, which converges with the line of interpretation developed here. From the point of view of a metaphysics according to which individuality itself is a mere appearance, while in essence all living beings make up a single, all-encompassing Will-to-live, punishment for self-assertion is inevitable. Insofar as an individual "affirms life with all its strength," it must "look at all the possible sufferings as actual."[80] In a manner that recalls both *On the Eve* and *Anna Karenina*, Schopenhauer appeals to the authority of "the prophetic poet Calderón, [who] speaks from this knowledge: 'For man's greatest offense/Is that he has been born.'"[81] It is precisely Anna's embrace of life and the will to life—understood in sentimentalist terms as the will to intimacy, sincerity, authenticity, and so on—that brings about her demise, trapped as she is between social ostracism and paranoid passion. As for the husband, the novel evacuates his authority by associating it with the authority of the bureaucratic state. The two moves, desocializing Anna's transgression and bureaucratizing Karenin's authority, create the social-imaginary conditions under which the wife's adultery is assimilated to the more general category of self-assertive individuation, while the punishing agency of the husband is displaced onto the occult "working out of things," the plot itself as the narrative instantiation of the Will. Tolstoy's novel, in other words, performs a sleight of hand, by which the exigent claims of a concretely instantiated substance (patriarchal family bolstered by the state) are occulted as the generalized condition of subjection/belonging to the all-powerful, overwhelming forces of nature, to the community of suffering mortals, to the unsafe refuge of the passions. Corresponding to this reduction of socially instantiated coercion to impersonal and therefore all the more irresistible force (some "phantom," some

"Vengeance is mine") is the stripping of the individual down to the status of a creature marked by primordial guilt.

* * *

The scenario of occult displacement—and its concomitant reduction of the individual to creaturely status—captures an essential feature of what I have been calling "sovereign mediation of intimate life." If, according to Carl Schmitt's classic definition, "sovereign is he who decides on the exception," then the subject of the sovereign is paradigmatically located at the site of the exception as well. This is to say that the sovereign and the subject, when they meet each other face to face, meet beyond the law and the symbolic order, as sheer capacity for violence on the one side and sheer exposure to it on the other. This latter condition of total exposure—beyond the protection of the legal or normative order—is the condition of what Giorgio Agamben has called "bare life." Bare life is the kernel of subjection in the individual that links her directly to sovereign violence; it is the irreducible kernel of creatureliness that exposes the subject to absolute power over life and death: "*The sovereign sphere is the sphere in which it is permitted to kill without committing homicide and without celebrating a sacrifice.*"[82] Bare life—the life that is socially and ritually void—is the proper domain of sovereign jurisdiction. The indifferent, impersonal violence of the volcano in Herzen's journal, the always already triumphant Fisherman-Death in Turgenev's novel, the fate-bearing, supremely authoritative epigraph in Tolstoy—all claim their subjects as "bare life."

At the outer—metaphysical—end of individuation stands the fate of a living organism over whom death hangs with the self-evident inevitability of poetic justice. But insofar as the texts considered here under the rubric of occult "displacement" zero in on the thematics of "life exposed to death," they present a paradigm case for the chapter as a whole. One way in which the overarching pattern can be formulated is this: The subject individuating himself or herself in the domain of intimate life falls under sovereign discretion and is, in that sphere, exposed to death; he or she dies, or is moribund, or is transfixed in melancholy by endlessly proliferating images of mortality and loss. At one point or another, the creaturely aspect emerges to the fore through images of physical breakdown or decline, making visible the surplus of sovereign violence—even where such violence is initially concealed: behind scenarios of magnanimous release (*Polinka Saks*), or proper management (*The Same Old Story*), or sheer chance (*On the Eve*), or psychological nuance (*Anna Karenina*), or social rivalry (*First Love*), or sentimental community (*Who Is to Blame?*). Surplus sovereignty, in turn, signals the triggering of the state of exception, the ascendance of a social imaginary within which the process of individuation in the intimate sphere is captured and its substantive stakes are laid bare.

Put differently, what we see is a form of *claiming* the individual, of reasserting her absolute belonging to a substance, thematized in familial-political-ontological terms. It is not that the individual encounters obstacles on his or her path to socialization; rather, through the workings of sovereign mediation, the individual is, as it were, "pulled back" violently into the parasocial domain of the family, allegorically coded as, and coding, the state. Hence, these texts' recursive structure: ancestors die but come alive as menacing statues, are left behind but haunt the protagonist's way; husbands release but all the more surely retain, let live but kill all the same; fathers withdraw but obtrude, forgive but eventually, ectopically, avenge. The actual, projected, or figurative death of the individual thus becomes readable not as the sign of the failure of the social order to accommodate her desire through one or another sociotope of aggregation but rather—within a differently configured, substantive, social imaginary—as the emblematic reminder of a nonindividuated state.

Nation

[CHAPTER FOUR]

Other Imagined Communities

Substantive Nationalism

As we survey the field of Russian realist fiction, we find, in addition to the *state* and the *family*, one other figure with far-reaching substantive associations: the *nation*. In fact, these three instances of substantive community often intermingle, investing visions of "intense association" with several layers of density, as if insisting that the communities at stake are tightly bound indeed: a polity, for example, that is also a nation and a family. Such forms of connectedness can be understood as a matter of feeling (one empathizes, senses a connection to one's fellow kinswomen, countrymen, fellow subjects of the state), of purely structural relations (one does not have to love one's kinsmen and hate outsiders, but at a time of war, one will defend the former and strive to defeat the latter), or of a metaphysical fact (the betrayal of one's links to the collective yields a kind of monstrosity, a transgression against the natural order). More often than not, though, the affective, structural, and metaphysical dimensions of substantive belonging reinforce one another, combining in various ratios. Under the pressure of such intensely overdetermined unities, it is no wonder that in narrative, scenarios of individuation (attempts to stand apart in self-sufficiency and self-affirmation) play out in highly dramatic ways: as antagonism, paradox, catastrophic reversal.

When it comes to the link between realist fiction and the imaginary of the nation, Benedict Anderson's now canonical lens of "imagined community" offers a useful starting point. In Anderson's account, "the nation," as an imagined sense of intense connection among people who may never actually meet, transpires at the point of convergence between "print capitalism" and "the fatal diversity of human language."[1] Print capitalism, in particular, with its corresponding forms, contents, and modes of distribution, generates the sense of a single social body, "a solid community moving steadily down (or up) history."[2] One example of a print medium that both generates and relies on a national imaginary is the modern novel, which represents distinct characters and events within the space-time of a society of a given nation.[3] The novel installs in the minds of its readers the paradoxical principle of connectedness among atomistically conceived individuals. Insofar as its form corresponds to the imaginary of the nation, the dominant chronotope of the novel is in a sense "flat": no place is superior to any other place a priori; no time is a priori special; no person occupying a given point on the coordinate plane belongs there inextricably.

To be sure, novelistic homogeneity of space and time is only a logical starting point, a spatiotemporal grid to be articulated differently by every text, whose unfolding produces a posteriori qualitative distinctions among spaces and times. Similarly presuppositional are atomistic individuals who will invariably come together into particular elaborations of gathering: the aggregations of needs, rights, common interests, and so on. One such elaboration in particular has been taken up by scholars of the European novelistic tradition, exploring the novel-nation nexus with reference to the nineteenth-century bildungsroman. Here, the nation serves as a kind of "spatial and political container" for the hero's path to maturity in the modern world.[4] The fictional narrative of personal development functions as a kind of synecdoche for the emergence of the nation as a whole: "the maturation of the protagonist and the modernization of the nation unfold as parallel narratives."[5] There is no maturity without the nation, so the argument goes, and those (mostly modernist) narratives that project wider, transnational worlds of capital circulation tend to present protagonists who remain eternally young and incomplete.[6]

Turning to our European case studies—all bildungsromane of sorts—we can observe how the modeling of the nation depends on the principles of social aggregation that underpin their respective narrative shapes. Balzac's *Père Goriot* gives us the nation as a unified, historically continuous, but highly dynamic system of needs, connecting diverse social classes, historical periods, and geographical areas into a single "community" of financial circulation and consumption. The novel shows how a single network of money and desire brings together Parisians and provincials, the ages of the Revolution, the Empire, and the Restoration, aristocrats old and new, members of the bourgeoisie and the petite-bourgeoisie, criminals, students—in short, the whole of "society" in the broad sense of the word it was just then acquiring. Likewise, Brontë's *Jane Eyre* presupposes and thus promotes the vision of a "national marriage market" based not only on increased spatial mobility[7] but also, more importantly here, on the conception of formal equality, a system of actualized right that takes precedence over distinctions of status and thus greatly expands the scope of available matches. The exemplary union between Jane and Rochester, moreover, takes place against the background of decidedly non-English alternatives: on Rochester's side, the Francophile would-be wife Blanche Ingram, the French lover Céline Varens, the Jamaican wife Bertha Mason; and on Jane's side, the missionary St-John Rivers about to depart for India.[8] The culminating unions in Goethe's *Lehrjahre* similarly transcend class boundaries, but here the terrain of bonding is less spiritual equality than the complementarity of temperamental dispositions and developmental trajectories, converging on the mysterious Society. The marriages at the end—Wilhelm's to Natalie, Therese's to Lothario, Lydia's to Jarno, Philine's to Frederick—are presented not as domestic but rather as sociable, a synecdoche of a (projected) national community that once again must exclude the foreigners Harpist and Mignon.[9]

The languages and social imaginaries of the nation in Russia emerge within the political framework of a paternalistically inflected dynastic realm and tend to be promoted by its rulers and ideologues.[10] Anderson appeals to Hugh Seton-Watson's term "official nationality" to designate the ideological maneuvers with which dynastic states attempted to neutralize the potentially explosive political consequences of nationalism.[11] As many scholars have observed, the trinitarian motto associated with the reign of Nicholas I and coined by his deputy minister of national education, Sergey Uvarov, in 1832—"Orthodoxy, Autocracy, Nationality [*narodnost'*]"—seeks preemptively to assimilate the new and potentially subversive member of the triad, *narodnost'*, to the other two terms, better known and legitimist in essence.[12] According to this formula, to be truly Russian, one must feel and act with undivided allegiance to the state, the czar, and official religion. Unlike the horizontal solidarity presupposed by the aggregative imaginary of the nation, the "nation" of "official nationality" gathers subjects around the sacralized body of the sovereign, who not only rules absolutely but also, doctrinally and charismatically, embodies the resulting community.[13]

Two years prior to the explicit formulation of the triadic doctrine, the semiofficial newspaper *Severnaia pchela* (*The Northern Bee*) published a report of Nicholas I's surprise visit to Moscow. Some of its language vividly testifies to the manner in which nationality crystallized in proximity to the ruler:

> It was just like a holiday [on the streets of Moscow]: everyone congratulated each other, a single thought animated all: it was not the subjects speaking of the sovereign, but children of their father. [...] We saw tears in [people's] eyes: such moments of national [*narodnoi*] love are precious, and that Sovereign knows the Russian soul who knows how to give [such moments] to his people [*narod*]. [...] All persons and ranks merged in a

single all-embracing feeling: this feeling is our glory as Russians. [...] We are confident that our feelings, even weakly conveyed, will find an echo in the heart of every Russian.[14]

National unity across "persons and ranks" transpires as an affective, filial convergence of the people on the figure of the sovereign. Thus conceived, the nation becomes visible at a special (*kairotic*) moment, a moment of the czar's nearly miraculous appearance in Moscow: according to the *Northern Bee*'s chronicler, he had arrived in Russia's old capital under the cover of night and was not even recognized by the Kremlin guards. The special moment of the czar's appearance binds the time of the nation together, invoking past victories and future glory, as well as the "unchanging Providential covenant," the promise of the people's flourishing under the protection of a righteous ruler. When it comes to space, the author emphasizes centrality: Moscow and the Kremlin, connoting Russia's ancient core, helpfully adumbrate the primordial and continuous character of the nation. Meanwhile, the newspaper itself—rather unlike Anderson's model of diverse events placed side by side according to the principle of mere "calendrical coincidence"[15]—conceives of local, Russian news as almost exclusively news of the czar and the royal court.

This official understanding of the nation did not remain unchallenged in the public sphere. Such challenges gained in energy and explicitness during the period of midcentury reforms. Olga Maiorova's discussion of the Millennium of Russia monument erected in 1862 in Novgorod highlights the expansion of the vision of the nation represented in it. Noteworthy in this context is the decision to include a number of public figures, writers and intellectuals, some with dissident reputations, who could now be regarded as active contributors to the project of nation building. The decision to leave out Novgorod's brutal sacker Ivan the Terrible while including the heroine of republican Novgorod's struggle against Muscovite rule, Marfa Posadnitsa, was likewise remarkable. Perhaps even more so was the initial decision, ultimately reversed, to exclude the recently deceased Nicholas I from the monument altogether. Still, on the whole, "commemorative symbolism was dominated by a historical narrative that identified the nation with the absolutist state and the autocracy."[16]

Nonofficial discussions in the recently liberalized press went further. Among other examples, Maiorova adduces Kostomarov, who in his capacity as a historian tended to draw a strict line of separation between the nation and the state.[17] In an 1860 monograph, titled "Thoughts on the Federative Principle in Ancient Russia," first published in the short-lived Ukrainian journal *The Foundation* (*Osnova*) in January 1861, the historian goes so far as to argue that had it not been for Mongol influence, the Slavic peoples would have developed another form of government—presumably a republican one, in accordance with their "native" predispositions.[18] No less scandalously, in the February 1862 issue of *Otechestvennye zapiski*, Kostomarov responds to plans for the aforementioned millennium monument with a painstaking historical critique of one of the founding myths of official nationality, the story of Ivan Susanin's sacrifice of his "life for the czar."[19] The essay triggered a series of rebuttals from such prominent historians as Sergei Soloviev and Mikhail Pogodin. When in 1866 Dmitry Karakozov's attempt to assassinate Alexander II was supposedly thwarted by Susanin's latter-day fellow native of Kostroma, Osip Komissarov, the cult of the peasant martyred for the reigning dynasty regained cultural momentum. Even in the face of critique, the association between the *narod* and the autocratic state remained tenacious.

One formidable attempt to drive a wedge between popular and autocratic-imperial conceptions of the nation can be found in Lev Tolstoy's *War and Peace* (1865–69). As Maiorova observes, Tolstoy's text presents the nation as an organism-like whole, leading a swarmlike, instinctual life, hostile or at best indifferent to administrative measures and official decrees. This independence becomes especially vivid in times of war, which delineates a "natural" boundary between those territories that the "people" regard as natively and primordially theirs and the significantly vaster areas subordinate to the imperial state.[20]

Still, even in opposition, the nation and the state continue to resemble each other structurally at the level of their respective social imaginaries. Both nation/*narod* and sovereign are construed as capable of bringing separate individuals into a single body endowed with charismatic visibility and implying a particular narrative shape. Two exemplary sequences from the novel make this especially clear. First, during the parade near Olmütz, Nikolai Rostov has an intense experience of encounter with the warrior-sovereign, Alexander I. The appearance of the czar breathes life into the lifeless body of the regiment. In his presence, this living body is one; individuals dissolve in it, and the sovereign has magical powers over it: to make it act according to his "word." The "word" of the monarch possesses total power over the whole, bypassing the individual wills of its constitutive parts, capable of driving it indiscriminately toward heroism or crime. Prominent here is the motif of joyful, delirious self-forgetfulness (*samozabvenie*), an affect expressed by Rostov's sole remaining wish pulsating through his mind: "just to die, to die for him!," realizing the metaphor of ecstatic dissolution of the self in the primordial, substantive whole.[21]

The second sequence of note involves Pierre Bezukhov's experiences

Nation: Other Imagined Communities   151

before and after the Battle of Borodino. Here, the focus is not on the sovereign but on the common people, yet analogous motifs show through:

> The deeper [Pierre] immersed himself in that sea of troops, the more he was overcome by anxious restlessness and a new joyful feeling he had never experienced before. This was a feeling similar to what he had experienced at the Slobodsky palace at the time of the sovereign's arrival—a feeling of the need to undertake something and sacrifice something. He now experienced a pleasant sense of awareness that everything that constitutes people's happiness, the comforts of life, wealth, even life itself, is nonsense, which is pleasant to throw away, in comparison with something… He was not concerned with what he wanted to sacrifice it for, but the sacrificing itself constituted a new, joyful feeling for him.[22]

Later in the text, Pierre fantasizes about being a simple soldier: "to enter that common life with my whole being, to be pervaded by what makes them that way. But how to cast off all that's superfluous, devilish, all the burden of the outer man?"[23] Individuality, marked by class belonging, by a specific lifestyle, by certain habits of body and mind, is here viewed as an impediment, preventing Pierre from giving himself over entirely to blissful unity with the common people. The motif of joyful sacrifice reappears later in the text, linked to some peculiarly "Russian" proclivity for testing one's "power and strength" through acts of renunciation. Posited here is some transindividual entity, a higher power to which the self is sacrificed; and through this sacrifice, the self and that entity (the substance, the sovereign, the nation) become one.[24]

These passages, framing the central battle of the novel, insistently refer us back to an earlier episode that depicts a gathering of the wealthy Russian estates at the Slobodsky Palace in Moscow. During this gathering, the local nobility and merchantry pledge generous support for the war effort, moving Alexander I to tears. Before the sovereign's arrival at the palace, Pierre gets into a debate with his fellow noblemen on the role of the nobility gathered there. In typical constitutionalist manner, he seeks to use the pretext of war and the czar's need for resources as a moment cautiously to assert the role of the aristocracy in affairs of the state. This position proves highly unpopular, far outdone by declarations like "We'll all stand up, we'll all go to the last man for our dearest tsar. […] We're Russian, and we won't spare our blood to defend the faith, the throne, and the fatherland."[25] By the time Alexander arrives, hears the size of the pledges and expresses heartfelt gratitude, Pierre has "no other feelings […] except the desire to show that it was all nothing to him, and he was ready to sacrifice everything."²⁶ The appearance of the sovereign is here, too, just like in the earlier episode involving Nikolai, a catalyst for the individual's sense of self-sacrificing belonging.

To belong is to sacrifice, to shed one's individuality—this is the social imaginary against the horizon of which Pierre experiences both his encounter with the Russian czar and with the Russian "people." The final paragraph of the Slobodsky Palace episode is telling: "The sovereign left the next day. All the assembled noblemen took off their uniforms, planted themselves at home or in the clubs again, and, groaning, gave their stewards orders about the militia, astonished at what they had done."²⁷ With the sovereign out of sight, everyone returns to consciousness of their own selves; the body politic falls apart into self-interested individuals, no longer in the grip of the desire to sacrifice. By remaining faithful to the self-sacrificing affect whose moment of origin coincides with the presence of the czar, Pierre proves his essential "Russianness."²⁸

The diegetic arc of the novel culminates, in the first epilogue, with a quarrel between Nikolai and Pierre over the formation of secret societies, vaguely oppositional to the state (and eventually leading to the Decembrist uprising). Nikolai remains firmly on the side of the czar, while Pierre proves faithful to his early republican leanings, adducing the example of the Prussian nationalist Tugendbund as a model for the kind of association he would like to form. Projected here is a confrontation in the political domain, portending a civil war that will sharply divide the body politic into friends and enemies and demand of both sides the ultimate sacrifice. Nikolai is willing to risk his life for the monarch; Pierre will risk his for the "civic nation."²⁹ Whether one hypostasizes the substance in the figure of the ruler or imagines it infusing the body of the nation, the imaginary of substantive belonging prevails. In this respect, Tolstoy's novel can serve as an example of how even a deliberate attempt to disarticulate the last two terms of Uvarov's triad (autocracy and nationality) is rerouted —at least at the level of the social imaginary, if not of explicit conceit—back toward identification between them. It thus alerts us to the possibility, explored in the rest of this chapter, that fictionalized Russian national belonging will frequently play out according to the substantive scenario of deindividuation, an ecstatic, traumatic, and fearsome loss of self.

One way to formulate the question that will preoccupy us below, then, is to ask how such a substantive imaginary of the nation might be imbedded in realist narrative. In Anderson's terms, this would imply asking what shape realist narrative might take within a social-imaginary field that combines the spatiotemporal coordinates of the nation with those of the dynastic realm. What if the atomistic, Cartesian social world assumed as a starting point by both the nation and the novel were traversed by a spatial imagination that privileged a qualitatively distinct, charismatic "high center" and a vision of time as prefigurative and recursive rather than sequential? What would realist representation of the nation look like if, instead of (or rather in addition to) ostensibly egalitarian,[30] spontaneous, and progressive narratives of socialization, it had to reckon with the motifs of charismatic prestige, administrative control, and the temporal short circuits of fate?

To address these questions, I will highlight four national scripts organizing several realist narratives from approximately the first decade of the Reform Era, just as the national question reached high urgency in the midst of the government's fitful attempts to enact social change. These four scripts represent distinct ways of "figuring" the nation in realist narrative. The first, represented here by Goncharov's *Oblomov* (1859), superimposes upon a vision of economic national integration the principle of providential state control, adumbrating a strong affinity-in-contradiction between the concept of a nation as a network of private individuals pursuing their own interests and despotic administrative power mobilizing nationhood "from above." The second national script—embedded in the important midcentury motif of Peter I as a national "Russian type" and animating prominent aspects of *Crime and Punishment* (1866)—explores the disjunctive amalgam between the figures of the ruler and the national substratum of the (common) people. The third—operative in Turgenev's *Spring Torrents* (1872) and in Dostoevsky's *The Idiot* (1869)—stages the allegory of the spell, by which a national substance embodied in a (sexually) magnetic woman pulls the protagonist back from his pursuit of personal fulfillment. Finally, the fourth script, organizing the kernel plotline of Goncharov's *The Precipice* (1869), tells the story of transgressive reenactment, in which an individual strays from, and is reabsorbed by, the primordial national substance buttressed by images of political and familial rule.

1. Mobilization

At first glance, Goncharov's *Oblomov* presents us with a paradigmatic case of a nation-building novel, setting the personal story of its characters against the background of the nation's broad temporal and spatial coalescence. The novel's central opposition between the incurable backwardness and immobility of the eponymous protagonist and the tireless activity of his forward-striding friend and mentor Stolz marks the point of historical inflection in the aftermath of the Crimean defeat and on the eve of the abolition of serfdom. Will the archaic and the stagnant be brought up to date? The novel's answer is both yes and no: yes, in objective-historical terms; no, when it comes to the individual person at stake. Stolz gives voice to this bifurcation in the mixed mode of a triumphalist elegy:

> You are done for, Ilya: it is useless to tell you that your Oblomovka is no longer in the wilds, that its turn has come, and that the rays of sunshine have at last fallen upon it! I shall not tell you that in another four years there will be a railway station there, that your peasants will be working on the line, and that later your own corn will be carried by train to the quayside. And then—schools, education, and after that—but no! You will be frightened at the dawn of new happiness; it will hurt your eyes that are unaccustomed to the bright light.[31]

The most backward and distant regions are being linked to the general life of the country. Railways, roads, labor, trade—all embodied in the figure of the paradigmatic *Homo oeconomicus* Stolz—bring about this spatiotemporal consolidation. The nation is becoming one at last. But Oblomov himself stays isolated and still. Long before the novel ends with his death, he begins hearing the verdict. First from his beloved: "it's no use—you are dead!" (362; 4:368); then from his friend: "Well, Ilya, you really are dead—you are done for!" (384; 4:391). The verdict is repeated numerous times; indeed, he pronounces it himself. When it comes to the national bildungsroman, the exact opposite of the standard pattern can be observed. Oblomov fails to mature or to assimilate to the progressive trajectory of the political community; national integration bypasses him, must happen at his expense. To be sure, our European texts also contain characters—foreigners, madwomen, creatures of transgression—who are marginalized and even killed off to adumbrate the protagonist's own successful trajectory of growth-accommodation. But killing off the protagonist himself has different resonances. We begin with something of a generic incongruity, then: a novel of successful national integration whose protagonist languishes and dies.

An early conversation between Oblomov and Stolz unfolds along the lines familiar from *The Same Old Story*. Oblomov shares with his friend his vision of the good life, a gentry idyll of harmony and peace; Stolz mocks the vision, diagnoses it as a kind of derangement (the notorious *oblomovshchina*); and offers an alternative understanding in its stead: life as ceaseless labor, labor for its own sake. What kind of labor, exactly? On this, the novel is rather vague: "[Stolz] has been a civil servant, retired, gone into business, and had actually acquired a house and a capital. He was on the board of some company trading with foreign countries. He was continually on the move." (161; 4:161). The most obvious answer to the question of Stolz's occupation is that he is a member of a (joint-stock?) trading company.[32] In the novel's drafts, his activity ranges more broadly but along similar lines. There, he is shown worrying that marriage would make it impossible for him to pursue his "social, civic labor [...] to go to Siberia, dig up gold, send shipments of wheat abroad, to participate in [joint-stock] companies, even to serve the state treasury [*sluzhit' kazne*], in the way in which he understood service."[33]

As the conversation continues, Oblomov questions his friend on the purpose of all this activity, assuming that it is directed at wealth and the comforts it affords. Stolz emphatically denies this: "[I work] for the sake of work itself and nothing else. Work means everything to me, it is the very breath of life—of my life at any rate" (182; 4:182). It is worth pausing on this apparent tautology: work for the sake of work itself, utterly disinterested work. In questioning his friend, Oblomov gets hold of a basic fact taken for granted by contemporary political economy: labor is hard; it requires physical exertion, which is inherently unpleasant, so only need (such a hunger, cold, unsatisfied desires) can make one work. As Jeremy Bentham puts it: "Aversion is the emotion, the only emotion, which labor taken by itself, is qualified to produce."[34]

How, then, do we make sense of Stolz's assertion about work? Max Weber's well-known account of the relationship between the Protestant ethic and the spirit of capitalism sets out with a similar puzzle. What accounts for the capitalist entrepreneur's deeply irrational commitment to rational economic activity, beyond all satisfactions and rewards? If you ask entrepreneurs themselves, many would likely respond "that business with its continuous work has become a necessary part of their lives."[35] In Weber's account, the statement conceals an internalized imaginary that treats rationally organized activity directed at worldly flourishing as contributing to the glory of God on earth, manifested not in the accumulated wealth but in the activity itself. This activity, in turn, confirms the active person in his status as the "tool of the divine will," a willing participant in the workings of the world as created by God. Weber once again: "God requires social achievement of the Christian because He wills that social life shall be organized according to His commandments, in accordance with [His glory]."[36] To refuse to take active part in this world would thus amount to a sacrilege.

Likewise, behind Stolz's formula of immanence—the creed of work for the sake of work—we can find an unspoken transcendent principle, grounding the injunction to economic activity without which life itself cannot be justified or even genuinely lived. The novel's drafts reveal the presence of a secularized recoding of the Protestant ethic casting glorification of divine providence as service to the state, a form of acclamation of the subsisting political order and an effort to expand its capacities and reach.³⁷ In attempting to stimulate Oblomov's "return to life," Stolz reminds him of his earlier interest in political economy and the Cameralist sciences of administration, and quotes back to him his earlier words:

> Didn't you say that Russia needs heads and hands, that it is a shame to crawl into a corner, when vast fields, sea shores, trade, farming, Russian science are calling us. We must release hidden springs, so that they will be filled with Russian power, so that Russian life will flow in a wide river and mix its waves with the life of all mankind, so that it will flow freely in its own ways in the Russian sphere, within the Russian borders, so that the giant will rise from his sleep.³⁸

And concerning a planned but never realized trip to Europe: "You considered it a preparatory course for the study of Russia, a necessity for a correct and deep understanding of Russia, for a methodical and conscientious development of Russian life, its resources, its forces. Why did you deceive me, your conscience, betray your duty, your obligation?"³⁹

Stolz's indignant invectives against his friend's indolence clarify the stakes of labor as a calling to service. Failing to be active, one fails to serve and therefore to fulfill one's mission in life, one's duty. Specifically, here, to serve ("as [Stolz] understood it") is to engage in one or another form of economic activity that contributes to the country's power and wealth. Audible in the compulsive repetition of "Russia" in the passages quoted above is the rhetoric of socioeconomic mobilization in the aftermath of the Crimean defeat and on the eve of major reforms. The image of a nation in peril—weakened, humiliated, in danger of falling into irremediable backwardness—heightens the substantive stakes of activity, sharpens the alternative between work-service-belonging and inactivity-treason-exclusion. Within this optic, military needs and national integration become impossible to tell apart: the roads and railroads that will connect Oblomovka to the rest of the country are the same ones that will make wartime mobilization—the slowness of which was seen as a major cause of the recent defeat—faster and more efficient. As we will see, the novel's peculiar—peculiarly substantive—national imaginary shows symptoms of being shaped within the force field of a state of exception triggered by military defeat and requiring full mobilization of national resources and forces.⁴⁰ Here, Schmitt and Weber converge, aligning capitalist development with service and, in line with the former's version of the secularization thesis, substituting God with the State in the moment of peril.

Though the published version of the novel made the link between

Stolz's economic activity and state service somewhat less explicit, its early readers quickly caught on. To many, Stolz appeared as a figure of governmental administration, a bureaucrat violently imposing proper forms on the inert and inchoate matter of Russian life embodied by the sleepy protagonist. For a number of readers, the novel invited comparisons with the recently published *One Thousand Souls*, especially comparisons between Kalinovich and Stolz. In a letter to Annenkov, Mikhail Saltykov-Shchedrin mentions an early episode in the novel, interpreting it as an allusion to Pisemsky's earlier text.[41] Here, a run-of-the-mill literary man, Penkin, recounts to Oblomov the plot of a short story he had recently written. In the story, a traveler happens to have seen the mayor of a town hitting local tradespeople. He complains to the governor, who launches an investigation, as a result of which it is revealed that the tradespeople are corrupt, sell rotten produce, and even cheat the state treasury. The beatings turn out to have been well deserved after all. Oblomov comments ingenuously: "So the mayor's blows play the part of Fate in the ancient tragedies?" (34; 4:26). Penkin enthusiastically agrees with the interpretation.

This by now familiar motif of the fate-bearing official returns in a more elaborate, narrativized form at the novel's end. There, Stolz protects Oblomov from extortion by appealing to his high connections in the civil service in order to get a legally binding IOU annulled and the culprit fired from his position at a government department. Only Stolz's reluctance to expose his friend to public embarrassment saves the villain from legal proceedings and imminent exile. Stolz's arrival comes just in time to prevent Oblomov's bankruptcy and spare the sympathetic reader the uncomfortable sight of a successful shakedown. But the execution of justice here is extrajudicial in nature and depends on high connections in the bureaucratic apparatus of the state.

The episode puts readers and reviewers on guard. Dobroliubov describes Stolz's rescue operation as "unceremonious," conducted, "according to Russian custom, without trial or investigation."[42] The historian and critic Alexander Miliukov compares Stolz's behavior under the circumstances to that of "minor despots, who, instead of taking the lawful path," act "through whimsy and by means of connections."[43] Miliukov continues in this vein:

> It is in these Stolzes that the bases of oppression so heavily burdening our society have lurked. It is from these gentlemen that there emerged those callous operators [*del'tsy*] who, in pursuit of an advantageous career, crush everything that comes their way; the leaders of the marching and writing phalanx, ready to arrange people like objects on their writing desks; dry bureaucrats, scourges of small bribes, and seekers of great ones; enemies

of everything that does not fit German decorum [*chinnost'*], ready to crush everything alive in the name of their discipline.⁴⁴

The telling, bureaucratic-imperial image of "the marching and writing phalanx," combined with the invocation of Stolz's Germanness, blends into a vision of the state as an implacable, alien, conquering force. Dmitry Pisarev summarizes the ostensible message of the novel thus:

> Russians! ... all of you are asleep, all of you are indifferent to the fate of the motherland, all of you are so stupid from sleep and fat, that I, the novelist, as a reproach to you, am forced to take my positive hero from among the Germans, just as your ancestors [...] called the Grand Prince, the gatherer of the Russian lands, from among the Germans.⁴⁵

The simile might seem far-fetched until we recall Oblomov's nearly tearful appeal to his proficient friend: "I know and understand everything, but I have no strength and no will of my own. Give me some of your will and your intelligence and lead me where you like" (183; 4:182). The national imaginary that we glimpse here runs counter to Anderson's paradigm of a flat, nonhierarchical aggregation linking distant places and simultaneous times into a densely populated model of the national-social whole. Instead, we find an imperial (Petrine, Varangian, etc.) imaginary in which the supremely competent foreign ruler gives form, energy, and power to an otherwise inert and inchoate popular mass.⁴⁶

The critics' tendency to read Stolz, contrary to all explicit textual indications, as a high-handed representative of the state finds support in the novel's widest narrative arc, which recapitulates the familiar motif of a triangulated rendezvous. The rendezvous is between Oblomov and Olga Ilyinskaya, a young woman to whom Stolz entrusts the task of stimulating his friend's dormant energies. Before leaving on a long business-related sojourn in Europe, Stolz instructs Olga "not to let [him] doze, not to allow him to sleep in the daytime, but to worry him, make him do things, give him all sorts of commissions," and leaves the country, expecting his friend to be brought back to life through lively social interaction with a young woman (222; 4:224). Stolz's approach to mentorship differs in telling ways from that of Pyotr Aduev. While Aduev works to restrain his pupil's "wildness," teaching him to control his thoughts, feelings, and physical movements, Stolz's task is, in a sense, the very opposite: to stimulate physical movement, feeling, and productive activity of some kind. The methods differ correspondingly: the elder Aduev oversees, instructs, mocks, lectures, prescribes; Stolz acts on his friend's environment, emboldens, goads, stimulates. Aduev's disciplinary motto is rationality, modernity, civilization; Stolz's biopolitical counterpart is labor and life.

Oblomov's acquaintance and subsequent falling in love with Olga initially produce the desired effects. His weariness and laziness disappear, he begins to read in earnest, introduces changes in his country estate, starts dressing like a man of the world. The following passage illustrates the mechanism of pastoral or biopolitical guidance with great vividness and precision: "What made him sit up even more than her reproaches was the realization that his weariness made her weary too, and she became cold and indifferent. Then he became full of life, strength and activity, and the shadow disappeared once more, and their feeling for one another was once again full of strength and vigor" (237; 4:240). The evident task here is not, as in *The Same Old Story*, to produce a docile, controlled, efficient body but to make it alert, energetic, mobile. And the path to achieving this goal is not chastisement, surveillance, and instruction, but the conferment, augmentation, or withdrawal of positive affect. Still, Oblomov experiences it all as arduous work. "What other sort of life and activity does Andrey want?" he muses. "Isn't love service?" (238; 4:240). The rhetorical question suggests that Oblomov, too, like the novel's reviewers, interprets Stolz's inducements in the Petrine spirit, as the demand of service to the fatherland. And in the same movement, it highlights the logic according to which failure in love is realist fiction's way of marking the protagonist's unfitness for active participation in the life of a national community.

A closer look at the trajectory of Oblomov's relationship with Olga yields a further important observation: that the absent coordinator of the rendezvous, Stolz, haunts it even in his absence. In this respect, the novel reprises the pattern of an earlier text with another paragon of German competence at its center: *Polinka Saks*. Like the protagonist of Druzhinin's novella, invisibly present everywhere his released wife and her new husband go, the shadow of Stolz accompanies Oblomov and Olga throughout. And as in the earlier text, here too, the haunting provokes expressions of passionate acclamation of the "absent coordinator" and contributes to—if not directly causes—the breakdown of the relationship he had enabled. So, for example, Olga demands that Oblomov's marriage proposal stay secret until he has fulfilled his absent friend's prescriptions: "Mr. Stolz wrote to you what you had to do in the country, didn't he?" To which Oblomov exclaims in despair: "if we are to listen to what Stolz says we'll never get as far as telling your aunt [of our plans to marry]" (289; 4:294). Olga persists in her demand, delaying the marriage to the point at which Oblomov begins to withdraw and hide. In other words, just as Polinka continues to belong to Saks, Zinaida to Volodya's father, Lizaveta Ivanovna to the elder Aduev, Tatyana to the nameless General, and Parasha to the Bronze Horseman, so also Olga belongs to Stolz from the start. It is always to the third instance, the older, more competent, stronger man, that the woman is ultimately consigned. It is up to him to grant the protagonist access to her, or to withdraw it, or to withdraw it in the processes of granting.

This capacity to unite or separate lovers serves both as an acclamation in itself and as a pretext for receiving further acclamation. Oblomov is not at all off the mark when, at a moment of panic, he guesses the identity of the person Olga has loved or will have loved all along:

> But what am I? Oblomov—and nothing more. Stolz, now, is a different matter: Stolz has intelligence, force, he knows how to govern [*upravliat'*] himself, others, destiny [*sud'boi*]. Wherever he goes and whoever he meets, he immediately has mastered them, playing people like musical instruments. And I? I can't get the better of [my servant] Zakhar even—or of myself. I am Oblomov! Stolz—good Lord, she loves him" (216; 4: 217-18).

Embedded within this act of acclamation is a gesture of self-denial. Oblomov here anticipates Volodya from *First Love*, who disavows his own feelings for Zinaida by comparing them with those of his father, which are ostensibly more real and intense. But the fact that Zinaida loves Pyotr Vasilievich, rather than his son, is at least established; Volodya only asserts the aptness and legitimacy of this fact. What makes Oblomov's interior monologue still more noteworthy is its capacity to anticipate (and thereby also to spur on) the outcome in advance, to see it as a foregone conclusion. In fact, Oblomov's suspicions of his own constitutional unfitness for the rendezvous make him regard himself as committing a transgression: "Let another man appear—and she will recognize her mistake with horror! How she will look at me then! How she will turn away! Awful! I am taking what does not belong to me! I am a thief!" (245; 4:249). As one might expect, then, Oblomov is later overjoyed to discover that Olga has married his superior friend. "Tell her," he implores Stolz, "that we were brought together only for the sake of putting her on the right path [to marrying Stolz] and that I bless our meeting and bless her on her new path in life!" (425; 4:433).

It is worth dwelling for a moment on the specific terms in which Stolz is acclaimed. He is said to be capable of governing himself and others; he plays people like musical instruments. The governmental, indeed despotic, overtones of these positive characterizations are of course impossible to overlook. Particularly striking is the suggestion—invoking Pushkin on Peter I ("vlastelin sud'by," "master of fate/destiny")—that Stolz is capable of governing destiny itself. Indeed, as we come to realize toward the end of the novel, a kind of predestination underpins the playing out of the romantic triangle. Oblomov, Stolz, and finally Olga all come to see the romance at the center of the novel as no more than a providential *felix culpa*, facilitating Olga's sentimental education and thus preparing her for marriage to Stolz.

Yet there is something peculiar about the turn taken by the providential schema in *Oblomov*. The peculiarity consists in the fact that instead of turning the protagonist's errors to his advantage, the overall pattern makes use of the erring protagonist and discards him. During the final exchange with Olga, Oblomov implores her to take him as he is, to love whatever is good in him. (364; 4:370). Olga's reply indicates that she had never loved the actual Oblomov, but only the one she and Stolz had hoped to create: a subject of desires and interests, an active, productive man—in other words, someone like Stolz. Instead of being brought into harmony with the subsisting order, Oblomov—the particular individual with his own capacities for life—is simply left out.

The forcefulness of this abandonment is still more evident in the final encounter between the two friends. Here, Stolz feels that "the gulf suddenly opened up before him and the 'stone wall' rose up and Oblomov did not seem to be there any longer, just as though he had vanished from sight or sunk through the floor" (475; 4:483). Yet Oblomov breathes, speaks, helps around the house, teaches his housekeeper-wife's children to read and count. Once again, we confront here a substantive social imaginary, with its stark dramas of inclusion/exclusion. Like the too-passionate Alexander in the well-regulated state, the too-passive Oblomov has no place in the economically mobilizing nation.[47] According to this substantive biopolitics, exclusion from the economic domain proves lethal for the excluded. If Oblomov cannot be *made* to *live* (in the economically robust sense of the word), he should be allowed to die.[48] When all or most Oblomovs die out and many more Stolzs ("under Russian names") are born, then according to the national imaginary here at play, Russia will finally come into her own (164; 4:164).

Still more must be said, however, about the workings of providence in *Oblomov*. Not only does it fail to benefit the protagonist; it benefits the providential agent-mentor himself. The resonances of such an unusual arrangement involve a bifurcating—indeed, paradoxical but by now familiar—vision of Stolz as both sovereign plotter, organizing and haunting the central relationship of the novel, and private person, internal to the relationship and standing to gain from its particular unfolding. This dynamic becomes explicit on the final pages of the novel, where (unsurprisingly for the reader of Goncharov's first novel) we get an account of Stolz's "management" of his wife:

> At first he had long to struggle with the vivacity of her nature, to check the fever of youth, to keep her impulses within definite bounds, and impart an even flow to their life, and that, too, only for a time. For as soon as he closed his eyes trustfully, an alarm was raised again, life was in full swing, some new question sprang from her restless mind and anxious heart: he had to calm her excited imagination, to soothe or rouse her pride. If she pondered over something, he hastened to give her the key to it." (444, 4:451)

As one might expect, Stolz's emphasis here is less on surveillance and control (Pyotr Aduev's specialization) than on the regulation of life forces: a little more here, a little less there; life—the life of the woman and the nation alike—must run its course, never stop. But it must run evenly, smoothly, without posing a threat to the individual organism or the general order. The more important point for our purposes is that Stolz appears to straddle the domains of the inside-private and outside-supervisory: a man who loves Olga and seeks happiness with her and at the same time regulates her vitality, administers her life.

In the final chapter of the novel, we learn that we had been dealing with a hybrid focalization all along, a story told both from an omniscient perspective and from Stolz's point of view (485; 4:493). Stolz continues to be located both "inside" (the text, the economy, the erotic relationship) and "above" (in the place of the author, the state, the matchmaker) to the end.[49] He thus enables a series of paradoxical equations according to which the prevailing social imaginary of the novel finally operates: egoistic activity *is* service, the economy *is* the state, national aggregation *is* imperial substance. It is probably in these equations that we find the solution to the puzzle troubling us throughout: Why do the novel's reviewers again and again construe Goncharov's paragon of a *privately* "active man" as an agent of the state? It is also here that we find the key to the constitutive exclusion of the protagonist from the nation-building narrative. When a national imaginary grounded in the sociotopes of civil society is in abeyance, an attempt to conceive of mobilization through individual activity recasts the individual (Stolz) as the sovereign, who alone both activates and acts. In the shadow of a substantive conception of the nation being mobilized, the man refusing or unable to act in a productively self-interested way (Oblomov) is reduced to the status of bare life, always already dead.

2. Amalgam

While the paradigm of national mobilization orchestrates the coincidence between the administrative state and the economically active individual, the figure of "amalgam" projects the nation as an imaginary blend between the figures of the sovereign and the primordial substratum of the "people." We have already glimpsed an element of this dynamic in the narrator's characterization of Russians in *War and Peace* as distinguished by their unusual capacity to renounce—and to revel in renouncing—all that is conventionally assumed to be precious: wealth, comforts, life itself (899-900; 11:360-61). In sacrifice, Russians discover a certain higher "power and strength" (*vlast' i sila*), the power to say no to all particular determinations. The narrator discloses the political imaginary underpinning these observations by recalling the royal appearance at the Slobodsky Palace. To sacrifice everything, one's life included, is to partake of the sovereign charisma, to become one with the sovereign. Or—and in this equivalence lies the hinge of the substantive imaginary here at stake—to become one with the nation (*narod*). The two domains, sovereignty and nationhood, intersect in the depicted individual at the point of his self-transcendence.

Several years later, in his *Diary of a Writer*, Dostoevsky would attempt to grasp the essence of the nation within the horizon of a similar script. Like Tolstoy and many others, he too asserts that the destiny of the Russian people will be resolved not in St. Petersburg, by the bureaucracy and/or the intelligentsia, but by the common people themselves. "And therefore every *new* feature, even the smallest, that serves to characterize these 'new people' may be worthy of our attention."[50] These considerations serve the narrator of the *Diary* as an introduction to the central anecdote of the entry: the story of the peasant, pseudonymously named "Vlas" (referring us to the protagonist of an earlier poem by Nikolai Nekrasov). In casting his exemplary peasant as a representative of the "new people," the narrator engages in deliberate catachresis, applying the term for radical members of the intelligentsia to supposedly archaic, apolitical, and mostly illiterate peasants. We shall shortly see how fruitful such a catachretic vision of the nation can be when it comes to historical as much as novelistic imaginaries.

Turning to the anecdote itself, Dostoevsky tells the story of a young peasant who comes close to committing a terrible sacrilege (shooting a gun at the Eucharistic wafer) on a dare but at the last moment has a vision of Christ on the cross and collapses unconscious. Dostoevsky's analysis of this real-life event resorts to a national psychology of excess, a characteristically national "urge to go beyond the limit, an urge for the sinking sensation one gets when one has come to the edge of an abyss, leans halfway over it, looks into the bottomless pit itself, and ... throws oneself headlong into it like a madman."[51] What fascinates Dostoevsky is that such a blasphemous act is committed not by a city-dwelling, German-reading atheist but by a devout peasant who up until the last moment perhaps harbored in his heart only the most pious feelings. Such people, he writes, can suddenly renounce their roots in "family, custom, God," and abandon themselves to the "maelstrom of violent and momentary negation and destruction of self that is so typical of the Russian national character at certain fateful moments in its existence."[52] True Russianness, then, is characterized by the ability to sever the connections with the national substance. Conversely, transgression of limits, rejection of the national soil, is something inherent in the soil itself.

In Tolstoy, an alienated, foreign-educated member of the nobility yearns to sacrifice all social attributes (wealth, status, comforts, power) for the sake of merging with the body of the nation. Dostoevsky adds another twist to this script by showing that belonging to the body of the nation itself presupposes the sacrifice of all that the nation ostensibly holds dear: "family, custom, God." The staging of Russianness is here more paradoxical than in *War and Peace*. Yet the two share the basic scenario of supreme daring, transgression of limits, negation of all worldly determinations. A certain charisma adheres to such acts, linking them to the political context of the state of exception (war in *War and Peace*, "certain fateful moments [in history]" in Dostoevsky), and connecting them further to the figure of the sovereign. In Tolstoy, this is made evident through repeated invocations of the episode in the Slobodsky Palace. And one need only look at Dostoevsky's earlier characterization of Peter I to appreciate the proximity, at the level of the national imaginary, between the exemplary peasant and the Westernizing czar:

> In the person of Peter we see an example of what a Russian can resolve to do when he develops for himself an absolute conviction and begins to feel that time has come and the new forces have ripened and manifested themselves within him. And it is frightening to conceive the extent to which the Russian is free in spirit, the extent to which his will is strong! Nobody has ever torn himself from the native soil the way he has sometimes had to, or veer to the side so sharply following his convictions.[53]

Here again, as in the earlier passages, Russianness expresses itself as a drama of excessive, overflowing strength, tearing, as it were, the native son out of his soil and through the ensuing crisis highlighting the soil's richness and power. The national drama of both the peasant and the sovereign is one of breathtaking individuation, the assertion of mastery over the existing order of things. To be Russian, according to this national imaginary, is neither to be dissolved in the traditional (communal) way of life nor to come together with others contractually, as an individual. Rather, to be Russian is to inhabit the state of exception in which all concrete determinations—including and especially traditional Russianness itself—are both canceled out and reasserted in an act of individual transcendence.

Dostoevsky is not alone in conflating the most un-Russian of Russian rulers with the figure of the Russian peasant—and correspondingly the most modern with the most primordial, the most individual with the most communal, the most artificial with the most authentic, and so on. Already Belinsky, in his review of *Sketches on the Battle of Borodino*, gestures in a similar direction, identifying Peter with the epic Russian hero (*bogatyr'*) Ilya Muromets, peasant, warrior, and saint. In Belinsky's account, Peter does not impose an alien order upon native life; rather, he releases the dynamic potential inherent in the nation to begin with. He is interpolated into the body of the nation and into the parallel biography of the epic hero—as their principle of motion.[54]

An analogous motif reappears in Turgenev's "Hor' and Kalinych" from *A Sportsman's Sketches* (1852). Recounting his conversations with the peasant Hor', the narrator pauses to comment with a kind of non sequitur:

> All his inquiries, I cannot recount, and it is unnecessary; but from our conversations I carried away one conviction, which my readers will certainly not anticipate [...] the conviction that Peter the Great was preeminently a Russian—Russian, above all, in his reforms. The Russian is so convinced of his own strength and robustness that he is not afraid of putting himself to severe strain; he takes little interest in his past, and looks boldly forward.[55]

Again, and still more explicitly here, Peter is placed squarely in the midst of the nation, characterized directly and polemically as Russian while, at the same time, Russianness is reconfigured in such a way as to make the emperor's figure unexceptional. Turgenev's Peter is Russian because he thinks and acts much like a Russian peasant, who, in turn, possesses abundant strength for deeds of Petrine overstepping.

The Peter-as-peasant-and-peasant-as-Peter topos represents an intriguing, paradoxical variation on the national-imaginary motif of unity between the sovereign and the nation. For Dostoevsky, in particular, this variation proved to be novelistically fruitful. We have already seen how in *Demons* the figure of Stavrogin combines elements of modern political charisma with those of folk legend and the tradition of peasant rebellion. An even more elaborate case of such an amalgam organizes *Crime and Punishment*, whose ambivalently acclaimed hero occupies the space of exception and, in transgressing against the national substance, demonstrates his belonging to it.

Like *Demons*, *Crime and Punishment* projects a vision of nearly total social collapse. Here, the status quo is flagrant exploitation and injustice, thematized immediately in the dire state of the Marmeladov family, living off their daughter Sonya's prostitution. What strikes Raskolnikov the most about the situation is the family's capacity to become accustomed to it.[56] Such, too, would have to be the conditions for the protagonist's acquisition of status in the world: he would have to be ready to sacrifice his sister Dunya to marital "prostitution" with a financially successful but thoroughly contemptible man. Unlike the Marmeladovs, Raskolnikov rejects this passively exploitative option and decides instead to take into his own hands the task of fixing it all, of reordering the world from the outside. The decision to start by a reckoning with a pawnbroker is apt: since at least Balzac's Gobseck, figures like her, taking financial advantage of other people's misfortunes, have been placed at the center of the system Rasklonikov finds so unbearably vile. The decision to begin with murder (rather than, say, with a robbery or theft) is appropriate for another reason: it creates the conditions for testing his fitness for the role of a man, whose capacity to introduce proper order correlates with his right to "take life and let live."

If the *social* conditions of Raskolnikov's act are clear from the start, its specifically *political* stakes become apparent during his first conversation with the investigator Porfiry Petrovich. Here, Raskolnikov reprises his earlier published argument that the "law-givers and founders of mankind" have the right to commit crimes whose nature and scale would be appropriate to the dimensions of the historical revolution they are destined to bring about. Raskolnikov says:

> I recall developing in my article the idea that all... well, let's say, the law-givers and founders of mankind, starting from the most ancient and going on to the Lycurguses, the Solons, the Muhammads, the Napoleons, and so forth, that all of them to a man were criminals, from the fact alone that in giving a new law they thereby violated the old one, held sacred by society and passed down from their fathers. (260; 6:199–200)

Raskolnikov tests himself against the paradigm of foundational politics represented by the figure of the great lawgiver. The lawgiver is at the same time a criminal who, in introducing new laws, spurns the laws of his fathers. The lawgiver acts from the place of normative exception, and so his actions invariably carry ambiguous ethical valences, depending on whether one views them from the perspective of their predecessors or successors.

This zone of ambiguity between a crime and a foundational political act is illuminated, for example, during Raskolnikov's walk to the apartment of the old pawnbroker he intends to murder. Here, he entertains plans for expanding the Summer Garden to include the Field of Mars and the garden of the Mikhailovsky Palace. The plan conjures up sovereign-imperial associations, echoing not only Georges-Eugène Haussmann's contemporary reconstruction of Paris under Napoleon III,[57] but also coinciding quite precisely with Peter I's original design of the city. Peter, the one lawgiver whose name does not make it to Raskolnikov's list, repeatedly appears in the notes to the novel as "the Dutchman-Peter," modeling the kind of world-transformative power Raskolnikov strives to possess. In Raskolnikov's own words from the notebooks: "I need power. [...] I want that everything I am seeing be different. [...] I don't want to dream; I want to act. [...] (The Dutchman Peter)." And a little later, in the third person: "Through his character, the novel expresses the idea of immeasurable pride, haughtiness, and contempt for this society. [...] Despotism is his [main] trait. [...] He wants to rule."[58] Within the imaginary regime of sovereignty, Raskolnikov's mental conflation between violent crime and the layout of the imperial capital suggests less a symptom of criminal psychopathology than an element in the coding of the crime as a political act.[59]

The tensions and ambiguities embedded in the novel's treatment of the crime tellingly manifest themselves in the protagonist's conflicted "play" with visibility. One episode stands out in this regard: the brief encounter between Raskolnikov, who has entered a tavern to look for accounts of his crime in newspapers, and the police clerk Zametov. In the course of the scene, Zametov suggests that the man who had killed the pawnbroker must have been an amateur and will surely be caught. Raskolnikov feels insulted, grows restless, and soon finds himself on the brink of admitting his guilt:

> A terrible word was trembling on his lips... another moment and it would jump out; another moment and it would let go; another moment and it would be spoken!
> "And what if it was I who killed the old woman and Lizaveta?" he said suddenly—and came to his senses.
> Zametov looked wildly at him and went as white as a sheet. (165; 6:128)

It is possible to read this scene, among similar others in which Raskolnikov brings himself to the edge of exposure, as an index of his conflicted desire to be apprehended. According to this interpretation—which arises by default within the horizon of novelistic psychosocial normativity—having committed the crime, Raskolnikov cannot bear the weight of the guilt and the isolation it imposes on him and begins to seek out exposure and punishment. The trouble with this interpretation is not only that Raskolnikov's feelings of guilt are explicitly ruled out (543; 6:417); the deeper issue is that it covers up the construction of the episode as a kind of scenario of power in which a witness is called upon to gaze spellbound at the hero, who flickeringly manifests himself as a superior being with power over life and death. Put another way, Raskolnikov's act of self-revelation is doubly emplotted. On the one hand, as a violation of the law committed by a private person—and this must remain hidden if the protagonist is to avoid getting caught. On the other hand, as the pivotal point in a certain scenario of power, which must by definition be performed in the open, publicly establishing the identity of the actor through the act. The crime thus conceived produces in the protagonist the contradictory desire at once to remain hidden and (not so much to get caught as) to be seen—and acclaimed.[60]

The interaction of these two social-imaginary regimes (those of social transgression on the one hand and of political sovereignty on the other) forms the dramatic kernel of the three conversations between Raskolnikov and Porfiry Petrovich. The encounters trace the investigator's struggle first to decode and then to realign the structure of the protagonist's subjectivity, including, and perhaps most prominently, his sense of time. Porfiry appears here as an exemplary "disciplinarian," less concerned with apprehending the criminal than with studying him, less driven to establish his formal identity than to get to the core of his way of thinking, less preoccupied with punishment than with correction and reform. The investigator thus anchors the techniques and articulates the values traditionally understood as novelistic: psychic transparency (to the omniscient gaze of the author/reader), malleability under the pressure of social interactions, openness in biographical time, and so on. Meanwhile, the protagonist adheres to a set of imaginaries associated with the regime of sovereignty: a vision of the subject as a mysterious source of exceptional, norm-destroying deeds, deeds that are on display for public viewing and acclamation (hence, the humiliating torment of having to hide) and thus establish, test, and fortify the identity of the doer.[61] Equally telling in this respect are the agonists' competing notions of identity in time. Porfiry is once again on the side of the novelistic impulse to see individuals as relatively mobile and fluid, insisting that confession and imprisonment would not empty Raskolnikov's life of meaning. For the investigator, the double murder, in other words, is only one among the many acts Raskolnikov will perform. For Raskolnikov himself, by contrast, the crime is *the* act, the ordeal of his "election" to sovereignty. Here, identity is given once and for all; it may be tested but not changed.[62] Porfiry keeps calling on Raskolnikov to be patient. The young man's most explicit reply appears in the notes: "Why be patient? The Dutchman [Peter]."⁶³

We might say, then, that the titular crime of the novel and the enigma of identity to which it gives narrative foundation can be specified as a locus of interference between the imaginaries of disciplinary and sovereign power. Here, the traditional nineteenth-century novelistic motif that may be designated as "the young man in the city" is traversed by the novelistically alien motif of "the acts of a foundational hero." The same incongruity can be articulated with reference to Anderson's distinction between the spatiotemporal coordinates of the nation as a social whole and those of the religious community and dynastic realm. The novel both asserts and struggles against sequential time and abstract, "ordinary" space, both wishes and refuses to regard its hero as a developing individual. Against homogeneous space, it posits the charismatic centrality of the protagonist; against developmental time—the *now* (accentuated by the hero's impatience and the density of narration both) on which the meanings of the future and the past converge.

This "now" is, moreover, the time of radical historical transition, time ripe with what Raskolnikov refers to as "a new word." In an article published three years prior to *Crime and Punishment*, Dostoevsky explores the dynamics of such times in Russian history with reference to the seventeenth-century religious Schism (*raskol*) and the reforms of Peter I. The two broadly speaking revolutionary events serve here as precedents for the equally radical contemporary upheavals of the early 1860s. The passage teems with expressions and motifs that reappear, sometimes verbatim, in the novel: the need for "fresh air" and the "new word," the powerful impulse to leave behind the old life that has become stifling. But more important for our purposes is the peculiar placement side by side of Peter and the Schism as twin phenomena of rejection and renewal, of national vitality and force.⁶⁴ Peter and the Schism—radical reform of the state apparatus and rebellious dissent among the common people—meet at the point of the nation's dynamism, name its capacity for self-transcendence.

It may thus not be necessary to search far for figurative meanings in the protagonist's name. In denoting the historical event itself, its stem roots the hero in the national soil just as his (theory of) crime links him to the theme of sovereignty and to Peter. At this point, then, it is helpful to recall that throughout much of the novel, while Raskolnikov wanders through the streets of St. Petersburg, the authorities already have the presumed murderer in custody. This is the schismatic (*raskolnik*) peasant Mikolka, who incurs the suspicions of the police by being in the wrong place at the wrong time and acting strangely in the aftermath of the murder. At a dramatic moment in Raskolnikov's interrogation, just as he seems ready to break down and admit his guilt, Mikolka pushes his way into the investigator's office and confesses to the crime he did not commit, substituting himself for the protagonist (351; 6:271).

Further parallels are drawn between the two, especially in the final conversation between Porfiry Petrovich and Raskolnikov. The investigator calls them both in turn "fantastic" (which is to say, strange, implausible) people and advises Raskolnikov to follow Mikolka's lead and "embrace suffering" (465: 6:352). Mikolka's (false) confession and Raskolnikov's crime alike are "fantastic" deeds beyond measure and beyond socially delineated limits of the self. And just as Mikolka replaces Raskolnikov in prison for much of the novel, so, having finally confessed his crime, Raskolnikov replaces Mikolka. The sequence of substitutions unfolding between a representative of the intelligentsia aspiring to sovereign status and the peasant dissenter seeking suffering culminates with Raskolnikov's transfiguration into the figure of the folk-mythological czar-redeemer, the epiphany of the Hidden One, greeted by the folkloric formula that roughly translates as: "Fee, fi, fo, fum, I smell the smell of a Russian man" (527; 6:406).

This final greeting is in fact prepared by a series of prior folkloric associations, linking Raskolnikov to the figure of the "hidden czar." During Raskolnikov's first visit to the police station, one of the officers addresses him ironically as a "bright young falcon" (*sokol iasnyi*). Porfiry himself ironically suggests that, to avoid mistakes, extraordinary people should wear distinctive clothes or be marked by brandings (*kleimy*) (262; 6:201). At a later point in the text, Porfiry speaks to Raskolnikov in the heightened register, delineating his future path: "Become the sun and everyone will see you" (460; 6:352). The images of the falcon, the branded one, and the sun—are all drawn from the depository of associations linked to the figure of royal power and impostorship.[65]

One final example of the novel's tendency to amalgamate images of sovereignty with those of national substance pertains to Raskolnikov's choice of murder weapon: specifically and emphatically an axe. In the epilogue, fellow prisoners from among the common people appear to mock him: "What did you take up an axe for; it's no business for a gentleman" (576; 6:418). Raskolnikov the "new man," who should be shooting a revolver (like Dmitry Karakozov some months after the publication of the novel) or throwing a bomb (like the regicides of the People's Will months after Dostoevsky's death), resorts to the common people's weapon of choice instead, the weapon of peasant mutiny. The novel dwells on this choice early on: "That the deed was to be done with an axe he had already decided long ago. He also had a folding pruning knife, but he could not rely on the knife and still less on his own strength, and therefore finally decided on the axe" (69; 6:57). A few paragraphs down, we find an odd account of Raskolnikov's misadventures with the murder weapon. He cannot get it where he had planned, is on the verge of giving up on the entire idea, and then, suddenly, finds the same weapon where he hadn't been looking. In the process of being denied and then granted, the axe acquires a magical status, which then narratively pays off at the moment of the murder itself, when the axe seems to strike Raskolnikov's victim on its own: "his own strength [seems] to have no part in it. But the moment he brought the axe down, strength was born in him" (76; 6:63). Thus, the "new" man's "old" weapon acquires a kind of fairytale quality; it wields itself and endows the person holding it with power.

In addition to the common-popular associations of the axe, as well as its folkloric function in the novel, we might recall here the image of Peter walking around incognito with an axe from Gogol's *Selected Passages from the Correspondence with Friends*: "This very sharp turn-around [*povorot*] in the whole state, produced by one person—and, moreover, by the czar himself, who magnanimously abandoned for a time his royal name, decided to try every craft himself, and with an axe in his hand to become foremost in every occupation, so as to prevent any disorders that tend to follow the slightest change in the form of government—this alone was a deed worthy of admiration."[66] The image is noteworthy in itself for the manner in which the axe functions as a symbolic hinge, conflating commoner with czar. Still more conspicuous in our context is the ostensible purpose with which the sovereign picks it up: to prevent disorder usually associated with rapid change. In the context of the Petrine myth, one is readily put in mind of the czar's personal axe-wielding participation in the execution of the rebel *Streltsy*.

Thus the signifier "Raskolnikov" transpires as an uncanny blend of images, mythemes, and motifs: a deracinated youth aspiring to sovereign exception and wielding the weapon of the demos, a catachretic "national persona," constructed at the site of an imaginary synthesis between the figures of the people (paradigmatically, the peasant) and the reformer-czar. The underlying fantasy here concerns the possibility of a violent suppression of unscrupulous social life through the figure of the sovereign-commoner, *a charismatic individual and a national substance both*. Such is the novel's idiosyncratic take on the official-nationality premise of unity between the rulers and the ruled. What we do not find here is anything like a story modeling national aggregation on the grounds of one or another sociotope of civil society. We don't have an account of individual development into the kind of person who would willingly become a member of a large group in pursuit of the common interest—though something like this is perhaps suggested by the figure of Raskolnikov's friend Razumikhin.

The notion of integrating the self-seeking individual into a national system of needs is dismissed early in the novel, together with the contemptible representative of its ideology, Pyotr Luzhin. Raskolnikov's concluding union with Sonya unfolds within the social-imaginary parameters that are starkly different from the Victorian vision of universality as actualized right. The affective foundations of sublime duty are replaced here by those of brotherly love (especially) for the unfortunate. Instead of an ascent to social respectability, we have utter social and geographic marginalization: a union of a murderer and a prostitute in Siberian exile, at the edge of the world. And rather than a vision of class reconciliation between the aristocracy and the middle class, we have a convergence between the "people," rooted in the Christian ways of life, and the intelligentsia, abjectly skeptical and rootless. This last model of national reconciliation, in any case, is where Dostoevsky explicitly directs his postemancipation hopes. But the novel relegates that plot line to the margins and presents a more paradoxical and dramatic allegory of the nation instead. This allegory is based on the projection of the transgressive act of self-uprooting as the most national act of all. In this act, the "alien" lawgiver and the "native" people stand to each other in the relationship of primordial unity in/though separation. It is in this scenario of national self-transcendence that the official nationalism's presumption of an unbreakable bond between the people and the sovereign comes to be novelistically conceived.

3. Spell

In the several paragraphs that *Crime and Punishment* allots to Raskolnikov's "post-conversion" relationship with Sonya, we are told that even his fellow prisoners from among the common people are better disposed to him now. To love Sonya, clearly, is to be one with the people, to realize Dostoevsky's hopes for national wholeness in which the Petrine intelligentsia would at last return to its roots. The Russian realist corpus abounds with such associations between the female heroine and the nation, often framed by scenarios of the uprooted protagonist's failure to be united to her.[67] Within this scenario, the question of belonging is substantively posed: one is either completely—physically, emotionally, by "flesh and blood"—united with one's female counterpart (the nation), or one is a desolate wanderer, a stranger in this world, doomed to a superfluous existence. We have already seen the plot of failed unification unfold within the "Russian on the rendezvous" paradigm. Turgenev's Asya is characterized as a "Russian girl" par excellence, while Chernyshevsky's take on that story and the entire lineage of failed Russian "Romeos" culminates with the urgent demand that the educated elites "come to terms" with the common people. Here, too, the standard realist courtship plot is diverted through allegorization into a national imaginary, organized around the rigid dualism of isolation and belonging.

The courtship strain in *War and Peace* partakes of this logic as well. Here, two prominent movements of the plot—Pierre Bezukhov's and Andrei Bolkonsky's relationships with the emblematically "Russian" Natasha Rostova and their attempts to reckon with the national cataclysm of the Napoleonic invasion—run in parallel to each other and contrast. In this respect, Andrei's "failure" to be united with Natasha corresponds to an episode in which he refuses to get into a pond filled to the brim with "the naked human bodies of soldiers flopping about in it, white with brick-red hands, faces and necks."[68] Worn out by the heat, but unable to go into the "dirty" pond, he decides to take a shower in his shed instead and, looking down at his naked body, thinks with revulsion: "Flesh, the body, *chair à canon*!"[69] The body is his, but it is also the body of the nation, constituted precisely by its status as cannon flesh in the time of war. This body and his are inseparable at this moment of universal peril, but he symbolically rejects the unity. It is of course the same "body" with which Pierre seeks to merge on the eve and in the aftermath of the Battle of Borodino, and while Andrei dies, Pierre "inherits" Natasha.

The two texts at issue in this section present somewhat more elaborate variations on the pattern of substantive national allegory. In both, we find a formidable female figure, tying the hero irremediably to her and thus standing in the way of what, in conventional realist terms, may be characterized as "fulfillment." The sequential, developmental character of national time—operative in Anderson's ideal-typical account of the nation-novel nexus—here proves illusory, loops back upon itself, and stages the mastery of the past over the present and the future. Likewise with space, which is, as it were, magnetized in such a way that, even at furthest remove, the fateful encounter with the charismatic heroine proves inevitable. This is the national-imaginary scenario of the *substantive spell*, according to which the nation is no longer a (welcoming) telos, but a (hostile) fate.

This pattern emerges with great clarity in Turgenev's *Spring Torrents*, which opens with an account of dawning love and then approaching marriage between a young Russian traveler, Dmitry Sanin, and the Italian young woman Gemma Roselli, in Frankfurt. We learn early on that the Italian family in which Sanin quickly begins to feel at home—the widowed mother, her daughter Gemma, her son Emilio, and the servant turned family friend Pantaleone—has deep roots in Italian politics. The now deceased husband and father, we are told, had been a republican, forced to leave his native land after the defeat of Napoleon and the reactionary measures by the newly reigning Austrian monarchy. Pantaleone appears to have been involved in planning an uprising in Modena in 1831. Gemma, too, is called a "republican" by her mother (perhaps as much for independence of character as for political views). And by the end of the novella, we learn that Emilio dies heroically fighting for the liberation of his native land under Garibaldi's command. Thus, Gemma is here an object of romantic attachment, a path to personal fulfillment, and an allegory of political freedom, human dignity, and European civilization.

Semes of "Russianness," by contrast, accrue to Maria Polozova, the woman with whom Sanin will in the end betray Gemma—and himself. She is endowed with "the overwhelming presence of a Russian, or perhaps gipsy, woman's powerful body in full flower."[70] She speaks "pure" Muscovite Russian "of a lower-class [*narodnogo*], not aristocratic sort" (131; 11:114). Unlike Sanin and the Italians, she does not like music, except for Russian folk dances and songs (136; 11:136). Just before their affair is consummated in the forest, she invokes the folk practice of *prisukha*, a kind of dark spell that attaches the beloved to the lover as if by force. Still more fundamentally, Polozova's "Russianness" is signified by hybridity. Layered on top of her folksiness, her "common" appearance, her disarming familiarity and directness are her perfect French, her allusions to Roman literature, her endless European sojourns. This incongruous coexistence of deeply native and haphazardly Western elements was designated as "monstrous" in Turgenev's earlier novel, *Smoke*.[71]

The nature of Polozova's magnetic appeal to Sanin is mysterious and mystified. Sanin himself is unable to understand what draws him to her, and finds himself on the verge of believing in the magic of *prisukha* (165; 11:146). Turgenev's early readers wondered what it was that allowed a man happily in love with Gemma to be seduced by Polozova in a matter of days.[72] As psychological verisimilitude encounters its limit, the allegorical dimension of the text emerges to the foreground. We are compelled to recognize that Sanin's "Russian" alternative embodies the pull of the national substance, always lurking around the narrative corner, ready to entrap the individual who, at the peak of happiness, has come to regard himself as self-sufficient and free. Neither self-sufficient nor free, the hero turns out to be rooted in the soil from which he came, drawn back into the orbit of a national curse, a collective sin, whose name is unambiguously pronounced.

This name, a political correlate of the occult *prisukha*, is "bondage." The motif appears at three decisive points in the text, all linked to the relationship between Polozova and Sanin. In order to marry Gemma and have the means to start a family with her, Sanin must sell his Russian estate, together with his serfs. By accident, he meets his old schoolmate, Polozov, who tells him that his wife may be willing to buy. When Sanin mentions his plan to Gemma's mother, the question of having to sell the serfs comes up. Profoundly uncomfortable, Sanin has nothing better to say than that he will make sure the purchaser is a decent person. Overhearing the conversation, the passionate Pantaleone pronounces his verdict: *barbari* (110; 11:96). Sanin recalls the verdict as he is trying to arrive at an agreement with Polozova, which involves counting the serfs and establishing the price for each (141; 11:123). At the end of the novella, he is himself described as a "bondsman, or serf" at whom Polozova looks with the smile of "the serf owner, of the sovereign lord and master" (169; 11:150). Serfdom emerges as a politically coded motivation for the plot's psychologically unmotivated pivot away from the path of autonomy and onto a trajectory of bondage. It thus thematizes the familiar structure of sovereign triangulation, with gender roles reversed. Here it is the hero, and not the heroine, who fatefully "belongs" to someone he doesn't love.

The decisive sexual encounter between Sanin and Polozova unfolds in the shadow of Virgil's narrative about the Trojan forefather of Rome, Aeneas, and Dido, queen of Carthage. Polozova herself alludes to the text, and later, inviting Sanin to follow her into the shadows of the forest, she calls him, in a whisper, "Aeneas" (167; 11:148). But *Spring Torrents* rewrites the civilizational myth in reverse. Rather than abandoning the barbaric princess to embark on his heroic mission, Turgenev's "Aeneas" will become fatefully attached.[73] When they return from the forest, he no longer has a will of his own:

> "I am going wherever you are, and I will be with you until you drive me away," he replied in despair, and pressed himself against the hands of his sovereign mistress [*vlastitel'nitsy*].
>
> She released her hands, placed them on his head and seized his hair with all ten fingers. [...] Her lips curled in triumph. Her eyes, so wide and shining that they looked almost white, showed only the pitiless torpor of one sated with victory. A hawk clawing at a bird caught in its talons sometimes has this look in its eyes. (168; 11:148)

The horizon of the Punic Wars—the proximate historical context in which the mythical encounter between Aeneas and Dido is narrated in Virgil—resonates here, as well, once again reversing the result as Russia-Carthage triumphs over Europe-Rome. And just as civilization is overtaken by "barbarism" (recall Pantaleone's "barbari!"), so also freedom by domination, and the protagonist by his "sovereign mistress"—a national substance whose prey he ultimately becomes. Eventually, Sanin follows Polozova back to Russia, with which he had planned decisively to part. Time and space loop in upon themselves. Apparently open to possibility and encounter at the beginning of the novel, space turns out to be fatefully warped, all paths leading back to the point of origin. Progressive biographical time, here associated precisely *not* with the Russian nation but with the West, is interrupted and drawn back into the orbit of the primordial national curse. And in the middle of it all, there arises before us an emblematic figure of a serf owner in an autocratic state, a ruler who is ruled, a lord whose price for lordship is his own enslavement.

Sanin's story is framed as a recollection. In the present, thirty years after the narrated events, we find him living in Russia, a gentleman in his fifties who has "managed to amass a considerable fortune" (176; 11:156). Returning from a pleasant sociable gathering, he collapses in an armchair, overcome by "taedium vitae," profound melancholy, and a sense of creaturely frailty. Rummaging through sundry mementos to distract himself from morbid thoughts, he discovers a little garnet cross that Gemma had given to him many years ago. His thoughts turn to the past, whose narration now appears as a kind of origin story, a genealogy of his destitution. The recollection inspires him to find Gemma, who has since moved to New York and lives there happily with her husband and children. As a sign of forgiveness, she sends him a photograph of her eighteen-year-old daughter, a bride, whom Sanin first mistakes for the young Gemma herself and to whom he sends a richly decorated garnet cross by way of a bridal gift. The novella ends with the reports of a rumor that Sanin had decided to sell his estates and emigrate to America. The concluding motif—embodied in the photograph, the cross, and yet another attempt to escape—is the motif of circularity. The novella ends with an odd tension between open-endedness and recursion: will Sanin's second escape be more successful than the first? Given that it is reported as a rumor, will such an attempt even be made? Regardless of the answer, the national-imaginary coordinates have not changed: freedom, life, progress are somewhere (increasingly) far away; here—only bondage, the mire of the past, and melancholy unto death.[74]

A similar pattern of national triangulation anchored in an occult notion of the spell organizes the central love intrigue of *The Idiot*. Making up the triangle are the novel's protagonist, Prince Myshkin, a young woman from a well-to-do and respectable family, Aglaya Epanchina, and the uncannily beautiful victim of a landowner's sexual exploitation, Nastasya Filippovna. The protagonist is positioned differently vis-à-vis the two women. In relation to Aglaya, Myshkin feels something akin to romantic love. She is, socially, the proper choice for him, the choice that those who represent the commonsense view of the subsisting social order can understand. At least on first approximation, Aglaya embeds the traditional novelistic plot of courtship and social integration. By contrast, Myshkin's feelings for

Nastasya Filippovna are of an indefinable, baffling quality. He is entranced by her photograph the moment he sees it, and hours after he meets her, he offers her his hand in marriage. He believes, contrary to all verisimilitude (but in accordance with the looping temporality of national soteriology), that he has seen her somewhere before. Nastasya Filippovna pulls him away from the "proper" romantic choice, though the name of the imponderable attraction here is no longer sexual passion but an equally overwhelming compassion, the drive to save and to redeem.

The social world of the novel is organized around the Epanchin family, which includes the wealthy and well-connected General Epanchin, his temperamental wife, Lizaveta Prokofyevna, and their three marriageable daughters, Alexandra, Adelaida, and Aglaya. A recent arrival from Switzerland, where he spent most of his childhood and adolescence in treatment from "falling sickness" and other ailments, Myshkin introduces himself to the family immediately upon arrival on the grounds of being a distant relative. He is a stranger to Russian society, from the conventional perspective of which his behavior is often inappropriate, overly democratic, too sincere, and at times provocatively naive. Yet from the day of his arrival, he manages to gain the Epanchins' guarded affections. And less than halfway through the novel, we find the beginnings of what may be regarded as the classical courtship plot: will Myshkin succeed or will he fail in securing Aglaya's hand in marriage?

The social-imaginary implications of this plot line, however, are ambiguous. On the one hand, it is linked to the problem of proper socialization, integration into decent society. The matriarchal Lizaveta Prokofyevna articulates this clearly as she tries to come to terms with the possibility that her youngest and most beautiful daughter—the jewel of the family—will marry the eccentric man "who neither knows society nor has any place in society."[75] Yet at the same time, the novel goes to great lengths to discredit the notion of respectability and decency by the lights of which the protagonist is being judged. From the very beginning, accepted versions of decency, propriety, seemliness, good taste, and solid order are associated with the most abhorrent actions, including, most importantly, Totsky's sexual exploitation of Nastasya Filippovna (41–42; 8:36–37). Once again, a panoramic mapping of contemporary Russian society reveals no solid foundations or bonds, pointing the way to total collapse, while keeping open the possibility of equally total, miraculous salvation.

Aglaya herself proves to be attuned both to social disorder and to the hero's special position within it. At a clandestine rendezvous, she draws on a series of contemporary novelistic topoi and journalistic clichés to express her distaste for conventionally decorous marriage and for her privileged and sheltered life more generally. She tells Myshkin that, on the basis of his nobility of heart and generosity of ideas, she has chosen him as a "friend" with whom she would elope, change her "social position," learn more about the world, and dedicate herself to doing something "useful" (426; 8:356–58). Like a number of other characters on other occasions, Aglaya mistakes Myshkin for a kind of "democrat" committed, one way or another, to the struggle against the reign of social privilege, hierarchy, and tradition. Insofar as this is a misunderstanding, however, it is only partially so. Myshkin's ideals do reach far beyond the available horizons of social life; his intentions vis-à-vis that world in no way involve the quest for worldly comforts or success. Instead, at stake is a soteriological narrative, the invention of a genuine (national) community whose prefiguration appears in the protagonist's prehistory in the Swiss Alps. There, recovering from his illness, Myshkin befriends a weak and consumptive young woman, Marie, who had been seduced and abandoned by a French traveling salesman and had become an outcast in her home town. Eventually, he succeeds in bringing together a community of children around the innocent victim. An attempt to perform an analogous miracle—this time, on the significantly broader and more treacherous terrain of contemporary Russian (mainly St. Petersburg) society—makes up the kernel of the other plot line, connected to Nastasya Filippovna: to reconcile Russian society with its own innocent victim, who has turned vengefully against it.[76]

The lexical aura surrounding Nastasya Filippovna—the excluded element, which must be kept out of sight in order to sustain a vision of social decorum—invokes scenarios of transgressive, scandalous action and excessive force (43; 8:37). Without a foothold in social normativity, without faith in social conventions, and without hopes for her own eventual resocialization, she threatens some imponderable, unspeakable offense against propriety, something that might deal a decisive blow to the order that excludes her. Here, for example, is a passage describing the "extraordinary" woman from the perspective of her childhood seducer, whose marriage to Alexandra Epanchina she now intends to prevent:

> On the other hand, his experience and profound insight into things told Totsky very quickly and with extraordinary sureness that he now had to do with a being who was completely out of the ordinary, that this was precisely the sort of being who would not merely threaten, but would certainly act, and above all would decidedly stop at nothing, the more so as she valued decidedly nothing in the [social] world [*v svete*], so that it was even impossible to tempt her. Here, obviously, was something else, implying some heartfelt and soulful swill—like some sort of romantic indignation, God knows against whom or why, some insatiable feeling of contempt that leaps completely beyond measure—in short, something highly

ridiculous and inadmissible in decent society, something that was a sheer punishment from God for any decent man to encounter. (43; 8:37)

Worth noting here is the occasion on which Nastasya Filippovna threatens to unleash her violence: her abuser's anticipated marriage. Throughout the novel, in fact, Nastasya Filippovna reveals herself as a serial preventer of marriages: she makes it impossible for Totsky to marry Alexandra Epanchina, for Evgeniy Pavlovich to marry Aglaya, and finally, after having plotted to bring about a union between Aglaya and Myshkin, subverts it too, just as it is about to be realized. The power to unite and divide, the behind-the-scenes manipulation of the visible social world, images of excessive power derived from her transcendence vis-à-vis the symbolic order—all mark her position at the point of exception, left out of the social world yet perpetually constraining and shaping it. Only occasionally do we glimpse her direct, almost blinding appearance, often registering it as shock, scandal, coercion, and command. One of the most impressive manifestations of power takes place during a late exchange between Nastasya Filippovna and Aglaya in the presence of Myshkin himself, who helplessly watches the conversation deteriorate into a brawl. In the course of the confrontation, Nastasya Filippovna warns her counterpart: "Or if you like, my girl, right now... I'll or-der him, do you hear? I'll simply or-der him, and he will drop you at once and stay with me forever, and marry me, and you'll run home alone!" (571; 8:474). At the end of the scene, something like that order is in fact issued—indeed, turned into an act of physical coercion: Nastasya Filippovna seizes Myshkin at the threshold as he rushes out in pursuit of the offended Aglaya.

Thus, while in the figure of the youngest Epanchin daughter, the hero is confronted with the horizon of socialization, Nastasya Filippovna places him into a relationship with sovereign power, articulating absolute demands, subjecting him to a fateful command. To inquire into the precise thematization of the substantive order ventriloquized through the figure of the abject-sovereign heroine is to appreciate the extent to which it partakes of the Dostoevskian national imaginary as outlined in the previous section. Nastasya Filippovna ceaselessly "poses riddles," "leaps out of measure," acts eccentrically, frustrates expectations, offends common sensibilities. For the protagonist, she constitutes the main object of decipherment, parallel to his attempt (as a kind of foreigner) to decipher Russia itself: "It's hard to unpuzzle [*razgadat'*] new people in a new land" (228; 8:190). Her blindingly beautiful face, her magnetic, mysterious eyes, her scandalous behavior—all raise her to allegorical status, reinforced by her triangulated position between the forces of redemption represented by Myshkin and those of perdition embedded in his infernal double, Rogozhin. Read in light of this juxtaposition, the novel poses the classic national-allegorical question of the nation's "whither."[77] Meanwhile, in relation to Myshkin, the heroine plays a role functionally and thematically analogous to that of Polozova vis-à-vis Sanin: she issues orders, subjugates the hero, claims him for herself, bars him from properly personal, private fulfillment. What most clearly distinguishes Nastasya Filippovna from Polozova is that the power she exercises over the protagonist is drawn from her status as a social outcast who thereby sets the standard for inclusion that would be absolute.

Myshkin's characterization, then, relies on a dual social imaginary: one in which the protagonist is conceived as a pursuer of individuated purposes and desires (centering on Aglaya, like Sanin's on Gemma) and the other as the bearer of a transpersonal and opaque commitment to—or condition of being fatefully given over to—a sovereign power that resides beyond and works against, individuation as such (Polozova, Nastasya Filippovna). When Evgeniy Pavlovich—the voice of measured common sense in the novel—questions Myshkin about his choice during the final confrontation, the latter is unable to explain it. Evgeniy Pavlovich cannot understand how Myshkin could have betrayed Aglaya, the girl who trusted him and to whom he had practically been betrothed, for a woman he didn't even love. "She deserves compassion..." Evgeniy Pavlovich exclaims. "But for the sake of compassion and for the sake of her good pleasure, was it possible to disgrace this other, this lofty and pure girl, to humiliate her before *those* arrogant, before those hateful eyes. How far can compassion go, then?" (581; 8:482).

The question touches on the absolute stakes of the substantive imaginary here at play.[78] Myshkin's mode of orienting himself in his triangular relationship with Nastasya Filippovna and Aglaya involves the sacrifice of all accepted principles of socialization—propriety, decorum, convention, institution—to the community of total mutual love and understanding, formed around the figure of the innocent victim. "Oh, if Aglaya knew, knew everything," Myshkin protests, bemoaning the misunderstanding between the two women, "that is, absolutely everything.... Why can we never know everything about another person when it's necessary, when the person is to blame!" (583; 8: 484). The purveyor of commonsense sociability Evgeniy Pavlovich fails to grasp such a demand. And when Myshkin suggests that he loves both women, his judicious counterpart wonders: "With two different loves of some sort? That's interesting... the poor idiot" (584; 8:485). This final dismissal notwithstanding, Myshkin's claim that his decision to marry Nastasya Filippovna should mean "nothing" as far as the mutual relationship among members of the triangle are concerned presupposes an imaginary of an "intense association" that tolerates no exclusions and clearly resembles the scenario of affective community we find in Herzen's *Who Is to Blame?* (582–84; 8:483–85). What dislodges the protagonist from the path of personal happiness and social integration is thus doubly thematized: as the formidable figure of a woman made of sovereignty and abjection and as an alternative model of harmonious community—nonexclusive, egalitarian, and heartfelt. Not society but the nation, substantively conceived, functions here as the ultimate social-imaginary horizon: not harmonization of passions and accommodation of desires, but the absolute demands of a substantive bond.

4. Reenactment

Of all the texts considered in this chapter, Goncharov's last novel, *The Precipice* (*Obryv*), unfolds most explicitly against the generic horizon of the bildungsroman. Here we get an extended account of Boris Raisky's childhood and youth, of his search for a calling and a romantic match. Yet Raisky's developmental path disintegrates into a series of episodic and unsuccessful endeavors: at a career in the military, in painting, in civil service, and so on. When we meet him at the beginning of the novel, he is already thirty-five years old, a dilettante, a bachelor, in the midst of yet another unsuccessful attempt at courtship. The novel's grotesque projection of social immaturity upon biological middle age signals a tension within the paradigm of social self-realization. Nothing adds up here; everything constantly changes but basically stays the same. Episode follows episode, retracing again and again the path from enthusiasm to disappointment and from erotic infatuation to boredom.[79]

Less than a quarter of the way into the novel, Raisky moves from St. Petersburg to his estate, Malinovka, inhabited by his distant relatives, the young women Vera and Marfenka and their guardian great-aunt, Tatyana Markovna (mostly referred to as "Grandmother"). It is here that Raisky finally achieves a sense of broader belonging. The manner of this discovery, however, is rather unconventional, reminiscent of initiation into a mystery cult. Raisky witnesses a triangular drama that, at least on the surface, involves Vera's sexual transgression with the political exile Mark Volokhov and both Vera's and Grandmother's suffering in the aftermath. Raisky does not stay in Malinovka but, as always, moves on, leaves for Europe, yet:

> Nowhere, amidst that ardent artistic life, did he betray his family, his group. [...] He wanted to absorb this eternal beauty of nature and art, to become saturated by the spirit of stony tradition and carry it all back with him there, to his Malinovka. [...] At his back they always stood there, ar-

dently beckoning—those three figures: his Vera, his Marfenka, and Grandmother. And behind them, drawing him even more powerfully, stood another gigantic figure, another magnificent "Grandmother"—Russia.[80]

The transfer of the novel's action from the imperial capital to the deep countryside, where alone something truly significant can happen, highlights the divergence between the kind of national imaginary on which *The Precipice* relies and the modernizing tendencies of the national bildungsroman. As the locus of essential Russianness, Malinovka is decidedly archaic; not, like Oblomovka in *Oblomov*, "backward," not superannuated, but rather primordial, a kind of imagined antiquity, accruing substantive social imaginaries and tragic plots. With this in mind, we can appreciate the importance of the otherwise minor figure of the classicist Kozlov, Raisky's old university friend who lives near Grandmother's estate and by the end of the novel moves in with her permanently. Kozlov emerges as a kind of scholarly spokesman for Malinovka, passionately articulating his faith in the coming "simplification":

> All this rubbish and pettiness into which modern man has been scattered will disappear. [...] The hands of fate will collect and fuse these historical fragments into a single mass, and, with time, colossal figures will once again be formed from this mass; an even, integral life will once again flow forth, which later on will come to form a second antiquity. (128; 7: 208)

By the end of the novel, Raisky is convinced that his Malinovka has already produced such colossal figures and already serves as the site for such a second antiquity. "My God...!" he exclaims with amazement, "Who would have thought that in this quiet neck of the woods such drama, such characters might be encountered. How enormous and terrible is simple life in the nakedness of its truth" (371; 7:675).

Construed as the privileged site of national belonging, Malinovka brings together imaginaries of family, state, and nation to create a richly resonant figure of substance. The estate is ruled—like "a small kingdom, wisely, economically, meticulously, but despotically and on feudal principles" (50; 7:58)—by the formidable matriarch Grandmother. The novel dwells on her methods of rule at length. We are told, for example, that she does not recognize official documents, claiming that "all the acts, records and documents were written on her conscience" (50; 7:58). When it comes to servants, she neither orders nor requests but "advises" that something be done. Yet she considers social roles to be set in stone and unalterable: "A butler, a footman, a servant, a housegirl—all these remained forever, despite everything [i.e., progress, enlightened ideas], a butler, a footman, a servant, and a housegirl" (52; 7:62). At times, she resembles a woman on one of the antique portraits hanging "in the gallery of ancestors"—and her appearance occasionally carries with it the air of "something powerful, dominating, proud" (56; 7:70).

Grandmother's attitude to local authorities deserves our attention as well. We learn that she considers every order issuing from them "an unlawful compulsion," refuses to pay fees, and is deaf to all discussions of "the common good" (57; 7:71). Grandmother's Malinovka-Russia is thus sharply distinguished from the bureaucratic machinery of the state and constructed as its patriarchal (or, as it happens, matriarchal) alternative: direct, practical rule oriented toward the well-being of the ruled and guided by instinctive adherence to custom. Invoking Weber's well-known classification, we can say that her rule is neither rational-bureaucratic nor charismatic, but rather traditional, based on the presumed authority of the immemorial past and symbolically reinforced by the antique portraits of ancestors, whom she occasionally resembles.[81]

At three points in the novel, the possibility of disobeying Grandmother is raised, with increasing seriousness. The first such episode involves Raisky's refusal of her generous offer to smoke in his room at night. After a short exchange, Grandmother's permission turns into a command, in response to which Raisky blows out the candle, signaling the end of the discussion. Getting into bed, Grandmother marvels: "How eccentric he is. He doesn't even obey Grandmother! What a strange person!" (135; 7:221). A more extended and, from the perspective of the novel's overall problematic, more pertinent episode treats a chaste rendezvous between the innocent younger sister Marfen'ka and her virtuous suitor, Vikent'ev. Unwittingly transgressing against tradition, the young man attempts to propose marriage directly to Marfen'ka, only to be rebutted by the scandalized girl, who is unable to imagine having such a conversation without Grandmother's knowledge. In the course of the brief exchange between them, Grandmother is mentioned nearly twenty times—all in connection with the question of her permission, approval, and forgiveness (267–70; 7:475–80).

Though in a comic key, the conversation touches on an important motif in the novel, that of sexuality as a dangerous force, threatening the overthrow of basic ethical-ontological norms. We have before us, moreover, the familiar pattern of authoritative mediation, the presence-even-in-absence of an imposing figure with power to unite or separate. This early episode anticipates what is probably the decisive scene of the novel, where Marfen'ka's older and more independent-minded sister Vera succumbs to her illicit passion for the "nihilist" Volokhov. Enveloped in an aura of terms such as "duty," "rules," "principles," "authority," and so on, Grandmother haunts the exchange between the more mature lovers as well. At one point, Volokhov suggests that they leave the environs of Malinovka together, mocking Vera for being afraid of Grandmother. Vera acknowledges that she is afraid, not, to be sure of Grandmother's rage, but of her suffering: "Oh no, she would permit it and what's more she would bless us, but she would die of grief! That's what I am afraid of!" (340; 7:614).

The statement distinguishes the dynamic of interdiction operative here from similar patterns within both charismatic and bureaucratic models of authority. Charismatic power—as with Pechorin or Raskolnikov, Saks or Polozova, Volodya's father or Nastasya Filippovna—is based on transcendent, near-miraculous exercise of brute, excessive force or equally unaccounted magnanimity, the capacity to dispose of lives, to unite or separate despotically, on the basis of personal majesty alone. Bureaucratic authority—as in the case of the elder Aduev, Kalinovich, or Karenin—relies on the imaginary of an impersonal ("impartial") rational order in the name of which the authoritative agent is assumed to speak and act. Grandmother's traditional rule, meanwhile, relies neither on reason nor on force but on the "personal loyalty" of the ruled.[82] Grandmother's "no" is lodged firmly in Vera's own heart, echoing Raisky's insight that the matriarch's "'despotism' is built on her tender, motherly sympathy, her tireless concern for the happiness of her beloved orphans" (243; 7: 430). Authority here is based on "principles of substantive ethical common sense" (Weber), which presumes the recognition of a basic commonality between the ruler and the ruled: both belong to the immemorial substantive tradition of togetherness. "Those subject to [traditional authority]," writes Weber, "are hence still members ['associates,' or 'fellows'—*Genossen*] of the group and not subjects."[83]

The novel's pivotal development introduces a further twist into the substantive reciprocity between Grandmother and Vera. Vera's sexual transgression turns out to be a reenactment of Grandmother's own similar act, committed many years ago. Transgression turns out to be constitutive of the substance itself, and, in the figure of Vera, comes back to haunt it. The haunting manifests itself in the extended descriptions of matriarch's grief in the aftermath of her ward's trespass:

> [Grandmother] opened the doors with her foot, proceeded to walk through all the rooms and the corridors, descended into the garden and kept on walking; it was as if a bronze monument had risen from its pedestal and had moved looking at no one and nothing. [...] It was as if it were not she who was striding there but one being carried by some external force. (367–68; 8:667)

Like the Bronze Horseman, only in reverse, at the decisive moment in the text, Grandmother finds herself between living woman and statue, the point at which substance crystallizes into an individual. The external force carrying her through Malinovka is the destiny of the community for which she is responsible and which she represents. The fate of the community is here inscribed on the body of the ruler, whose status as such now becomes explicit. Again and again, these dramatic passages, focalized through awestruck Raisky, call Grandmother a "tsaritsa," an "empress of sorrow," linked as if in a direct line of descent to countless precedents in world (but especially Russian) history: "And as if alive, the shades of other great suffering women came crowding around [Raisky]: of Russian [*tsaritsy*], forced by their husbands' will to become nuns but retaining their spirit and power even in their cells; and other [*tsaritsy*] who at fateful moments had stood at the head of their kingdom and saved it" (368; 7:669).[84]

Vera's act, then, sets substance itself in motion, and in this she differs starkly from the novel's main, or framing, protagonist, Raisky. In fact, in Vera and Raisky, the novel juxtaposes two imaginaries of individuality. One, pertaining to the hero of the failing bildungsroman, can be understood as aggregative in principle, atomistic, but incapable of projecting any of the standard sociotopic scenarios of cohesion. Raisky himself is writing just such a novel. He has collected a wealth of material: character portraits, landscape descriptions, scenes, conversations; but he is unable to make a whole. The novel within the novel reflects back on the protagonist himself: the world to which he contributes his disjointed pursuits does not contain providential guarantees. We are as far as possible from the ideal-typical model according to which it is sufficient for the individual simply to be himself or herself in order for things around them to work out for the best. Hence, Kozlov's—and with him, the novel's—yearning for holistic antiquity.

Vera's story presents a different scenario—not of individuality taken for granted, but of individuation as a problem. In other words, Vera inhabits the world—the substantive, traditional world of Malinovka as an archaic family-polity-nation—in which her private affairs are not merely her own. What she does pertains not only to her personal happiness or unhappiness but to the essential makeup of the order as a whole. She not only acts but also *enacts*, brings into visibility a deed concealed as it were since the creation of the world, Grandmother's "original sin." Her transgression reawakens an original imbalance in substance.

By contrast with rootless Raisky's harmless meandering, rooted Vera's ostensibly personal choice threatens to lay waste to the entire realm:

> [Grandmother's] kingdom was falling; her house was becoming empty. [...] She was wandering alone through the ruins. [...] The spirit of peace, pride and prosperity had disappeared from the happy nook. She saw a waking dream—a terrible dream which she later related to Raisky—how her kingdom was falling to pieces and an abomination of desolation would take its place in the near future. (369–71; 7:670–73)

By heightening the stakes of Vera's act well out of the range of realist conventions, such passages emphasize the substantive nature of her guilt, positing a body politic so "intensely associated" that the act of self-assertion triggers within the association a far-reaching disturbance.[85] Vera's imponderable link to Grandmother is thus enacted in the ambiguity of her "fall." Her transgressive act is an act of her individual will, but it is also, at the same time, the vehicle for the staging of the power of the communal. The act is prepared by an extended involvement with the carrier of radical modernity, Volokhov, yet it awakens the ancestral past. It is a single event, an episode of an individual's life, but it is also a reenactment of a prior event—the original "fall" of Grandmother herself. The national time that links Vera to Grandmother is, despite the young woman's modern ideas and independent habits, not progressive and developmental, but prefigurative.

In concluding, the novel leaves behind its dramatic language and plot and tells of Vera's gradual recovery, hinting at her eventual marriage to the landowner-industrialist Tushin. Tushin easily overlooks her downfall, and she is promised (if not quite granted) generically standard domestic happiness. Yet the overwhelming focus and symbolic weight of the narrative rests on the tragic Vera-Volokhov-Grandmother triangle, on the scene of transgression, capable of illuminating the true nature of the offended order and of making it tremble. Vera's affair with Volokhov, then, is doubly coded. It constitutes one episode among others in a long life, an act to which the social world finds a way to adjust. But it also marks a decisive moment of truth, revealing once and for all that the bonds between the individual and the (national) community are indissoluble and interior to both.

The final sentences of the novel, describing Raisky's sojourn in Europe, accumulate names of "intense association" in a kind of crescendo, taking us from "family," to "group," to "nation"—all localized in the deep countryside of Malinovka, embodied in the towering figure of Grandmother and conceived within the parameters of traditional political rule. The image of this "deep nation" emerges as an effect of a drama of individuation: a free act, the consequences of which highlight the self-asserting individual's rootedness in substance. Unsatisfied with novelistic aggregation of episodes and scenes, Raisky yearns for a unifying "drama" or "tragedy" and finds it at last in the story of Vera's trespass, Grandmother's grief, and their reconciliation. The story does not allow him to discover, as a national bildungsroman might, the proper purpose of his life. Rather, by witnessing the drama of Malinovka as the site in which the major anxieties of individuation are staged and pacified, Raisky discovers what it means to have roots. The final words of the novel assert that—though by no means actually show how—such a discovery can allow the hero to stay on his meandering course without falling into superfluity and alienation. The upheaval of Malinkovka has at least afforded him a glimpse of what true belonging to a national community might look like, an insight that he finds both fearsome and sustaining.

* * *

Scenarios of *mobilization*, *amalgam*, *spell*, and *reenactment* stage the nation within the horizon of a distinctive social imaginary, in which individuals make up national communities not through social aggregation but through political belonging. Central here, in others words, is not the tendentially horizontal relationships of individuals to each other unfolding within the parameters of one or another civil society sociotope, but a starkly binary relationship of individuals to the figure of the sovereign embodying a substance. Such binarism does not preclude or replace more dispersed forms of sociality, but rather *deforms* them, imposes its exigencies on the represented social field: triangulates romantic affinities, transfixes narrative attention, predetermines outcomes of social interactions, and so on. And it is on these deformations that the central dramatic interest of these texts depends.

By contrast with Anderson's chronotopes of the nation—linear, progressive time and homogeneous, empty space—we therefore find projections of time and space, coagulating around emphatically construed figures of authority. Authority does not accrue to such figures in accordance with accepted social conventions (we only need to think of the "kept woman" Nastasya Filippovna, or the kopekless former student and murderer Raskolnikov) but due to their capacity for embodying the nation substantively construed. In chronotopic terms, such authority tends to anchor moments of temporal recursion and spatial magnetism. Temporal recursion characterizes narratives that cast the protagonist's present as fatefully haunted by the grievous past or the imperative future. Thus, we follow protagonists, often at the moment of peak self-assertion, overtaken, brought low, *claimed* by a hostile (national) fate or a forgone (national) conclusion. Whether the nation's temporal center of gravity is located with the primordial past or the compulsory future, the individual's trajectory invariably experiences its ruinous-redemptive pull.

In spatial terms, too, our national-substantive scripts depend on the revelation of the center's proximity (or even internality) to the individual, a center of immense gravity that threatens to absorb all personal purposes and pursuits. The city and the countryside, capital and periphery, home country and abroad, geocultural diversity and simultaneity still constitute a kind of background spatial imaginary of these texts. But the shape that stands out against this background suggests that the center is in fact everywhere or, rather, that it is always there wherever individuation is taking place. This paradoxical construal of the mobile center transpires at the point of interference between the national and the dynastic-religious conceptions of community: thoroughly secularized, indifferent space permits any segment of it to be invested with charismatic prestige. Whether the basis of that prestige is thematized as despotic modernization, the substratum of the people, psychosexual bewitchment, or traditional rule—it comes into view in the scenario of a heightened encounter with a national substance akin to, and rhetorically conflated with, those of the family and the state: instances of "intense association," in relation to which no externality can, for better or for worse, be indefinitely sustained.

Précis

[CHAPTER FIVE]

Poetics and Politics
in Russian Realism

Tragic Affinities

Early in Sophocles's *Antigone*, during a speech in which he proclaims himself ruler of Thebes and forbids the burial of Polyneices, Creon sets the discursive ground for his subsequent clash with Antigone over the proper application of the word *philos* ("friend," "relation," "dear one"). He addresses the chorus as follows:

> A man who rules a state
> And will not steer the wisest course,
> But is afraid, and says not what he thinks,
> That man is worthless; and if any holds
> A friend [*philon*] of more account than his own city,
> I scorn him; for if I should see destruction
> Threatening the safety of my citizens,
> I would not hold my peace, nor would I count
> That man my friend [*philon*] who was my country's foe,
> Zeus be my witness. For be sure of this:
> It is the city that protects us all;
> She bears us through the storm; only when she
> Rides safe and sound can we make loyal friends [*philous*].[1]

At issue in the correct use of *philia* is the question of what constitutes the ultimate locus of human togetherness. *Antigone* presents us with two competing visions: one based on belonging to the city (*polis*); the other on belonging to the family, or kin. Antigone claims that her sisterly duty is to Polyneices, her *philos* in the sense of kinsman. Creon counters that true *philia* can be found only among loyal citizens of the city/state. This contestation itself—the possibility that *philia* could name an intense bond among members of more than one type of collectivity—reorients the term from describing the *what* of a given community to designating its *how*, not the institutional form it takes but the type of connectedness that organizes it, its basic social imaginary. *Philia* can be found wherever a specific relationship between the individual and the community (a state, a family, a tribe, a nation, a religious group, etc.) obtains, a relationship in which the separation between them is only provisional and in which the sublime sight of the individual's reabsorption into the collective solicits ambivalent acclamation. The individual thus becomes the site of the community's encounter with itself.[2]

In *Antigone*, family kinship and *polis* meet and struggle on the social-imaginary terrain of *philia*. Since the contemporary association between kinship and *philia* is standard, Creon's is the more surprising use of the term.[3] From his point of view, to act by driving a wedge between the categories of "loved one" and "city," to assert the existence of an exigent bond independent of the state, is to undermine the very foundations of political order. Creon annexes the concept of *philia* for the *polis* in the context of a *state of exception*: a war—partly a civil, fratricidal one—has just concluded; a new ruler has just ascended. War, royal fratricide, and interregnum, all endow the problem of political order with special urgency; Antigone's deliberately "private," kinship-centric act is thus emplotted as a crime against the state. It is not opposed, as it might be in a novel, by the acts of other individuals pursuing their similarly personal interests and goals, but by the violent injunction against all interests other than those of the polity itself.

The conflation of *polis* with *philia*—still striking in *Antigone*—becomes commonplace in patriarchalist justifications of monarchical power. We see this in Belinsky's Hegel-inspired fusion of the two substantive unities of the family and the state: "Spiritual kinship [within the state] is sacred for the very reason that it derives from that of flesh and blood. In the same way, for the same reason, the state is a rational and therefore a sacred phenomenon because its beginnings are found in the natural-familial kinship of a people."[4] The analogy produces and relies on a common denominator, the social imaginary of an intense, primordial, and indissoluble bond. Following Hegel, who is himself inspired by Sophocles, Belinsky calls this bond "substance." It is that horizon of togetherness against which individuation transpires as tragedy.

Tragedy makes *philia* visible as the site of a basic antagonism (exclusion and instability), in which a certain substance, an "intense association," is posited as that in relation to which all externality is hostile. Such antagonism produces the merely private person as the enemy. Or, put another way, such antagonism turns the particular as such—individual desires, pursuits, and so on—into a threat to the reigning order of things. As an enemy and a threat to the substantive or political grouping, the individual—or rather that in the individual which remains merely private, impossible to universalize (passion, impulse, self-assertion, transgression, etc.)—becomes a matter of essential concern to the order itself. We find, in other words, a profound entanglement between the individual and the *philial* community, such that the individual's separateness, her constitutive exclusion, is precisely what makes her matter urgently to the order that now turns out to be vulnerable, at the level of its very foundation, to that private individual's statements and deeds.

Something like this notion of tragic individuation underpins much theorizing about the genre, philosophical and philological alike. Nietzsche formulates this principle with characteristic provocativeness in *The Birth of Tragedy*: "The Greeks simply *could* not suffer individuals on the tragic stage."[5] This claim, referring to the ineluctability of the chorus in early Attic tragedy, receives a more scholarly gloss from the classicist Jean-Pierre Vernant: "Neither the individual nor his internal life had acquired enough consistency and autonomy to make the subject the center of the decision from which his actions were believed to emanate. Cut off from his familial, civic and religious roots the individual was nothing; he did not find himself alone, he ceased to exist."[6] Vernant's account of the logic of tragic action relies on a fundamental distinction—and convergence—between the hero's *ethos*, his explicitly presented and socially acknowledged individual character, and "his" *daemon*, his deep ontological entanglement in the destiny of a city or a clan. The hero's actions are to be understood on both of these levels at once: agential, self-motivated, conscious on the one hand, and imponderably caused, blindly consequential on the other. Thus understood, the tragic hero appears to be both "broader" than the novelistic individual and, at the same time, less concentrated, more diffuse. The boundaries of the tragic individual are blurry; she "shades" into the community and "echoes" through to its foundational past.

The tragic individual thus bears an affinity for the figure of the sovereign, in whom the body politic acquires human shape. This mixture of the human-particular and the universal-political is rife with tragic explosiveness. In an appendix to a recent intervention on sovereignty and tragedy, the classicist Glenn Most supplies a list of forty-seven speaking kings in thirty-three extant Attic tragedies. Most's point: that tragedy insistently stages the self-willed actions of monarchs, unaware of the constraints under which they act. "As soon as [the king] begins to make his decision about the present," Most writes, "it is discovered that some powerful, maleficent force from the distant past—an oracle, a curse, a crime—is reaching inescapably into that present to determine his choices and their outcomes in a way that makes a mockery of his human freedom."[7] An oracle, a curse, a crime, we might add, that paradigmatically involve members of the family and the ruling house—founders and ancestors—who had at some point in the more or less immemorial past introduced an imbalance in the ontological-political order, of which the transgressing sovereign of the unfolding tragedy is now the instantiation.

Most explains the transhistorical appeal of Attic tragedy, as well as the survival of the genre itself, by invoking the temptation, felt by individuals ancient and modern alike, of unconstrained power and unmediated control.[8] This notion of tragic action as a response to the anthropologically constant desire for, and fear of, ungovernable individuality guides a prominent strain of scholarship on the genre. What contributors to this interpretative tradition tend more or less tacitly to assume is the historical universality of the freestanding individual. This assumption, in turn, naturally permits genre designations like "tragic realism," in which "tragic" stands for what is universally human (typically, the overweening but vulnerable individual), while "realism" names the particular, historically conditioned medium within which that universal experience plays out.[9]

Yet as we have glimpsed in Nietzsche and Vernant, an equally formidable tradition of thought on tragedy militates against such universalism.[10] Particularly pertinent in our context is Nancy Armstrong and Leonard Tennenhouse's recent discussion of the notions of sovereignty and individuality in early modern England. Here, the authors insist that "the protagonists of Jacobean tragedy have little if anything to do with the individual that serves as the metaphysical envelope for the modern 'self,' 'consciousness,' or 'immaterial spirit,' except insofar as they gave Shakespeare occasion to imagine a world stripped of the metaphysical hierarchy essential to its form."[11] Underpinning their narrative is the historical trajectory from tragic to novelistic imaginaries of individuality: from the individual as a problem, a crisis in the onto-political order of the world, to the individual as an a priori presupposition, the minimal unit of social life.

This historicist approach alerts us to the dividing line between (tragic) sovereignty and (novelistic) individuality, no matter how acquisitive, ruthless, and overweening the latter might be. In our terms, the distinction can be drawn with reference to the corresponding social imaginaries that delineate and define the two categories: while the destiny of the sovereign correlates directly with the cosmic-political order, the path of the individual presupposes the emergent notion of society as an aggregate of self-standing units. In tragedy, the acts of the sovereign—or, more broadly, acts within the zone of sovereignty—threaten to undermine metaphysical hierarchy and bring about the (partial, temporary) collapse of the polity as a whole. The acts of an individual (in the novel) can encroach upon another individual or transgress against social norms, but the normative framework as such stays more or less intact.

Thus understood, tragedy's link to the problematics of sovereignty signals an affinity for matters of the state, made visible at the moment of peril in its capacity as the locus of total belonging, charismatic violence, and spectacular scenarios of power—the state, in other words, precisely in its sovereign, rather than institutional or procedural, mode. It is in this spirit that Foucault speaks of the "tragic harshness of the state," which manifests itself in a situation of crisis and constitutes "a particular way for the sovereign to demonstrate in the most striking way possible, the irruption of *raison d'État* and its prevalence over legitimacy."[12] The state's manifestation of the violence underpinning lawful order is, in Foucault's view, the paradigmatic subject matter of tragedy, ancient, Renaissance, and neoclassical: "Just as in politics *raison d'État* manifests itself in a kind of theatricality, so [tragic] theatre is organized around the representation of the *raison d'État* in its dramatic, intense, and violent form of the *coup d'État*."[13]

The tragedy of politics is here at the center of Foucault's analysis of state power. The politics of tragedy, conversely, occupies Franco Moretti in his essay "The Moment of Truth." Reflecting on the prevalence of modern tragedy in Germany and Scandinavian countries by contrast with its paucity in such "strongholds of the novel" as England and France, Moretti suggests that "the symbolic power of tragic form is inversely proportional to the real power of the state. When the state is stable and strong, a national culture does not have to bother about it, and it evolves in a fundamentally unpolitical fashion: whence the anti-heroic conventions of the novelistic worldview, one of the greatest stabilizing factors of Modernity."[14] Moretti's hypothesis—that tragic discourse is indexed to the prevalence, within a given culture, of a certain modality of state power—appears fruitful. My emphasis on modality here has to do with the basic ambiguity in the concept of "strength" when applied to the state. The state may be "strong" in the sense of aggressively interventionalist and repressive, or it may be "strong" enough to obviate the need for such interventions, to appear gentle and weak. It is this latter, far-reaching, and mostly noncoercive state that, as we have discussed with reference to Gramsci in chapter 1, creates the conditions for a relatively apolitical culture and the novel as its representative form. Conversely, tragedy is likely to flourish in cultural contexts in which the state is conspicuous and momentous.

With this we come in a sense full circle. Russian culture in the age of realism was produced and received in contexts systemically shaped by strict censorship, precipitant journal closures, periodic arrests and imprisonments of pivotal figures within the publishing world, and so on. At the same time, individual writers and readers came to know the state intimately, at times as a kind of elementary force rife with peripety (*Naturgewalt*, *fatum*), shaping, reshaping, making, and unmaking their personal biographies. Such sovereign mediation of culture was of course not as commonplace as in the previous century of court drama and the laudatory ode, but it was therefore all the more salient in the age of the prose tale and the novel, when private life had become both the object of literary representation and the site of its reception. Thus, if the hypothesis linking tragedy to the prominence of sovereign power in the cultural domain stands, we should find elements of tragic sociality—understood as a historically variable but up to a point persistent manner of imagining human togetherness through the construction of character, plot, and affect—playing prominent structuring roles in Russian realist texts. Then, Belinsky's reconciliation-period articles will have turned out both symptomatic and prescient. Symptomatic, because they present us with an image of a cultural producer urgently preoccupied with the figure of the autocratic state while formulating an idiosyncratic vision of the tragic novel as the genre of contemporary actuality par excellence. Prescient, because, as we have already seen and as we shall see in greater detail in what follows, many prominent realist (and protorealist) Russian texts would go on to stage the reduction of everyday social interactions to the *philial* paradoxes of absolute (non)belonging and sovereign mediation, and, in the process, to introduce elements traditionally associated with tragic character (*ethos*), plot (*mythos*), and affect (*pathos*) into the fabric of realist narrative about contemporary social life. Similarly apt again is Pavel Annenkov's suggestion that Russian literature has been shaped by a tendency toward an antique "simplification" of social conditions, the erasure of a boundary between the political and the private. As members of the educated elite, these critics and others could not fail to be attuned to the cultural prominence of the state—pregnant with dramatic possibilities—as the imaginary locus of universal belonging and sovereign coercion both.

What comes next, then, is an attempt to describe some of the distinctive formal features through which the resulting hybrid social imaginary manifests itself in the corpus of Russian realist texts discussed in the previous chapters. For this task, neither the plain universalism that asserts tragedy's transhistorical capacity to chastise individualist overreach, nor the strict historicism that firmly fixes genres and forms to "endemic" historical moments appears adequate. Rather, what is required is a poetics attuned to the tensions arising from the persistence, or reemergence, of historically distant genres, forms, and social imaginaries within individual texts and literary movements alike, a poetics, in other words, that approaches literary texts as historically stratified, containing and often uncomfortably mixing differently oriented visions of human togetherness.[15]

Ethos (Sovereignty Effects)

Realist fiction—Western European and Russian alike—tends to exclude, or at least to relegate to the margins, direct and explicit representations of political rule. Most of the cases we have considered in the previous chapters follow this trend. Several counterexamples from the 1830s, however, are illuminating. Pushkin's *Bronze Horseman* culminates with the confrontation between Eugene and the statue of the emperor, whose violent burst into the diegetic present during the scene of the chase exposes the fundamental duality of sovereign power traced by Kantorowicz in *The King's Two Bodies*. In the image of the enraged Horseman galloping through the night we have stately order irrupting into—and revealing itself to be—violence. The emperor's "odic" body politic rushes down from the pedestal and into Eugene's "novelistic" world, acquiring the characteristics and exuding the affects of a body natural. Something similar happens in *The Captain's Daughter* on a number of levels at once. Pugachev's claims to the throne pose a fundamental question: To which natural body does the political body adhere? The puzzle is repeatedly enacted in the text, as the two competing rulers appear to the protagonists first in "natural" and then in "political" guises (Pugachev as a simple Cossack guide and as Peter III, Catherine as a kindly lady in the garden and as the majestic empress). The proliferating crises of rule in *The Captain's Daughter* signal the subjection of the private lives of their protagonists—the average people that populate realist fiction—to sovereign mediation. We might say that both Eugene and Grinev unwittingly stray into, stumble upon—or realize they have all along inhabited—the zone of sovereignty that reroutes their stories and reshapes their lives.

By "zone of sovereignty" I mean a semantic space—created in the accrual of textual indices—in which the narrative's more standard realist preoccupations with private pursuits undergo a stark deformation under the influence of substantive social imaginaries. In the more straightforward cases just recalled, a hero or heroine comes into literal proximity with representatives of state power—a point at which a new, political, dimension of the character and its destiny comes to light. Eugene's confrontation with the czar supplants and retrospectively recodes his dreams of personal happiness; the relationship between Masha and Grinev experiences the warping effects of absolute power; the arrival of the Government Inspector/Impostor (re)organizes the lives of the town's officials; Andriy's deadly subjection to his father's power reinterprets his romantic attachment as a political crime and, in the same move, enacts the paradigmatic prerogative of the sovereign, derived by Giorgio Agamben from the father's right over the life of his son in Roman law; and so on. In these more explicit cases, the zone of sovereignty is directly associated with the state of exception: a disaster, a war, rampant government corruption, threatening the social order as a whole. Under such conditions, individuality becomes unsustainable as a premise and is replaced by the problem of individuation: a deep and characteristically tragic enchantment with, and skepticism about, the freestanding self.

Within a more entrenched realist hermeneutic, still more deeply committed to the representation of ordinary life, the problematics of sovereignty undergo a more thorough "censorship" at the level of genre and style. Few sovereigns remain to be acclaimed or provoked (of course *War and Peace* immediately comes to mind as an exception). Yet as we have seen, the discourse of sovereignty remains detectable and continues to play an active (de-)formative role vis-à-vis the more standard novelistic material it inhabits. Zones of sovereignty in Russian realism coalesce out of realist "sovereignty effects" that, at pivotal points in the narratives, set ostensibly ordinary characters apart and endow them with an aura of wonder and dread. This aura, in turn, accrues to them due to their contact with one or another figuration of *philial* order: the state, the (state-as-)family, the (state-as-)nation. In this section, I examine three such sovereignty effects—"rhetorical heightening" in the discourse surrounding a central character; "scenarios of power" in which the character is involved, or to which he or she is subjected; and the character's "occulting," its relegation to a transcendent, mystical, or mystified realm vis-à-vis represented social space—all of which rely on and at the same time register a disturbance in the depository of standard realist devices and motifs.

1. RHETORICAL HEIGHTENING

A shift in stylistic register often signals a character's entry into the zone of sovereignty, which is frequently also the zone of his or her demise. Such moments of rhetorical heightening lift the individual out of the narrowly private domain, endowing his or her strivings and frustrations with more than individual stakes. This turns out to be a rather cumbersome procedure at times, capturing the attention of contemporaries and provoking censure on aesthetic grounds. These moments of awkwardness mark the generic hybridity of the texts, the unease within which the realist and the tragic are sutured together, leaving a visible scar. Two well-known cases of the protagonist's incongruous heightening should be mentioned at the outset: the sudden reversal in the characterization of Eugene Onegin in chapter 8 of Pushkin's novel in verse and a similarly unexpected reevaluation of Rudin in Turgenev's novel.

Onegin's rehabilitation is set in an exchange between a hypothetical member of the public and the embodied narrator. At the sight of Onegin, the nameless socialite pronounces a judgment, echoing Tatyana's earlier suspicion that he is a "mere parody" of Western literary prototypes:

> Is he the same, or is he learning?
> Or does he play the outcast still?
> In what new guise is he returning?
> What role does he intend to fill?
> Child Harold? Melmoth for a while?
> Cosmopolite? A Slavophile?
> A Quaker? Bigot?—might one ask?
> Or will he sport some other mask?[16]

The tirade goes on until the narrator cuts it short:

> But why on earth does he inspire
> So harsh and negative a view?
> Is it because we never tire
> Of censuring what others do
> Because an ardent spirit's darling
> Appears absurd or overbearing
> From where the smug and worthless sit?
> Because the dull are cramped wit?
> Because we take mere talk for action,
> And malice rules a petty mind?
> Because in trite the solemn find
> A cause for solemn satisfaction,
> And mediocrity alone
> Is what we like and call our own?[17]

In the previous chapter, Tatyana's suspicions of Onegin's stylized persona meet with the narrator's confirmation and approval. But in these new verses, the judgment is contemptuously dismissed. Here, Onegin is elevated over the social world he inhabits. Whatever his flaws may be, he is not to be judged in the gossipy tones of social mores and conventions. More surprisingly still, Onegin is now endowed with an "ardent spirit's daring"—certainly an odd way of describing the meandering, jaded protagonist of the first seven chapters.[18] At stake, as we saw in chapter 3, are not merely passionate feelings but a whole sentimental predicament, rife with political overtones. By entering into a triangular relationship with Tatyana and the nameless General to whom she now "belongs," Onegin becomes exposed to sovereign mediation coded in sentimental language.

The sound of the General's clinking spurs, the image of heavenly thunder, and the hero's conclusive paralysis—all join together to project the elevated predicament of subjection to a tragic fate.

We have already touched on rhetorical heightening in *Rudin*. Here again, critics were puzzled by a tonal change, signaling, about three-quarters into the novel, a reversal of judgment and, in the end, a comprehensive rehabilitation of the protagonist. To recall Northrop Frye's well-known classification, we seem to move here from a low-mimetic to a high-mimetic mode, from a realist, novelistic protagonist whose qualities don't exceed those of the social average to the tragic hero who, while subject to human frailty, nevertheless rises above his social milieu.[19] The notion that Bakunin's imprisonment may have had something to do with the novel's shift in attitude toward the hero, though impossible to verify, illuminates a general predicament in which such a text as *Rudin* would be produced and received: the need to read and write members of the educated elite as both individuals in society and subjects of the monarch, with relatively petty stakes accruing to the former position and significantly higher (sometimes life-and-death) ones to the latter.

Somewhere halfway between *Onegin* and *Rudin*—both chronologically and generically—stands Herzen's *Who Is to Blame?* Here, sentimentality and politics are equally explicit in their alliance against the vapid world of social aggregation. Once again, however, we are confronted with the problem of "two heroes." In an otherwise enthusiastic review of the novel, Belinsky criticizes Herzen for his failure consistently to observe the requirements of "realist" characterization. According to Belinsky, the protagonist appears to us in part 1 of the novel in the appropriately prosaic, ironized guise of a young man whose upbringing and education have not prepared him for useful activity in contemporary Russia. In part 2, however, Beltov reappears as a kind of Pechorin-like higher being, bound to remain inactive in a drab and stagnant world that does not deserve him. Belinsky hints at the reasons for this change: Beltov needed to be lifted up into a higher register in order to prepare him for the encounter with the spiritually superior Lyuba.[20] This insight, in turn, proves consistent with the reading of the text as a hybrid of two social imaginaries: the vision of an egoistically fragmented social world in part 1, and the horizon of philial sentimental community as an alternative *polis* in part 2. Framed in this way, the rhetorical heightening of the protagonist coincides with his entry into the "zone of sovereignty," the zone he had sought from the beginning, where the paradoxes of the body politic—in this case, the failure to harmonize the fulfillment of each with the fulfillment of all—dramatically play out. The heightened language now converging on Beltov serves to clarify the meaning of his intrusion into the Krutsifersky household. We are not dealing here with a case of toxic boredom but with an attempt to divert a thwarted political project into the domain of intimate life. The Romantic provenance of this elevated language, with its projection of abstract, metaphysical alienation, is here endowed with concrete content. This content is not so much *social* in character, not a matter of social position and upbringing, which, as Belinsky implied, need not induce overwrought rhetoric. Rather, the language of Romantic alienation invokes here a *political* horizon, which, as such, brings with it the grandiloquence of universality, an aura of proximity to where the most urgent dramas of human togetherness play out. It is within this horizon that the novel reconstitutes Beltov as the more-than-individual protagonist of what the narrator himself calls a "modern tragedy."[21]

More jarring perhaps than any of the cases we have considered so far is the labored recoding of "Kalinovich" in part 4 of *One Thousand Souls*. Again, critics were taken aback by the evident incompatibility between the two versions of the protagonist: a pedestrian parvenu throughout and a larger-than-life statesman at the end. To recognize that the two are actually one is to appreciate the "constructive function" of the two-bodies paradigm of sovereignty vis-à-vis the text as a whole, to see how the tragic paradoxes of violence and law, legitimacy and impostorship deform the novelistic material cathected on conflicts between the intimate and the social, between conscience and ambition. The stylistic price of this deformation proves high. The shift from the sober, ironic, at times coarse language of the first three parts to the melodramatic diction of part 4 is arresting. At one point, beset by the intrigues of his enemies, Kalinovich exclaims: "I feel clearly, I almost see that at this very moment, somewhere in the sky, by some mysterious twist of fate, a turning-point in my life is taking place. Whether for better or for worse, I don't know, but a terrible turning-point, terrible."[22] This supernatural attunement to the mysteries of fate places Kalinovich above the normative jurisdiction of society and, as it were, directly under the jurisdiction of the stars, in the place of the tragic ruler, mediating between the heavenly order of the divine and the political order of the human. The histrionic straining of the language signals the effort with which a broadly realist texture of the narrative accommodates visions of "substantive" protagonists not strictly limited by their psychosomatic boundaries but blending into, and internalizing, the political order as such.

Rhetorical heightening as a correlate of a character's ascent to the status of sovereign more-than-individuality also accompanies the goodhearted Tatyana Markovna's transformation into tragic-monumental Grandmother-Russia. Walking, statuelike, through her realm and hallucinating its desolation, Grandmother comes to embody the entire social order, concentrically embracing the family, the estate, the town of Malinovka, and the empire as a whole. This transformation takes place at the cost of a (once again, critically censured) shift in stylistic register, and it elevates the event of Vera's ostensibly personal "fall" to the status of a state of emergency, a danger to the polity as a whole. The sight of Grandmother's grief fills Raisky with "astonishment" and "dread" and convinces him that he is witnessing a "tragedy." We may recall here Raymond Williams's observation that tragic action zeroes in neither on what the protagonist does nor on what the protagonist undergoes, but rather on what transpires (in the community) *through* the protagonist.[23] The explosion of heightened rhetoric yielded by this conflation of person and polity once again pushes the text out of strictly realist confines, testifying to the discomfort with which "realist" discourse incorporates manifestations of a *philial* social imaginary, in which the body natural may at any moment be pervaded and set in motion by the political body.

2. SCENARIOS OF POWER

The affinity of these strategies of stylistic heightening with tragic poetics emerges most clearly in the bond between rhetorical heightening and fateful downfall. This script enacts the dynamics of sovereignty in two basic ways. A character might be raised to the position of sublime dignity and power only to be chastened, humbled, or unmasked. Such is the case with the statesman Kalinovich, whose omnipotence as a governor lasts but a short while; with Beltov, whose quest for an alternative community issues in misery and death; with the Government Inspector, who appears in the guise of the harebrained Khlestakov; with the exalted Grandmother, who turns out to have been the original "sinner" after all. Alternatively, a character might be dignified by—and be undone though—a confrontation with a figure endowed with supreme authority. We see this with Onegin, elevated in anticipation of an encounter with the General's sovereign "no!"; or with Rudin, whose rhetorical rehabilitation is indexed to his exile and finally to his futile and heroic death in political struggle. In each case, stylistic elevation signals a transition from prosaic-novelistic to tragic social imaginaries and a corresponding transformation of a self-enclosed individual, acting in an aggregative social space and in more or less linear biographical time, into one whose dramatic reversals of fortune register the ironies and contradictions of sovereign power and substantive belonging.

Rhetorical heightening marks the intrusion of another world into the world of the realist everyday. It thus produces and reflects a fundamental feature of what I have called the "zone of sovereignty"—its position at the point at which an unworldly entity (the political body) is manifested in a worldly/realist form. In the context of Russian imperial history, Richard Wortman has described "scenarios of power" through which monarchs have attempted to achieve similar catachrestic effects:

> Carefully staged ceremonies and celebrations, the coronations foremost among them, demonstrated the monarch's power of control and direction, providing a simulacrum of a political order responding to his will. [...] Imagery and pageantry made it clear that Russian monarchs were neither bound by the limits of the everyday nor subject to mundane judgment. Representation lifted them into a realm of the sublime.[24]

As we have seen, such scenarios of power permeate the corpus of Russian realist texts in forms that were considerably more variegated than their official public deployment would allow. Even an incomplete list of pivotal, structurally significant dramatizations of authority in the corpus of texts assembled here attests to their wide-ranging nature. Here we have Peter's statue coming alive and chasing Eugene through the streets of the city and Eugene's submissive meekness in the aftermath ("His worn-out cap he then would raise,/Cast to the ground a troubled gaze"); the somber announcement of the real Inspector's arrival and the mute scene of petrification acclaiming it; the elder Aduev's implacable omniscience and his nephew's astonished dejection; male physical force and legal power in *Boyarschina*, and the lifeless body of the woman on whom such power is exercised; the father's taming of both woman and horse in *First Love*, and their devoted acceptance of his power; Polozova's clawlike fingers in Sanin's hair, and his eager abasement; Raskolnikov claiming the right over life and death, and the novel's shocking near-affirmation of this right. These diagrams of power, ranging from "benevolent" displays of supremacy that promote in the subject feelings of loving allegiance to directly coercive expressions of force that paralyze the subject with mystical dread, mark the outer boundaries of the social-imaginary space allotted to the figure of sovereignty in Russian realist fiction: rule legitimized with reference to the welfare of the ruled and acclaimed by veneration and love, and rule legitimized through the exercise of sheer power and acclaimed with melancholy helplessness and morbid terror. In each case we find distinctive relationships between the staging of transcendence or sublimity, on the one hand, and spectatorial witnessing or acclamation, on the other. The two axes of the scenario are inseparable, depend on each other, and interact to produce specific affects and motifs of power as it relates to the depicted world over which it is proclaimed to be sovereign.

One particularly intricate projection of power—connoting a vision of rule legitimized with reference to the welfare of the ruled and sealed by their veneration and love—can serve as a model for the more general dynamics of display and acclamation inherent in Russian realist imaginaries of sovereignty. This is the enactment of magnanimity, organizing "sovereign-subject" relations in *Polinka Saks*, *The Precipice*, and *Demons*, as well as, more marginally, in several other texts. We find what is probably the simplest manifestation of this pattern in *The Precipice*, where, as we have seen, Vera's reluctance to go against Grandmother's rules is based not on an explicit prohibition or the fear of punishment, but on concern for the welfare of the matriarch. The specific form taken by Vera's acclamation is thus distinct from mere assertion of another's external power over oneself. Instead, we have an enactment of a deeply interiorized authority, based in a conviction of its willingness to sacrifice itself for the sake of its subjects.

The entire sequence depicting Grandmother's grief-stricken wanderings through the estate fulfills Vera's prophesy and plays out the script according to which the ruler's power expresses itself as the capacity for taking on the burden of the subject's suffering and guilt. In a characteristically paradoxical fashion, such exculpation results in the subject's self-abasement. Explicitly forgiven by Grandmother, Vera feels for the very first time the full extent of the matriarch's superiority to herself.[25] This is the paradigmatic effect of magnanimous power: that those who are released from authority feel all the more bound by it and those who are forgiven, more guilty. In *The Precipice*, this script is taken to its limit with Grandmother's admission of her own "primordial" guilt. On the one hand, this restores the young woman's confidence in herself: if Grandmother could survive and flourish in the shadow of her "sin," so can Vera. On the other hand, the admission seals Vera's obedience to Grandmother, fully internalizes it. "You are a saintly woman!" she acclaims upon hearing Grandmother's secret. "There is no mother like you… If I had really known you… would I ever have left off submitting to your will?"[26]

The culminating sections of *Polinka Saks*, too, stage magnanimous display, reinforced and complicated here by an association of ostensibly benevolent power with images of enigma and dread. The preparations for the scene in which the formidable husband grants release to his unfaithful wife are dilated and loaded with the gothic paraphernalia of terror. Through Polinka's and Galitsky's letters, we have access to the outward actions of the husband, whose intentions remain hidden from them and the reader alike. In anticipation of the dimly defined "event," Saks looms over the lovers as a man "capable of anything." The lovers fully expect him to resort to violence (after all, he has already killed someone in a duel) and even acknowledge his right to do so. The decor of the old, beautiful, but decrepit house in which the ritual of emancipation takes place appears to us as an odd mixture of motifs. The house is associated with the age of Catherine II and appears to contain the busts of American founding fathers, yet its Enlightenment connotations blend with, are in fact overwritten by, the atmosphere of gloom and the foreboding of violence. This fusion of images, invoking both coercion and release, foreshadows the effects of the verdict itself. Once again, at the moment of magnanimous release, the subject is granted special insight into the essence of her liberator-sovereign. Just as Vera understands Grandmother at the moment when Grandmother "lowers" herself to Vera's level (both are sinful), so Polinka grasps the depth and nature of her husband's love when he lets her go. And just as Vera proclaims that had she truly known Grandmother, she would have never disobeyed her, so, from the very moment of her release, and for the first time, Polinka begins to belong to her husband irrevocably. Still, the formula of magnanimous domination underpinning the central conflict of *The Precipice* is complicated in *Polinka Saks* by stronger emphasis on arcane mystery and threat. Here, the greater the sovereign's capacity for violence, the more magnanimous his refusal to exercise it; the more magnanimous the sovereign, the more insuperable and (indirectly) violent his will.

A similarly structured case of magnanimous display organizes the pivotal scene of the slap in *Demons*. Here the emphasis falls on the act of self-mastery in which the offender is spared, pardoned, or released. This act, once again, results not in the diminution but in the accrual of power to the figure of the sovereign:

> The first to lower his eyes was Shatov, obviously because he was forced to lower them. Then he slowly turned and walked out of the room, but not at all with the same gait as he had just had when approaching. He was walking softly, his shoulders hunched up somehow especially awkwardly, his head bowed, and as if he were reasoning something out with himself. He seemed to be whispering something. He made his way carefully to the door without brushing against anything or knocking anything over, and he opened the door only a very little way, so as to be able to squeeze through the crack almost sideways. (10:166; 205–6)

This painstaking description of the effect of Stavrogin's self-mastering inaction on Shatov highlights the resulting abasement of the offender. His gait changes from rebellious to docile; he appears crushed by the encounter, retreats in confusion, touched, like Pushkin's "poor Eugene," by a kind of submissive madness. During the ensuing nocturnal conversation between them, Shatov will proclaim, in part on the basis of this display of "limitless power," that Stavrogin alone is chosen to raise the banner of the Russian national god.

In his farewell letter to Darya Shatova, Stavrogin repeats the word "magnanimity" (*velikodushie*) six times. He claims that magnanimity is precisely what he lacks, by contrast with "strength" or "power" (*sila*), which is something he has in excess. In order to appreciate the difference between the classical enactment of magnanimity and Stavrogin's display of self-possession, we might turn to a text Dostoevsky deeply admired, Pierre Corneille's tragedy *Cinna ou la Clémence d'Auguste* (1641). In an 1840 letter to his brother Mikhail, Dostoevsky enthusiastically praises the play and points out for particular appreciation the moment when the emperor Augustus forgives the political conspirators Cinna and Emilie for plotting to assassinate him:

> I'm master of myself as of the world;
> I am. I wish to be. O days to come,
> Preserve for ever my last victory!
> I triumph over the most righteous wrath
> That ever can be handed down to you.
> Cinna, let us be friends. This I entreat...[27]

The staging of self-mastery in Corneille signifies the existence of a principle that supersedes the offended individual himself. The rebels are pardoned for the sake of the stability of the state, which is thus placed beyond the persons of both Octavian and Cinna. Or, put another way, pardon marks the site other than the person of the ruler himself, at which sovereignty is ultimately located. In showing himself able—unlike the rebels—to act on behalf of the state, the sovereign demonstrates his legitimacy. Magnanimity presupposes arcane supremacy, the right to kill or to pardon, but Corneille's Augustus de-emphasizes this power, covers it up, privileging the welfare of the polity instead. By contrast, throughout the novel, Stavrogin repeatedly refuses to take upon himself the weight of an "idea": the national idea, the revolutionary idea, the Christian idea, and so on. The emphasis here is precisely on what remains covered up in magnanimity: the "privacy" of sovereign power, its hiddenness in the opacity of the self, its arbitrariness, its indifference to techniques of explicit legitimation.

3. OCCULTING

With *Demons*, then, we approach yet another set of devices for the production of sovereignty effects. These devices present power as transcendent, beyond the comprehension of those who come in contact with it and therefore more or less beyond their ability to challenge it. A clear distinction is established between merely private individuals and those only partially individuated figures who embody a substantive or *philial* principle, the body politic as a whole. In this confrontation, the difference between the private and the political is often both reasserted and erased. Private individuals turn out to have all along been only apparently so; in actuality, within the state of exception, they are directly exposed to the power of the ruler. Meanwhile, the substance-bearing sovereign turns out to have all along been merely "private," incapable of embodying the body politic fully and without excess; the *reason* of state is inevitably also its *blow*. The tension between the spectacular and the privy modalities of power manifests itself in projections of the occult, in which the source of power "appears" as hidden, placed in the narrative's shadow, operating behind the scenes. Properly speaking, this hiding prepares spectacular revelation; together, the hiding and the revelation frequently constitute the narrative's basic plot.

Pegged to the figure of the sovereign, such a plot is best understood as fateful, in accordance with Pushkin's designation of Peter I as "the sovereign of fate" (*vlastelin sud'by*) and with Gogol's comment that the state, represented by the real Inspector, appears as the "*fatum* of the ancients." Peter and the Inspector remain hidden from the protagonists' view until, their "mind[s] unclouding," they confront these fate-bearing figures as what has befallen them all along. Konstantin Saks's mysterious machinations procuring the divorce culminate in a spectacular reappearance that settles his wife's fate; Pyotr Aduev's predictions foreshadow the life trajectory of his nephew; the father's seduction of Zinaida in *First Love* takes place behind Volodya's back and, at the moment of revelation, delivers a fateful blow; the absent Stolz first enables, then haunts and attenuates the relationship between Oblomov and Olga; Nastasya Filippovna spins behind-the-scenes intrigues promoting the courtship plot between Myshkin and Aglaya but reappears at the end to break it up. In short, elements of occlusion accompany almost every "sovereignty effect" and contribute to creating every "zone of sovereignty" arising within the corpus of texts I have considered. In most cases, such elements coincide with patterns of fateful emplotment: the invisible is what structures the manifest world as well as what undermines that structure.

Stressing the prominence of the invisible, of what is beyond the purview of everyday social interactions, the sovereignty effect of occulting transpires as the shimmering manifestation of the numinous at the meeting point of revelation and concealment. The resulting combination emerges with great vividness in *First Love*. The father's charismatic sway over humans and beasts correlates with his capacity to stay out of sight. Sovereignty effects are timed to his rare and spectacular appearances, which also punctuate and organize the plot. The father's culminating enactment of power—the blow of the whip that submits his headstrong lover—appears to Volodya only dimly, as actions of a higher being, acting in the realms of the occult. As a result, his own passion for Zinaida begins to appear to him as insignificant and childish "in comparison with that other, unknown something, at which I could scarcely guess and which terrified me like an unfamiliar, beautiful but ominous face which one tries in vain to make oneself see in the twilight" (200; 6:361). The tangled language of the sentence mimics the workings of a consciousness dazzled by the encounter with the supernatural—a pivotal encounter that seals his fate as the sort of man who, at the age of forty, will exclaim, "And what has come of all that I hoped for?" (202; 6:363).

Volodya's father is (at least tendentially) exempted from participation in the world of social competition. At the same time, he functions as the point of articulation for the interactions that unfold before us. Like his imperial namesake in *The Bronze Horseman*, he is both character and plot. At its outer limit, such a figure can vanish altogether, depositing itself entirely in what appears as an impersonal order of things. We have encountered this metamorphosis in texts that hand familial authority over the transgressing woman to an impersonal jurisdiction. Memorable instances of such familial occulting organize major plot lines in *On the Eve* and *Anna Karenina*, where the role of the sovereign prohibition (whose original source derives from the state-family complex) is transferred to the occulted figures of the Fisherman-death and the depersonalized "Vengeance is mine."

An episode from *Who Is to Blame?* exposes the mechanism of such supplementation, or relay, with great clarity. One of the novel's many biographical digressions, this episode tells of an encounter, sometime in the 1770s, between Beltov's uncle, at the time a young lieutenant of the Guards, and "a tall, stately man [...] wrapped in his bearskin coat." One winter day, the two strangers become involved in a sleigh race on Nevsky Prospect. When the lieutenant wins the race, the mysterious stranger roars in a "lion-like voice" and strikes the other's coachman (and glancingly, the lieutenant himself) with a whip. The two get into a combative exchange, and in the heat of the moment, the young man misses some hints at his competitor's fearful status. At the end of the exchange, the massive gentleman contemptuously shows the lieutenant his fist, "as large as an elephant's foot," and drives away. The lieutenant follows his rival in the hopes of discovering where he lives and challenging him to a duel, but the discovery dissuades him. Instead, he decides to write him a letter but is soon placed under arrest and exiled to a distant fortress, from which he returns only years later, somewhat deranged (146–47; 4:88—89).

The outsized proportions of the man, the leonine voice, the notorious bearskin, the free wielding of the whip, the inaccessibility and even the unmentionable character of his residence—all placed against the historical backdrop of the reign of Catherine II, and still more precisely in the 1770s—point to the figure of the empress's most illustrious and broadly mythologized favorite, Grigoriy Potemkin. What appears as a competitive encounter between two members of the nobility, with its rules of engagement and rituals of combat, turns out to be an utterly asymmetrical confrontation between an individual and the absolute power of the state. Such power manifests itself at the moment when it can no longer be seen. It appears as sovereign insofar as it is exluded from direct competition and confrontation. It vanishes as something one might resist and reappears as that to which one must succumb. It dissolves into sheer impersonal force, the order of things, which, like a blow of fate, can forever alter the life of the subject confronting it. We have seen such occulting at work in Herzen's discussion of Bryullov's *The Last Day of Pompeii*, where power appears and at the same time hides as sheer *Naturgewalt*.

Mythos (Telling Philia)

The concluding sentences of George Eliot's *Middlemarch* (1872) recall the novel's prologue, which first establishes an ambiguous link between the novel's heroine, Dorothea Brooke, and the early modern saint Theresa of Avila. What connects Dorothea to her monastic forebear is that she, too, with her "young and noble impulse,"[28] seeks "illimitable satisfaction" and strives after a "rapturous consciousness of life beyond self."[29] But the latecoming heroine, the heroine of a modern novel, authors no "far-resonant action," accomplishes no "long-recognizable deed"; she is, in the end, "foundress of nothing."[30] Subjectivity plays out differently in the modern world, and action adopts a different shape: "A new Theresa will hardly have the opportunity of reforming a conventual life, any more than a new Antigone will spend her heroic piety in daring all for the sake of a brother's burial: the medium in which their ardent deeds took shape is forever gone."[31] We are in the world of interlocking privacies, of aggregations and diffusions, of actions tightly entwined, none superfluous and none decisive. The point is not so much that Dorothea has been confined to the domestic sphere, not that she ends up, disappointingly for some, a wife. The point rather is that the "domestic sphere," the sphere of small, private acts is projected outward onto the entire social world, in which neither "ideally beautiful," nor "heroic," nor "historic" events can take place. The medium for them, we are told, "is forever gone." This medium was a kind of substance, a "coherent social faith and order which could perform the function of knowledge for the ardently willing soul."³² Within such an order, one may speak of a great transgression, for example, or a foundational act. Without it—only a great convergence of "insignificant people's" "daily words and deeds," private but "incalculably diffusive."

Contrast this vision of aggregative connectedness with the tendency of the texts in our corpus to reduce the complex social space of a narrative to an encounter within the zone of sovereignty. This "simplified" social imaginary—what, following Belinsky and Hegel, I have called "substance," or in the language of Attic tragedy, *philia*—transpires in the unfolding of plot. Unlike the developmental and/or disillusioning trajectories of the realist novel, in which social connections ramify and accumulate as an increasingly intricate world of linkages comes into view while the protagonist acquires a more richly socialized identity, the telling of *philia* operates in reverse. In a single blow, it strips the protagonist of social ties, transfers her into the rarefied domain of sovereignty, and leaves her in the grip of the one relationship that matters: the relationship of belonging/nonbelonging to one or another thematic instantiation of *philia* (the state, the family, the nation). To be sure, this reduction—which Annenkov casts as the erasure of the boundary between the private and the political—often takes place against the horizon of novelistic-realist sociality, which is the very thing being simplified, or reduced. What we have in such cases is a dynamic hybrid, in which novelistic narrative material is deformed by *philial* emplotment.

To illustrate the workings of such hybridity, we may recall the idiosyncratic composition of *The Precipice*. The novel's apparent hero, Raisky, a failing novelist himself, cannot make the episodes of his life—much like the episodes of his novel—come together into a meaningful whole. Neither a developmental nor a properly disillusioning narrative emerges. Instead, Raisky is supplanted by another protagonist, anchoring a different kind of plot. Her story unfolds within a more compact social space—literally, because she acts within the confines of Malinovka, but also structurally and symbolically, because her drama unfolds within a *philial* triangle, in which her Grandmother's patronymic is the name of Vera's forbidden object of love (Tatyana Markovna-Mark Volokhov). Vera's plot is not, like Raisky's, sequential and episodic, but rather recursive. Self-willed movement forward turns into a retracing of age-old steps. In rebelling against Grandmother, Vera becomes her. And this convergence takes place at the point of original disorder, Grandmother's own similar transgression in the past. In Raisky's biography, the novel depicts a failure to gain a sense of meaningful belonging from the confluence of individuals and their diffusive acts. To compensate for this failure, it produces a "drama" or "tragedy" that stages the recoiling of action upon the individual in such a way as to disclose the individual's rootedness in a collective destiny. In this manner, character and plot are interwoven: sovereignty effects rely on specific narrative shapes, which, in turn, crystallize around moments of rhetorical elevation, enactments of power, and figurations of the occult.

Narrative reversal (*peripeteia*) and recognition (*anagnorisis*) constitute the means by which the tragic plot expands the acting individual beyond the confines of inner life and intention. Aristotle defines *peripeteia* as a "shift of what is being undertaken to its opposite."[33] This shift is in turn linked—conceptually, though not always in practice—to the parallel transition from "ignorance to awareness."[34] *Anagnorisis* is paradigmatically the recognition "either of blood ties or of hostility."[35] The direction of the movement matters less than the centrality of *philia*: after all, latent in the recognition of hostility, too, is, as Gerald Else glosses it, "a passage into enmity of natural philoi."[36] We might say, in other words, that *peripeteia* marks the transferal of the protagonist's action from one social imaginary into another, forcing him to reinterpret the nature of his relationship to his lifeworld. The movement from ignorance to knowledge involves the recognition that whatever the hero might have believed, he was all along acting within the social space marked by the intense association of substance. In Aristotle's own favored example, Oedipus comes to recognize himself as having acted in a much more compact, denser world than he had imagined, in a world in which his bond with others is more direct, immediate, and exacting than he suspects.

Understood as a catastrophic straying onto the social imaginary of substantive belonging, *peripeteia* triggers a retroactive recognition that one has not traveled far, has not become separate, has not escaped the *philial* domain. Such is the case with *Taras Bulba*'s Andriy, who at the pivotal moment of the narrative encounters his enemy as his father: "*I begot you, and now I shall kill you!*"[37] Pyotr Aduev comes to recognize at last that his deliberate quest for rational usefulness in all areas of life has caused him, perhaps irreparably, to harm his own wife. Emancipated to personal happiness, Polinka Saks dies from the recognition that her kinship ties to her statesman-husband cannot, in the end, be broken. Young Volodya's first attempt to step beyond the limits of the family through an exogenous erotic attachment is thwarted by the appearance of his father. The moment of *peripeteia*-recognition extinguishes the social-imaginary horizon of mature socialization and desiring competition, replacing it with another, narrower horizon of defiled familial relations: the man he intended to kill was his father; the woman he desired is his father's woman. The network of variegated personal relationships turns out to be no more than a decoy, distracting our attention from the essential and sharply abbreviated world of substantive bonds. What against the broad horizon of aggregative order might seem like legitimate desiring competition, against the horizon of *philia* threatens socio-ontological breakdown, insinuating the outrages of parricide and incest.

In *One Thousand Souls*, narrative reversal turns into subject matter for explicit reflection. Here again, projections of state majesty present the privileged site for the play of *peripeteia* and recognition. As in Gogol, the state may be said to make two appearances here, both times in the concluding fourth part of the novel. First, the scene is set for the hero's arrival in the provincial town in the capacity of a newly appointed vice-governor. The reigning governor of the province appears to be as invulnerable as he is corrupt, but the narrator foretells his imminent downfall: "It was obvious that he was unbreakable. But, say what you will, there is always something sinister, something fateful when we have reached the highest summits…" (364; 3:357).

The old governor is indeed brought down, as the bearer of the "impartial idea of the state" reclaims to it the illicitly private lives of its servants. Yet Kalinovich, too, fails to escape his predecessor's fate. As soon as he has been appointed governor, he begins to anticipate his fall: "I have begun to believe in forebodings, and just now, explain it as you will […] I have so strong a sensation of being in the grip of some inexplicable fear that I feel clearly, I almost see, that at this very moment, somewhere in the sky, by some mysterious caprice of fate, a turning-point in my life is taking place […], a fearsome turning-point, fearsome" (364; 3:533). This characteristically overblown (from the perspective of realist aesthetics) thematization of tragic *peripeteia* highlights an essential point: that the conflict between the state and those who act like private individuals (e.g., the corrupt old governor) is redoubled in the paradox of power underpinning the workings of the state itself. The sovereign both belongs and does not belong in the state; in acting on behalf of the state, he inevitably transcends it, draws on the surplus of "privacy" at the occult locus of exception, and must pay the price for this transcendence.[38]

The workings of narrative reversal, coinciding with the recognition of a *philial* bond that stands in the way of individual self-assertion, stage the condensation of the social space of action, as if recalling the protagonist "home." Just this sort of summons organizes the narrative of *Spring Torrents*, enacting the ascendance of *philia* under yet another name. Here again we find a hero who believes himself capable of self-determination, of tracing his own path in life, specifically, of marrying a foreigner and settling abroad. Yet in typically tragic fashion, the means of the hero's escape guide him back into the trap he is trying to flee. In order to marry Gemma and gain the means to support a family, he must sell his serfs. This need leads him in turn into the fateful embrace of the buyer Polozova. The signified "Russia" is constituted in the disturbing conflation of the signifiers "Polozova" and "serfdom," terms that complement each other as character and associated motif. Polozova is serfdom is Russia, and in attempting to sell his serfs, Sanin himself becomes a "bondsman."[39] The *peripeteia* at the center of the novella—the "shift of what is being undertaken [the sale of serfs and thus the renunciation of the national past] to the opposite [one's own bondage to the very thing one wants to renounce]"[40]—here renders the problematic of belonging literal. Like Volodya from *First Love*, like the officials from *Government Inspector*, Sanin believes he belongs to himself. Instead, he belongs to the dark national past, a belonging that is narrated in substantive terms as the unfolding of an archaic, jealous fate.

These instances of tragic *peripeteia* in the corpus of Russian realist texts alert us to the miasmatic character of its underlying conception of reality. Tragic miasma—a form of thoroughgoing pollution or defilement affecting an entire community and stemming from an act of sacrilege, contact with impurity, or murder (especially within the family)[41]—manifests itself as a unity, at the moment of narrative reversal, between action and recoil, hero and substance. Jean-Pierre Vernant's discussion of miasma in Attic tragedy is illuminating in this regard:

> Certain actions that run counter to the religious order of the world contain an unpropitious power that quite overwhelms the human agent. [...] The action does not so much emanate from the agent as if he were its origin; rather, it overwhelms and envelops him, engulfing him in a power that affects not only him but a whole sequence of actions of greater or less duration that are influenced by him. The effects of the defilement thus cover a field of action in which the constituent parts and moments are all connected. [...] The objects on which the power of the *daimōn* works comprise a whole more or less extensive system of human, social, and cosmic relations the order of which has been upset by the sacrilegious disruption. Basically, it is this disorder that the defilement makes manifest through all the various concrete forms it adopts.[42]

Miasma, then, names a vision of sociality that presumes the participation of the entire *philial* grouping in the action and destiny of a single individual. This participation becomes evident in the manner in which what appears to be a subjectively originated action turns out, at the moment of *peripeteia*, to have all along been entangled in substantive disorder. The disorder does not start with the act but congeals in it. Here, straightforward notions of individual responsibility and moral guilt become inapplicable as such.

We may recall in this context the reaction of Vladimir Petrovich's audience in the epilogue added to the French and German translations of *First Love*: "You yourself are not to blame for anything, but one can feel some general, national guilt, something like crime. [...] Something is rotten in the state of Denmark."[43] The nature, let alone the cause, of the defilement is here difficult to identify precisely. How far back does it go? In what does it consist? All we know is that Vladimir Petrovich's story unfolds under the influence of—and, in fact, embodies—a national-political contagion. The main narrative part of the tale contains still more explicit invocations of this predicament, especially as articulated by the sober medical doctor, Lushin. On several occasions throughout, Lushin tries to prevent Volodya's entanglement with Zinaida. "The atmosphere of this place isn't healthy for you," he repeatedly warns the young man. "Believe me, you could catch an infection" (171; 6:39). Lushin's predictions come true; Volodya catches an "infection"—one of melancholy impotence in the face of despotically wielded power—and never fully recovers from it. And the fact that Volodya is "not to blame for anything" is both the cause and the symptom of the infection itself.

Miasma manifests itself in narrative as recursion. Temporally, this can mean that the transgressing person is both the originator of a defilement and the conveyor of it. She is, we might say, deindividuated within it, both cause and consequence, both self and others.[44] This temporal configuration emerges with great vividness in the entanglement between Vera's and Grandmother's parallel trespasses in *The Precipice*. In light of the matriarch's hallucinatory vision of Malinovka as a desecrated wasteland and in light of the discovery of the matriarch's "original sin," the path of causation loops in on itself: Has Malinovka fallen into "an abomination of desolation" because of what Vera has done, or does Malinovka, in ruins for at least a generation, inevitably beget her act? The uncertainty circles around the moment of original defilement, which has echoed through generations and has overtaken the heroine like a tragic *philial* curse.

Herzen frequently refers to such contagion as history's capacity to "enter into the blood" of its willing and unwilling participants. Just as temporal distinctions between present and past are difficult to sustain within the social imaginary presupposed by the telling of miasmatic pollution, so also spatial boundaries, particularly the boundaries between individuals and the surrounding world, prove radically permeable. A passage from *My Past and Thoughts*, set in reactionary Paris in the aftermath of the "June days" of 1848, can serve as an illustration. Emotionally crushed by the defeat of the revolution and the violence unleashed on the rebellious workers, Herzen decides to withdraw from politics and history into private life, an intimate circle of family and friends. This resolution is, in retrospect, presented as an act of hubris: "Seeing that all was tumbling into ruins, I wished to save myself, to begin a new life, to get away with two, three others [...]. With this *faro da me*, my boat was bound to be wrecked on submerged rocks, and wrecked it was. I survived, it is true, but lost everything...."[45] The incident takes place at a Paris train station, where a small group of close friends, cold and dejected at the prospect of indefinite separation, witnesses an ugly scene of a fight between two drunken old men wandering in from the street. This minor episode of arbitrary violence, complete with details of the head hitting the stone "with a sharp, jarring sound," the blood pouring on the floor, the vicious crowd attacking the "victor" turns, for Herzen, into an omen:

> Every man who has had much experience remembers days, hours, a succession of scarcely noticed moments, at which a break begins, at which the wind blows from a different quarter; these signs and warnings do not come by chance at all: they are consequences, from which in turn come the first embodiments of what is ready to burst into life, manifestations of what is secretly fermenting and exists already. We do not notice these physical tokens, but laugh at them as we do over a spilt salt-cellar, or an extinguished candle, because we consider ourselves incomparably more independent than we really are, and proudly desire to govern our lives ourselves.[46]

The miasmatic intrusion of contemporary Paris, with its odor of recent blood and defeat, into the vulnerable atmosphere of personal relationships foreshadows the entrance of political reaction into Herzen's household in the shape of the treacherous "petit-bourgeois" poet Georg Herwegh—here cast as a herald of the reactionary turn in French politics, carrying emotional and physical devastation into Herzen's personal life.[47] Once again, the narrative pattern of *peripeteia* and the social imaginary of miasma intersect, confirming the status of the political domain as substantive, forcefully claiming the individual at the very moment of his self-assertion. Herzen's circular, miasmatic guilt consists in having attempted to assert his independence from the political struggles of the time, just as the dreary outcome of the struggles—a dictatorship of petit-bourgeois indifference to politics—has come to reign over France in the figure of Louis Napoleon. Here, as elsewhere—and we find more or less elaborated cases of miasma in most of the works in our corpus—tragic pollution can be understood as a representational mode for staging the paradoxes of individuation within the parameters of *philia*.

Pathos (Affecting Power)

What does (recognition of) substantive belonging feel like? Or: what does it feel like to be (or be confronted by) a sovereign, to find oneself in the field of sovereign power? The culminating stanzas of *The Bronze Horseman* provide a clue. In a flash of clarity—"his mind unclouding"—Eugene recognizes himself as a political being whose apparently private life, crushed by blind elemental forces, has all along been unfolding in "that square," under the gaze and within the jurisdiction of the Horseman.[48] When the protagonist shakes his fist at the czar, he acts out the consequences of a recoding in which natural disaster and the blind, impersonal misfortune it brings are now registered as the personal act of the divine ruler, the "mortal god."[49] The sequence recapitulates the tale at a higher level of explicitness, rewriting Eugene's attempt at self-determination as a threat to the sovereign, the impersonal flood as the personal chase, and madness as the abjection of the cowed subject. The sequence presents belonging as a kind of direct, visually coded, and rhetorically heightened tableau of the consequences of sovereign power, whose workings congeal in the vision of the hero's calamity.

We are speaking here of what is known within the tragic tradition as *pathos*, a spectacle of divinely inflicted suffering that may or may not be represented as in some sense deserved, but whose horror exceeds the calculus of justice as mortals understand it.[50] When it comes to spectacles of tragic *pathos*, the Greek chorus (to an extent modeling the experience of the audience) frequently expresses profound ambivalence: horror and fascination at once. Thus, the chorus in Oedipus: "What cruel spirit [*daemon*] with superhuman leap/Came to assist your grim destiny?/ Ah, most unhappy man!/But no! I cannot bear even to look at you,/Though there is much that I would ask and see and hear./But I shudder at the very sight of you."[51] The chorus (together with the audience) feels horror at the sight of the protagonist's suffering, combined with wonder at the manifestation of the awesome power of the divine. The fate of the individual is the stage upon which divine preponderance is displayed. Witnessing the suffering of the heroine, hearing her lamentations, woven into those of the chorus, the audience is reassured that the gods exist, their supremacy manifest in the very lack of consideration for the human measures of fairness.

A kind of choral discourse is operative in *The Bronze Horseman* as well, inviting the reader to partake of sublime dread at the sight of the supreme power expressed in the protagonist's misfortune: "How awesome in the gloom he rides!/What thought upon his brow resides/His charger with what fiery mettle,/His form with what dark strength endowed!" The acclamation occurs precisely at the moment when Eugene recognizes the

Horseman as the cause of his misfortunes and just before he utters his reckless challenge. In fact, the entire sequence of recognition, acclamation, challenge, and chase can be described as an unfolding of a single *pathos* in which both the protagonist's suffering and the ascendancy of power inflicting it are at their most vivid.

As a projection of the experience of catastrophic belonging, *pathos* designates less a determinate emotion than a generalized, but in each case specifically articulated, *affect*, a being-affected by *philia*, whose proximity is registered in a psychosomatic way.[52] Such registering takes the ambiguous form of activity/passivity, corresponding to the moment of indistinction between *ethos* and *daemon*, the self-willed and the externally determined.[53]

> His breath congealed in him, he pressed
> His brow against the chilly railing,
> A blur of darkness overveiling
> His eyes; a flame shot through his breast
> And made his blood seethe. Grimly lowering,
> He faced the haughty image towering
> On high, and fingers clawed, teeth clenched,
> As if by some black spirit wrenched,
> He hissed, spite shaking him: "Up there,
> Great wonder-worker you, beware! ..."

Here we have an example of how, within the parameters of *pathos*, suffering a devastating fate can, by way of a series of subtle modifications, reappear as rebellious action. Such transformation is in the nature of affect itself as a state "prior to the distinction between activity and passivity."[54] The depiction of Eugene's protest is somatic: his clenched teeth and clawed fingers, his shuddering body and boiling blood are as much a matter of being invaded by a kind of "black spirit" (*siloi chernoi*) as it is the body bracing for a rebellious act. Noteworthy here is the modification of affect that occurs along with the political recasting of natural disaster. The death of Parasha in the flood drives Eugene into a state of profound melancholy: deafened by the noise of inner anguish (*shumom vnutrennei trevogi*), he does not distinguish his path, does not feel pain, but bears his "luckless span" (*neschastnyi vek*) dumbly, neither beast nor man, neither dead nor alive (*ni zhitel' sveta, ni prizrak myortvyi*). The moment of recognition, transplanting the flood from the register of elemental disaster into the register of political confrontation, results in a flash of mania, a burst of heat, of energy, a seizure, a quickening of force. This movement on the terrain of *pathos* from melancholy to mania corresponds to what Fredric Jameson has called the "chromaticism" of affect, its tendency for infinitesimal differentiation in which each preceding moment differs from the next by a subtle modification of intensity, ranging "up and down the bodily scale from melancholy to euphoria."[55]

The choice to designate the experience of substantive belonging as a certain kind of affect does not entail here anything like an assertion of its radical privacy or its essentially asemiotic nature: we are after all dealing with shared verbal constructions. At stake, rather, are several features that distinguish affect as a mode of representation of experience from the more standard uses of "emotion." *Pathos* is a kind of affect insofar as it is genuinely psychosomatic: not mental, or inward alone, but also bodily, physical. As such, *pathos* is both passive-suffering and active-violent, like Oedipus's self-blinding, or Ajax's slaughter of cattle and herdsmen, or Pentheus's dressing like a maenad. This in turn implies fluidity: affect circulates through the psyche/soma in such a way that it crosses boundaries among more determinate emotions and sensations; for example, pain becomes rage, becomes heat, becomes indignation, dread, flight—all as a single process without distinct demarcations. Finally, and most importantly for our purposes, *pathos* is affect insofar as it points to the experience of "being affected," of something (miasmatically) transgressing the boundaries of the individual, retroactively exposing the assumption of the bounded, self-sufficient, or isolated self as an illusion.

The locus of the affect of sovereign power, in other words, is not the body proper, but the point of intersection between the psychosomatic individual and the *philial* substance. To say that we are dealing with affects, rather than "emotions," is to stress that instead of presupposing distinct, psychically delimited individuals at the outset, we must reckon with the problem, the drama, and here specifically the *pathos* of individuation. Within the representational domain of *pathos*, a particular affective state or movement marks a specific experience of being claimed by substance and so also a specific way of being entangled with the dual figure of community and coercion.

The modulations of *pathos* that we will encounter in the rest of this section mark distinctive alignments between the acting/suffering individual and the substantive order in which they act/suffer. A vivid illustration of such variety can be found in three consecutive drafts of the dramatic confrontation between Eugene and the statue of Peter. Next to Pushkin's original version of the scene, we may place his own attempt to rewrite it in response to objections from the censor (presumably, Nicholas I himself) and, further still, Vasiliy Zhukovsky's edits, which appear in the posthumous publication of the poem in 1837. Here are the three texts in respective sequence:

1. Кругом подножия кумира	2. Безумец бедный обошел	3. Безумец бедный обошел
Безумец бедный обошел	И надпись яркую прочел	Кругом скалы с тоскою дикой
И взоры дикие навел	И сердце скорбию великой	И надпись яркую прочел
На лик державца полумира	Стеснилось в нем. Его чело	И сердце скорбию великой
Стеснилась грудь его. Чело	К решетке хладной прилегло	Стеснилось в нем. Его чело
К решетке хладной прилегло	Глаза подернулись туманом…	К решетке хладной прилегло
Глаза подернулись туманом,	И дрогнул он — и мрачен стал	Глаза подернулись туманом
По сердцу пламень пробежал,	П<е>ред недвижным великаном	По членам холод пробежал
Вскипела кровь. Он мрачен стал	И перст с угрозою подъяв	И дрогнул он — и мрачен стал
Пред горделивым истуканом	Шепнул, волнуем мыслью черной	Пред дивным русским великаном
И, зубы стиснув, пальцы сжав,	"Добро строитель чудотворный!	И перст свой на него подняв
Как обуянный силой черной,	Ужо тебе…" Но вдруг стремглав […] (5:499)	Задумался. Но вдруг стремглав […] (5:519)
"Добро, строитель чудотворный! —		
Ужо тебе!… И вдруг стремглав […] (5:148)		

A number of these changes are what we might expect. "Proud idol" (*gordelivyi istukan*) for Peter turns into the more innocuous "motionless giant" in Pushkin's revision and into the downright reverential "wondrous Russian giant" in Zhukovsky. Eugene's wild gaze at the visage of the "sovereign of half the world" disappears in the latter two versions, and in Zhukovsky, so does the challenge itself. What is more pertinent for our purposes, however, is the editing (self-censoring) work that takes place at the level of affect.

In his revision, Pushkin imbues the descriptions of Eugene's feelings with a new air of "great sorrow" (*skorbiu velikoi*); Zhukovsky keeps the sorrow and, as if that is not sign enough of Eugene's dejection, adds "anguished sadness" (*s toskoiu dikoi*). The power that takes hold of Eugene at the moment of the challenge changes from "force" (*sila*) to thought (*mysl'*) in Pushkin's edits and then altogether vanishes in Zhukovsky, replaced by Eugene's losing himself in thought, becoming pensive (*zadumalsia*). The revisions display two parallel movements: the temperamental taming of the protagonist, accompanied by his privatization, his withdrawal into himself. Zhukovsky's version also completely eliminates the sense of possession by an external force, as well as all action and speech. And as we move from the original to the published version, we find a corresponding reduction in levels of heat: first there is fire in the heart and boiling blood, then nothing but a shudder, and finally, with Zhukovsky, a straight reversal of the original: a chill running through his limbs. If we take into account the presence in all three versions of the touch of the brow against the chilly railing, then the burst of heat in the original draft marks Eugene's momentary separation from the object world, while the gradual cooling in the second and third drafts blends him back into his environment. What we thus find in the sequence of versions increasingly acceptable to the state is the steering of Eugene's *pathos*—his recognition of belonging to Peter's polity—down the chromatic scale, from dangerous mania to docile melancholy.[56]

1. MANIA

Tableaux of mania register the dramatic coincidence of individual and substance, the affect of daemonic possession, the self's expansion beyond the limits of mere individuality. Here, a character becomes the site at which substance manifests itself, pervading the individual as a force, a fit of frenzy, a burst of heat, pushing him out beyond the boundaries of his prior habitus. The individual feels and acts, as it were, in a state of exception, proves capable of shocking feats, risks everything, acts "beyond measure"—because he no longer acts alone. This is what happens when Eugene steps over the boundary separating his private existence from the substantive-political domain. Within the zone of sovereignty, he is seized by "a black force," the force that might be designated as "rage" but in the end exceeds clear definition. In the language of affect, this is deindividuating *pathos*, the starkly depicted state of recognition that one has all along been subject to a fate.

Scenes of mania rely on a range of figural devices that designate suprapsychological effects. The character grows in size, is physically elevated, moves galvanically, hardens to stone, steel, bronze, becomes radiant, terrifying, is no longer constrained by social norms or even physical limitations, is capable of anything, is ready and willing to die. In a diary entry, Elena Stakhova compares her suitor, the honest young historian Bersenev, to the Bulgarian revolutionary Insarov: "You [Bersenev] may be more learned than he is, cleverer even—but somehow you seem small beside him. When he talks of his country he grows and grows and his face becomes finer, and his voice turns to steel."[57] Insarov's superiority—if it can even be understood as such—has nothing to do with his personal, individual characteristics: he may not be as learned, or intelligent, or even as sensitive and kind as Bersenev. The difference is conceived figuratively in terms of size, grandeur, energetic charge, both of which accrue to Insarov insofar as he is attuned to—and channels—the will of the "*It*," rather than his own individual will.[58]

By contrast with the staid description of Insarov's national-emancipatory mania, the extensive account of Grandmother's manic walk through Malinovka is rhetorically profuse. Here the dynamic of deindividuation comes through with still greater clarity. As Grandmother herself asserts, she is not walking alone; another, more than human power quickens (in) the old woman. The narrator confirms: "It was as if it were not she who was striding there but one being carried by some external force."[59] Compare the description of Raskolnikov's murderous blow: "his own strength seemed to have no part in it. But the moment he brought the axe down, strength was born in him" (76; 6:63). Within the parameters of mania as it is taken up in our texts, the moment of suffering a fate and the moment of the transgressive act need not be distinguished at all. What matters is a heightened vision of a doing that is also a suffering, an image of substance acting in the individual.

Indeed, mania stages extreme proximity, to the point of indistinction, between character and substance. Telling in this regard are episodes in which such proximity transpires as an encounter with the figure of the sovereign, whose acclamation involves the wish or act of self-annihilation on the part of the acclaiming subject. We may recall, for example, Prince Galitsky's desire to die for the magnanimous Saks, or Polinka's actual death, precipitated by her husband's magnanimity. During the scene of the Olmütz troop review in *War and Peace*, Nikolai Rostov wishes with his whole being to die for the sovereign. To die for the sovereign here is to merge with him, to become one with something infinitely great: "Every general and soldier sensed his own nullity, aware of being a grain of sand in this sea of people, and at the same time sensed his strength, aware of being part of this enormous whole."[60] Nullity and greatness, pleasure and pain, self and other—easily blend together in the *pathos* of mania. Its heightened affective range, the energetic surge building up in the subject from proximity to the sovereign or to substance, can resolve in any number of determinate, intensely felt emotions (rage, rapture, gratitude, readiness, and so on) and precipitant, liminal acts (self-sacrifice, rebellion, a feat of unlikely physical endurance, and so on).

The famous episode of the oath on Sparrow Hills from Herzen's *My Past and Thoughts* will serve here as the final illustration of the way in which the *pathos* of mania is textually produced. The passage opens the dominant trajectory of the memoir as a whole, an account of the formation of a Russian revolutionary, the story of his personal life woven into history and guided by political struggle.

> Flushed and breathless, we stood mopping our faces. The sun was setting, the cupolas glittered, beneath the hill the city extended farther than the eye could reach; a fresh breeze blew on our faces, we stood leaning against each other and, suddenly embracing, vowed in sight of all Moscow to sacrifice our lives to the struggle we had chosen.

The scene may strike others as very affected and theatrical, and yet twenty-six years afterwards I am moved to tears as I recall it; there was a sacred sincerity in it, and our whole life has proved this. But apparently a like destiny defeats all vows made on that spot; Alexander was sincere, too, when he laid the first stone of that temple, which, as Joseph II said (though then mistakenly) at the laying of the first stone in some town in Novorossiya, was destined to be the last.

We did not know all the strength of the foe with whom we were entering into battle, but we took up the fight. That strength broke much in us, but it was not the strength that shattered us, and we did not surrender to it in spite of all its blows. The wounds received from it were honorable. Jacob's strained thigh was the sign that he had wrestled with God.

From that day the Sparrow Hills became a place of worship for us and once or twice a year we went there, and always by ourselves [...].

Five more years passed. I was far from the Sparrow Hills, but near me their Prometheus, A. L. Vitberg, stood, austere and gloomy. In 1842, returning finally to Moscow, I again visited the Sparrow Hills, and once more we stood on the site of the foundation stone and gazed at the same view, two together, but the other was not Nick. [...]

Schiller remained our favorite. [...] My ideal was Karl Moor, but soon I was false to him and went over to Marquis of Posa. I imagined in a hundred variations how I would speak to Nicholas, and how afterwards he would send me to the mines or the scaffold. It is a strange thing that almost all our day-dreams ended in Siberia or the scaffold and hardly ever in triumph; can this be the way the Russian imagination turns, or is it the effect of Petersburg with its five gallows and its penal servitude reflected on the young generation?"[61]

Around the central tableau of the oath, the passage accumulates increasingly broad horizons: autobiographical, historical, and mythological. Organizing the proliferation of allusions is the motif of sacrifice in an unequal struggle against oppressive authority: the two boys following the Decembrists' exemplary struggle against autocracy; the marquis of Posa conspiring against (and, momentarily, with) the emperor Phillip II, Prometheus defying Zeus, Jacob wrestling with God—all struggles that highlight the intimacy between the struggling parties. Jacob wrestles with God only to receive his new name from him; Posa is at one point Phillip's only trusted adviser; Zeus and Prometheus hold the keys to each other's destinies; the enlightened Decembrists are creatures of the modernizing autocracy. The struggle brings the individual into maximal proximity to the substantive order—construed in politico-theological terms—against which he or she is waging the struggle. This proximity makes it difficult to distinguish between suffering and apotheosis, but this is precisely the point; it is how mania is made.

2. DEADLOCK

Moving down the chromatic scale of Russian realist *pathos*, on the way from mania to melancholy, we encounter a series of prominently positioned scenes in which protagonists find themselves paralyzed, deadlocked in an encounter with a more or less internalized obstacle to their desire. Unlike mania, with its momentary quickening of vitality, accompanied by the language of psychosomatic fervor and daemonic possession, deadlock is the affect of restriction, of constraint, of the inability to act upon one's impulse, an incapacity to recognize it, or even to feel it at the appropriate time. In narratives privileging the thematics and containing the tableaux of deadlock, figurations of substance (the body politic) tend to appear dispersed or dislocated from the site at which the protagonist's desire is blocked.

A mixed or transitional case, somewhere between mania and deadlock, can be found in *Eugene Onegin*, whose final scene presents a spectacle (quoted in full in chapter 3) of the rejected protagonist's *pathos*: "She left him then. Eugene, forsaken,/Stood seared, as if by heaven's fire./How deep his stricken heart is shaken!" We find here no direct confrontation of the sort with which *The Bronze Horseman* culminates. But a horseman—the stately, nameless general-husband with clanking spurs—does enter at the very moment Tatyana (who has been "given" to him) vanishes. The confrontation between Eugene and the husband is merely glancing here. Eugene's misery seems more private, mediated through Tatyana's dutiful faithfulness and his own earlier mistake: his failure—from fear of losing his "hateful freedom"—to love Tatyana when she was free to be his. In retrospect, the later prohibition illuminates the earlier failure, as if at the beginning, too, she could not be his—only that impossibility was lodged inside him, internalized as a kind of fear or hesitation, an inner constraint, rendered explicit with the appearance of its objective correlate, the General, at the novel's conclusion.

The case of *Rudin* reprises the pattern of belated recognition. Here, too, as in *Onegin*, the original blockage of feeling receives an adequate explanation only at the end, when the hero's failure to feel and act out passionate love for Natalya gains a more than purely characterological dimension, appearing instead as an expression of a deeply internalized, politically inflected substantive deadlock. In light of the image of the protagonist, broken and on his way into exile, and later still, dying in futile defeat on the Parisian barricade, his failure at romantic love reappears as a proleptic symptom of internalized constraint. Meanwhile, the moment of the blockage itself is replete with the language of tragic *pathos*: "My God! My God! ... It's so cruel! ... It's such a sudden blow! ... Why should we be made so miserable! ... My head's in such a whirl, I can't think of a thing.... I can only feel my misery!" (125–26; 5:279)

An especially telling case of deadlock structures the dynamics of Oblomov's romance with Olga. One morning, at what is in retrospect the high point of their relationship, the happy lover awakens in a despairing mood. His ruminations quickly lead him to the following conclusion:

> No, you can't live as you like, that's clear. [...] You will fall into a chaos of contradictions which no human intellect, however profound and daring, can unravel! One day you desire something, next day you get what you so passionately desired, and then you curse life because it has been fulfilled—that is what comes from your arrogant and independent striding into life, from your willful *I want to*. (244; 4:247)

The language of tragic hubris, inappropriate for the situation at first glance, nevertheless registers the point at which inner, merely psychological reservations come to light as internalized responses to an external prohibition. More precisely, it turns out to be impossible to tell what comes first: the *fact* that the woman "belongs" to a (superior) other or the *feeling* that one's relationship with her constitutes a transgression. Oblomov thinks of his relationship with Olga as theft; he thinks of the need to break the relationship off as his duty. What at the moment sounds like a hysterically overblown rationalization for fleeing the responsibility of a relationship turns out, by the end, to be an appropriate act of deferral to the prerogatives of his accomplished friend. The narrator exclaims in disbelief: "What was the cause of all this? What ill wind had suddenly blown on Oblomov? What clouds had it brought? And why did he assume so sorrowful a burden?" (244; 4:248). A sudden change in weather, a poisoning—these are the metaphors with which the novel marks the affective, transindividual dimension of Oblomov's deadlock: his exposure to the forces of mediation enveloping his life and claiming him, demanding that he give Olga up, out of duty.

Provoked by Rudin's predicament and anticipating Oblomov's, Chernyshevsky makes the logic underpinning these narratives explicit. "The Russian at a Rendezvous" presents a theory of deadlock as a depletion of affect accompanying the kind of substantive belonging that is both coercive and "out of range," unavailable for direct confrontation. In Chernyshevsky's account, the personal and the political mix in the experiences of genuine passion or love to the point of indistinguishability. Love is both an allegory and a symptom of politics. Love that in some way transgresses social norms (parental prohibition, differences of station, etc.) means, at least where Chernyshevsky is concerned, revolution. The fact that Russian writers find it hard to tell stories of "our best men" heeding the demands of such love is linked at the root with their exclusion from political action. Deadlock—the experience of one's own incapacity for love/politics—is the affect of such exclusion.

Polemically, Chernyshevsky's portrait of the Russian at the rendezvous constitutes an attack on a certain generation of gentry intelligentsia to which the authors and protagonists mentioned in the article belong. We may find it surprising, then, to discover a similar dynamic play out in the work of a next-generation radical activist such as Sleptsov. Yet *Hard Times* concludes with a similar characterological twist. The rendezvous takes place in Riazanov's room, where Marya Shchetinina confesses her wish to become his friend and lover. Riazanov does not appear to reciprocate her impulse. Dejected and disappointed, Shchetinina steps toward the door, and we witness the following scene: "'I wish you success,' he said without stirring from his place as she was leaving the room; almost at the same moment he hurled [*shvyrnul*] the book, with all his might under the table; seizing his hair with both hands he rushed forward but then stopped, dropped his hands, shook his head, smiled, and began pacing the room."[62]

What makes such a violent outbreak particularly conspicuous is that throughout the novel, Riazanov is restrained and ironically uninvolved. The passage is structured as a dramatization of a powerful impulse, frustrated from within. In the original, the two opposing vectors are separated by an ellipsis—"rushed forward... but then stopped"—dilating the space of mysteriously motivated hindrance. The reader is compelled to search for reasons of Riazanov's refusal to obey his impulse, but in accordance with the poetics of the tableau, the hints are only external: "dropped his hands," "shook his head," "smiled," "began pacing"—all they do is sustain our attention on the mystery itself. The solution to the mystery cannot be found "inside" Riazanov; as the context in which Shchetinina makes her offer suggests, we are once again dealing with a borderline phenomenon: psychic and political both. In the midst of a countrywide reaction, with its leaders imprisoned, exiled, or dead, the radical movement is devastated. Riazanov himself, haggard and in poor health, seems to have come to Shchetinin's estate fleeing police surveillance.

We find Riazanov in a comparable state of agitation only once more in the course of the novel. In that earlier episode, he picks up a recently arrived volume of a St. Petersburg journal, finds his own article in it, and begins to compare it with his original manuscript. Evidently discovering important changes made by the censors, he hurls (again: *shvyrnul*) the volume toward the window and sinks deep into thought.[63] The two outbursts share more than might appear at first glance. They both feature affective responses to defeat, projected as a violent curbing of impulse or expression. The directness and explicitness of the early sequence, though inevitably mindful of the censors, sheds light on the later episode, in which no explicit link is established between the defeat of the revolutionary movement and Riazanov's failure at the rendezvous. In this way, the text creates an affective continuum between personal and political failure, staging the incursion of substance into self.

The movement from mania to deadlock involves a degree of disengagement from the sphere of the political proper—the sphere of foundation, crisis, rebellion, and so on. Yet as the domain of political authority recedes from the field of representation, we do not find characters liberated to pursue their desires, for better or for worse. In scenarios of deadlock, the body politic is far away yet very close: the external aura of substantive meaningfulness and belonging fades, even as the experiences of constraint and coercion "enter into blood." Safer than violent mania, deadlock does not devastate but just as surely deadens.

3. LANGUISHING

If (predominantly male) deadlock stages substantive prohibition internalized at the level of individual desire and action, (predominantly female) languishing registers similar internalization at a still deeper level, the level of the individual's vital forces. Tableaux of languishing show the heroine in a state of profound lethargy: her head droops, her eyes are dull, her skin pale; her movements are slow; she is pensive but cannot concentrate on her thoughts. Here is Polinka Saks, describing her state following the divorce:

> I have a pain in my chest and at times a fever. That's not too important… but sometimes I fall into a stupor, walk around all day as if in a fog… Certain fragments of thoughts run through my mind night and day; sometimes I sit for hours at a time staring at one and the same place, thinking about nothing at all. (104–5; 54)

Illness (in fact, illness unto death), stupor, generalized weakness and dejection, dispersed thinking, heart palpitations—all the major components of the relevant affect are here. Added to them, too, is the key to her condition, her magnanimous ex-husband's parting threat, which continues to haunt her as an ominous vestige of his power and his love. Saks kills her by letting her go, and the text manages to have it both ways: to stage the statesman-husband's absolute power over her life and death and to assert the enlightened character of that power. Languishing here is coded as the state of being—and at the same time of needing to be—ruled. The predicament of the languishing subject is one in which she would not know what to do with her freedom.

Pyotr Aduev's wife says this much directly. Looking at her "lifeless, dim eyes," "her face, totally devoid of the animation of thought and feelings," her "apathetic pose and sluggish movements," Aduev vaguely grasps her condition as the outcome of having lived in "a fortress which [...] had been made impregnable to temptation from the outside, while inside, it was patrolled and barricaded against all legitimate expression of feeling" (322–23; 1:459). The fortress, walled off and vigilantly guarded inside, figures not only a particular type of family life but also the structure of the languishing subjectivity itself, one that is not only externally constrained and isolated but thoroughly overseen and "disabled" from within. By comparison with Druzhinin, Goncharov presents us with a less spectacular but no less effective form of power. It goes about things in a different way but achieves similar results when it comes to mastering its "subject."

Unlike mania and deadlock, which anchor temporally condensed, "intensive" instances of *pathos*, languishing (along with melancholy) undramatically distends in time. The narrator of *Who Is to Blame?* comments explicitly to this effect. One night, poisoned by jealousy, Krutsifersky keeps watch over his sleeping wife, staring at her "with such hatred and ferocity that had he not subscribed to the peace-loving customs of our age, he would have smothered her in bed just as the Venetian Moor did Desdemona." But: "our modern tragedies do not end so drastically" (266; 4:190). Krutsifersky smothers Lyuba more slowly, with his own self-sacrificing misery. "Today it occurred to me," she writes in her journal, "that self-sacrificing love is nothing more than an extreme form of egoism, and that great humility and meekness are merely a terrible form of pride or disguised harshness" (263; 4:186). The disguise drops off momentarily with the Shakespearean allusion to *Othello*, establishing a continuum that links the husband's murderous rage to his self-destructive despair and, in turn, to Lyuba's own appearance at the end of the novel as a "dying young woman with sunken cheeks, enormous sparkling eyes and hair tumbling down onto her shoulders" (289; 4:209). Aduev, Saks, and Krutsifersky represent three distinct types of power: the power of rational discipline, of enlightened magnanimity, and of sentimental entanglement. Yet the outcomes are strikingly consistent: extended tableaux of languishing in which the heroine finds herself drained of life and moribund. This deathward movement exposes the surplus of sovereign power—the power "to let live and make die"—behind these ostensibly milder, less dramatic manifestations of control.

A more explicit relationship between the *pathos* of languishing and proximity to naked power organizes much of Pisemsky's *Boyarshchina*. The heroine appears from the start as a pale, thin woman with a sickly flush on her cheeks and a sad expression on her face, as if in the grips of some "secret grief." We then become acquainted with the story of her marriage, insisted upon by her father, whom she obeys like "a new Tatyana," only to become so thin from grief as to be unrecognizable during her wedding. She is then beaten and thrown out of her home by her husband, met by her lover with the demand that she belong to him "like property," must hide out in the field when her husband brings the police to her lover's house, is abandoned by her lover, pursued by the lascivious Count Sapega, who acts under cover of being a father figure and recruits the state apparatus in his effort to possess her. Declining, bedridden, mad, and finally dead, her *pathos* registers a cumulative substance, connecting father, husband, lover, aristocrat, and the state—all wielding exceptional power over her, exposing her to the elements, to rage, to lust, as bare life.

This emphasis on exposure, on the loss of protection within the symbolic order, allows *Boyarshchina* to add an extra twist to the dynamics of female languishing. Highlighted here is the fact that the jurisdiction of death-dealing power extends beyond the threshold of the woman's home. The predicament is registered with great precision in *Anna Karenina* by the heroine's sister-in-law as that of being "nobody's wife." To be nobody's wife is to lose all grounding in the symbolic, to become a mere living thing. As it turns out, this condition matches Anna's organizing characterological trait: her vitality itself, the animation that waxes and wanes, and at least initially falls within the jurisdiction of her husband. Languishing, "extinguished in her or hidden somewhere far away" under his administration, it is powerfully released outside it, but at the price of desocialization. Distilled to bare life, Anna reappears at the end as a disfigured carcass on the rail tracks, testifying to the fact that the power remains in force even if no one acts to assert it. This culminating tableau makes visible the power of the husband to kill the adulterous wife (à la Dumas's *L'homme-femme*), while rarefying it to the sheer predicament of suffering a fate.

Our texts repeatedly produce stark representations of languishing to mark the traversal of (female) life by sovereign power. Whether such power appears as disciplinary, magnanimous, sentimentally binding, or even altogether depersonalized, the heroine's listlessness unto death discloses the kernel of sovereign violence more or less concealed in the familial dynamics to which she is subjected. These tableaux momentarily freeze and expose to contemplation the schema of substantive belonging, within which the heroine is revealed as both less and more than an individual: less insofar as she is reduced to sheer vitality exposed to death; more because in the space of that exposure, she is claimed by a force that is daemonically outside, against, and within her at once.

4. MELANCHOLY

The affective movement from mania to melancholy traverses the territory between the two bodies of the king, a kind of *continuum in which the protagonist is determined as a ratio of substance to creature*. Acting within, or on behalf of, the body politic, the protagonist manifests that weighty body through heightened rhetoric, infused with sublimity, universality, and force. Reduced to the status of the body natural, the hero/ine succumbs to helplessness in the face of death, blind and indifferent nature, and the vanity of earthly things. Walter Benjamin's account of the conception of kingship in German Baroque tragic drama (*Trauerspiel*) highlights this latter melancholy modality in particular. In Benjamin's reading, the tragic drama of the German Baroque registers a crisis in the theocratic notion of kingship: the separation of the sovereign's absolute civil authority from the authority of the church.[64] The sovereign now becomes a wholly earthly ruler, whose divine extraction is belied by his status as a mortal being. This immanent conception of kingship engenders a peculiar anxiety associated with the sovereign's irreducibly "private," extralegal, and yet defining capacity to decide in vital matters of the state. The sovereign's indecisiveness, his excesses, his vulnerability to intrigue, his exposure to the vagaries of fate—all testify to the "antithesis between the [political] power of the ruler and his [personal] capacity to rule."[65] The vision of the collapse and disintegration of the sovereign, his reduction to creaturely privacy corresponds, in turn, to the devolution of history as it were "back" into nature. When the sovereign, who "holds the course of history in his hands like a scepter,"[66] rages and dies, then "human actions are deprived of all value."[67] Melancholy is the generalized affect accompanying the realization that the sovereign is, in a sense, always already dead, drawing all worldly things with him into oblivion. Put another way, melancholy links the evanescence of the body politic to the loss of symbolic investment in all spheres of existence.

Benjamin's account of tragic melancholy as a response to the crisis of theocratic rule has proved productive beyond the German Baroque. Moretti appeals to Benjamin in his analysis of Elizabethan tragic theater's concern with the reduction of the sovereign to "his physical and private person."[68] Foucault detects a similar preoccupation in Racine, whose tragedies focus on "the moment when the sovereign, the possessor of public might, is gradually broken down into a man of passion, a man of anger, a man of vengeance, a man of love, incest, and so on."[69] In the Russian context, Kirill Ospovat makes extensive use of Benjamin's analysis in his readings of mid-eighteenth-century theater and *The Bronze Horseman*.⁷⁰ When it comes to the Russian realist tradition, too, melancholy proves an extraordinarily widespread affect, linked to the depiction of private life from the perspective that privileges substantive belonging. Here, the dramatic collapse of the body politic onto the body natural reappears as an image of a dismal life cut off (ambiguously liberated) from the (manic) exigencies of political striving. In his article on *Woe from Wit*, Belinsky contrasts the poetry of actuality found in the tragic *Taras Bulba* with Gogol's own fundamentally melancholy "Tale of How Ivan Ivanovich Quarreled with Ivan Nikiforovich." The tale of the absurd quarrel between two neighbors and friends, the quarrel that drags on into their old age, ends on a rainy day: "Those fields again, with black plowed patches in places, showing green in others, the drenched cows and jackdaws, monotonous rain and a tearful sky without one ray of sunlight.... It is a dreary world, gentlemen."⁷¹ Belinsky comments: "Yes! It is sad to think that the human being, this most noble vessel of spirit, can live and die as a ghost and in the ghostly [*v prizrakakh*], without even suspecting the existence of actual [*deistvitel'noi*] life."⁷²

Actual life for Belinsky is, as we have seen, the life of substance, or polity, the conscious life of participation, to whatever extent possible, in the affairs of the state. What falls away from substance, is vanity of vanities, comic on the surface, but essentially melancholy. Toward the end of *The Same Old Story*, the disillusioned Alexander briefly leads such a ghostly existence, avoiding contact with his uncle and apparently content with the life of idleness and isolation. This final act of protest, this refusal to take part in his mentor's disciplinary scripts, brings with it some relief, and a great deal of despair: "Before him stretched raw reality, as boundless as a steppe. Oh God, the sheer immensity of that space! What a grim and joyless prospect! The past has perished, the future had been destroyed, happiness did not exist" (244; 1:389). Or: "He was afraid of wanting things, knowing that at the very moment when what you wished for is in your grasp, fate will snatch it from you and present you with something quite different, which you have absolutely no desire for" (245; 1:390). And again: "What was wonderful yesterday is worthless today; what you wanted yesterday, you don't want today; yesterday's friend is today's enemy" (272; 1:414). Alexander's disengagement from his uncle, his attempt to finally lead an independent life, coincides with the proliferation of melancholy laments about the transience of life and the vagaries of fate. Outside the family and the state, outside the substantive bonds that painfully constrain him (and in the end assimilate him without a remainder), the protagonist finds himself in an existential vacuum, exposed in "a boundless steppe" to the unfathomable laws of decomposition.

A similar socioaffective distribution structures *Who Is to Blame?*, whose protagonist succumbs to grief precisely in the interval between his unrealized desire to serve the state and his emotional entanglement with the Krutsiferskys. We find a fully realized tableau of melancholy in a scene where Beltov gazes at his portrait as a youth, sent to him from Switzerland by his dying mentor M. Joseph:

> "Then," thought Beltov as he looked reproachfully at the portrait, "then I was only fourteen. Now I am over thirty. What lies ahead? Nothing but a vast, gray mist, a dull, monotonous continuation of the present. It is too late to begin a new life, but it is no longer possible to continue the old one. How many beginnings have I made! How many people have I met! Yet everything has resulted in idleness and loneliness…" (225; 4:152)

The elegiac mood of this passage, mourning both the death of his beloved teacher and the vanishing into the past of his youthful, hopeful self, frames the expression of melancholy *pathos* that in turn characterizes the protagonist's experience of exclusion from the realm of meaningful activity. His failure to find an occupation outside state service takes him down a meandering path of transitory occupations, encounters, and interests—until, that is, his introduction to the Krutsiferskys. Once again, we find a parallel between politics and love, service of the state and sentimental drama. As we have seen, the failures, too, are parallel. But what lies between them—where the aggregative realm of the social might be found, where the premise of individuality is taken for granted—is still worse than failure: it is life under the sign of *vanitas*, in the shadow of death.

Turgenev's *First Love* offers a still more elaborate example of melancholy *pathos*, together with its detailed genealogy. The dizzying succession of death scenes at the end of the tale begins with the death of Volodya's father. The diagnosis of apoplectic stroke, as well as the first lines of an unfinished letter ("My son [...] beware a woman's love, beware that happiness, that poison....") designate this death as a death of passion (200; 6:362). That the overweening father must die—that passion and death, in their interconnectedness, signify creaturely frailty from which even the sovereign is not exempt—emblematizes the psychopolitical workings of melancholy. The father's death opens the floodgates of death imagery—first Zinaida's, then that of an old woman—commented upon by the mournfully contemplative hero-narrator: "So that's how it's all worked out! It's to this that that young, ardent, brilliant life has come after all its haste and excitement! In thinking this I imagined to myself those features so dear to me, those eyes, those curls all locked away in a narrow box in their damp underground darkness" (201; 6:363). The downfall of the father-sovereign triggers a process of melancholy contagion, which culminates in universal creaturely solidarity in death. "In Trauerspiel," writes Benjamin, "[death] frequently takes the form of a communal fate, as if summoning all the participants before the highest court."[73]

The mood of all-embracing melancholy at the end of the tale casts a backward, elegiac shadow over the narrative as a whole. Exiled from the realm of significant action, Volodya confronts a world in the grips of mysterious forces beyond his control; the world is de-formed and de-realized (producing a social realism of shadows) by the hidden machinations in the background. The narrative lingers lovingly on the standard realist subject matter now rendered utterly weightless: the world of objects, feelings, gestures, settings—all mourned as what has never been real to begin with: "Even then, in that light-minded time of youth, I was not deaf to the sad voice that called to me [...] from beyond the grave" (202; 6:363). The melancholy narrator gives us the social world, the world of "realism," as irreal, subject to the workings of the occult sphere imaged as the sphere of violence, vitality, and the will. All life, sucked out of the social/private domain, has been concentrated there, at the site of the political allegory, where "autocratic" fathers and self-styled "queens" live all too intensely and die young.

Toward the end of *Anna Karenina*, Konstantin Levin—happy husband, proud father, conscientious landowner, and good man—is haunted by thoughts of death and on the verge of suicide. In a noteworthy late scene, Levin observes peasants at work on his estate with a melancholy gaze:

> Why are they bustling about and trying to show me their zeal? Why is this woman toiling so? ... Today or tomorrow or in ten years they'll bury her and nothing will be left of her, nor of that saucy one in the red skirt who is beating the grain from the chaff with such a deft and tender movement. She'll be buried, too, and so will this piebald gelding—very soon.... He'll be buried, and Fedor, the feeder, with his curly beard full of chaff and the shirt torn on his white shoulder, will also be buried.... And above all, not only they, but I, too, will be buried and nothing will be left.[74]

Through much of the novel, Levin is preoccupied with the "peasant question," the question of their poverty and his wealth, and of the "unfair advantages" he is uncomfortable enjoying. He considers several solutions to this problem. One, occurring to him after he witnesses a similar, but more joyfully focalized scene of peasant labor earlier in the novel, is simply to change his "so burdensome, idle, artificial and individual life into [the peasants'] laborious, pure and common, lovely life" (275; 18:291). Another solution involves writing a book on political economy in which proper relations to the land and those who work it could be outlined: "Instead of poverty—universal wealth, prosperity; instead of hostility—concord and the joining of interests. In short, a revolution, a bloodless and great revolution, first in the small circle of our own region, then the province, Russia, the whole world" (344; 18:363). But Levin settles on the third solution: to accept that nothing can be done. He does not lead a bloodless revolution or join the joyful, common life of peasant labor. Instead, he marries Kitty and takes good care of his estate so as to be able to pass it on, intact, to his children.

Yet personal happiness turns out not to be enough, and so at the end, he casts his melancholy gaze on the peasants who work for him, kills them off one by one, along with the animals, and, for good measure, buries himself. What accounts for the reemergence of melancholy *pathos* at what one might expect to be the high point the hero's biography? Why is it impossible simply to assume—as many a Western European novel does—that it is a good and right thing for there to exist happy, wealthy, benevolent, and virtuous gentlemen with thriving families and fertile fields? Belinsky's para-Hegelian dictum continues to hold: nonsubstantive, merely private life—life that is not preoccupied with the question of the common good and is excluded from the zone of political sovereignty—is melancholy and ghostly.

The final sections of the novel establish a curious parallelism between supposedly countrywide enthusiasm for the coming war with Ottoman Turkey and Levin's realization that one must live not "for the stomach" but "for the soul." The juxtaposition of these two themes at the conclusion of the novel is not accidental. At stake in both cases is a disavowal of private interests for the sake of a higher unity. Levin's older half brother, Sergei Ivanovich, claims that the entire Russian people is united in a feeling of solidarity with the Slavic peoples' sufferings under the Ottoman yoke. "All the most diverse parties in the world of intelligentsia, so hostile before, have merged into one," he says. "All discord has ended, all social organs are saying one and the same thing, everyone has felt the elemental power that has caught them up and is carrying them in one direction" (808; 19:390). Before us is the familiar situation of wartime social unity, a universal, manic sense of being carried along, all together, by an elemental force.

Levin remains indifferent to this substantive option and pursues another one instead. Walking away from an enlightening conversation with a peasant, he feels a growing commitment to "[living] for God and not for [his own] needs" (797; 19:379). He believes he has at last come to recognize "the Master," to whom he is ready to sacrifice the demands of his self-interest. National unity (in war) and human brotherhood (in God) both counteract the melancholy that arises as the affect of private mortality. Both, too, are accompanied by images associated with mania: the elemental power bringing all Russians together as described by Sergey Ivanovich, and Levin's excitement at the thought of service to the divine, which has "the effect of an electric spark in his soul, suddenly transforming and uniting into one the whole swarm of disjointed, impotent, separate thoughts" (794; 19:376).

In an 1883 review of *Anna Karenina* alongside Turgenev's *Virgin Land* (1877) and *The Brothers Karamazov*, Nikolai Strakhov sets out to understand the reasons for Levin's puzzling predicament at the end. Why, he asks, would this happy, wealthy, educated man who has everything he has ever wanted still entertain thoughts of suicide? "If my life and happiness is the sole purpose of life," writes Strakhov in an attempt to respond, "then this purpose is so pitiful, so fragile, so obviously unachievable that it can only invoke despair, can only weigh on a person, rather than inspire him."[75] Levin's subjection to death, in other words, has something to do with his incapacity, until the moment of final "conversion," to conceive of himself as part of that which does not die. Melancholy is here the affect of privacy regarded from the standpoint of substance. In dwelling on the protagonist's perplexing condition at the end—why, if he is happy, is he so sad?—the novel registers the affective price paid by the protagonist for leading the kind of life that finds no legitimate foundation in the novel's underlying social imaginary. Within the parameters of this imaginary, the private individual—however satisfied and fulfilled in his personal pursuits—is grasped as the outcome of the most extreme and successful form of oppression in which sovereignty both vanishes from view and reappears as the deathward trajectory of the creature. Such is the verdict of a narrative form lodged at the intersection between novelistic realism and the imaginary exigencies of substantive belonging.

Discipline and *Pathos*

In connection with the novels of Émile Zola, Fredric Jameson describes Western realist fiction's tendency to treat affect as something to be controlled, regulated, and disciplined. Only as a result of such a painstaking effort does the acceptable individual come into being in the first place. This is achieved in "the mastering of affect [...] by the bourgeois ideology of the body and its training, manners, stances and practice."[76] More recently, Audrey Jaffe has explored the Victorian novel's articulation of affect to class and class to affect, resulting in a vision of the poor as "in thrall to impulse and desire, to an animality assumed to be their inherent affective state," while casting model members of the middle and upper classes as capable of rising above "their own immediate, instinctive responses."[77] The movement from a cluster of affects to a socialized individual is a developmental movement "upward," a process of integration into a group, and the precondition for social mobility. How this process unfolds varies from text to text. Drawing on our Western case studies, we can see how the protagonists gradually master impulse, passion, and vitality, channeling them into respective scripts of aggregative socialization. Rastignac learns what and how to desire by imitating the desires of others and by learning what it takes to succeed without running afoul of the legal order. Jane learns to discipline her inborn passion, to internalize the harsh limitations imposed upon it by human and divine law. With proper guidance, Wilhelm proves able, up to a point at least, to channel his inchoate generous impulses into the broader and more predictable course of enlightened social improvement. The Western model can thus be described as tracing the success (or, in some cases, failure) of the process by which the subject sublimates inchoate affect on the way to becoming a socialized individual.

That sheer affect is dangerous and must be controlled is a thought one can encounter in our Russian realist corpus as well—most insistently, perhaps, in Alexander Aduev's "civilizing process." Yet far more prominent than this is a different affective structure, the workings of *pathos* that transfixes the body/psyche of a character as the locus at which a kind of substance is made visible. To undergo *pathos* is to be traversed, and claimed, by a certain type of belonging. As such, it is an experience of meaningfulness and coercion both, blending together in unstable, uncertain proportions so as to highlight the splendor and the misery of being connected in an absolute and therefore conflict-ridden way to an intense association that at pivotal points makes it difficult to specify the very boundaries of the individual. As an affectively articulated point of indistinction between self and substance, scenes of *pathos* serve as sites for the staging of the sovereignty effect, interpreting the individual as the space of contestation between body politic and body natural: "Am I a trembling creature or do I have the right?"

Raskolnikov's stark alternative marks the outer boundaries of the modern social imaginary converging on the figure designated as "citizen subject" by Étienne Balibar. Commenting on a passage from Rousseau's *Social Contract*, Balibar writes: "Precisely in his capacity as 'citizen,' the citizen is (indivisibly) *above* any law, otherwise he could not legislate, much less constitute [...]. In his capacity as 'subject' (that is, inasmuch as the laws he formulates are imperative, to be executed universally and unconditionally, inasmuch as the pact is not a 'vain formula') he is necessarily *under* the law."[78] The dualism is resolved in Rousseau by placing the citizen neither below nor above, but precisely at the level of the law—a solution that generates further dilemmas that bear an affinity with the problematics of hegemony, enfranchisement, and discipline, and play out, among other places, on the terrain of European realist fiction. Raskolnikov's question, meanwhile, cracks the figure of the "citizen subject" open, revealing, as it were, "inside" it a different social-imaginary persona: that of the "sovereign-creature." The hero's formula suggests that the only alternative to full sovereignty (with the right to "take life and let live") is creaturely abjection, the abjection of a merely private person who, by virtue of being merely private, has no reason to exist at all.

Articulated to this figure of the sovereign-creature are the multiple tableaux of *pathos*, spanning the chromatic range from the mania that accompanies the experience of direct confrontation or merging with the body politic, to the melancholy of exclusion from political life and significant action. At each pole, the other is present in its negation: one "has the right," is the sovereign insofar as one has ceased, in a moment of mania, to feel the weight of creaturely frailty; one is "a trembling creature" when one's experience of exclusion and subjection is so deep that it appears to be as inescapable as physical suffering and death. Between these poles, we have a wide variety of affective inflections marking the traversal of the individual by substance, more and less subtle, more and less dramatic, and more or less temporally condensed.[79] In *mania*, substance (thematized as polity, family, or nation, or constructed as a hybrid of these) transfixes the individual in a scene of dramatic encounter: possession, embodiment, collision—all figuring a crisis in the zone of sovereignty. In *deadlock*, the individual finds himself, at a turning point in his biography, affected at a distance; the sovereign "no" is spoken from within, appears as a character flaw, a psychic attenuation. *Languishing* makes visible upon the body of the heroine the workings of sovereign power, variously thematized but invariably domestic. Languishing is the affect of subjection within the household, which functions simultaneously as a displacement of political power and its reduction to essence: the paterfamilias as the original despot, his dependents constituted, in their exposure to his authority, as bare life. *Melancholy*, finally, marks the absolute outer reaches of substance, its vanishing into the elements. On the side of the subject, *melancholy* marks the emergence of the private person as the outcome of domination through exclusion. It thus delineates the Russian counterpart—produced within the horizon of a distinctive social imaginary oriented toward the state (and substantive order more broadly)—of that pivotal figure of European realism: the individual pursuing, with varied success, his or her "happy objects"[80] within a social world made up of similarly engaged individuals. Within the purview of a social imaginary that habitually yields sovereignty effects, *melancholy* marks the bearer of private life as a body natural, a creature whose ultimate end and purpose is death.

Making the State Visible [EPILOGUE]

One way to formulate the overriding concern of this study is to ask what happens to the realist project of social hermeneutics when it is undertaken in an environment that stimulates social imaginaries articulated to the political authority of the state. I have tried to show that the crossing of literary realism with sovereignty-oriented imaginaries yields distinctive formal responses to many of the central social dilemmas of modern life. In the bleak light of Russia's military aggression in Ukraine, accompanied by state-of-exception-style stifling of dissent, proliferating economic violence, and coercive social atomization at home, it may be tempting to understand this distinctiveness as a symptom of some ostensibly inherent or historically stable national culture, or "mentality." I hope that this is not the spirit in which this book is read, especially since such cultural or civilizational essentialism informs the bellicose myths currently purveyed by the Russian state itself. Rather, I would like to suggest that the imaginaries registered in our corpus of texts are rooted in and constitute responses to a historically concrete conjuncture that is, like every such conjuncture, both unique and partially iterable. I also hope to have made clear the extent to which these responses themselves are diverse, ranging among, and at times combining, scripts of resistance, critique, compromise, accommodation, and so on. What unites them and makes them distinctive is their tendency to see the state—sovereign power as the site of substantive belonging—as an unsurpassable horizon of modern sociality.

Broadly understood as an ensemble of institutions with a socially accepted function of making and enforcing decisions on a given population on behalf of its "common interest," the political state has for centuries constituted such a horizon for European and Russian societies alike.[1] The state's capacity to enforce decisions (sovereignty) and its claim to embody the common good (substance) as well as its claim to social legitimacy (representation) were not unique to the Russian empire, but they did draw the uniquely relentless attention of Russian realist imaginaries of the social. Such attention, in turn, yielded a distinctive range of images, rhetorical registers, narrative shapes, and structures of feeling, offering an especially clear-eyed, sober view of modern society, skeptical of hasty assumptions that despotic domination has been tamed and that the problem of collective welfare is a priori unresolvable or resolved. What takes place here is akin to the process Roberto Schwarz has described with reference to postcolonial Brazilian reception of European liberalism. Ill-fitting in a slave-owning and patronage society, these "misplaced ideas" are relativized and exposed as ideological obfuscations—not only in relation to the realities of their new setting but also, in a kind of critical boomerang effect, in relation to the realities at their (European) source. Schwarz describes the resulting effect as "an emptying out of what is already hollow."[2]

In recent years, a number of social theorists have spoken of the need to conceptualize the contemporary social formation in the West as "posthegemonic," characterized by the "withering of civil society" and the corresponding transition from disciplinarity, mediated through institutions, to direct surveillance and control.[3] This new predicament exposes subjects to power not as institutionally defined, disciplined individuals but as sheer contingent identities, characterized by anonymity and infinite mobility, and subject to flexible control within the parameters of neoliberal state governance. The resulting configuration posits the subject who is at once depoliticized and ruled directly, despotically, like a member of the household by the *pater familias*. The state of exception becomes the norm and reaches "maximum worldwide deployment."[4]

Referring to something like this context twenty years ago, Eve Kosofsky Sedgwick wonders what the point might be in producing critical genealogies of the welfare state and its "pastoral" practices at the time when such states are being rapidly dismantled and we witness everywhere the "ethos where forms of violence that are hypervisible from the start may be offered as an exemplary spectacle rather than remain to be unveiled as a scandalous secret."[5] What appears "hollow" in this situation, then, is the very assurance that sovereign power is something we have put behind us, that it is no longer our problem, that it belongs in the past, somewhere else, or, ideally, both. Such assurances are repeatedly belied by our texts, which suggest that certain elements of the modern social imaginary—the faith in the elemental status of the individual, in the providential workings of the market and of social aggregation more generally, in the intrinsic meaningfulness and value of private life and personal happiness—do not protect but more thoroughly expose us to manifestations of exceptional violence. Depending on the social formation of which it constitutes an indispensable part, such supreme authority may manifest itself in direct and spectacular forms under the generalized state of exception, or as preshaping apparently "natural" economic and social outcomes, or insinuating itself into the process of "constitution and reproduction of social classes."[6]

The critical or paranoid perspective offered by a prominent strain within Russian realism, its obsessive "seeing through to" and "making visible" domination, can nevertheless be complemented by its utopian or reparative tendencies.[7] Prominent among these would be the emphasis on substantive, or political, belonging, understood as the locus of collective meaning and the common good. In the context of a neoliberal denigration of the political,[8] the Russian realist recourse to political affects, personas, and plots as well as its generative location at the political heart of things can—despite but also because of the evident exigencies endowing it with historically specific and therefore privative forms—recall us to the hope of a genuinely common life. In these ways and others, the eccentric social hermeneutics of Russian realism can be read as more than a mere historical curiosity stretching our assumptions about what realist fiction tends to register and what to disregard, but also as an interlocutor for an estranged, bifocal reflection on our own social predicaments today.

Acknowledgments

This book took shape under the influence of countless exchanges with friends and colleagues within and outside institutional settings. Very early on, before a single word of it had been written, Michael Holquist demanded explanations and offered warm encouragement. I am grateful for his mentorship and friendship, which will always be among the fondest of memories. Likewise early and throughout, Nasser Zakariya was there to read rough drafts and talk through them, then read and talk through later versions. Over the years, it has become impossible to do any thinking or writing without his direct or latent participation. Alyx Cullen has been an inexhaustible source of ideas and a stronghold of relentless affection and support. Her intellectual curiosity, thoroughness in research, and commitment to her projects have set a high standard for my own. I am very fortunate to be sharing my life and work with her.

Among the many settings that enabled this project to take shape, I would like to mention with special gratitude the Working Group in Historical Poetics. Its participants, Luba Golburt, Kate Holland, Michael Kunichika, Boris Maslov, Jessica Merrill, and Victoria Somoff, have all read and commented on parts of this book. Regular exchanges with Boris Maslov, in the context of the working group, of coauthoring, and of coteaching, and outside any particular institutional context, have generated a special mix of collaboration, friendship, and ongoing debate—all invigorating and productive for this project and many others. Michael Kunichika responded to parts of the book, early and late, and has been as insightful and generous an interlocutor as one could possibly wish. Sharing thoughts and exchanging ideas on nineteenth-century fiction with Kate Holland has become second nature.

Parts of the project were presented at events organized by Ilya Bendersky, Natalia Borisova, Sara Dickinson, Özen Nergis Seckin Dolcerocca,

Anatoliy Korchinksy, Radik Lapushin, Anne Lounsbery, Boris Maslov, Riccardo Nicolosi, Kirill Ospovat, Harsha Ram, Valeria Sobol, Lina Steiner, Alexey Vdovin, and Kirill Zubkov. My warmest thanks to them all, as well as to Michael Finke, Jennifer Flaherty, Bella Grigorian, Lilya Kaganovsky, Olga Maiorova, Harriet Murav, Irina Paperno, and Schamma Schahadat, whose insightful observations at these events have helped me formulate and clarify aspects of the project. Over the years, the project has benefited from the generosity of Harsha Ram, who has read and commented on earlier versions of many sections of this book, which owes its current shape in significant part to his engagement. Jennifer Flaherty has been a frequent and formidably thoughtful interlocutor on matters proximately and distantly related to the book. Kirill Ospovat's rich and expansive feedback and patient encouragement (shading into exhortation) have been as helpful in improving the manuscript as his own like-minded projects have been inspiring.

Along with Boris Maslov and Kirill Ospovat, Alexey Vdovin and Masha Salazkina read the entire early version of the manuscript (overlong and unedited!) and offered many insightful suggestions for improvement. Traces of collaboration with Alexey and of his work more generally are evident throughout the book. At pivotal points, Masha was there to talk through matters of method and theory, as she had been since the days of graduate school.

At later stages of work, I benefited from the engagement, encouragement, and advocacy of Caryl Emerson and Jeanne-Marie Jackson. I am grateful to Nan Z. Da and Anahid Nersessian, editors of the Thinking Literature series, and Alan Thomas and Randy Petilos at the University of Chicago Press, for their belief in the project and their light-handed but firm and incisive guidance for its improvement. Much of whatever improvement has been made I owe to the engagement and erudition of anonymous reviewers for the University of Chicago Press, to Bud Bynack, who helped shorten the manuscript with patience and humor, and to Charles Dibble for his quick, keen, and charitable copyediting. Many thanks also to Brianna Philpot for her early editorial help.

I am grateful to my colleagues and friends at New York University, Eliot Borenstein, Rossen Djagalov, Yanni Kotsonis Anne Lounsbery, Chistina Vatulescu, and Maya Vinokour, for sharing their scholarly expertise, practical wisdom, companionship, and hospitality. I feel fortunate to work in a department that is imbued with so much spirit of cooperation and mutual aid. To my family, Sam Kliger, Olga Kliger, Marius Talochka, Hannah Kliger, Daniel Kliger, and Joseph Kliger I owe long-standing and multifarious gratitude—among other things, for the many ways they urged me to complete this book. To Sasha Kliger, a special thanks for growing up into a person from whose example I constantly learn. My mother, Tatyana Harash, did not live to see me begin this project, but her spirit, at once skeptical and earnest, accompanied its writing all the way.

Fellowships from the National Humanities Center, from New York University's Center for the Humanities, and from the Wissenschaftskolleg zu Berlin afforded time and stimulating environments for writing. I would like to thank in particular friends from Berlin—Gabriel Abend, Michel Durinx, Adrian Favell, Ilya Kalinin, Elena Kalinina, Christopher Kelty, Hannah Landecker, Sabina Leonelli, Teresa Castro Martin, Sean McMahon, Jessica Metcalf, Maxim Osipov, Anthony Ossa-Richardson, Plum Ossa-Richardson, David Nirenberg, Nuno Ramos, Sandra Antunes Ramos, Sophie Roux, Kulbhushansingh Suryawanshi, and Sofia Torallas Tovar—many of whom read parts of the book or helped me think through aspects of it, shared their own work, and, on the whole, made up a world of cooperative thinking and living with creativity and joy.

* * *

Early versions of portions of this book have appeared as "Sovereignty and the Novel: Dostoevsky's Political Theology" in *Dostoevsky at 200*, ed. Katherine Bowers and Kate Holland (Toronto: University of Toronto Press, 2021); "Distsiplinarnoe gosudarstvo i gorizonty sotsial'nosti: *Obyknovennaia istoriia* i poetika evropeiskogo realizma" in *Russkii realizm XIX veka: Obshchestvo, znanie, povestvovanie* (Moscow: NLO, 2020); "Scenarios of Power in Turgenev's *First Love*: Russian Realism and the Allegory of the State" in *Comparative Literature* (March 2018); "Tragic Nationalism in Dostoevsky and Nietzsche" in *Dostoevsky and Nietzsche*, ed. Jeff Love and Jeffrey Metzger (Evanston, IL: Northwestern University Press, 2016); "Hegel's Political Philosophy and the Social Imaginary of Early Russian Realism" in *Studies in Eastern European Thought* (March 2014); "Resurgent Forms in Ivan Goncharov and Alexander Veselovsky: Toward a Historical Poetics of Tragic Realism" in *Russian Review* (Fall 2012); and "Genre and Actuality in Belinsky, Herzen, and Goncharov: Toward a Genealogy of the Tragic Pattern in Russian Realism" in *Slavic Review* (Spring 2011).

Notes

Introduction

1. I draw most directly on the elaborations of the term found in Cornelius Castoriadis, *The Imaginary Institution of Society*, trans. Kathleen Blamey (Cambridge: Polity, 1987), 135–46; and Charles Taylor, *Modern Social Imaginaries* (Durham, NC: Duke University Press, 2004), 23–30.

2. Fredric Jameson, *The Political Unconscious: Narrative as a Socially Symbolic Act* (Ithaca, NY: Cornell University Press, 1981), 70. Jameson uses "must" instead of "can," and I subscribe to that stronger claim as well, but this is not the place to recapitulate the far-reaching argument, and for my purposes here the more limited formulation is sufficient.

3. We may recall, for example, Raymond Williams's observation that "from Dickens to Lawrence, over nearly a hundred years," fiction was most urgently preoccupied with the question of sociable living: "For this is a period in which what is meant to live in a community is more uncertain, more critical, more disturbing as a question put both to societies and to persons than ever before in history." See Williams, *The English Novel: From Dickens to Lawrence* (London: Hogarth, 1984), 12.

4. Lauren M. Goodlad, "Worlding Realisms Now," *Novel: A Forum on Fiction* 49, no. 2 (August 2016), 190.

5. I use the Marxist-structuralist term "social formation" to mean a historically concrete articulation of semiautonomous social, political, economic, and cultural-ideological domains. See, for example, Barry Hindress and Paul Q. Hirst, *Pre-capitalist Modes of Production* (London: Hanley; and Boston: Routledge and Kegan Paul, 1975), 13.

6. Pierre Bourdieu, *The Logic of Practice*, trans. Richard Nice (Stanford, CA: Stanford University Press, 1990), 53.

7. Indeed, in the context of this particular instantiation of nineteenth-century fiction, we are compelled to reconsider the very keystone of realism's social imaginary as it tends to be understood in mainstream scholarship: the figure of the individual. If my project has any merit, Nancy Armstrong's claim that "the novel was not made to think beyond the individual," for example, will have to be revised. See Armstrong, *How Novels Think: The Limits of Individualism from 1719–1900* (New York: Columbia University Press, 2006), 25.

8. The metaphor of literary history as a history of generals is found in Yuri Tynianov's

essay "On Literary Evolution." See Tynianov, *Permanent Evolution: Selected Essays on Literature, Theory and Film*, trans. and ed. Ainsley Morse and Philip Redko (Boston: Academic Studies Press, 2019), 267. Strictly speaking, of course, many of the authors discussed in this book are major, canonical figures with oversized cultural status. Tynianov's (and the Russian Formalists') project, however, is not to leave such figures out of literary history altogether, but to make sense of the fact that they, too, are subject to transpersonal, collective logics governing the literary process, in which their creations can, without shocking anyone's sensibilities, appear side-by-side with work by ostensibly "secondary" and "tertiary" authors: Pushkin next to Druzhinin, Tolstoy next to Sleptsov, and so on.

9. On the Russian formalist concepts of "deformation," "constructive function," and "orientation," see Tynianov, *Permanent Evolution*, especially the essays "Literary Fact," "The Ode as an Oratorial Genre," "On Literary Evolution," "Problems of the Study of Literature and Language" (with Roman Jakobson), and "Interlude."

10. It would be impossible to give an exhaustive list of scholars whose expertise in thick historical and literary-historical analysis of works and bodies of work belonging to nineteenth-century Russian realism has been indispensable for my thinking about the period. Their work is acknowledged throughout, in the body of the book as well as in the notes.

11. Fernand Braudel, *On History*, trans. Sarah Matthews (Chicago: University of Chicago Press, 1980), 3.

12. In a recent book dedicated to the study of turn-of-the-nineteenth-century British and French detective and spy fiction, Luc Boltanski makes a like-minded attempt to explore "the relation between the emergence of a literary form and the development of modes of governance that constituted the political environment for that genre." Specifically at stake for Boltanski are the two traditions' divergent representations of society, corresponding to the respective governmental approaches adopted by the two states. See Boltanski, *Mysteries and Conspiracies: Detective Stories, Spy Novels and the Making of Modern Society*, trans. Catherine Porter (Malden, MA: Polity, 2014), 26.

Chapter One

1. Georg Wilhelm Friedrich Hegel, *Elements of the Philosophy of Right*, trans. H. B. Nisbet, ed. Allen W. Wood (Cambridge: Cambridge University Press, 1991), 20.

2. Shlomo Avineri, *Hegel's Theory of the Modern State* (New York: Cambridge University Press, 1972), 123.

3. Yuri Mann, *Russkaia filosofskaia estetika* (Moscow: Iskusstvo, 1969), 235. Belinsky was understood in this way both by his contemporaries and by later scholars. Writing from abroad, Nikolai Stankevich asks Timofey Granovsky to convey this message to Belinsky and Mikhail Katkov, who, in his view, misunderstood Hegel's concept of *Wirklichkeit* by taking it to refer, simply, to "exterior being," or empirical immediacy. See also D. I. Chizhevsky, *Gegel' v Rossii* (St. Petersburg: Nauka, 2007), 159. Gustav Shpet in his article "K voprosu o gegel'ianstve Belinskogo" shows less interest in the correctness of Belinsky's interpretations than in their national and cultural symptomatics. See G. Shpet, *Ocherk razvitiia russkoi filosofii*, vol. 2 (Moscow: Rossiiskaia politicheskaia entsiklopediia, 2008-2009), 100-184. For more recent accounts of Belinsky's "reconciliation period," see Vadim Shkolnikov, "The Philosophical Cap of Yegor Fjodorovič or

Becoming Belinskij," *Studies in East European Thought* 65, nos. 3-4 (2013): 175-87; and Ilya Kliger, "Hegel's Political Philosophy and the Social Imaginary of Early Russian Realism," *Studies in East European Thought* 65, nos. 3-4 (2013): 189-99.

4. Allen W. Wood, editor's introduction in Hegel, *Elements of the Philosophy of Right*, x.

5. Vissarion Belinsky, "Borodinskaia godovshchina. V. Zhukovskogo," in *Polnoe sobranie sochinenii v 13i tomakh*, vol. 3, *Stat'i i retsenzii. Piatidesiatiletnii diadiushka, 1839-1840* (Moscow: Akademiia nauk, 1953), 242.

6. Belinsky, 3:246.

7. Belinsky, 3:246.

8. Belinsky, 3:247.

9. Belinsky, 3:247.

10. Hegel, *Elements of the Philosophy of Right*, 313; Allen W. Wood, *Hegel's Ethical Thought* (New York: Cambridge University Press, 1990), 240; Avineri, *Hegel's Theory of the Modern State*, 187.

11. Hegel, 203.

12. Hegel, 276. See Shlomo Avineri, *Hegel's Theory of the Modern State*, 133-34.

13. A discussion of civil society as the negation of Hegelian *Sittlichkeit* within *Sittlichkeit* itself can be found, for example, in Jean Cohen and Anthony Arato, *Civil Society and Political Theory* (Cambridge, MA: MIT Press, 1992), 95.

14. Belinsky, *Polnoe sobranie sochinenii*, vol 3, 338. Belinsky uses the term *grazhdanskoe obshchestvo* ("civil society") in its Hegelian sense, for example, in his unfinished article on "The Idea of Art" ("Ideia iskusstva"), written in 1841. His later appeals to *sotsial'nost'* (something like "social-mindedness") and *obshchestvennost'* (something like "the public") tend to refer, respectively, to the notions of social harmony (or "socialism") and the public sphere.

15. Vissarion Belinsky, "Ocherki Borodinskogo srazheniia (vospominaniia o 1812 gode). Sochineniia F. Glinki, avtora 'Pisem russkogo ofitsera.' Moskva. 1839," in *Polnoe sobranie sochinenii v 13i tomakh*, vol. 3, *Stat'i i retsenzii. Piatidesiatiletnii diadiushka, 1839-1840* (Moscow: Akademiia nauk, 1953), 343.

16. Georg Wilhelm Friedrich Hegel, *Phenomenology of Spirit*, trans. A. V. Miller (New York: Oxford University Press, 1979), 267-89. See also G. W. F. Hegel, *Hegel's Aesthetics: Lectures on Fine Art*, trans. T. M. Knox, 2 vols. (Oxford: Clarendon Press, 1988), 2: 1194-95.

17. In the account given in *Phenomenology*, the first step towards the establishment of what will later be called civil society is taken in the immediate aftermath of the collapse of the Greek city-states, namely in the figure of the "legal person" that arises in the context of Roman law. See Hegel, *Phenomenology of Spirit*, 290-94.

18. Belinsky, *Polnoe sobranie sochinenii*, 3:331-32.

19. Vissarion Belinsky to Mikhail Bakunin, September 10, 1838, in *Polnoe sobranie sochinenii*, vol. 11, *Pis'ma. 1829-1840* (Moscow: Akademiia nauk, 1956), 285.

20. The term "realism" (*realizm*) does not appear broadly in literary-critical discourse in Russia before the middle of the century. The first literary-critical use of the term is usually attributed to Pavel Annenkov, whose "Notes on Russian Literature from 1848," published in *Sovremennik* (1849, no. 1), allude, in turn, to Alexander Herzen's more expansively philosophical use of the term in *Letters on the Study of Nature* (1846). This latter text provides an overview of the long tradition of philosophical realism cul-

minating with Hegel. Herzen uses *"realizm"* to refer to the kind of intellectual stance that boldly and soberly confronts *"deistvitel'nost'."*

21. Vissarion Belinsky, "Razdelenie poezii na rody i vidy," in *Polnoe sobranie sochinenii*, vol. 5, *Stati' i retsenzii, 1841-1844*, 25, 28. See also "Mentsel, kritik Gete" in *Polnoe sobranie sochinenii*, 3:411–12.

22. Vissarion Belinsky, "Stat'i o Pushkine: Stat'ia sed'maia," in *Polnoe sobranie sochinenii*, vol. 7, *Stat'i i retsenzii, 1843: Stat'i o Pushkine, 1843-1846*, 406. "Drama," for Belinsky, is paradigmatically "tragedy."

23. Belinsky, "Gore ot uma," in *Polnoe sobranie sochinenii*, 3:440.

24. Belinksy, 3:439.

25. Belinksy, 3:439.

26. Belinksy, 3:445.

27. Belinksy, 3:445.

28. Belinksy, 3:445.

29. For a discussion of the complex relationship between tragedy and the novel in Hegel and German romantic aesthetics more broadly, see Richard Halpern, *Eclipse of Action: Tragedy and Political Economy* (Chicago: University of Chicago Press, 2017), 196–98.

30. For Hegel's account of the difference between (ancient) fate and (modern) providence, see Georg Wilhelm Friedrich Hegel, *The Encyclopaedia Logic*, trans. T. F. Geraets, W. A. Suchtig, and H. S. Harris (Indianapolis, IN: Hackett, 1991), 222–23.

31. Hegel, 222–23.

32. Hegel, *Hegel's Aesthetics*, trans. Knox, 1:593.

33. Jürgen Habermas, *The Philosophical Discourse of Modernity: Twelve Lectures (Studies in Contemporary German Social Thought)*, trans. Frederick G. Lawrence (Cambridge, MA: MIT Press, 1990), 37.

34. Hegel, *Elements of the Philosophy of Right*, 220–21.

35. Hegel, 229–33. My use of masculine pronouns is indexed to Hegel's notion that only men make up the membership of civil society. On tradition, innovation, and contradictions in Hegel's account of gender relations, see Wood, *Hegel's Ethical Thought*, 243–46.

36. Hegel, *Elements of the Philosophy of Right*, 240.

37. Hegel, 240.

38. Hegel, 226.

39. Hegel, 273. In Hegel's account, the aggregation of common interest marks the boundary between civil society and the state (278). "In our modern states," Hegel writes, "the citizens have only a limited share in the universal business of the state; but it is necessary to provide ethical man with universal activity in addition to his private end. This universal [activity], which the modern state does not always offer him, can be found in the corporation" (273). Meanwhile, the police, which Hegel defines as an institution of the executive branch of the state, charged with ordering and regulating the always more or less chaotic life of the system of needs, is "the state insofar as it relates to civil society." Quoted in Wood, *Hegel's Ethical Thought*, 283.

40. Hegel, 273.

41. Kenneth Westphal, "The Basic Context and Structure of Hegel's *Philosophy of Right*," in *The Cambridge Companion to Hegel*, ed. F. C. Beiser (New York: Cambridge University Press, 1993), 247.

42. Hegel, *Elements of the Philosophy of Right*, 224, 226, 240.

43. For a like-minded observation, see Terry Pinkard, *Hegel's Naturalism: Mind, Nature, and the Final Ends of Life* (Oxford: Oxford University Press, 2013), 156.

44. See György Lukács, *The Young Hegel: Studies in the Relations between Dialectics and Economics*, trans. Rodney Livingstone (Cambridge, MA: MIT Press, 1977), 400. "Animal kingdom of the Spirit" is Hegel's designation, in *Phenomenology of Spirit*, of what he will, in *Philosophy of Right*, call "the system of needs." Following Lukács's earlier observations on the novel, Lucien Goldmann argues that "there is a rigorous homology between the literary form of the novel [...] and the everyday relation between man and commodities in general, and by extension between men and other men, in a market society." See Goldmann, *Towards a Sociology of the Novel*, trans. Alan Sheridan (London: Tavistock, 1974), 7. Franco Moretti addresses the role of the market as a site of narrative innovation in Balzac and elsewhere in *The Way of the World: The Bildungsroman in European Culture* (New York: Verso, 2000), 142–48, and in *Atlas of the European Novel: 1800-1900* (New York: Verso, 1999), 109–10. Catherine Gallagher, Mary Poovey, and many others have explored the affinities between the European (mostly Victorian) novel and contemporary discourses of political economy. See Gallagher, *The Body Economic: Life, Death, and Sensation in Political Economy and the Victorian Novel* (Princeton. NJ: Princeton University Press, 2008); and Poovey, *Making a Social Body: British Cultural Formation, 1830–1864* (Chicago: University of Chicago Press, 1995).

45. Peter Brooks, *The Melodramatic Imagination: Balzac, Henry James, Melodrama, and the Mode of Excess* (New Haven, CT: Yale University Press, 1995), 143.

46. Honoré de Balzac, *Père Goriot*, trans. Burton Raffel, ed. Peter Brooks, Norton Critical Editions (New York: W. W. Norton, 1997), 26.

47. Balzac, 169–70.

48. Balzac, 89.

49. Balzac, 90.

50. Fredric Jameson's thesis on the fundamentally suprasubjective character of desire in Balzac is illuminating in this connection. Indeed, within the framework of the system of needs, the so-called centered subject proves impossible to sustain. Such a subject, after all, depends on the universality of the law. See Fredric Jameson, *The Political Unconscious: Narrative as Socially Symbolic Act* (Ithaca, NY: Cornell University Press, 1981), 179.

51. Charlotte Brontë, *Jane Eyre*, 3rd Norton Critical Edition (New York: W. W. Norton, 2016), 8.

52. Brontë, 12.

53. Brontë, 216.

54. Brontë, 269.

55. Brontë, 270.

56. On the complex relationship of unity-in-opposition between Jane and Bertha, see Sandra Gilbert and Susan Gubar's classic *The Madwoman in the Attic: The Woman Writer and the Nineteenth-Century Literary Imagination* (New Haven, CT: Yale University Press, 1979), 360. On self-government in *Jane Eyre* and the British novel more broadly, see Nancy Armstrong, "The Fiction of Bourgeois Morality and the Paradox of Individualism" in *The Novel*, vol. 2: *Forms and Themes*, ed. Franco Moretti (Princeton, NJ: Princeton University Press, 2006), 349–88. Susan Fraiman sums up an important

line of the novel's interpretation, which describes it as a narrative of bourgeois female subjectivity acquired at the expense of her foils: a woman from the working class (Grace Poole) and the "aboriginal" woman (Bertha Mason). See Fraiman, *Unbecoming Women: British Women Writers and the Novel of Development* (New York: Columbia University Press, 1993), 118.

57. On the sociotope of "common interests" underpinning the representational fabric of realist fiction, see Marc Redfield, *Phantom Formation: Aesthetic Ideology and the "Bildungsroman"* (Ithaca, NY: Cornell University Press, 1996); Bruce Robbins, *Upward Mobility and the Common Good: Toward a Literary History of the Welfare State* (Princeton, NJ: Princeton University Press, 2007); and Zarena Aslami, *The Dream Life of Citizens: Late Victorian Novels and the Fantasy of the State* (New York: Fordham University Press, 2012).

58. Johann Wolfgang von Goethe, *Wilhelm Meister's Apprenticeship*, ed. and trans. Eric A. Blackall with Victor Lange (Princeton, NJ: Princeton University Press, 1995), 302.

59. Joseph Vogl, *Specters of Capital* (Stanford, CA: Stanford Univerity Press, 2014), 27.

60. Goethe, *Wilhelm Meister's Apprenticeship*, 263.

61. Goethe, 265.

62. Goethe, 266.

63. Goethe, 335.

64. Westphal, "The Basic Context and Structure of Hegel's *Philosophy of Right*," 259.

65. Karl Marx, *Critique of Hegel's "Philosophy of Right,"* ed. Joseph O'Malley, trans. Joseph O'Malley and Annette Jolin (New York: Cambridge University Press, 2009), 76.

66. Karl Marx, "On the Jewish Question," in *The Marx-Engels Reader*, 2nd ed., ed. Robert C. Tucker (New York, London: W. W. Norton, 1978), 46.

67. Marx, *Critique of Hegel's "Philosophy of Right,"* 79.

68. Shlomo Avineri, *The Social and Political Thought of Karl Marx* (New York: Cambridge University Press, 1968), 23.

69. Antonio Gramsci, *Selections from the Prison Notebooks*, ed. Quintin Hoare and Geoffrey Nowell-Smith (New York: International, 1989), 263.

70. Gramsci, 258–59.

71. Gramsci, 260.

72. Gramsci, 242.

73. Gramsci, 242.

74. Moretti, *The Way of the World*, 53.

75. Jameson, *The Political Unconscious*, 152.

76. Louis Althusser, "Ideology and Ideological State Apparatuses (Notes towards an Investigation)," in *Lenin and Philosophy and Other Essays*, trans. Ben Brewster (New York: Monthly Review Press, 2001), 142.

77. Althusser, "Ideology and Ideological State Apparatuses," 182.

78. See the relevant discussion of "expressive" and "structural" causality in Louis Althusser and Étienne Balibar, *Reading Capital*, trans. Ben Brewster (New York: Verso, 2009), 206–7.

79. Jameson, *The Political Unconscious*, 153–54.

80. Catherine Gallagher, "The Rise of Fictionality," in *The Novel*, vol. 1, *History, Geography, and Culture*, ed. Franco Moretti (Princeton, NJ: Princeton University Press, 2007), 345–47.

81. Poovey, *Making a Social Body*, 21.

82. Nancy Armstrong, *How Novels Think: The Limits of Individualism from 1719-1900* (New York: Columbia University Press, 2006), 29.

83. Michel Foucault, *Discipline and Punish: The Birth of the Prison*, trans. Alan Sheridan (New York: Penguin Random House, 2019), 221.

84. Michel Foucault, *The Birth of Biopolitics: Lectures at the Collège de France, 1978-1979*, trans. Graham Burchell (New York: Palgrave Macmillan), 283.

85. Foucault, 296.

86. Michel Foucault, *Society Must Be Defended: Lectures at the Collège de France, 1975-1976* (New York: Picador, 1997), 175; Foucault, *Discipline and Punish*, 193. Foucault comments extensively on the affinities between sovereignty and tragedy, and, briefly, on the links between discipline and the novel.

87. D. A. Miller, *The Novel and the Police* (Berkeley: University of California Press, 1989), 27-32.

88. Miller, 23.

89. Lauren M. E. Goodlad, *Victorian Literature and the Victorian State: Character and Governance in a Liberal Society* (Baltimore: Johns Hopkins University Press, 2004), 14.

90. Walter Bagehot, *The Works and Life of Walter Bagehot*, vol. 2, *Historical and Financial Essays*, ed. Mrs. Russell Barrington (London: Longmans, Green, 1915), quoted in Goodlad, *Victorian Literature and the Victorian State*, 16.

91. Bagehot, *The Works and Life of Walter Bagehot*, 2:16.

92. Goodlad, *Victorian Literature and the Victorian State*, 20-21.

93. Goodlad, 63.

94. Goodlad, 25.

95. Emily Steinlight, *Populating the Novel: Literary Form and the Politics of Surplus Life* (Ithaca, NY: Cornell University Press, 2018), 12.

96. Hannah Arendt, *The Human Condition* (Chicago: University of Chicago Press, 1958), 38-49.

97. Arendt, 40.

98. Gramsci, *Selections from the Prison Notebooks*, 238.

99. With regard to qualifications, see, for example, Adele Lindenmeyr, "'Primordial and Gelatinous'? Civil Society in Imperial Russia," *Kritika* 12, no. 3 (2011): 713. Lindenmeyr diagnoses a normative and teleological tendency underpinning the "absence" topos in Russian imperial historiography: the absence of the middle class, the absence of rights and freedoms, the absence of civil society, and so on. Her overview of some recent attempts to rectify the situation by exploring elements of a public sphere independent of the state suggests that whether civil society in Russia could be characterized as "primordial and gelatinous" ultimately depends on how robustly one defines the term. If evidence of relatively flourishing salons, charitable organizations, voluntary associations, commercial activity, and the press is sufficient, then there is no reason to deny elements of civil society to imperial Russia. But if we set the standard at "equality before the law and security of rights," then "primordial and gelatinous" no longer seems altogether inappropriate. Indeed, while terms like *obshchestvo* ("good society," "high society," "lettered public"), *publika* (the public), *obshchestvennost'* (socialness, or the public), *sotsial'nost'* (social harmony) and *narod* (the people as a whole, or the common people) were widely used to refer to various aspects and dimensions of col-

lective life, none of them habitually referred to anything like a vision of private persons with property rights entering into self-interested but socially normalized interactions with each other.

100. Marc Raeff, "The Well-Ordered Police State and the Development of Modernity in Seventeenth- and Eighteenth-Century Europe: An Attempt at a Comparative Approach," *American Historical Review* 80, no. 5 (1975): 1241.

101. Marc Raeff, *The Well-Ordered Police State: Social and Institutional Change through Law in the Germanies and Russia, 1600-1800* (New Haven, CT: Yale University Press, 1983), 250. See also Alfred J. Rieber, *The Imperial Russian Project: Autocratic Politics, Economic Development, and Social Fragmentation* (Toronto: University of Toronto Press, 2017), 357; and the classic, if somewhat tendentious, claims in Richard Pipes, *Russia under the Old Regime* (New York: Penguin, 1974).

102. See, for example, Elise Kimerling Wirtschafter, *Social Identity in Imperial Russia* (Dekalb: Northern Illinois University Press, 1997).

103. Christopher Ely, "The Question of Civil Society in Late Imperial Russia," in *A Companion to Russian History*, ed. Abbott Gleason (Malden, MA: Wiley Blackwell, 2014), 236.

104. Ely, 239.

105. See Viktor Zhivov, "Osobyi put' i puti spaseniia v Rossii," in *Osobyi put': Ot ideologii k metodu* (Moscow: Novoe literaturnoe obozrenie, 2018), 55-105.

106. Zhivov, 89.

107. Oleg Kharkhordin, "What Is the State? The Russian Concept of *Gosudarstvo* in the European Context," *History and Theory* 40, no. 2 (May 2001), 227.

108. Yanni Kotonis, *States of Obligation: Taxes and Citizenship in the Russian Empire and Early Soviet Republic* (Toronto: University of Toronto Press, 2014), 20.

109. Michael Cherniavsky, *Tsar and People: Studies in Russian Myths*, 2nd ed. (New York: Penguin Random House, 1969), 88.

110. Viktor Zhivov, "Gosudarstvennyi mif v epokhu Prosvescheniya i ego razrushenie v Rossii kontsa XVIII veka," in *Razyskaniia v oblasti istorii i predystorii russkoi kul'turi* (Moscow: Iazyki slavianskoi kul'tury, 2002), 445-46.

111. Zhivov, 455-56.

112. Clifford Geertz, "Centers, Kings and Charisma: Reflections on the Symbolics of Power," in *Local Knowledge: Further Essays in Interpretive Anthropology*, 3rd ed. (New York, Basic Books, 1985), 122-23.

113. Vasily Zhukovsky, *Polnoe sobranie sochinenii i pisem*, vol 14, *Stikhotvoreniia, 1797-1814*, ed. O. B. Lebedev and A. S. Ianushkevich (Moscow: Iazyki slavianskoi kul'tury, 2004), 40-41.

114. See Armstrong, "The Fiction of Bourgeois Morality," 372-79.

115. I borrow this suggestive formula from Ranajit Guha's classic Gramscian analysis of British colonial rule in India. Elaborating on the meaning of the phrase, Guha writes: "As an absolute internality, the colonial state was constructed like a despotism, with no mediating depths, no space provided for transactions between the will of the rulers and that of the ruled." Guha, *Dominance without Hegemony: History and Power in Colonial India* (Cambridge, MA: Harvard University Press, 1998), 65.

116. Boris Chicherin, "Pis'mo k izdateliu," in *Golosa iz rossii*, ed. A. I. Gertsen and N. P. Ogarev (Moscow: Nauka, 1976), 56. The article was published two years later in London, avoiding censorship.

117. Chicherin, 60.
118. Chicherin, 67.
119. Chicherin, 77.
120. Chicherin, 99.
121. Quoted in Andrei Teslia, "Zapreshchennaia 6-ia stat'a I. S. Aksakova iz tsykla 'O vzaimnom otnoshenii naroda, obshchestva i gosudarstva,'" *Sotsiologicheskoe obozrenie* 11, no. 2 (2012), 61.
122. Quoted in Teslia, 57.
123. Teslia, 49.
124. Fyodor Dostoevsky, *A Writer's Diary*, ed. Gary Saul Moson and Kenneth Lantz, trans. Gary Saul Morson (Evanston, IL: Northwestern University Press, 2009), 397.
125. Fyodor Dostoevsky, *Polnoe sobranie sochinenii*, vol. 22, *Dnevnik pisatelia za 1876 god. Ianvar'-aprel'* (Moscow: Akademiia nauk, 1981), 81-82.
126. Dostoevsky, *Polnoe sobranie sochinenii*, vol. 22, *Dnevnik pisatelia za 1876 god. Ianvar'-aprel'*, 356.
127. Alexander Herzen, *Polnoe sobranie sochinenii*, vol. 7, *O razvitii revoliutsionnykh idei v Rossii: Proizvedeniia, 1851-1852 godov* (Moscow: Akademiia nauk, 1956), 251.
128. Pavel Annenkov, "Delovoi roman v nashei literature," *Atenei* 2 (January-February 1859): 248.
129. Annenkov, 253.
130. Annenkov, 254-55.
131. Annenkov, 255.
132. Annenkov, 250.
133. Benjamin Constant, "De la liberté des Anciens comparée à celle des Modernes, discours prononcé à l'Athénée Royal de Paris" in *Benjamin Constant: Oeuvres complètes*, vol. 15, *Brochures politiques, 1819-1821*, ed. Kurt Kloocke and Paul Delbouille (Boston: De Gruyter, 2017), 296.
134. In the context of an autocracy, Annenkov's invocation of the (emblematically, if not often actually) republican "ancients" may be puzzling at first glance. Yet what seems to matter to him more than differences among political constitutions is the writer's sense of proximity to the domain where matters important to the community are decided and from where the most meaningful and consequential actions flow.
135. On the relationship between eighteenth-century Russian literature and the state, see, among others, Yuri Tynianov, "Oda kak oratorskii zhanr," in Tynianov, *Poetika, Istoriia literatury, Kino* (Moscow: Nauka, 1977), 227-52; G. A. Gukovsky, *Russkaia literatura XVIII veka* (Moscow: Aspekt Press, 1999); Lev Pumpianskii, "Mednyi vsadnik i poeticheskaia traditsiia XVIII veka," in *Klassicheskaia traditsiia: Sobranie trudov po istorii russkoi literatury* (Moscow: Iazyki russkoi kul'tury, 2000), 158-96; Viktor Zhivov, "Gosudarstvennyi mif v epokhu prosveshcheniia i ego razrushenie v Rossii kontsa XIII veka," in *Razyskaniia v oblasti istorii i predistorii russkoi kul'tury* (Moscow: Iazyki slavianoskoi kul'tury, 2002), 439-60; Harsha Ram, *The Imperial Sublime: A Russian Poetics of Empire* (Madison: University of Wisconsin Press, 2006); Kirill Ospovat, *Terror and Pity: Alexander Sumarokov and the Theater of Power in Elizabethan Russia* (Boston: Academic Studies Press, 2016); and *Pridvornaia slovesnost': Institut literatury i konstruktsii absoliutizma v Rossii serediny XVIII veka* (Moscow: NLO, 2020).
136. See William Mills Todd III, *Fiction and Society in the Age of Pushkin: Ideology, Institutions, and Narrative* (Cambridge, MA: Harvard University Press, 1986).

137. Nikolai Engel'gardt, *Ocherk istorii russkoi tsenzury v sviazi s razvitiem pechati (1703-1903)* (St. Petersburg: Bibliopolis, 2016), 152.

138. Engel'gardt, 194.

139. Ekaterina Pravilova, *A Public Empire: Property and the Quest for the Common Good in Imperial Russia* (Princeton, NJ: Princeton University Press, 2014), 220.

140. Ivan Turgenev, *Polnoe sobranie sochinenii i pisem*, vol. 4, *Povesti i rasskazy. Stat'i i retsenzii, 1844-1854* (Moscow: Nauka, 1980), 606.

141. Sergei Mel'gunov, "Mysli vslukh ob istekshem tridtsatiletii Rossii," in *Golosa iz Rossii*, vol. 1, facsimile ed. (Moscow: Nauka, 1974).

142. For more on Goncharov's work as a censor and especially on his hopes and disappointments with regard to the possibility of conciliatory mediation between the literary field and the state, see Kirill Zubkov, "Mezhdu vlastiami i pisatel'skim mirom: I. A. Goncharov i liberal'nye proekty tsenzurnykh reform, 1858-1859 gg," in *Chiny i muzy: Sbornik statei* (Moscow: Marina Batasova, 2017).

143. *Proekt ustava o knigopechatanii* (St. Petersburg: Imperatorskaia akademiia nauk, 1862), 71-73.

144. Charles A. Ruud, "Russia," in *The War for the Public Mind: Political Censorship in Nineteenth-Century Europe*, ed. Robert J. Goldstein (Santa Barbara, CA: Praeger, 2000), 244-45.

145. W. Gareth Jones, "Politics," in *The Cambridge Companion to the Classic Russian Novel*, ed. Malcolm V. Jones and Robin Feuer Miller (New York: Cambridge University Press, 2006), 63.

146. William Mills Todd III, "The Ruse of the Russian Novel," in *The Novel*, vol. 1, *History, Geography, and Culture*, ed. Franco Moretti (Princeton, NJ: Princeton University Press, 2007), 409.

147. For the imperial literary elite, in Alexander Etkind's words, "the boundary between the office and the prison was strangely unstable." See Etkind, *Internal Colonization: Russia's Imperial Experience* (Malden, MA: Polity, 2011), 159.

148. Marc Raeff, *Origins of the Russian Intelligentsia: The Eighteenth-Century Nobility* (Boston: Mariner, 1966), 119.

149. Zhivov, "Gosudarstvennyi mif," 445-47. On the overlapping of Christian and civic notion of duty, see Boris Maslov, "Ot dolgov khristianina k grazhdanskomu dolgu (Ocherk istorii kontseptual'noi metafory)," in *Ocherki istoricheskoi semantiki russkogo iazyka rannego novogo vremeni* (Moscow: Iazyki slavianskoi kul'tury, 2009).

150. Richard Wortman, *The Power of Language and Rhetoric in Russian Political History: Charismatic Words from the 18th to the 21st Centuries* (New York: Bloomsbury, 2017), 49-83.

151. Irina Reyfman, *How Russia Learned to Write: Literature and the Imperial Table of Ranks* (Madison: University of Wisconsin Press, 2016), 43. Reyfman observes that the writers' "participation in the service hierarchy was not only strongly expected by others, including but not limited to the state, but often avidly desired by the writers themselves."

152. Nikolai Gogol, *Sobranie sochinenii v shesti tomakh*, vol. 6, *Izbrannye stat'i i pis'ma* (Moscow: Khudozhestvennaia literatura, 1959), 228-29.

153. Alexander Herzen, *Polnoe sobranie sochinenii*, vol. 13, *Stat'i iz Kolokola i drugie proizvedeniia, 1859-1860 godov* (Moscow: Akademiia nauk, 1958), 196.

154. Ivan Turgenev, *Polnoe sobranie sochinenii i pisem*, vol. 11 (Moscow: Nauka, 1983), 218.

155. Alexander Herzen, *My Past and Thoughts: The Memoirs of Alexander Herzen*, vol. 1, trans. Constance Garnett, trans. revised Humphrey Higgins (London: Chatto and Windus, 1968), 72. For a brief discussion of the popularity of the figure of Schiller's Posa in elite early nineteenth-century circles, see Yuri Lotman, "The Decembrist in Everyday Life: Everyday Behavior as a Historical-Psychological Category" in Lotman and Boris Uspensky, *The Semiotics of Russian Culture*, trans. Ann Shukman (Ann Arbor: University of Michigan Press, 1984), 95–149.

Chapter Two

1. Vissarion Belinsky, "Ocherki Borodinskogo srazheniia (vospominaniia o 1812 gode). Sochineniia F. Glinki, avtora 'Pisem russkogo ofitsera.' Moskva. 1839." *Polnoe sobranie sochinenii, v 13i tomakh*, vol. 3, *Stat'i i retsenzii. Piatidesiatiletnii diadiushka, 1839–1840* (Moscow: Akademiia nauk, 1953), 440.

2. Belinsky, 3:334.

3. Georg Wilhelm Friedrich Hegel, *Elements of the Philosophy of Right*, trans. H. B. Nisbet, ed. Allen W. Wood (Cambridge: Cambridge University Press, 1991), 361.

4. Belinsky, *Polnoe sobranie sochinenii*, 3:345.

5. See Ernst Kantorowicz, *The King's Two Bodies: A Study in Medieval Political Theology* (Princeton, NJ: Princeton University Press, 2016), 23.

6. Carl Schmitt, *Political Theology: Four Chapters on the Concept of Sovereignty*, trans. George Schwab (Chicago: University of Chicago Press, 1985), 6.

7. Carl Schmitt, *The Concept of the Political*, trans. George Schwab (Chicago: University of Chicago Press, 2007), 38.

8. Schmitt, 22.

9. Nikolai Gogol, *The Complete Tales of Nikolai Gogol*, vol. 2, ed. Leonard J. Kent, trans. Constance Garnett (Chicago: University of Chicago Press, 1985), 107.

10. Gogol, 2:108.

11. For a more detailed discussion of the language of the verse tale, see Lev Pumpiansky, "'Mednyi vsadnik' i poeticheskaia traditsiia XVIII veka," in *Klassicheskaia traditsiia: Sobranie trudov po istorii russkoi literatury*, 158–97.

12. On the poetics of the state of exception in Pushkin's "Petersburg Tale," see Kirill Ospovat, "Kumir na bronzovom kone: Barokko, chrezvychainoe polozhenie i estetika revoliutsii," *Novoe literaturnoe obozrenie* 149, no. 1 (2018): 49–73. See also T. Grob and R. Nikolosi, "Rossiia mezhdu khaosom i kosmosom (O peterburgsom navodnenii, literaturnom mife goroda i povesti A. S. Pushkina 'Mednyi vsadnik,')" in *Sushchestvuet li Peterburgskii tekst?*, ed. V. M. Markovich and V. Shmid (St. Petersburg: Izdatel'stvo S-Peterburgskogo universiteta, 2005), 124–53; David Bethea, "'Mednyi vsadnik': Peterburgskii tekst i mifopoeticheskoe myshlenie Pushkina," in *Sushchestvuet li Peterburgskii tekst?*, ed. V. M. Markovich and V. Shmid (St. Petersburg: Izdatel'stvo S-Peterburgskogo universiteta, 2005), 170–92.

13. On free indirect discourse in the poem, specifically in connection with its emergent realist representation of the protagonist, see Boris Maslov, "Metapragmatics, Toposforschung, Marxist Stylistics: Three Extensions of Veselovsky's Historical Po-

etics" in *Persistent Forms: Explorations in Historical Poetics*, ed. Ilya Kliger and Boris Maslov (New York: Fordham University Press, 2015), 150–55.

14. See Wacław Lednicki's discussion of this ambiguity in Lednicki, *Pushkin's Bronze Horseman: The Story of a Masterpiece* (Berkeley: University of California Press, 1955), 50–52. See also Kevin M. F. Platt's nuanced analysis in Platt, *Terror and Greatness: Ivan and Peter as Russian Myths* (Ithaca, NY: Cornell University Press, 2011), 60–64. On the tensions between subduing and unleashing, which structures the poem and emerges in the process of transplantation of the European imperial statuary tradition to Russia, see David Bethea, "The Role of the Eques in Pushkin's *Bronze Horseman*," in *Pushkin Today*, ed. David Bethea (Bloomington: Indiana University Press, 1993), 99–118.

15. Giorgio Agamben, *Homo Sacer: Sovereign Power and Bare Life*, trans. Daniel Heller-Roazen (Stanford, CA: Stanford University Press, 1998), 37.

16. Nikolai Gogol, *Polnoe sobranie sochinenii v 14 tomakh*, vol. 5, *Zhenit'ba: Dramaticheskiye otryvki i otdel'nyye stseny* (Moscow: Institut russkoi literatury, 1949), 144.

17. Gogol, 5:144.

18. Gogol, 5:146.

19. For a discussion of Khlestakov's symbiotic link to the Nicholaevian state, see Yuri Lotman, "O Khlestakove," in *Izbrannye stat'i*, vol. 1, *Stat'i po semiotike i tipologii kul'tury* (Tallinn: Alexandra, 1992), 361–62.

20. See G. A. Gukovsky, *Realizm Gogolia* (Moscow: Khudozhestvennaia literatura, 1959), 441–46; Yuri Mann, *Poetika Gogolia* (Moscow: Khudozhestvennaia literatura, 1988), 235.

21. Nikolai Gogol, *Polnoe sobranie sochinenii*, vol. 4, *Revizor* (Moscow: Institut russkoi literatury, 1951), 114. This is Gogol's own formulation.

22. Charlotte Brontë, *Jane Eyre*, 3rd Norton Critical Edition (New York: W. W. Norton, 2016), 137.

23. For an extended juxtaposition between Goncharov's first novel and Goethe's celebrated bildungsroman, see Elena Krasnoshchekova, *Roman vospitaniia (Bildungsroman) na russkoi pochve* (St. Petersburg: Izdatel'stvo "Pushkinskogo fonda," 2008), 125–77.

24. Ivan Goncharov, *The Same Old Story*, trans. Stephen Pearl (Richmond, UK: Bunim and Bannigan, 2017), 62; I. A. Goncharov, *Polnoe sobranie sochinenii i pisem v dvadtsati tomakh*, vol. 1, *Obyknovennaya istoriya; Stikhotvoreniya; Povesti i ocherki; Publitsistika, 1832–1848* (St. Petersburg: Nauka, 1997), 126–27. Subsequent references to these editions will be given parenthetically in the body of the text in the form (62; 1:126–27).

25. Fredric Jameson, "The Experiments of Time: Providence and Realism," in *The Novel*, vol. 2, *Forms and Themes*, ed. Franco Moretti (Princeton. NJ: Princeton University Press, 2007), 95–127.

26. See Richard Wortman, *The Power of Language and Rhetoric in Russian Political History: Charismatic Words from the 18th to the 21st Centuries* (New York: Bloomsbury, 2017), 73. For an invocation of the image of St. Petersburg itself as a pedagogue, see Pavel Annenkov, "Khudozhnik i prostoi chelovek: iz vospominanii ob A. F. Pisemskom," in *Literaturnye vospominaniia* (Moscow: Khudozhestvennaia literatura, 1960), 498.

27. Joan Brooks, "Obyknovennaia istoriia odnogo chitatelia 'Mednogo vsadnika,'" *NLO*, no. 6 (2010).

28. See Joan Brooks's discussion of the novel's incorporation of *The Bronze Horseman* as a subtext.

29. This is the line of interpretation adopted by early reviewers of the novel. See in particular Vissarion Belinsky, "Vzgliad na russkuiu literaturu 1847 goda: Stat'ia vtoraia," in *Polnoe sobranie sochinenii*, vol. 10, *Stat'i i retsenzii, 1846-1848* (Moscow: Akademiia nauk, 1956), 328.

30. See especially D. Blagoi, *Sotsiologiia tvorchestva Pushkina: Etiudy* (Moscow: Federatsiia, 1929), 263-328.

31. Norbert Elias, *The Civilizing Process: Sociogenetic and Psychogenetic Investigations*, ed. Eric Dunning, Johan Goudsblom, and Stephen Mennell, trans. Edmund Jephcott (Oxford: Blackwell, 2000), 398.

32. Lidiya Lotman characterizes the collision between the nephew and the uncle, the country and the city, in sociohistorical terms as a contrast between feudal and bourgeois perceptions of the world and ways of life. At stake in her analysis is a stageist opposition between relative progress and historical atavism. My own invocation of the "feudal" kernel in Alexander acquires its specific meaning from being conceived within the horizon of the modern state's "civilizing mission." See L. M. Lotman, "I. A. Goncharov," in *Istoriia russkoi literatury*, vol. 3, *Rastsvet realizma*, ed. F. Ia. Priima and N. I. Prutskov (Leningrad: Nauka, 1982), 160-202. A number of more recent interpretations of the novel have tended to depoliticize and even dehistoricize Alexander's trajectory by treating it as either a universal story of human maturation or the tale of an idealist devoid of genuine creative capacity. See, for example, Krasnoshchekova, *Roman vospitaniia (Bildungsroman) na russkoi pochve*, 125; M. V. Otradin, *Proza I. A. Goncharova v literaturnom kontekste* (St. Petersburg: Izdatel'stvo Sankt Peterburgskogo universiteta, 1994), 70-71.

33. On the nature of Lizaveta's condition, see Valeria Sobol, *Febris Erotica: Lovesickness in the Russian Literary Imagination* (Seattle: University of Washington Press, 2009), 115-18.

34. For a more extended discussion of the place of tragedy in the entire corpus of texts at issue in this book, see the concluding chapter 5.

35. Michel Foucault, *Security, Territory, and Population: Lectures at the Collège de France, 1977-1978*, ed. Michel Senellart, trans. Graham Burchell (New York: Palgrave Macmillan, 2009), 257.

36. Foucault, 263.

37. For a discussion of the reception of Balzac in mid-century Russia and by Pisemsky in particular, see Kirill Zubkov, *Molodaia redaktsiia Moskvitianina: Estetika, poetika, polemika* (Moscow: Biosfera, 2012), 92-99.

38. See Kirill Zubkov, "Roman A. F. Pisemskogo 'Tysiacha dush' i p'esy o chinovnikakh vtoroi poloviny 1850-kh godov," *Russkaia literatura*, 2009, no. 4: 95-106; Kirill Zubkov, "Pushkinskaia traditsiia v romane A. F. Pisemskogo 'Tysiacha dush,'" *Russkaia literatura*, 2010, no. 3: 95-105.

39. Alexey Pisemsky, *One Thousand Souls*, trans. Ivy Litvinov (New York: Greenwood Press, 1969), 395; Alexey Pisemsky, *Sobranie sochinenii v deviati tomakh*, vol. 3 (Moscow: Pravda, 1959), 389. Subsequent references to these editions will be given parenthetically in the body of the text in the form (395; 3:389).

40. Indicative, in this respect, is the complicated history of the novel's composition.

Begun in 1853 and published in 1858, the novel straddles an important historical transition. The boundary between the first three parts of the novel (the narrative of social ambition) and part 4 (the drama of state power) converges with the historical appearance on public stage of a new type of official, the liberal bureaucrat, selflessly fighting to eradicate bureaucratic abuses in the name of the idea of a well-regulated state. As Kirill Zubkov has convincingly shown, part 4 of the novel is thus drawn into a polemic about the figure of the "honest bureaucrat," staged and restaged in the drama of the late 1850s. See Zubkov, "Roman A. F. Pisemskogo"; Zubkov, "Pushkinskaia traditsiia," 105.

41. Annenkov, "Delovoi roman v nashei literature," *Atenei* 2 (January–February 1859): 263–64.

42. Annenkov, "Khudozhnik i prostoi chelovek," 514.

43. Dobroliubov, "Literaturnye melochi proshlogo goda." N. A. Dobroliubov, *Sobranie sochinenii v 9 tomakh*, vol. 4. *Stat'i i retsenzii. Ianvar'–Iiun' 1859* (Moscow, Leningrad: Khudozhestvennaia literatura, 1962), 106. For a brief overview of the novel's critical reception, see O. Timashova, "Roman Pisemskogo 'Tysiacha dush' v otzyvakh sovremennoi emu kritiki," *Izvestiia Saratovskogo universiteta. Novaia Seriia, Seriia "Filologiia. Zhurnalistika"* 16, no. 2 (2016): 174–79.

44. Fyodor Dostoevsky, *Polnoe sobranie sochinenii*, vol. 14, *Brat'ia Karamazovy, knigi I–X* (Leningrad: Nauka, 1976), 58; Fyodor Dostoevksy, *The Brothers Karamazov*, trans. Richard Pevear and Larissa Volokhonsky (New York: Penguin Random House, 2002), 62.

45. Dostoevsky, *Polnoe sobranie sochinenii*, 14:59–60; Dostoevsky, *The Brothers Karamazov*, 64.

46. Viktor Zhivov, "Gosudarstvennyi mif v epokhu prosveshchenia i ego razrushenie v Rossii kontsa XVIII veka" in *Razyskaniia v oblasti istorii i predystorii russkoi kul'turi*, 456–57.

47. Goncharov, *The Same Old Story*, 274–75; Goncharov, *Polnoe sobranie sochinenii i pisem v dvadtsati tomakh*, 417.

48. For existing work on Dostoevsky's political theology, see *Dostoevsky's Political Thought*, ed. Richard Avramenko and Lee Trepanier (Washington, DC: Lexington, 2013); Ilya Kliger, "Sovereignty and the Novel: Dostoevsky's Political Theology," in *Dostoevsky at 200: The Novel and Modernity*, ed. Katherine Bowers and Kate Holland (Toronto: University of Toronto Press, 2021), 196–219.

49. Igor Volgin, *Poslednii god Dostoevskogo: Istoricheskie zapiski* (Moscow: AST, 2010), 30–40.

50. These notes contain a kind of metaplot for the last three novels Dostoevsky had yet to complete, as well as, retroactively, for the two major novels that came out in the 1860s, *Crime and Punishment* (1865) and *The Idiot* (1868). For a more detailed discussion of Dostoevsky's notes on *The Life of a Great Sinner*, see Kate Holland, *The Novel in the Age of Disintegration: Dostoevsky and the Problem of Genre in the 1870s* (Evanston, IL: Northwestern University Press, 2013), 49–57.

51. Fyodor Dostoevsky, *Polnoe sobranie sochinenii*, vol. 9 (Leningrad: Nauka, 1974), 130.

52. See the discussion of *Crime and Punishment* in chapter 4.

53. Dostoevsky, *Polnoe sobranie sochinenii*, 9:486.

54. Dostoevsky, *Polnoe sobranie sochinenii*, 10:143; Fyodor Dostoevsky, *Demons*,

trans. Richard Pevear and Larissa Volokhonsky (New York: Vintage Classic, 2010), 179. Subsequent references to these editions will be given parenthetically in the body of the text in the form (179; 10:143).

55. On geographical symbolism, in accordance with which significance accrues to characters associated with the empire's "center," see Anne Lounsbery, "Dostoevskii's Geography: Centers, Peripheries, and Networks in *Demons*," *Slavic Review* 66, no. 2 (Summer 2007): 211–29.

56. The comparison of Russian social life with a cheap show house, or circus, a *balagan*, appears to have been common throughout the century. Recall, for example, Vasily Zhukovsky's similar use of the term, discussed in chapter 1.

57. For a detailed account of the multiple folk and theological associations attached to the figure of Stavrogin, see Linda Ivantis, *Dostoevsky and the Russian People* (New York: Cambridge University Press, 2008), 117–27.

58. Boris Uspensky and Viktor Zhivov, *"Tsar and God" and Other Essays in Russian Cultural Semiotics*, ed. Marcus C. Levitt, trans. Marcus C. Levitt, David Budgen, and Liv Bliss (Boston: Academic Studies Press, 2012), 10. On the vicissitudes of secularization of monarchical power under Peter I, see also Michael Cherniavsky, *Tsar and People: Studies in Russian Myths*, 2nd ed. (New York: Penguin Random House, 1969), 88.

59. Ernst Zitser, *Transfigured Kingdom: Sacred Parody and Charismatic Authority at the Court of Peter the Great* (Ithaca, NY: Cornell University Press, 2004), 145–46.

60. Uspensky and Zhivov, *"Tsar and God,"* 8. Ilya Kalinin argues along similar lines that "impostorship merely exposes the emptiness of the foundations on which 'true' authority rests." See Kalinin, "On gran' khotel steret' mezh tem, chem byl i chem kazalsia": Raby, samoderzhtsy i samozvantsy (dialektika vlasti). Stat'ia pervaia," *Novoe literaturnoe obozrenie* no. 6 (2020): 534–61. In a different context, Mikhail Bakhtin notes the motif of pretendership in one of Raskolnikov's dreams, linking it to the dream of the False Dmitry in Pushkin's *Boris Godunov*: "Before us is the image of communal ridicule on the public sphere decrowning a carnival king-pretender." Bakhtin, *Problems of Dostoevsky's Poetics*, ed. and trans. Caryl Emerson (Minneapolis: University of Minnesota Press, 1984), 168. For more comments on the motif of pretendership (again, in the context of carnival decrowning) in Dostoevsky, see Mikhail Bakhtin, *Sobranie sochinenii v semi tomakh*, vol. 5, *Raboty 1940-kh–nachala 1960-kh godov* (Moscow: Russkie slovari, 1996), 43–44. Harriet Murav dedicates a detailed discussion to the topic of pretendership in *Demons*, once again linking the protagonist-pretender to *Boris Godunov* and, more broadly to the historical period of the Time of Troubles. See Murav, *Holy Foolishness: Dostoevsky's Novels and the Poetics of Cultural Critique* (Stanford CA: Stanford University Press, 1992), 99–123. In an attempt to make sense of the "Ivan Tsarevich" motif in *Demons*, Olga Maiorova provides an especially pertinent account of the broader postemancipation mytheme of royal pretendership in Maiorova, "Tsarevich-samozvanets v sotsial'noi mifologii poreformennoi epokhi," in "Kul'turnye praktiki v ideologicheskoi perspektive. Rossia XVII-nachalo XX veka," special issue, *Rossia/Russia* 3, no. 11 (1999): 204–32. In Maiorova's account, the motif invokes contemporary folk legends conflating various members of the royal family with leaders of past peasant uprisings and sectarian leaders in the figure of the sovereign-redeemer. One important distinction that emerges in the process is between bureaucratic and popular notions of monarchical rule. The pretender-redeemer-czar's legitimacy is ev-

idently based on his messianic charisma rather than on legality or reason. For the role of schismatic-revolutionary imaginaries of sovereignty, see Irina Paperno, "The Liberation of Serfs as a Cultural Symbol," *Russian Review* 63, no. 4 (October 2004): 421–36.

61. Schmitt, *Political Theology*, 13.

62. Schmitt, 36.

63. Franco Moretti, *The Way of the World: The Bildungsroman in European Culture* (New York: Verso, 2000), 53.

64. I borrow this term from the well-known essay by Roland Barthes, "The Reality Effect," in *The Rustle of Language*, trans. Richard Howard (Berkeley: University of California Press, 1989), 141–48.

65. See B. M. Eikhenbaum, "Geroi nashego vremeni" in *Stat'i o Lermontove* (Moscow: Akedemiia nauk, 1961), 250–51.

66. Mikhail Lermontov, *A Hero of Our Time*, trans. Natasha Randall (New York: Penguin, 2014), 150; M. Iu. Lermontov, *Sochineniia v shesti tomakh*, vol. 6, *Proza, pis'ma* (Moscow, Leningrad: Akademiia nauk, 1957), 332. Subsequent references to these editions will be given parenthetically in the body of the text in the form (150; 6:332).

67. Belinsky, *Polnoe sobranie sochinenii*, 4: 234–35.

68. Stepan Shevyrev, "Geroi nashego vremeni," *Moskvitianin*, part 1, no. 2 (1841), 529–30.

69. Eikhenbaum, "Geroi nashego vremeni," 253–58.

70. For an excellent analysis of "Taman'" in light of the problematic of the "imperial uncanny," see Valeria Sobol, "The Uncanny Frontier of Russian Identity: Travel, Ethnography, and Empire in Lermontov's "Taman'," *Russian Review* 70 (January 2011), 65–79.

71. For a discussion of this episode in light of imperial conquest, see Peter Scotto, "Prisoners of the Caucasus: Ideologies of Imperialism in Lermontov's 'Bela,'" *PMLA* 107, no. 2 (March 1992), 246–60, 252.

72. Pechorin's tendency to "go native" is discussed in Susan Layton, *Russian Literature and Empire: Conquest of the Caucasus from Pushkin to Tolstoy* (Cambridge: Cambridge University Press, 1994), 215–16.

73. On theatricality in "Princess Mary," see William Mills Todd III, *Fiction and Society in the Age of Pushkin* (Cambridge, MA: Harvard University Press, 1986), 152–61.

74. Belinsky, *Polnoe sobranie sochinenii*, 4:253.

75. The genealogy of Lermontov's psychological prose has been frequently linked to the French tradition of the "roman d'analyse," in particular to Benjamin Constant's *Adolphe* (1816) and Alfred de Musset's *La Confession d'un enfant du siècle* (1836). See, for example, E. I. Kiiko, "'Geroi nashego vremeni' Lermontova i psikhologicheskaia traditsiia vo frantsuzskoi literature." *Lermontovskii sbornik* (Leningrad: Nauka, 1985) 181–93. Symptomatic differences emerge against the background of obvious similarity. While both French novels are organized around conflict between the domains of the intimate and the social, the Russian instantiation of psychological-analytical prose displays a veritable fascination with the hero's exercise of unlimited power in the context of imperial conquest.

76. Ivan Turgenev, *Rudin*, trans. Richard Freeborn (New York: Penguin Random House, 1975), 62; Ivan Turgenev, *Polnoe sobranie sochinenii i pisem*, vol. 6 (Moscow: Nauka, 1981), 270. Subsequent references to these editions will be given parenthetically in the body of the text in the form (62; 6:270).

77. Victor Ripp observes that the reversal of judgment at the end of the novel is diegetically undermotivated, comparing it to the gift of divine grace. See Victor Ripp, "Turgenev as a Social Novelist: The Problem of the Part and the Whole," in *Literature and Society in Imperial Russia*, ed. William Mills Todd III (Stanford, CA: Stanford University Press, 1978), 252.

78. See, for example, Chernyshevsky's article on Nathaniel Hawthorne, Nikolai Chernyshevsky, "Sobranie chudes: Povesti, zaimstvovannye iz mifologii. Sochineniia amerikanskogo pisatelia Natanielia Gotorna," in *Polnoe sobranie sochinenii v 15-i, tomakh*, vol. 7, *Stat'i i retsenzii, 1860–1861*, ed. V. Ia Kirpotin, B. V. Koz'min, and P. I. Lebedev-Polianskii (Moscow: Gosudarstvennoe izdatelstvo khudozhestvennoj literatury, 1950), 449. See also Nikolai Chernyshevsky, *Polnoe sobranie sochinenii v 15-i, tomakh*, vol. 1, "Denvniki," "Iz avtobiografii," Vospominaniia, ed. V. Ia Kirpotin, B. V. Koz'min, and P. I. Lebedev-Polianskii (Moscow: Gosudarstvennoe izdatel'stvo khudozhestvennoi literatury, 1939), 738–40.

79. Aleksandr Druzhinin, "Povesti i rasskazy I. S. Turgeneva," in *Sobranie sochinenii A.V. Druzhinina*, vol. 7, ed. N. V. Gerbel' (St. Petersburg: Tipografiia imperatorskoi akademii nauk, 1865), 371–73.

80. For a narrative of the novel's fitful composition history, see Turgenev, *Polnoe sobranie sochinenii i pisem*, 6:560–71.

81. Vasily Sleptsov, "Trudnoe vremia," in *Russkie povesti XIX veka 60kh godov*, vol. 1 (Moscow: Khudozhestvennaia literatura, 1956), 213–14; Vasily Sleptsov, *Hard Times: A Novel of Liberals and Radicals in 1860s Russia*, trans. Michael Katz (Pittsburgh, PA: University of Pittsburgh Press, 2016), 7. Subsequent references to these editions will be given parenthetically in the body of the text in the form (7; 213–14).

82. See the discussion of this passage in William K. Brumfield, *Sotsial'nyi proekt v russkoi literature XIX veka* (Moscow: Tri kvadrata, 2009), 223–24.

83. See Nancy Armstrong, *Desire and Domestic Fiction: A Political History of the Novel* (New York: Oxford University Press, 1990) for discussions of the role of literacy and reading in replacing other, more politically explosive forms of leisure.

84. For an analysis of the whole range of hidden references to contemporary political realities, see Korney Chukovsky, "Tainopis' 'Trudnogo vremeni'" in *Liudi i knigi shestidesiatykh godov* (Leningrad: Izdatel'stvo pisatelei v Leningrade, 1934), 203–39.

Chapter Three

1. Robert Filmer, *Patriarcha, or the Natural Power of Kings* (London, 1680), 12–13.

2. John Locke, *Two Treatises of Government and a Letter concerning Toleration*, ed. Ian Shapiro (New Haven, CT: Yale University Press, 2003), 123.

3. Locke, 106.

4. Locke, 133–35, discussed in Michael McKeon, *The Secret History of Domesticity: Public, Private and the Division of Knowledge* (Baltimore: Johns Hopkins University Press, 2006), 122–34.

5. Charles Taylor has characterized this later approach as a tendency to treat "political society [...] as an instrument for something prepolitical," which is to say, for the benefit of individuals with inborn and inalienable rights. Taylor, *Modern Social Imaginaries* (Durham, NC: Duke University Press, 2003), 19.

6. Ian Watt, *The Rise of the Novel: Studies in Defoe, Richardson and Fielding* (Berkeley:

University of California Press, 2001), 141. See also McKeon on Defoe in *The Secret History of Domesticity*, 15.

7. Lynn Hunt, *The Family Romance of the French Revolution* (Berkeley: University of California Press, 1992), 20.

8. Hunt, 25.

9. Hunt, 34.

10. Tony Tanner, *Adultery in the Novel: Contract and Transgression* (Baltimore: Johns Hopkins University Press, 1979), 103.

11. Tanner, 229.

12. Bruce Robbins's account of the figure of the older woman facilitating the young man's worldly success is telling in this regard. We might extrapolate to say that the "good mother" tends to supplant the "bad father," at least tendentially, as the representative of the world's response to the hero's desire. See Robbins, *Upward Mobility and the Common Good: Toward a Literary History of the Welfare State* (Princeton, NJ: Princeton University Press, 2007), 37–66.

13. George Eliot, *Middlemarch*, ed. Rosemary Ashton (New York: Penguin Random House, 2003), 477.

14. Nikolai Karamzin, *Karamzin's Memoir on Ancient and Modern Russia: A Translation and Analysis*, trans. Richard Pipes (Ann Arbor: University of Michigan Press, 2008), 197.

15. Whether this was done in accordance with or against Karamzin's own wishes remains a matter for scholarly debate. See, most recently, Mikhail Velizhev, "Politik ponevole? Istoriograf, monarkh i publichnaia sfera v Rossii nachala XIX veka," *Novoe literaturnoe obozrenie* 151, no. 3 (June 2018), 186–203.

16. Vissarion Belinsky, "Ocherki Borodinskogo srazheniia (vospominaniia o 1812 gode). Sochineniia F. Glinki, avtora 'Pisem russkogo ofitsera.' Moskva. 1839," in *Polnoe sobranie sochinenii v 13i tomakh*, vol. 3, *Stat'i i retsenzii. Piatidesiatiletnii diadiushka, 1839–1840* (Moscow: Akademiia nauk, 1953), 334.

17. In *The Philosophy of History*, Hegel does assert that the first states were essentially patriarchal, but there is little implication that this could be relevant to the legitimacy of modern monarchies. See Georg Wilhelm Friedrich Hegel, *The Philosophy of History*, trans. J. Sibree (New York: Dover, 2004), 112.

18. Nikolai Gogol, *Selected Passages from Correspondence with Friends*, trans. Jesse Zledin (Nashville, TN: Vanderbilt University Press, 1969), 59.

19. See also Richard Wortman's discussion of this episode in Wortman, *Scenarios of Power: Myth and Ceremony in Russian Monarchy from Peter the Great to the Abdication of Nicholas II*, abridged ed. (Princeton, NJ: Princeton University Press, 2006), 161.

20. Nikolai Kostomarov, "Syn," in *Kudeyar, Syn, Kholop, Sorok let: Roman i povesti* (Moscow: Charli, 1994), 252.

21. Kostomarov, 344.

22. For an insightful, differently angled comparison between the Russian and the Victorian traditions of family novels, see Anna Berman, "The Family Novel (and Its Curious Disappearance)," *Comparative Literature* 72, no. 1 (2020): 1–18. For a still more thorough comparative study of English and Russian family fiction based on extensive material, see Anna Berman, *The Family Novel in Russia and England, 1800–1880* (Oxford: Oxford University Press, 2022). For a discussion of female friendship as an alternative form of community, particularly prominent within the Russian literary tradition,

see Anne Eakin-Moss, *Only among Women: Philosophies of Community in the Russian and Soviet Imagination* (Evanston, IL: Northwestern University Press), 2020.

23. Roman Jakobson, *Language and Literature*, ed. Krystyna Pomorska and Stephen Rudy (Cambridge, MA: Belknap Press, 1990), 321–25.

24. Yuri Lotman's reading of *The Captain's Daughter* as an averted tragedy highlights the humanist-optimistic "content" of the narrative at the expense of its evidently substantivist-political "form." See Lotman, "Ideinaia struktura 'Kapitanskoi dochki,'" in *Pushkin: Biografiia pisatelia; Stat'i i zametki, 1960–1990*. "Evgenii Onegin" Kommentarii (St. Petersburg: Iskusstvo, 1995), 212–36.

25. Margaret Cohen, *The Sentimental Education of the Novel* (Princeton, NJ: Princeton University Press, 2002), 65.

26. Alexander Pushkin, *Eugene Onegin*, trans. James Falen (New York: Oxford University Press, 1998), 207. For an account of Pushkin's engagement with contemporary French sentimental fiction, see Hilde Hoogenboom, "Sentimental Novels and Pushkin: European Literary Markets and Russian Readers," *Slavic Review* 74, no. 3 (Fall 2015): 553–74.

27. Cohen, *The Sentimental Education of the Novel*, 66.

28. V. K. Küchelbecker, *Puteshestvie. Dnevnik. Stat'i*, ed. N. V. Korolyova and V. D. Rak (Leningrad: Nauka, 1979), 100.

29. Pushkin, *Eugene Onegin*, 243.

30. Pushkin, 210. Boris Gasparov has argued on the basis of lexical resemblance that the loud ringing of the spurs with which the arrival of the General is announced creates associations with the supernatural statue figures of both *The Stone Guest* and *The Bronze Horseman*. See B. M. Gasparov, *Poeticheskii iazyk Pushkina kak fakt istorii russkogo literaturnogo iazyka* (St. Petersburg: Akademicheskii proekt, 1999), 274–75.

31. Nikolai Chernyshevsky, *Polnoe sobranie sochinenii v 15-i, tomakh*, vol. 5, ed. V. Ia Kirpotin, B. V. Koz'min, and P. I. Lebedev-Polianskii (Moscow: Gosudarstvennoe izdatelstvo khudozhestvennoi literatury, 1950), 168.

32. Chernyshevsky, 5:174.

33. I. S. Turgenev, *Polnoe sobranie sochinenii i pisem*, vol. 9 (Moscow: Nauka, 1982), 374–75. Needless to say, such an epilogue and, in particular, the concluding quote, would appear unacceptable to the Russian censors.

34. Ivan Turgenev, *First Love and Other Stories*, trans. Richard Freeborn (New York: Oxford World Classics, 2008), 184–85. I. S. Turgenev, *Polnoe sobranie sochinenii i pisem*, vol. 9. *Povesti i rasskazy, 1860–1867* (Moscow: Nauka, 1865), 54. Subsequent references to these editions will be given parenthetically in the body of the text in the form (184–85; 9:54).

35. While the reference to Anthony is explicitly made by Zinaida herself, the parallel with Caesar emerges more subtly in the course of several passages, with two scenes montaged together: one in which Volodya witnesses Zinaida's astonishment at the sight of his dashing father, and the next, immediately after the chapter break, where we see him, in the state of "despairing numbness" read again and again in his history textbook: "Julius Caesar excelled in military valor" (156–57; 9:21–22). Afanasiy Fet's translation of *Anthony and Cleopatra* came out in the February 1859 issue of *Russkoe slovo*. Still earlier, Fet had read the play to Turgenev.

36. For what happens when the horse is allowed too much freedom, see I. A. Kry-

lov, *Sochineniia v 2-kh tomakh*, vol. 2 (Moscow: Khudozhestvennaia literatura, 1984), 545–46.

37. For a more detailed discussion of the tale, see Ilya Kliger, "Scenarios of Power in Turgenev's *First Love*: Russian Realism and the Allegory of the State," *Comparative Literature* 70, no. 1 (2018): 25–44.

38. This, as well as the other cases of triangulated desire we have considered, represents a special case of what Eve Sedgwick famously described as the sublation of heterosexual desire by homosocial networks, "trafficking" women. And once again, the difference is telling: rather than a matter of social and financial alliance (and rivalry) between men, the female heroine in the Russian version of the triangle (which one may be tempted to call *homopolitical*, rather than homosocial), becomes a pretext for staging the encounter between the sovereign and the male. See Eve Kosofsky Sedgwick, *Between Men: English Literature and Male Homosocial Desire*, 30th anniversary ed. (New York: Columbia University Press, 2015).

39. René Girard, *Deceit, Desire, and the Novel: Self and Other in Literary Structure*, trans. Yvonne Freccero (Baltimore: Johns Hopkins University Press, 1976), 59.

40. Alexey Pisemsky, *Sobranie sochinenii v 9 tomakh*, vol. 1, Boyarshchina: Roman. Vinovata li ona: Zapiski. Tiufiak: Povest'. (Moscow: Pravda, 1959), 79. Subsequent references to this edition will be given parenthetically in the body of the text.

41. See O. B. Kafanova, "Zhorzh Sand i russkaia literatura XIX veka (1830–1860 gg.)," PhD diss. (Tomskii gosudarstvennyi pedagogicheskii universitet, 1999), 218–19. See also Lesley Singer Herrmann, "George Sand and the Nineteenth-Century Russian Novel: The Quest for a Heroine," PhD diss. (Columbia University, 1979), 70–73.

42. George Sand, *Indiana*, 2 vols. (Paris: Felix Bonnaire, 1838), 1:104–5.

43. Sand, 1:105.

44. Sand, 2:103.

45. Pisemsky, *Sobranie sochinenii*, 1:32.

46. Sand, *Indiana*, 2:79.

47. Michel Foucault, *Discipline and Punish: The Birth of the Prison*, trans. Alan Sheridan (New York: Penguin Random House, 2019), 49.

48. A. V. Druzhinin, *Povesti, Dnevnik*, ed. B. F. Egorov and V. A. Zhdanov (Moscow: Nauka, 1986), 10; Aleksandr Druzhinin, *Polinka Saks and the Story of Aleksei Dmitrich*, trans. Michael Katz (Evanston, IL: Northwestern University Press, 1992), 26–27. Subsequent references to these editions will be given parenthetically in the body of the text in the form (10; 26–27).

49. The links between *Polinka Saks* and *Jacques* have received much scholarly attention. See, for example, O. B. Kafanova, *Zhorzh Sand i russkaia literatura XIX veka (Mify i real'nost')*, 1830–1860 gg. (Tomsk: Tomskii gos. pedagog. univ., 1998), 237–40; B. F. Egorov, "Proza A.V. Druzhinina" in Druzhinin, *Povesti, Denvnik*, 432–35; and Dawn D. Eidelman, *George Sand and the Nineteenth-Century Russian Love-Triangle Novels* (Lewisburg, PA: Bucknell University Press), 1994.

50. Michel Foucault, *The Birth of Biopolitics: Lectures at the Collège de France, 1978–1979*, ed. Michel Senellart, trans. Graham Burchell (New York: Picador, 2010), 313.

51. Foucault, 65.

52. For still more far-fetched enactments of control, see the unrealized plan for a dramatic version of *Polinka Saks* in A.V. Druzhinin, "Zamysel dramy o sem'e Saksov," in *Povesti, Dnevnik*, 416–18.

53. A.N. Ostrovsky, *Polnoe sobranie sochinenii v 12i tomakh*, vol. 2 (Moscow: Iskusstvo, 1974), 448.

54. Michel Foucault, *Security, Territory, Population: Lectures at the Collège de France, 1978-1979*, ed. Michel Senellart, trans. Graham Burchell (New York: Picador, 2009), 313.

55. See Sara Ahmed, *The Promise of Happiness* (Durham, NC: Duke University Press, 2010).

56. Like the pattern of the failed rendezvous, the three governmental models of early realist "domestic fiction"—nakedly coercive, bureaucratic-disciplinary, and enlightened-paternalistic—extend far beyond the texts here analyzed in some detail. Thus, Pisemsky's focus on sheer coercion, motivated by jealousy in particular, reaches back at least as far as Pushkin's *Gypsies* (1824), Lermontov's *Masquerade* (1835), and Dostoevsky's *The Landlady* (1847) and extends forward to include Pisemsky's own *Bitter Fate* (1859) and Alexander Ostrovsky's *Sin and Sorrow Are Common to All* (1863). The archaic aura of this script suits it for Romantic "ethnography," "frenetic" drama, Pisemsky's "primitivist" prose, realist drama thematizing the life of the common people, and Dostoevsky's gothic tale. Meanwhile, Druzhinin's tale of the self-effacing husband reemerges in such later texts as Tolstoy's *Family Happiness* (1859), Mikhail Avdeev's *The Reef* (1860), and Turgenev's *Punin and Baburin* (1874), whose heroines literally or figuratively "return" to their significantly older husband-mentors after a more or less extended period of more or less explicitly permitted passionate straying. A similar trajectory of permissiveness, straying, and return, though with the figure of the husband replaced by that of a matriarchal grandmother, is at play in Goncharov's last novel, *The Precipice* (1869), of which more will be said in chapter 4. As for *The Same Old Story*'s script of raison d'état disciplinarity, it finds a distant though very prominent echo in the figure of the statesman-husband in *Anna Karenina* (1878), of which more shortly.

57. Alexander Herzen, *Who Is to Blame?*, trans. Michael R. Katz (Ithaca, NY: Cornell University Press, 1984), 145; Alexander Herzen, *Polnoe sobranie sochinenii*, vol. 4, *Khudozhestvennye proizvedeniia, 1841-1846* (Moscow: Akademiia nauk, 1955), 87. Subsequent references to these editions will be given parenthetically in the body of the text in the form (145; 4:87).

58. Jürgen Habermas, *The Structural Transformation of the Public Sphere*, trans. Thomas Burger (Cambridge, MA: MIT Press, 2000): 47.

59. George Sand, *Jacques* (Paris: Calmann Lèvy, 1889), 350.

60. Nancy Armstrong, "The Fiction of Bourgeois Morality and the Paradox of Individualism," in *The Novel*, vol. 2, *Forms and Themes*, ed. Franco Moretti (Princeton, NJ: Princeton University Press, 2007), 378.

61. Martin Malia, *Alexander Herzen and the Birth of Russian Socialism* (New York: Grosset and Dunlap, 1965), 259.

62. Malia's suggestion that "for Herzen, the only 'moral' solution would have been for Liubov to go off with her love and let Krutsifersky find solace in 'general interests'" (270) misses this more radical dimension of the text, its interest in the possibility of an alternative emancipated community.

63. Mediating between French political sentimentalism of the eighteenth century and this mid-nineteenth-century Russian novel are the more contemporary socialist doctrines in 1830s France, especially the work of Pierre Leroux—a major influence on Sand and Herzen alike. Irina Paperno characterizes the kernel of Leroux's influence

succinctly, stating that his "vision of social harmony in a collective was an expansion of the private ideal of emotional harmony in a love triangle." Paperno, "Introduction: Intimacy and History; The Gercen Family Drama Reconsidered," *Russian Literature* 61, nos. 1-2 (January-February 2007): 9.

64. William M. Reddy, *The Navigation of Feelings: A Framework for the History of Emotions* (Cambridge: Cambridge University Press, 2001), 181.

65. Reddy, 164.

66. Tony Tanner, *Adultery in the Novel: Contract and Transgression* (Baltimore: Johns Hopkins University Press, 2020), 231.

67. Alexander Herzen, *Sobranie sochinenii*, vol. 2, *Stat'i i fel'etony, 1841-1846; Dnevnik, 1842-1845* (Moscow: Institut mirovoi literatury im. A.M. Gor'kogo, 1954), 229.

68. Alexander Herzen, "Novaia faza v russkoi literature," in *Sobranie sochinenii*, vol. 18, *Stat'i iz Kolokola i drugie proizvedeniia 1864-1865 godov* (Moscow: Institut mirovoi literatury im. A.M. Gor'kogo, 1959), 188; Alexander Herzen, *Sobranie sochinenii*, vol. 7, *O razvitii revoliutsionnykh idei v Rossii. Proizvedeniia 1851-1852 godov* (Moscow: Institut mirovoi literatury im. A.M. Gor'kogo, 1956), 331.

69. On Insarov as the first explicitly political hero in the history of the Russian novel, and on the social foundation of the contrast between him, on the one hand, and Shubin and Bersenev, on the other, see Lev Pumpiansky, "Romany Turgeneva i roman 'Nakanune': istoriko-literaturnyi ocherk," in *Klassicheskaia traditsiia: Sobranie trudov po istorii russkoi literatury* (Moscow: Iazyki russkoi kul'tury, 2000), 394-99.

70. Ivan Turgenev, *On the Eve*, trans. Gilbert Gardiner (New York: Penguin Random House, 1950), 29; I. S. Turgenev, *Polnoe sobranie sochinenii i pisem*, vol. 8, *Nakanune. Gamlet i Don-Kikhot. Ottsy i deti 1859-1861* (Moscow: Nauka, 1964), 14. Subsequent references to these editions will be given parenthetically in the body of the text in the form (29; 8:14).

71. For a discussion of the motif of guilt in *On the Eve*, see Viktor Markovich, *Turgenev i russkii realisticheskii roman XIX veka (30-e-50-e gody)* (Leningrad: Izdatel'stvo leningradskogo universiteta, 1982), 169-86. Markovich regards the outbreak of metaphysical guilt toward the end of the novel as in a sense displacing the political problematics of the earlier parts. I attempt to understand that displacement itself in political terms.

72. N. A. Dobroliubov, "Kogda zhe pridet nastoiashchii den'?" in *Literaturnaia kritika*, vol. 2 (Leningrad: Khudozhestvennaia literatura, 1984), 204.

73. See Irene Masing-Delic, "The Aesthetics of Liberation: Insarov as Tristan," *Die Welt der Slaven* 32, no. 1 (1987): 59-77.

74. On fateful plotting in *Anna Karenina*, see Vladimir Alexandrov, *Limits to Interpretation: The Meaning of Anna Karenina* (Madison: University of Wisconsin Press 2004), 276-89.

75. Leo Tolstoy, *Anna Karenina*, trans. Richard Pevear and Larissa Volokhonsky (New York: Penguin Random House, 2000), 290; Lev Tolstoy, *Polnoe sobranie sochinenii*, vol. 18, *Anna Karenina, chast' 1-4* (Moscow, Leningrad: Khudozhestvennaia literatura, 1934), 306-7. Subsequent references to these editions will be given parenthetically in the body of the text in the form (290; 18:306).

76. Lev Tolstoy, *Polnoe sobranie sochinenii*, vol. 20, *Anna Karenina. Chernovye redaktsii i varianty* (Moscow, Leningrad: Khudozhestvennaia literatura, 1939), 16, 25.

77. Reddy, *The Navigation of Feelings*, 145.

78. For a discussion of the undoing of Anna's "social self," see Harriet Murav, "Law as Limit and the Limits of the Law in *Anna Karenina*," in *Approaches to Teaching Tolstoy's Anna Karenina*, ed. Liza Knapp and Amy Mandelker (New York: Modern Language Association of America, 2003), 74–82.

79. Boris Eikhenbaum, *Lev Tolstoi, semidesiatye gody* (Leningrad: Sovetskii pisatel', 1960), 200–202.

80. Arthur Schopenhauer, *World as Will and Representation*, vol. 1, trans. E. F. J. Payne (New York: Dover, 1969), 353.

81. Schopenhauer, 1:355.

82. Giorgio Agamben, *Homo Sacer: Sovereign Power and Bare Life*, trans. Daniel Heller-Roazen (Stanford, CA: Stanford University Press, 1998), 83; italics in the original.

Chapter Four

1. Benedict Anderson, *Imagined Communities: Reflections on the Origin and Spread of Nationalism* (New York: Verso, 2016), 46.

2. Anderson, 26.

3. Anderson, 25.

4. Jed Esty, *Unseasonable Youth: Modernism, Colonialism, and the Fiction of Development* (New York: Oxford University Press, 2013), 47.

5. Esty, 58.

6. While allowing for the appearance in nineteenth-century fiction of colonial echoes (as discussed, for example, by Edward Said, Gayatri Spivak, and Fredric Jameson), Esty observes that the texts' "closural process drives home the underlying idea that animating conflicts (at the thematic level) and contradictions (at the socio-symbolic level) are resolved through an alignment between the protagonist's end-narrative in time and the nation's boundary-limit in space." Etsy, 50. Similar arguments have been advanced in relation to another historical context altogether, that of decolonizing nationalism. See Pheng Cheah, *What Is a World? On Postcolonial Literature as World Literature* (Durham, NC: Duke University Press, 2015), 239.

7. Franco Moretti, *Atlas of the European Novel: 1800–1900* (New York: Verso, 1999), 15.

8. See a more detailed discussion of this dynamic in Patrick Parrinder, *Nation and Novel: The English Novel from Its Origins to the Present Day* (New York: Oxford University Press, 2008), 202–8.

9. On the national and international dimension of Goethe's novel, see Tobias Boes, *Formative Fictions: Nationalism, Cosmopolitanism, and the Bildungsroman* (Ithaca, NY: Cornell University Press, 2012), 63–69.

10. For a helpful account of the seeds of nation-thinking in the concept of *otechestvo* (fatherland), see Oleg Kharkordin, "What Is the State? The Russian Concept of *Gosudarstvo* in the European Context," *History and Theory* 40, no. 2 (May 2001): 220.

11. Anderson, *Imagined Communities*, 86.

12. Nicholas Riasanovsky, *Nicholas I and Official Nationality in Russia, 1825–1855* (Berkley: University of California Press, 1967), 124.

13. Andrei Zorin, *By Fables Alone: Literature and State Ideology in Late-Eighteenth–Early-Nineteenth-Century Russia*, trans. Marcus C. Levitt (Boston: Academic Studies

Press, 2019), 350. See also Ronald Grigor Suny, "Thinking about Feelings: Affective Dispositions and Emotional Ties in Imperial Russia and the Ottoman Empire," in *Interpreting Emotions in Russia and Eastern Europe*, ed. Mark D. Steinberg and Valeria Sobol (Dekalb: Northern Illinois University Press, 2011), 114.

14. *Severnaia pchela*, March 15, 1830.

15. Anderson, *Imagined Communities*, 33.

16. Olga Maiorova, *From the Shadow of Empire: Defining the Russian Nation through Cultural Mythology, 1855–1870* (Madison: University of Wisconsin Press, 2010), 71. For some negative responses to the Millennium monument from a more popular-nationalist perspective, see Richard Wortman, *Scenarios of Power: Myth and Ceremony in Russian Monarchy from Peter the Great to the Abdication of Nicholas II*, abridged ed. (Princeton, NJ: Princeton University Press, 2006), 216.

17. Maiorova, *From the Shadow of Empire*, 80.

18. Nikolai Kostomarov, "Mysli o federativnom nachale drevnei Rusi," in *Istoricheskie monografii i issledovaniia Nikolaia Kostomarova*, vol. 1 (St. Petersburg: Tipografiia tovarishchestva Obshchestvennaia pol'za, 1863), 41.

19. Nikolai Kostomarov, "Ivan Susanin. Istoricheskoe issledovanie," in *Istoricheskie monografii i issledovaniia Nikolaia Kostomarova*, vol. 1 (St. Petersburg: Tipografiia tovarishchestva Obshchestvennaia pol'za, 1863), 477–504.

20. Maiorova, *From the Shadow of Empire*, 147.

21. Leo Tolstoy, *War and Peace*, trans. Richard Pevear and Larissa Volokhonsky (New York: Vintage, 2011), 245–46; trans. emended; Lev Tolstoy, *Polnoe sobranie sochinenii*, vol. 9, *Voina i mir*, vol. 1, 300–301.

22. Tolstoy, *War and Peace*, 752–53; Tolstoy, *Polnoe sobranie sochinenii*, 11:184.

23. Tolstoy, *War and Peace*, 842; Tolstoy, *Polnoe sobranie sochinenii*, 11:293.

24. Tolstoy, *War and Peace*, 899–900; Tolstoy, *Polnoe sobranie sochinenii*, 11:360–61.

25. Tolstoy, *War and Peace*, 679; Tolstoy, *Polnoe sobranie sochinenii*, 11:95.

26. Tolstoy, *War and Peace*, 681; Tolstoy, *Polnoe sobranie sochinenii*, 11:98.

27. Tolstoy, *War and Peace*, 681; Tolstoy, *Polnoe sobranie sochinenii*, 11:98.

28. Lina Steiner offers an intriguing Herderian reading of the way nation/totality and selfhood come together in *War and Peace*. See Lina Steiner, *For Humanity's Sake: The Bildungsroman in Russian Culture* (Toronto: University of Toronto Press, 2011), 108–29.

29. Susanna Rabow-Edling, "The Decembrist and the Concept of a Civic Nation," *Nationalities Papers* 35, no. 2 (May 2007): 369–91.

30. "Ostensibly" because, of course, depending on the European text, many are selected for constitutive exclusion: those who are stubbornly transgressive, fail to develop, lack proper sensibility, and so on.

31. Goncharov, *Polnoe sobranie sochinenii*, vol. 4, *Oblomov: Roman v chetyrekh chastiakh* (St. Petersburg: Nauka, 1998), 484. Ivan Goncharov, *Oblomov*, trans. David Magarshack (New York: Penguin, 2005), 475–76. Subsequent references to these editions will be given parenthetically in the body of the text in the form (475–76; 4:484).

32. See Liudmilla Geiro's painstaking examination of all the available evidence in "Roman I. A. Goncharova 'Oblomov,'" in I. A. Goncharov, *Oblomov* (Leningrad: Nauka, 1987), 534–35.

33. Goncharov, *Polnoe sobranie sochinenii*, vol. 5, *Oblomov: Roman v chetyriokh chastiakh, Rukopisnye redaktsii* (St. Petersburg: Nauka, 2003), 239.

34. Quoted in Catherine Gallagher, *The Body Economic: Life, Death, and Sensation in Political Economy and the Victorian Novel* (Princeton. NJ: Princeton University Press, 2008), 24.

35. Max Weber, *The Protestant Ethic and the Spirit of Capitalism*, trans. Talcott Parsons (London: Routledge Classics, 2005), 32.

36. Weber, 64.

37. For a political-theological reading of glory as acclamation, see Giorgio Agamben, *The Kingdom and the Glory: For a Theological Genealogy of Economy and Government* (Stanford, CA: Stanford University Press, 2020), 197–259.

38. Goncharov, *Polnoe sobranie sochinenii*, 5:205.

39. Goncharov, 207.

40. For a differently configured but complementary reading of the place of political economy in *Oblomov*, see Anne Lounsbery, "The World on the Back of a Fish: Mobility, Immobility, and Economics in *Oblomov*," *The Russian Review* 70, no. 1 (January 2011), 50–60.

41. Goncharov, *Polnoe sobranie sochinenii*, vol. 6, *Oblomov: Roman v chtyrekh chastiakh, Primichaniia* (St. Petersburg: Nauka, 2004), 211–12. For more on the Penkin passage as an allusion to *One Thousand Souls*, see Zubkov, "'V samom dele real'noe napravlenie': 'Oblomov' i tvorchestvo A.F. Pisemskogo," ed. S. N. Gus'kov, S. V. Denisenko, N. V. Kalinina, A. V. Lobkareva, and I. V. Smirnova, *Oblomov: Konstanty i peremennye. Sbornik nauchnykh statei* (St. Petersburg: Nestor-Istoriia, 2011), 145–46.

42. M. V. Otradin, ed., *Roman I. A. Goncharova "Oblomov" v russkoi kritike* (Leningrad: Izdatel'stvo Leningradskogo universiteta, 1991), 63.

43. Otradin, 138.

44. Otradin, 138.

45. Otradin, 96.

46. Audible here and elsewhere in the critical discussions of Stolz and Kalinovich are echoes of contemporary debates on the figure of the enlightened bureaucrat as a potential agent of national regeneration. See Nikolai L'vov, "Neskol'ko slov o komedii 'Chinovnik,'" *Sovremennik* (May 1856), no. 6, part 3, 242. For a detailed reconstruction and analysis of the discourse surrounding dramatic representations of the enlightened bureaucrat, see Kirill Zubkov, *Stsenarii peremen: Uvarovskaia nagrada i evoliutsiia russkoi dramaturgii v epokhu Aleksandra II* (Moscow: Novoe literaturnoe obozrenie, 2021), 155–200. See also Bruce Lincoln's observation on the role of "enlightened bureaucrats" in implementing the reforms of the 1860s: "Although dedicated to renovating and transforming the Russian Empire, they remained autocratic servants of an autocratic master, and their approach to the Great Reforms was dominated by that single characteristic." Lincoln, *In the Vanguard of Reform: Russia's Enlightened Bureaucrats 1825–1861* (DeKalb: Northern Illinois University Press, 1982), 167.

47. For a recent discussion of the significance of such passivity for the novel's treatment of the developing noble estate consciousness, see Bella Grigoryan, *Noble Subjects: The Russian Novel and the Gentry, 1762–1861* (DeKalb: Northern Illinois University Press, 2018), 103–17.

48. Michel Foucault, *Society Must Be Defended: Lectures at the Collège de France, 1975–1976*, ed. Mauro Bertani and Allessandro Fontana (New York: Picador, 2003), 247.

49. It is this position of outsideness that accounts for the lack of both narration and description when it comes to the figure of Stolz. See Anne Lounsbery, "The World on

the Back of a Fish: Mobility, Immobility, and Economics in *Oblomov*"; and Vadim Shneyder, *Russia's Capitalist Realism: Tolstoy, Dostoevsky, and Chekhov* (Evanston, IL: Northwestern University Press, 2021), 24–25.

50. Fyodor Dostoevsky, *A Writer's Diary*, ed. Gary Saul Morson and Kenneth Lantz, trans. Gary Saul Morson (Evanston, IL: Northwestern University Press, 2009), 160; Fyodor Dostoevsky, *Polnoe sobranie sochinenii*, vol. 21, *Dnevnik pisatelia, 1873; Stat'i i zametki, 1873–1878* (Leningrad: Nauka, 1980), 34.

51. Dostoevsky, *A Writer's Diary*, 161; Dostoevsky, *Polnoe sobranie sochinenii*, 21:35.

52. Dostoevsky, *A Writer's Diary*, 161; Dostoevsky, *Polnoe sobranie sochinenii*, 21:35. For an insightful discussion of some of these passages, see Nancy Ruttenberg, *Dostoevsky's Democracy* (Princeton, NJ: Princeton University Press, 2010), 187–92.

53. Fyodor Dostoevsky, *Polnoe sobranie sochinenii*, vol. 18, *Stat'i i zametki, 1845–1861* (Leningrad: Nauka, 1978), 55–56.

54. Belinsky, *Polnoe sobranie sochinenii*, 3:345.

55. I. S. Turgenev, *Polnoe sobranie sochinenii i pisem*, vol. 4, *Zapiski okhotnika 1847–1874* (Moscow: Nauka, 1963).

56. Fyodor Dostoevsky, *Crime and Punishment*, trans. Richard Pevear and Larissa Volokhonsky (New York: Vintage, 1993), 27; Fyodor Dostoevsky, *Polnoe sobranie sochinenii*, vol. 6, *Prestuplenie i nakazanie* (Leningrad: Nauka, 1973), 25.

57. See Adele Lindenmeyr, "Raskolnikov's City and the Napoleonic Plan," in *Fyodor Dostoevsky's "Crime and Punishment": A Casebook*, ed. Richard Peace (New York: Oxford University Press, 2006), 37–49.

58. Dostoevsky, *Polnoe sobranie sochinenii*, vol. 7, *Prestuplenie i nakazanie: Rukopisnye redaktsii* (Leningrad: Nauka, 1973), 153, 155. For further invocations of Peter-the-Dutchman, see pp. 189, 190 of the same volume.

59. Much has been made of Raskolnikov's preoccupation with the figure of Napoleon, but it is important to distinguish among the various valences of the "Napoleonic myth" mobilized by different novelists and in different novelistic traditions. For the protagonists of Balzac, Napoleon symbolizes the unscrupulous energy of a parvenu; for Stendhal's heroes, he stands for spontaneity, impetuousness, and valor; for Raskolnikov, Napoleon is first and foremost a criminal lawgiver, a usurper-sovereign, a(n) (impostor) redeemer. See Yuri Lotman, "Siuzhetnoe prostranstvo russkogo romana XIX stoletiia," in *Izbrannye stat'i (v 3-kh tomakh)*, vol. 3, *Stat'i po istorii russkoi literatury: Teoriia i semiotika drugikh iskusstv. Mekhanizmy kul'tury. Melkie zametki* (Tallinn: Aleksandra, 1993), 91–106. In this respect, Peter, especially Peter as a "Dutchman" provides an equally appropriate paradigm case. And indeed, though only the former makes into the final text, both receive several mentions in the notebooks. For Petrine subtexts in *Crime and Punishment*, see Clint Walker, "On Serfdom, Sickness, and Redemption: The Peter the Great Subtext in *Crime and Punishment*," *Dostoevsky Studies*, n.s. 13 (2009): 93–108. On Peter I in the context of Dostoevsky's relationship to Pushkin, see Gary Rosenshield, *Challenging the Bard: Dostoevsky and Pushkin, a Study of Literary Relationship* (Madison: University of Wisconsin Press, 2013). And, most recently, with reference to the subtext of *The Bronze Horseman*, see Kathleen Scollins, "From the New Word to the True Word: The *Bronze Horseman* Subtext of *Crime and Punishment*," *Russian Review* 78, no. 3 (July 2019): 414–36.

60. Hence, too, the ambiguity of searching for one's crime in the newspapers to be-

gin with: Is it to make sure he is not a suspect, or is it to find the mark he left in the universe of public deeds?

61. I can do no more here than suggest a relationship between the notion of sovereignty as the source of exception and Mikhail Bakhtin's well-known thesis on the unfinalizable nature of Dostoevsky's heroes. The unfinalizable self, the self that inevitably breaks out of societal norms and expectations, evidently bears at least a structural resemblance to the self of the unlimited ruler, the one who gives laws rather than obey them.

62. To be sure, the protagonist and the investigator should not be regarded as pure embodiments of the imaginaries of sovereignty and disciplinarity, respectively. Raskolnikov, for one, turns out to lose control of the crime and must in the aftermath reckon with the need to keep it secret. On the other hand, Porfiry Petrovich invokes the solar metaphor in relation to his suspect and acclaims him in other ways. Dostoevsky, *Crime and Punishment*, 460; Dostoevsky, *Polnoe sobranie sochinenii*, 6:351. The investigator's penchant for seeing the crime less as a moral outrage or an infringement of the law than as an episode in Raskolnikov's—after all "exceptional"—biography also indicates his partiality for at least an attenuated interpretation of the protagonist within the regime of sovereignty.

63. Dostoevsky, *Polnoe sobranie sochinenii*, 7:189.

64. Dostoevsky, "Dva lageria teoretikov (Po povodu 'Dnia' i koi-chego drugogo)," *Polnoe sobranie sochinenii* 20 (1861): 14–15.

65. B. A. Uspenskij, "Tsar and Pretender: *Samozvančestvo* or Royal Imposture in Russia as a Cultural-Historical Phenomenon," trans. David Budgen, in *Semiotics of Russian Culture*, ed. J. M. Lotman and B. A. Uspenskij (Ann Arbor: University of Michigan Press, 1984), 264–65.

66. Nikolai Gogol, *Selected Passages from Correspondence with Friends*, trans. Jesse Zledin (Nashville, TN: Vanderbilt University Press, 1969), 200; Gogol, *Vybrannye mesta iz perepiski s druz'iami* in *Polnoe sobranie sochinenii v 14i tomakh*, vol. 8, *Stat'i* (Moscow: Akademiia nauk, 1952), 370.

67. For illuminating accounts of this pattern, see Ellen Rutten, *Unattainable Bride Russia: Gendering Nation, State, and Intelligentsia in Russian Intellectual Culture* (Evanston, IL: Northwestern University Press, 2010); Aleksei Makushinsky, "Otvergnutyi zhenikh, ili osnovnoi mif russkoi literatury XIX veka," *Zarubezhnye zapiski*, no. 5 (2006); Yuri Lotman, *V shkole poeticheskogo slova: Pushkin, Lermontov, Gogol'* (Moscow: Prosveshchenie, 1988), 325–48.

68. Tolstoy, *War and Peace*, 703; Tolstoy, *Polnoe sobranie sochinenii*, 11:124–25.

69. Tolstoy, *War and Peace*, 704; Tolstoy, *Polnoe sobranie sochinenii*, 11:125.

70. Ivan Turgenev, *Spring Torrents* (New York: Penguin Random House, 1980), 126; I. S. Turgenev, *Polnoe sobranie sochinenii i pisem*, vol. 11, *Povesti i rasskazy (1871–1877)* (Moscow: Akademiia nauk, 1961), 110. For a recent analysis of *Spring Torrents* as a political allegory, see Alexey Vdovin and Pavel Uspenskij, "'First Love Is Exactly Like Revolution': Intimacy as Political Allegory in Ivan Turgenev's Novella *Spring Torrents*," *Slavic Review* 80, no. 3 (Fall 2021), 504–22.

71. Turgenev, *Polnoe sobranie sochinenii i pisem*, 9:172.

72. Turgenev, *Polnoe sobranie sochinenii i pisem*, 11:462–66.

73. For a discussion of the ideology of gender implicit in the image of Dido in Tur-

genev, see Jane Costlow, "Dido, Turgenev, and the Journey toward Bedlam," *Russian Literature* 29, no. 4 (May 1991): 395–408. For a discussion of memory and forgetting in *Spring Torrents*, in connection with Virgil's epic, see Boris Maslov, "Gniozda klochnei i rokovye retsidivy," in *Russkii realizm XIX veka: obshchestvo, znanie, povestvovanie*, ed. M. Vaysman, A. Vdovin, I. Kliger, and K. Ospovat (Moscow: Novoe literaturnoe obozrenie, 2020), 543–45.

74. For a like-minded reading of Turgenev's earlier novel *Smoke*, see Boris Maslov, "'Zhilishche tishiny preobratilos' v ad': O sud'be starorezhimnykh poniatii v Novoe vremia," in *Poniatiia, idei, konstruktsii: ocherki sravnitel'noi istoricheskoi semantiki*, ed. Iu. Kagarlitskii, D. Kalugin, and B. Maslov (Moscow: Novoe literaturnoe obozrenie, 2019), 346–56.

75. Fyodor Dostoevsky, *The Idiot*, trans. Richard Pevear and Larissa Volokhonsky (New York: Vintage, 2012), 508; Fyodor Dostoevsky, *Polnoe sobranie sochinenii*, vol. 8, *Idiot* (Leningrad: Nauka, 1973), 421. Subsequent references to these editions will be given parenthetically in the body of the text in the form (508; 8:421).

76. For a more detailed account of the parallels between the story of Marie and Myshkin's adventures in Russia, see W. J. Leatherbarrow, *Fyodor Dostoevsky: A Reference Guide* (Boston: G. K. Hall, 1990), 110.

77. The allegorical Russianness of Nastasya Filippovna comes through still more clearly if we take into consideration the novel's clear genealogical link to Dostoevsky's tale *The Landlady* (1847). Like the earlier, explicitly national-allegorical Katerina, who speaks the stylized language of Russian folklore, Nastasya Filippovna stands between the dark, archaic, powerful, and in the end murderous Rogozhin (Murin in *The Landlady*) and the redemptive but ultimately powerless Myshkin (Ordynin), dramatizing the fate of the nation hanging in the balance between salvation and perdition. For an analysis of *The Landlady* as national-political allegory, see Rudolf Neuhauser, "*The Landlady*: A New Interpretation," *Canadian Slavonic Papers/Revue Canadienne des Slavistes* 10, no. 1 (Spring 1968): 42–67.

78. For a discussion of the extent of compassion in Dostoevsky's poetics in the context of his polemics with Tolstoy's views on the war in the Balkans, see Jens Herlth, "'Na kakom rasstoianii konchaetsia chelovekoliubie?' Tolstoi i Dostoevskii v 1877 godu: sotsial'naia epistemologiia romana," *Novoe literaturnoe obozrenie* 155, no. 1 (January 2019).

79. Given Raisky's artistic aspirations, there is of course the possibility that the novel might be organized within the horizon of the bildungsroman's sub- (or, some would argue, anti-) genre, the *Künstlerroman*. This possibility has to be dismissed as well, since Raisky's talented but dilettantish dabbling with painting, music, literature, and sculpture displays no signs of artistic maturation.

80. Ivan Goncharov, *The Precipice*, trans. and ed. Laury Magnus and Boris Jakim (Ann Arbor, MI: Ardis, 1994), 423; Ivan Goncharov, *Polnoe sobranie sochinenii i pisem v dvadtsati tomakh*, vol. 7, *Obryv*, ed. T. A. Lapitskaya and V. A. Tunimanov (St. Petersburg: Nauka, 2004), 772. Subsequent references to these editions will be given parenthetically in the body of the text in the form (423; 7:772).

81. Max Weber, *The Theory of Social and Economic Organization*, ed. Talcott Parsons, trans. A. M. Henderson and Talcott Parsons (New York: Free Press, 1964), 341–58.

82. Weber, 341–58. In fact, these three types of authority may mix in various proportions in the examples here adduced and in others. The most common admixture of all is that of the most representationally impactful charisma.

83. Weber, 346.

84. The novel's drafts insist on the link between Grandmother and the *tsaritsy* of the past still more emphatically. See Ivan Goncharov, *Polnoe sobranie sochinenii i pisem v dvadtsati tomakh*, vol. 8, *Obryv: Kniga 1* (St. Petersburg: Nauka, 2008), 419.

85. The price for achieving such a projection, the price for positing an identity between the political and the libidinal within a realist novel about contemporary life (i.e., in the context in which the actual destruction of Malinovka as a result of Vera's actions would be unwritable) is the tremendous, indeed grotesque, compensatory exertion of rhetorical heightening, resorting to methods of the "frenetic school" of the 1830s, long since in disgrace among Russian writers of prose and directly attacked by Goncharov himself already in his first novel. Thus, one of the novel's early critics, N. V. Shchelgunov, makes the following biting observation: "Was it worth living for twenty years in order to turn off onto the retrograde path, in order to defend in 1869 what was mocked and considered antiquated in 1847?" See *I. A. Goncharov v russkoi kritike: Sbornik statei*, ed. M. Ia. Poliakov and S. A. Trubnikov (Moscow: Khudozhestvennaia literatura, 1958), 258.

Chapter Five

1. Sophocles, *Antigone; Oedipus the King; Electra*, ed. Edith Hall, trans. H. D. F. Kitto (New York: Oxford University Press, 1998), 8–9.

2. Simon Goldhill writes: "As a nephew Polyneices should be regarded as a philos to Creon. As an enemy to the city, Polyneices has forfeited his claim on Creon's sense of duty. Such, once more, is the polarizing force of the vocabulary of *philos* and *ekhthros* [enemy]. Indeed, for Creon the correct establishment of the state is the very condition of possibility of having *philoi* at all. Unlike Homer and unlike Antigone, for Creon it is the *polis* and not the *oikos* [household] which offers the institutional basis of *philia*. [...] It is the correct use of the term *philos* which is being set at stake." Simon Goldhill, *Reading Greek Tragedy* (New York: Cambridge University Press, 1986), 94.

3. Debates on the meanings of *philia* in classical Greece continue. When it comes to its use in tragedy, however, Elizabeth S. Belfiore has assembled overwhelming evidence allowing us to link the term paradigmatically with kinship relations, extending to relations of marriage, *xenia* (roughly, host/guest-friendship), and suppliancy. See Elizabeth S. Belfiore, *Murder among Friends: Violations of* Philia *in Greek Tragedy* (New York: Oxford University Press, 2000).

4. Vissarion Belinsky, "Ocherki Borodinskogo srazheniia (vospominaniia o 1812 gode). Sochineniia F. Glinki, avtora 'Pisem russkogo ofitsera.' Moskva. 1839," in *Polnoe sobranie sochinenii v 13i tomakh*, vol. 3, *Stat'i i retsenzii. Piatidesiatiletnii diadiushka, 1839–1840* (Moscow: Akademiia nauk, 1953), 331.

5. Friedrich Nietzsche, "The Birth of Tragedy from the Spirit of Music," in *Basic Writings of Nietzsche*, ed. Walter Kaufmann, trans. Walter Kaufmann (New York: Modern Library, 2000), 73.

6. Jean-Pierre Vernant, "Intimations of the Will in Greek Tragedy," in *Myth and Tragedy in Ancient Greece*, trans. Janet Lloyd (Princeton, NJ: Princeton University Press, 1990), 82.

7. Glenn W. Most, "Sad Stories of the Death of Kings: Sovereignty and Its Constraints in Greek Tragedy and Elsewhere," in *The Scaffolding of Sovereignty: Global and*

Aesthetic Perspectives on the History of a Concept, ed. Zvi Ben-Dor Benite, Stefanos Geroulanos, and Nicole Jerr (New York: Columbia University Press, 2017), 72. David Quint discusses a version of this tension between self-affirmation and constraint in Shakespeare and French neoclassical theater in Quint, "The Tragedy of Nobility on the Seventeenth-Century Stage," *Modern Language Quarterly* 67, no. 1 (March 2006): 7–29. Walter Benjamin's classic analysis in *The Origin of German Tragic Drama* places the concept of sovereignty at the center of his analysis of the Baroque *Trauerspiel*.

8. Most, "Sad Stories of the Death of Kings," 70.

9. See Erich Auerbach, *Mimesis: The Representation of Reality in Western Literature*, trans. Willard R. Trask (Princeton, NJ: Princeton University Press, 2013), 465–66. Generalizing from Auerbach's discussion of Stendhal, John Orr construes tragic-realist sensibility as an attunement to the individual's alienation in bourgeois society. Orr, *Tragic Realism and Modern Society: Studies in the Sociology of the Modern Novel* (Pittsburgh, PA: University of Pittsburgh Press, 1978), 14. For like-minded accounts of "tragic realism" and "modern tragedy," see also Raymond Williams, *Modern Tragedy*, ed. Pamela McCallum (Peterborough, Ontario: Broadview, 2006); Jeannette King, *Tragedy in the Victorian Novel: Theory and Practice in the Novels of George Eliot, Thomas Hardy and Henry James* (New York: Cambridge University Press, 1980); and Terry Eagleton, *Sweet Violence: The Idea of the Tragic* (New Haven, CT: Yale University Press, 2022). Soviet literary criticism tended to endow tragic alienation in the realist novel with a parallel but opposite historical vector. While for Auerbach and Orr, among others, the alienated individual typically bears the obsolescent values of aristocratic society, Soviet critics tend to regard the tragic hero as someone born prematurely, with the social conditions not yet ripe for the emergent values he or she bears. See, for example, Maria Kurginian, *Chelovek v literature 20go veka* (Moscow: Nauka, 1989), 370.

10. See, for example, George Steiner, *The Death of Tragedy* (New York: Open Road Media, 2013), 3–10, 106–28; György Lukács, *The Theory of the Novel*, trans. Anna Bostock Berger (Cambridge, MA: MIT Press, 1977), 31; Walter Benjamin, *The Origin of German Tragic Drama* (New York: Verso, 2009), 101. Hegel is here a major point of reference. For Hegel, the Greek tragic character is best understood as a vessel for an "ethical power," a substantive principle embedded in the social world itself: "it is not this particular individual who acts and is guilty; for as this self he is only the unreal shadow, or he exists merely as a universal self, and individuality is purely the formal moment of the action as such, the content being the laws and customs which, for the individual, are those of his class and station [*seines Standes*]." Georg Wilhelm Friedrich Hegel, *Phenomenology of Spirit*, trans. A. V. Miller (New York: Oxford University Press, 1979), 282.

11. Nancy Armstrong and Leonard Tennenhouse, "Sovereignty and the Form of Formlessness," *Differences: A Journal of Feminist Cultural Studies: The Future of the Human* 20, nos. 2–3 (2009): 171.

12. Michel Foucault, *Security, Territory, and Population: Lectures at the Collège de France, 1977–1978*, ed. Michel Senellart, trans. Graham Burchell (New York: Picador, 2009), 265.

13. Foucault, 265.

14. Franco Moretti, "The Moment of Truth," in *Signs Taken for Wonders: Essays in the Sociology of Literary Forms*, trans. Susan Fisher, David Forgacs, and David Miller (New York: Verso, 1988), 253.

15. Alexander Veselovsky, who coined the term "historical poetics" and laid the ground for its development, spoke of the social "demand" of the times, which brought back into cultural relevance half-forgotten, or awakened slumbering, forms. On Veselovsky and the tradition of historical poetics, see *Persistent Forms: Explorations in Historical Poetics*, ed. Ilya Kliger and Boris Maslov (New York: Fordham University Press, 2015).

16. Alexander Pushkin, *Eugene Onegin*, trans. James Falen (New York: Oxford University Press, 1998), 188; Alexander Pushkin, *Polnoe sobranie sochinenii v deviatnadtsati tomakh*, 6:168.

17. Pushkin, *Eugene Onegin*, 189; Pushkin, *Polnoe sobranie sochinenii*, 6:169.

18. Nabokov comments: "such phrases are really smuggled in here only to create the right atmosphere for and prepare the transition to Onegin's passionately falling in love with Tatyana." Aleksandr Pushkin, *Eugene Onegin. A Novel in Verse*, trans. Vladimir Nabokov, vol. 2, *Commentary and Index* (Princeton, NJ: Princeton University Press, 1975), 161. Lotman speaks more broadly of "the tendency of the eighth chapter toward the 'rehabilitation' of the hero." See Yuri Lotman, *Pushkin. Biografiia pisatelia. Stat'i i zametki 1960–1990. "Evgeniy Onegin" Kommentarii* (St. Petersburg: Iskusstvo, 1995), 715.

19. Northrop Frye, *Anatomy of Criticism: Four Essays* (Princeton, NJ: Princeton University Press, 2020), 33–34.

20. Vissarion Belinsky, "Vzgliad na russkuiu literaturu 1847 goda: stat'ia vtoraia," in *Polnoe sobranie sochinenii*, vol. 10, *Stat'i i retsenzii, 1846–1848* (Moscow: Akedemiia nauk, 1956), 322.

21. Alexander Herzen, *Who Is to Blame?*, trans. Michael R. Katz (Ithaca, NY: Cornell University Press, 1984), 266; Alexander Herzen, *Polnoe sobranie sochinenii*, 4:190.

22. Alexey Pisemsky, *Sobranie sochinenii v deviati tomakh*, vol. 3 (Moscow: Pravda, 1959), 448; Alexey Pisemsky, *One Thousand Souls*, trans. Ivy Litvinov (New York: Greenwood Press, 1969), 453.

23. Raymond Williams, *Modern Tragedy*, ed. Pamela McCallum (Peterborough, Ontario: Broadview, 2006), 55.

24. Richard Wortman, *Scenarios of Power: Myth and Ceremony in Russian Monarchy from Peter the Great to the Abdication of Nicholas II*, abridged ed. (Princeton, NJ: Princeton University Press, 2006), 1.

25. Goncharov, *Polnoe sobranie sochinenii*, 7:672; Goncharov, *The Precipice*, 370.

26. Goncharov, *Polnoe sobranie sochinenii*, 7:687; Goncharov, *The Precipice*, 378.

27. Pierre Corneille, *The Cid/Cinna/The Theatrical Illusion*, trans. John Cairncross (London: Penguin, 1975), 189; Pierre Corneille, *Corneille's Cinna ou la Clémence d'Auguste*, ed. John E. Matzke (Boston: D. C. Heath, 1905), 91. "Only offended angels speak this way," comments young Dostoevsky. F. M. Dostoevsky, *Polnoe sobranie sochinenii*, vol 28.1, *Pis'ma, 1832–1859* (Leningrad: Nauka, 1985), 71. For a more detailed discussion, see Ilya Kliger, "Sovereignty and the Novel: Dostoevsky's Political Theology," in *Dostoevsky at 200: The Novel and Modernity*, ed. Katherine Bowers and Kate Holland (Toronto: University of Toronto Press, 2021).

28. George Eliot, *Middlemarch*, ed. Rosemary Ashton (New York: Penguin Random House, 2003), 869.

29. Eliot, 25.

30. Eliot, 25–26.

31. Eliot, 896.

32. Eliot, 25.

33. Aristotle, *Poetics*, trans. Gerald F. Else (Ann Arbor: University of Michigan Press, 1967), 35.

34. Aristotle, 36.

35. Aristotle, 36.

36. Gerald F. Else, *Aristotle's Poetics: The Argument* (Cambridge, MA: Harvard University Press, 1957), 350.

37. Nikolai Gogol, *The Complete Tales of Nikolai Gogol*, vol. 2, ed. Leonard J. Kent, trans. Constance Garnett (Chicago: University of Chicago Press, 1985), 108 (emphasis added).

38. See Kirill Zubkov, "Povesti i romany A.F. Pisemskogo 1850-kh godov: Povestvovanie, kontekst, traditsiia," PhD diss. (St. Petersburg State University, 2011), 149. What undoes Kalinovich is the internality to him of what he fights against: his dishonest marriage to Polina makes him vulnerable at the end.

39. I. S. Turgenev, *Polnoe sobranie sochinenii i pisem*, 11:150; Ivan Turgenev, *Spring Torrents* (New York: Penguin Random House, 1980), 169.

40. Aristotle, *Poetics*, 35.

41. Robert Parker defines miasma as "a condition that has some, and usually all, of the following characteristics: it makes the person affected ritually impure, and thus unfit to enter a temple; it is contagious; it is dangerous, and this danger is not of familiar secular origin. Two typical sources of such a condition are contact with a corpse, or a murderer." See Robert Parker, *Miasma: Pollution and Purification in Early Greek Religion* (Oxford: Clarendon Press, 1983), 3–4.

42. Jean-Pierre Vernant, *Myth and Society in Ancient Greece*, trans. Janet Lloyd (New York: Zone, 1988), 134–35.

43. I. S. Turgenev, *Polnoe sobranie sochinenii i pisem*, vol. 9 (Moscow: Nauka, 1982), 374–75.

44. Vernant, *Myth and Society*, 126.

45. Alexander Herzen, *Polnoe sobranie sochinenii*, 10:234; Alexander Herzen, *My Past and Thoughts: The Memoirs of Alexander Herzen*, 4 vols., trans. Constance Garnett, trans. revised Humphrey Higgins (London: Chatto and Windus, 1968), 2:853.

46. Herzen, *Polnoe sobranie sochinenii*, 10:230; Herzen, *My Past and Thoughts*, 2:848.

47. For discussions of the family drama in terms of genre, and, especially, of tragedy, see N.V. Dulova, "Poetika 'Bylogo i dum' A.I. Gertsena," PhD diss. (Irkutsk University, 1998); Ilya Kliger, "Auto-historiography: Genre, Trope, and Modes of Emplotment in Aleksandr and Natal'ja Gercen's Narratives of the Family Drama," *Russian Literature* 61, nos. 1–2 (January–February 2007): 103–38.

48. Alexander Pushkin, "The Bronze Horseman," in *Collected Narrative and Lyrical Poetry*, ed. and trans. Walter Arndt (Woodstock, NY: Ardis, 2002), 436–38.

49. This is Thomas Hobbes's resonant expression, echoed in numerous eighteenth-century odes dedicated to Peter I. Thomas Hobbes, *Leviathan*, ed. C. B. Macpherson (Harmondsworth: Penguin, 1968), 227.

50. Thomas Gould, *The Ancient Quarrel between Poetry and Philosophy* (Princeton, NJ: Princeton University Press, 2014), ix–xxvii.

51. Sophocles, *Antigone; Oedipus the King; Electra*, 92.

52. On *pathos* and *philia* in Aristotle, see Else, *Aristotle's Poetics: The Argument*, 414.

53. For a more detailed discussion of *ethos* and *daemon* in Attic tragedy, see Vernant, "Intimations of the Will in Greek Tragedy" in *Myth and Tragedy in Ancient Greece*, 82.

54. Brian Massumi, "Autonomy of Affect," *Cultural Critique*, no. 31 (September 1995): 93.

55. Fredric Jameson, *Antinomies of Realism* (New York: Verso, 2013), 47.

56. For a like-minded discussion of melancholy in *The Bronze Horseman*, see Kirill Ospovat, "Kumir na bronzovom kone: Barokko, chrezvychainoe polozhenie i estetika revoliutsii," *Novoe literaturnoe obozrenie* 149, no. 1 (2018): 49–73.

57. Ivan Turgenev, *On the Eve*, trans. Gilbert Gardiner (New York: Penguin Random House, 1950), 119; I. S. Turgenev, *Polnoe sobranie sochinenii i pisem*, 8:82.

58. Turgenev, *On the Eve*, 120; Turgenev, *Polnoe sobranie sochinenii*, 8:83.

59. Goncharov, *The Precipice*, 368; Goncharov *Polnoe sobranie sochinenii*, 7:667.

60. Leo Tolstoy, *War and Peace*, trans. Richard Pevear and Larissa Volokhonsky (New York: Vintage, 2011), 244–45; Lev Tolstoy, *Polnoe sobranie sochinenii*, 9:299.

61. Herzen, *Polnoe sobranie sochinenii*, 8:81–84; Herzen, *My Past and Thoughts*, 69–72.

62. Vasily Sleptsov, *Hard Times: A Novel of Liberals and Radicals in 1860s Russia*, trans. Michael Katz (Pittsburgh, PA: Pittsburgh University Press, 2016), 181.

63. Sleptsov, *Hard Times*, 168–69.

64. Benjamin, *The Origin of German Tragic Drama*, 65.

65. Benjamin, 70.

66. Benjamin, 65.

67. Benjamin, 139.

68. Franco Moretti, *Signs Taken for Wonders*, trans. Susan Fisher, David Forgacs, and David Miller (New York: Verso, 1988), 51.

69. Michel Foucault, *Society Must Be Defended: Lectures at the Collège de France 1975–1976*, ed. Mauro Bertani and Alessandro Fontana, trans. David Macey (New York: Picador, 1997), 176.

70. See Kirill Ospovat, *Terror and Pity: Aleksandr Sumarokov and the Theater of Power in Elizabethan Russia* (Boston: Academic Studies Press, 2016); Ospovat, "Kumir na bronzovom kone," 49–73.

71. Nikolai Gogol, *Polnoe sobranie sochinenii v 14i tomakh*, vol. 2, *Mirgorod*, ed. V. V. Gippius (Moscow: Izdatel'stvo akademii nauk, 1937), 276; Nikolai Gogol, *Diary of a Madman, The Government Inspector, and Selected Stories*, trans. Ronald Wilks (New York: Penguin Classics, 2006), 77.

72. Belinsky, *Polnoe sobranie sochinenii*, 3:444.

73. Benjamin, *The Origin of German Tragic Drama*, 136.

74. Lev Tolstoy, *Polnoe sobranie sochinenii*, 19:375; Tolstoy, *Anna Karenina*, 793.

75. Nikolai Strakhov, "Vzgliad na tekushchuiu literaturu" in Strakhov, *Literaturnaia kritika* (Moscow: Sovremennik, 1984), 403.

76. Jameson, *Antinomies of Realism*, 65.

77. Audrey Jaffe, "Affect and the Victorian Novel," in *The Palgrave Handbook of Affect Studies and Textual Criticism*, ed. Donald R. Wehrs and Thomas Blake (New York: Palgrave Macmillan, 2017), 717.

78. Étienne Balibar, *Citizen Subject: Foundations for Philosophical Anthropology*, trans. Steven Miller (New York: Fordham University Press, 2016), 33.

79. I have chosen to mark two intermediary points on the continuum, which would certainly yield itself to a still more detailed parsing as well.

80. See Sara Ahmed, *The Promise of Happiness* (Durham, NC: Duke University Press, 2010).

Epilogue

1. My definition of the state draws on Bob Jessop, *State Power: A Strategic Relational Approach* (Cambridge: Polity, 2008), 9.

2. Roberto Schwarz, *Misplaced Ideas: Essays on Brazilian Culture*, ed. John Geldson (London: Verso, 1992), 7.

3. Michael Hardt, "The Withering of Civil Society," *Social Text*, no. 45 (Winter 1995): 27–44.

4. Giorgio Agamben, *State of Exception*, trans. Kevin Attell (Chicago: University of Chicago Press, 2005), 87.

5. Eve Kosofsky Sedgwick, *Touching Feelings: Affect, Pedagogy, Performativity* (Durham, NC: Duke University Press, 2003), 140.

6. Nikos Poulantzas, *State, Power, Socialism*, trans. Patrick Camiller (London: Verso, 2014), 27.

7. The terms "paranoid" and "reparative" are Sedgwick's.

8. See Wendy Brown, *In the Ruins of Neoliberalism: The Rise of Antidemocratic Politics in the West* (New York: Columbia University Press, 2019).

Index

actuality: Belinsky vs. Hegel on, 5–6, 10–18, 76, 194; poetry of, 228; in *Rudin*, 90–91; Russian, 7, 128; in *Same Old Story*, 67; and state (Belinsky), 38, 76, 90. *See also* realism, Russian; realism, Western

affect. See *pathos*

Agamben, Giorgio: on sovereignty, 58–59, 75; on "bare life," 144; on paternal prerogative, 195–96

aggregation
— in civil society (Hegel et al.): of actualized right, 6, 19, 21, 23–24, 62, 136; of common interest, 6, 19–21, 24–27, 62 136; of "system of needs," 6, 20, 21, 136. *See also* civil society
— national, 147–148, 158, 162, 171, 185, 187
— social, 7, 12, 15, 18, 19–21, 28, 30, 34, 40, 46, 53, 55–56, 98, 99, 100, 104, 114, 145, 192, 198, 200, 207–208, 210, 229, 233, 236

Aksakov, Ivan, 41–42

Alexander I, Emperor, 55, 100, 150

Alexander II, Emperor, 42, 45, 49–50, 51, 55, 75, 150

allegory
— in Balzac, 99
— national, 146–88
— political: Chernyshevsky on, 109–10; in Dostoevsky, 172, 179–80; Herzen on, 134–35; in Pisemsky/Sand, 118–19; in Pushkin, 57–58, 108; in Sleptsov, 91–92; in Turgenev, 88, 110–14, 139, 172–74, 230
— of Russia, 174, 179–80, 181–87, 270n77

Althusser, Louis, 29–30

ambition, 22, 70–74, 86, 117, 130, 199, 256n40

Anderson, Benedict, 7–8, 146–48, 152, 158, 169, 173, 187

Annenkov, Pavel, 44–47, 74–76, 245n20, 251n135

Arendt, Hannah, 34

Aristotle, *Poetics*, on *anagnorisis* and *peripeteia*, 209–10

Armstrong, Nancy, 30, 40, 99, 192, 243n7

authority. *See* power

autocracy, 3, 9, 11, 35–50, 103, 111, 148–50, 176, 194, 220, 230, 251n134, 267n46

Avineri, Shlomo, 27

Bakhtin, Mikhail, 257n60, 269n61

Bakunin, Mikhail, as model for Turgenev, 90, 198

Balibar, Étienne, on "citizen subject," 233

Balzac, Honoré, *Père Goriot*, 21–22; authoritative father becomes "economic man" in, 99; happiness in, 136; mentorship in compared with Pisemsky's, 71; national imaginary in, 147; "system of needs" in, 6

bare life, 144, 162, 226, 234. *See also* Agamben, Giorgio
Battle of Borodino, 11, 12, 150–51, 165, 173. *See also* war
Belfiore, Elizabeth, on *philia* in Greek tragedy, 271n3
Belinsky, Vissarion: criticizes Herzen, 198–199; equates Peter I with Russian peasant, 165; fuses family and state, 190; on God transposed as czar/father, 101; and Hegel, 5–6, 10–12, 13–18, 101, 244n3, 245n14; on political life vs. melancholy, 228, 231; as prescient, 18, 194; reviews Lermontov novel, 86; on Russian state as charismatic locus, 38; on Russian state, substantive unity of, 54–56; on *Taras Bulba*, 16, 54, 228; "Woe from Wit," 228
Bell, The (Herzen and Ogarev), 50
Benjamin, Walter: on death as communal fate, 230; on kingship and tragic melancholy, 227
Bentham, Jeremy: on labor, 155; panopticon of, 31
Bible, Jacob wrestling with God, 220. *See also* myth
Bildung, 35, 52, 69–70
bildungsroman, 24–25, 61, 64–65, 67, 68, 81, 128, 147, 154, 181–82, 185, 187
binarism, of individuals to sovereign, 187
Braudel, Fernand, 9
Brontë, Charlotte, *Jane Eyre*, 22–24; "actualized right" in, 6, 21, 23, 24, 62, 147–48; equality in, 23, 147–48; father absent from, 99; happiness in, 136; patriarchal authority neutralized in, 99–100; portrayal of nation in, 147–48
Brooks, Peter, 21
Bryullov, Karl, *The Last Days of Pompeii* (painting), 134–35

Calderón de la Barca, Pedro, 143
Catherine II, Empress, 107, 121, 195, 203, 207
censorship, mid-19th-century Russian: and copyright, 47–48; czar's association with, 47, 48–49; "double," in Turgenev, 90; of *Bronze Horseman*, 216–18; and literature's influence, 48–49; of Pisemsky, 115; of resistance to power (Herzen), 134–35; in Sleptsov, 95, 223–24
Cherniavsky, Michael, 37
Chernyshevsky, Nikolai, 109–10, 113, 115, 222–23, 172–73
Chicherin, Boris, 41
civil society: in Belinsky, 13–14, 18, 245n14; in European novels (nineteenth century), 28–35, 99–100; Gramsci on, 27–28, 35; Hegel on, 6, 12–21, 55, 246n35n39; Marx on, 27; narratology of, 17–26; in Russia, 35–36, 39–46, 74, 249n99; and the state, 26–28, 32–34, 53, 55. *See also* aggregation; nation, the; state, the
Cohen, Margaret, 99, 107, 108, 115–16, 131
"common good," vis-a-vis Russian and Western absolutism, 36–37
Constant, Benjamin, 46
Corneille, Pierre, *Cinna* or *La Clémence d'Auguste*, magnanimity in, 204
coup d'état: in *One Thousand Souls*, 74–76; vs. peace and order (Foucault), 69–70, 72; and tragedy (Foucault), 193
courtship: in *The Idiot*, 176–77; "deformed" (Turgenev, Tolstoy), 91, 109, 113, 173; as national imaginary (Tolstoy), 173
czars. *See individual names*; autocracy; monarchy; sovereign/sovereignty; state, the

"deformation," 7, 81, 82; defined, 4–5, 53; *philial* emplotment and, 208–9; of private pursuits, 195; rhetorical (Pisemsky), 199; of realistic fiction, 18, 53, 181–82, 185; of social interactions, 187
Dickens, Charles, 33, 100
discipline, 7, 37, 43, 74, 232–34, 236; in *Crime and Punishment*, 168–69; Foucault on, 30–31, 56, 119, 125; in Miller,

D. A., 31–32, 63–64; in *Same Old Story*, 61–65, 115, 125–26, 159, 225, 228; in Sleptsov, 92; Zhivov on, 36

Dobroliubov, Nikolai: on Insarov, 139; on "literature of exposure," 75–76; on Stolz, 157; "What Is Oblomovitis?," 109

Dostoevsky, Fyodor: biography, 50; *Brothers Karamazov*, political theology in, 76–77, 78; *Crime and Punishment*, 79, 165–72, 201, 219, 233–34; *Demons*, 79–85, 165, 203–204; *Diary of a Writer*, on civil society, 42; *Diary of a Writer*, on peasant as basis of nation, 163–64; *The Idiot*, 176–81, 205, 270n77; *The Life of a Great Sinner*, 78

Druzhinin, Alexander
— *Polinka Saks*: compared with Sand, *Jacques*, 121–23; languishing in, 224–25; mania in, 219; sovereign mediation in, 119–23; violence vs. magnanimity in, 202–3
— review of Turgenev, *Rudin*, 90–91

Dumas, Alexandre *fils*, 142–43

Eikhenbaum, Boris, 86; on epigraph to *Anna Karenina*, 139, 142–43

Elias, Norbert, 66

Eliot, George, *Middlemarch*: aggregative connectedness in, 207–8; husband effaced in, 100

Engel'gardt, Nikolai, 47

equality: Arendt on, 34; in *Jane Eyre*, 23–24, 147–48

family: authority of converges with political, 101, 115–27; incest within, 124, 126; and state, 12–16, 21–22, 57–58, 97–145, 194; state-nation as collective imaginary (Goncharov), 181–87. *See also* patriarchalism; triangulation; women

fate: *anagnorisis* of, 218; "*fatum* of the ancients," 15, 17, 58, 76, 135, 205; Hegel vs. Belinsky on, 17, 18; of individual vs. divine power, 214; inscribed on ruler (Goncharov), 185; Lermontov on, 87–90; mysteries of (Pisemsky), 199; nation as hostile, 173–81; and rendezvous motif, 138; Russian official actualizing (Goncharov), 157; and sovereign, 205

fathers. *See* family; patriarchalism

Fedorov, Nikolai, 43

fiction. *See* fiction, realist; novel, realist; novel, the

fiction, realist, 2, 5, 6, 18–19, 33–34, 63–64, 195, 263n56
— and civil society, 20–53
— Russian: of collectivity/substantive community, 53 and passim; scenarios of power in, 201–4; nation in, 146–88; *pathos* and sovereignty effect in, 233–34; state-culture knot, 47–53
— Western European vs. Russian: on affect and socialization, 232–33; on courtship, 109; on happiness, 135–37; on nationality, 147–48; on *pathos*, 234; on patriarchalism, 105

See also individual author names; family; novel, realist; state, the

Filmer, Robert, 97

Flaubert, Gustave, 99

force. *See* coup d'état; power; violence; war

Foucault, Michel: on breaking down of sovereign, 227; on "governmental reason," 69, 122; on necessary limitations of government, 122; on raison d'état, 68–70, 193; on sovereign power and "discipline," 31, 119, 125, 127; on tragedy of politics, 193

freedom. *See* individuation

French Revolution: and effacement of father, 98, 99; sentimentalism/paranoia of, 131–32

Frye, Northrop, 198

Gallagher, Catherine, 30, 247n44

Geertz, Clifford, 38

Girard, René, 114–15

Glinka, Fyodor, *Sketches*, Belinsky on, 54–56

Glinka, Mikhail, *A Life for the Czar*, 102

280 Index

Goethe, Johann Wolfgang von
— on happiness, 136
— *Wahlverwandtschaften*, paternalism in, 99, 133–34
— *Wilhelm Meisters Lehrjahre*, 24–26: "common interest" in, 6: effacement of father in, 99: happiness in, 136: mentorship in, 62: national community in, 148
Gogol, Nikolai: *An Author's Confession*, 50–51; *Government Inspector*, 59–60, 73, 76, 79, 81, 200, 201; on literature as service to state and God, 51; political "finalization" in, 87; *Selected Passages from a Correspondence*, on conflation of commoner with czar, 171; *Selected Passages from a Correspondence*, on state-family parallelism and self-sacrifice, 101–2, 103; "Tale of How Ivan Ivanovich Quarreled with Ivan Nikiforovich," 228; *Taras Bulba*, 16, 54, 57, 61, 209, 228
Goldhill, Simon, 271n2
Goldmann, Lucien, 247n44
Goncharov, Ivan: as censor, 48; *Oblomov*, 153, 62, 182, 205, 222; *The Precipice*, 181–87, 199–200, 202, 208–9, 212, 218–19; *The Same Old Story*, 61–69, 81, 116, 125–26, 201, 225, 228
Goodlad, Lauren, 32–33
government. *See* state, the
Gramsci, Antonio, 27–28, 35

Habermas, Jürgen, 18
happiness: as command, 123; domestic, 57, 70, 95, 133, 186, 195, 208; in European realist fiction, 136; in *Anna Karenina*, 231–32; "promise of," 126; in *On the Eve*, 136–39; sacrifice of, 107, 121–22
Hegel, G. W. F.: and Belinsky, 5–6, 10–11, 13–15, 17–18, 53, 55, 101, 190, 231, 244–45n3; Chicherin draws on, 41; on civil society and sociotopes, 12–13, 18–22; Gramsci critiques, 27–28; on Greek tragic hero, 272n10; levels of aggregation in society, 19–20, 22–27, 136; Marx critiques, 26–27; *Phenomenology of Spirit*, 14; *Philosophy of Right*, 12–13, 18–21, 26–27; on reconciliation in civil society, 14–15; on Sophocles, *Antigone*, 14, 15, 68, 190; on war, 11–12, 55
hegemony: bourgeoisie and (Gramsci), 27–29; vs. dominance post emancipation, 92–94; dominance without, 35–53; and power, in European novel, 100. *See also* state, the
Herzen, Alexander
— on civil society as "invisible state," 43–44
— on end of serfdom, 51
— gentry-state relations in, 51–52
— on *The Last Day of Pompeii*, 134–35
— *My Past and Thoughts*: hubris in, 212–13; mania in, 219–21; *Don Karlos* in, 51–52
— *Who Is to Blame?*: hero's elevation in, 198; melancholy *pathos* in, 229; as "modern tragedy," 198–99; occulting in, 206–7; political community as substantive refuge in, 127–33; *Wahlverwandtschaften* in, 134
Hobbes, Thomas, 22, 40, 74
Homo oeconomicus, 25, 31, 57, 71, 73, 99; mentor figure as (Goncharov), 153–62
Homo politicus, 57, 72, 129, 135
Hunt, Lynn, 98

individuation: as catastrophic, 54–57, 127, 131–33, 144–46; and deindividuation 152, 219; dramas of, 104, 146, 185–87; and familial authority, 124–27, 144–46, 185; *pathos* and, 216; practices of, 36; and sovereign power, 180; and state as substantive community, 54–61, 185, 188; and substantive belonging, 138; and tragedy, 190–91, 196, 213; types of, 46. *See also* substance
"intense association," 56, 57, 59, 98, 104, 131, 133, 146, 180, 186, 188, 190, 209. *See also* substance
interregnum, crisis of (Belinsky, Schmitt), 55–56. *See also* state, the
Ivan IV, Emperor, rule as negative precedent, 42, 149

Ivan VI, Emperor, in Dostoevsky, *The Idiot*, 79

Jaffe, Audrey, on class and affect in Victorian novel, 232–33
Jakobson, Roman, "The Statue in Pushkin's Mythology," 105–6
Jameson, Fredric, 247n50; on "chromaticism" of affect, 215–16; on realist novel and hegemony, 29; on subjective centeredness, 30; on Western realism and affect, 232
Jones, Gareth, on writers and czars, 49

Kantorowicz, Ernst, 195
Karakozov, Dmitry, 150
Kharkhordin, Oleg, on autocracy and common good in Russia, 37
kingship. *See* autocracy; monarchy; sovereign/sovereignty
Komissarov, Osip, 150
Kostomarov, Nikolai: critiques the Susanin myth, 150; on nation vs. state, 149–50; *The Son*, father/sovereign vs. patricide/rebellion in, 103–4
Kotsonis, Yanni, 37
Küchelbecker, Wilhelm, on Pushkin, 108

Last Days of Pompeii, The (Bryullov painting), and sovereign power, 134–35
law: citizen/subject and, 233–34; and discipline (Sleptsov), 92–93; in Hegel, 13–14, 19–20; human vs. divine in *Antigone*, 14, 233; and lawgiver (*Crime and Punishment*), 166–68; and sovereignty, 37–38, 49, 56, 58–60, 69, 74–75, 84, 166–68; and violence, 58–59, 75, 87, 93, 144, 193, 195, 199; universality of (*Père Goriot, Jane Eyre*), 22–24
Lermontov, *A Hero of Our Time*, 85–88
Lindenmeyr, Adele, 249–50n99
Locke, John, 97–98
Lotman, Lidiya, 255n32
Louis Napoleon, 213
love: and government of women, 115–127; and politics, 101–2, 129, 130, 131, 133, 137–38, 140–43, 159, 222–23, 229; and sovereign mediation, 105–15. *See also* happiness
Lukács, György, 21, 247n44, 272n10
Lunin, Mikhail, 80, 83

Maiorova, Olga, 149, 150, 257–58n60
Malia, Martin, 130
marriage: in *Demons*, 82–83; in European fiction, 147–48; in *The Idiot*, 177–79; in *Jane Eyre*, 23; in *Oblomov*, 160–61; in *Père Goriot*, 21–22, 71; sovereign mediation on, 107, 121; in *Who Is to Blame?*, 128, 132, 134
Marx, Karl: *Critique of Hegel's Philosophy of Right*, 26–27; "On the Jewish Question," 27
matriarchy, in Goncharov, *The Precipice*, 181–87. *See also* patriarchalism; women
mediation
— authoritative, 184–87
— in European vs. Russian fiction, 44–45, 53
— sovereign/paternal, 100–105; displacement scenario, 133–44; by government, 115–27; interdiction scenario, 105–115; refuge scenario, 127–33
See also triangulation
Mel'gunov, Nikolai, 48
mentorship: disciplinary and biopolitical, 158–59; in European realist novels, 61–62; in *Oblomov*, 153–62; in *One Thousand Souls* and *Père Goriot*, 70–71; patriarchal, 62–4, 67–8, 69, 119–121; in *Who Is to Blame?*, 128–29
miasma, tragic, 211–14, 274n41. *See also* tragedy
Miliukov, Alexander, 157
Miller, D. A., 31–32, 63–64, 126
monarchy: Belinsky vs. Hegel on, 11; and elite interdependence, 47, 52, 104; powers of in imperial Russia, 37–38. *See also individual names*; autocracy; sovereign/sovereignty; state, the
Moretti, Franco, 28, 193, 227, 247n44
Most, Glen, 191–92
Muromets, Ilya, 165

282 Index

myth: civilizational, 57, 175; of czar-redeemer, 170, 171; national, 150; of paternal authority, 98–99; Petrine, 50, 63, 171; of state, 38, 77, 102; statuary (Pushkin), 105–6. *See also* realism, Russian; statues

Nabokov, Vladimir, on Pushkin, 108
Napoleon Bonaparte, in Dostoevsky, 79, 173, 268n59
nation, the
— in Aksakov, 41
— allegorized in fiction, 146–88
— in Chicherin, 42
— distinguished from state, 149–51
— embedding in realist narrative, 152–87; amalgam between sovereign and people, 162–72; under power of spellbinding women, 172–81; reenactment scenario, 181–87; mobilization scenario, 153–62
— as hostile fate, 173–81
— individuation and, 186–87
— in Kostomarov, 103
— personal development parallels growth of, 147
— providential state control and (*Oblomov*), 153–62
— sacrifice and, 150–52, 163
— sovereign embodies, 148–49, 165
— "spell" allegory and, 172–81
— transgressive reenactment and (Goncharov), 181–87
— work as service to (Goncharov), 155–57
See also sovereign/sovereignty; state, the; substance

Naturgewalt, 134, 138–39, 194, 207. *See also* power; violence
Nicholas I, Emperor, 8, 55, 63, 65, 103, 105, 149, 220; censors Pushkin, 216; surprise visit to Moscow, 148–49; triadic doctrine of, 148, 152
Nietzsche, Friedrich, on tragic individuation, 191
novel, realist
— "administrative" (Russian), 44–45
— Belinsky vs. Hegel on, 17

— and bourgeois hegemony (Jameson), 29
— British, and governmentality, 32–33
— and civil society (Moretti), 28
— French sentimental (Sand), Russians "rewrite," 107–8, 115–27
— and Hegel's civil society aggregates, 22–26
— and the police (Miller), 31–32
— as social art form (Arendt), 34
— socio-historical effects of, 29–30
— Western European: accommodations in, compared with Pisemsky's, 71; on affect/socialization, 232–33; on human needs vs. society's demands, 44–45; modeling of nation in, 147–48
See also individual authors; fiction, realist
novel, the: British et al., eighteenth century, on autonomy of intimate relations, 98; British/French, patriarchy in, 97–100; desire/triangulation/mediation in modern (Girard), 114–15; individual within, 29–30; novel within (*The Precipice*), 185. *See also* fiction, realist; novel, realist

Ogarev, Nikolai, 51
opera, 54–56
Ospovat, Kirill, 228
Ostrovsky, Aleksandr, 124
Otrep'ev, Grigoriy, in Dostoevsky, 80

pathos: as affect, 215–18; and belonging, 233; deadlock as aspect of, 221–24, 234; defined, 214, 233; and discipline, 232–34; languishing as aspect of, 224–27, 234; mania as aspect of, 218–21, 234; melancholy as aspect of, 227–32, 234; in Pushkin, from manic to melancholic, 216–18; in Pushkin, from melancholic to manic, 215–16; and sovereignty, 234. *See also* substance
patriarchalism, 57, 97–100, 101, 103–4, 105–15, 113–15, 136–37, 141. *See also* family; power; sovereign/sovereignty; triangulation; women
"peasant question" (Tolstoy), 230–31
peasants: attempt to discipline

(Sleptsov), 91–94, 120; conflated with Peter I, 164–65, 171; Vlas (Dostoevsky), 163–64; substitutes for member of intelligentsia (Dostoevsky), 163, 169–70, 172. *See also under* Turgenev, Ivan

peripeteia, in Russian realist fiction, 209–12. *See also* tragedy

Peter I: Belinsky on, 13–15; conflated with Russian peasant, 164–65, 171; in Dostoevsky, 78–80, 164, 167, 169; and law/violence (Pushkin), 58–59; Annenkov on Kalinovich as, 75; Pushkin on, 205; Russian state under, 35, 42, 57, 95; and Schism (Dostoevsky), 169; statue of, as Bronze Horseman, 58, 59, 61, 65, 70, 112, 217. *See also* autocracy; monarchy; sovereign/sovereignty

Peter III (impostor), 106, 107, 195

Peterson, Nikolai, 42–43

philia, 189–191, 194, 208–212, 215, 271n2. *See also* substance

Phillip II, Emperor, 220–221

Pisarev, Dmitry, 158

Pisemsky, Alexey: *Boyarshchina*, 116–19, 201, 226; *One Thousand Souls*, 44, 70–76, 157, 199–200, 210, 255–56n40

poetics: "historical," 272–73n15; realist, individuation and state of exception within (Schmitt), 57–61, 87

Pogodin, Mikhail, 150

political theology: Belinsky and, 101; in Dostoevsky, 76–84; in Gogol, 77–78; in Goncharov, 78; in Herzen, 220–21; in Pisemsky, 78; in Pushkin, 77; in Schmitt, 81, 156; in Turgenev, 115

politics/political. *See* nation, the; power; sovereign/sovereignty; state, the

Poovey, Mary, 30, 247n44

Potemkin, Grigoriy, 207

power: and domestic fiction, 115–27; magnanimous, 200–205; in nineteenth-century British/French/German fiction, 64, 99–100; personal and political conflated (Lermontov), 86–88; political, intrudes onto romance, 105–9; private vs. spectacular, 205–7; "scenarios of," 201–4; self-mastery as, 84–85, 204; sovereign, disciplinary and biopolitical, defined (Foucault), 31; sovereign's (*see* power, sovereign's); as threat (Attic tragedy), 192; as transcendent, 204–5; unlimited, 84–85, 88, 134–35, 192, 200–201. *See also* autocracy; monarchy; patriarchalism; sovereign/sovereignty; state, the; violence; war

power, sovereign's, 7–8; and bare life (Agamben), 144; benevolent/laissez-faire, 119–24; disciplinary power and, 169; as force of nature, 134–35, 138; invisible, 205–7; languishing and, 225–27; and national belonging, 7–8, 56, 95, 146; during "states of exception," 56–85; as transformative, 195–96; undermined, 97–98; victimizes women, 115–27; as violent, 56–57, 134–35; during war, 54–55

providence: as government/sovereign, 59, 149, 153, 155; husbands as, 122, 161; as market, 19, 236; in modern novel (Hegel), 17; in *Oblomov*, 153, 155, 160–61; as society, 33, 35, 62; vs. fate (Hegel), 17; in *Wilhelm Meisters Lehrjahre*, 25

Pugachev, Emelian (Peter III), 106–7

Pushkin, Alexander

— Belinsky on, 15–16

— biography, 50

— *The Bronze Horseman* ("Petersburg Tale"); Jakobson on, 105–6; *pathos* in, 214–18; order vs. force in, 69–70, 195; political vs. private in, 57–59, 65; revisions of, 216–18; "scenario of power" in, 201; "zone of sovereignty" in, 195. *See also* Peter I; statues

— *The Captain's Daughter*, 106–7; "zone of sovereignty" in, 195

— *Eugene Onegin*: deadlock in, 221; hero's elevation in, 197–98, 200; triangulation in, 107–8, 197–98

— *The Golden Cockerel*, Jakobson on, 105–6

— *The Stone Guest*, Jakobson on, 105–6

284 Index

Racine, Jean, 227
Raeff, Marc, 35
Razin, Stepan, "in" Dostoevsky, 78, 80
realism, defined, 1–2. *See also* realism, Russian; realism, Western
realism, Russian, 4, 6–8, 10–53, 245–46n20
— compared with French sentimental novel (Sand), 107–8, 115–27
— compared with Western counterpart, 79, 100, 105, 232–34
— "deformed" by political theology (*Demons*), 81–82, 187
— early psychological (Lermontov), 88
— individuation within "state of exception," 56–57
— as lens on the present, 236–37
— melancholy widespread in, 228–32
— origin of, 10
— critical vs. "utopian" aspects in, 237
— on patriarchal/political power, 100–145, 193–94
— perspectives on human togetherness in, 194–234
— "reality effects" in, 85–96
— "sovereignty effects": "occulting" in, 204–7; *pathos* and, 233; "rhetorical heightening" in, 196–200; "scenarios of power" in, 200–204
— tragic elements of, 194–234; *ethos*, 195–207; *mythos*, 207–213; *pathos*, 214–18
See also individual authors; actuality; fiction, realist; novel, realist; power; tragedy
realism, Western: compared with Russian counterpart, 53, 79, 105, 232–34; Foucault and, 30–31; individualism within, 56; "tragic realism," 192, 272n9, 272n10
reason: in civil society (Hegel), 18–19; governmental (Foucault), 122; of state (Foucault), 69, 95, 205; state-civilizing and sacred (*Same Old Story*), 61–62, 67, 69, 78
Reddy, William, on sentimentalist political ethos, 131–32, 141–42

religion. *See* myth; political theology; salvation
rendezvous, as motif in Russian realism, 109–15, 138, 158–60, 172, 222–24. *See also* Chernyshevsky, Nikolai
Richardson, Samuel, 98
Romanov, Mikhail Fyodorvich, 102
Rousseau, Jean-Jacques: *Julie, ou La Nouvelle Héloïse*, "good" father in, 98; *Social Contract*, 233
Russia. *See* state, Russian
Russian realism. *See* realism, Russian

Saint-Pierre, Bernardin de, 98, 101
Saltykov-Shchedrin, Mikhail, 157
salvation: and discipline in West vs. Russia, 36; monarch and, 38, 40; and state, 69, 77. *See also* mythology; political theology
Sand, George: and familial authority, 116; Herzen draws on, 129, 130; *Indiana*, 117–19, 122, 124; *Jacques*, 121–24, 126, 129, 262n49
Schiller, Friedrich, 51–52
Schmitt, Carl, 56, 58, 75, 81, 144, 156
Schopenhauer, Arthur, 143–44
Schwarz, Roberto, 236
Sedgwick, Eve, 236, 262n38
sentimentality, in fiction, 107–108, 115, 117, 118, 123–27, 129–34, 139, 141–43, 197–98, 225–26, 229
Seton-Watson, Hugh, on "official nationality," 148
Severnaia pchela, on Nicholas I's visit to Moscow, 148–49
Shakespeare, William: *Hamlet* quoted in Turgenev, 111; Henriad "in" Dostoevsky, 80, 84; *Othello* in Herzen, 225; tragedies compared with modern counterparts, 133
Shevyrev, Stepan, 86
Sleptsov, Vasily, *Hard Times*, 91–95, 223–24
social imaginary: and civil society, 14, 100, 97–98; cultural production in Russia in the age of realism and, 3–4, 6, 51–53, 91; defined, 1; in Belinsky vs.

Hegel, 15, 18, 208; in Foucault, 30–31, 122; in Hegel, 18–21, 22; individual in, 21, 57, 97–98, 145, 152, 161, 187, 192, 233–34, 243n7; *philia* as, 199, 200, 208, 213; and sociotopes, 18–26; and state, 8, 9, 53, 56, 66, 235; substantive, 8, 12, 14, 18, 53, 60, 91, 104, 131, 133, 145, 161, 181, 182, 187, 209; tragic, 14, 15, 132, 182, 194, 200; Victorian, 32–33, 172

Soloviev, Sergei, 150

Sophocles, *Antigone*: Hegel on, 14, 15; *polis* conflated with *philia* in, 189–90; subjectivity in, 207; theme in Goncharov, 67–68

sovereign/sovereignty: ambiguity in, 74; Belinsky vs. Hegel on, 11–12; benevolent/revered, 201–4; charisma of, 38, 40, 52, 74, 78, 80, 82, 150–52, 163, 171, 184, 188, 193; conflated with father (Gogol et al.), 19, 57, 101–4; as convergence of law and violence, 40, 58–59; as convergence of spiritual and secular, 80–81 (*see also* political theology); and creature, 233–34; and crime, 168–69; death of (Belinsky on), 55–56; and deindividuation, 150–52, 163; "election" and, 81; elevation into as lethal (tragic), 196–200; and exception (Schmitt), 81–82 (*see also* state[s] of exception); father/spouse as, 57, 111–14, 116–19, 121–23; father/spouse as, abstractly, 127–33; in Greek tragedy (Most), 191–93; and God/czar/father continuum, 63, 101–2, 113–14; as God figure, 37–38, 59, 101–2; and "Homo sacer," 144; as impostor (Gogol), 59–60; and interdiction, 105–115, 184; and melancholy, 227–2; and nation, 148–49, 162–72; *pathos* within, 234; power (*see* power, sovereign's); vs. private individual(s), 56–61, 70, 81–82, 95–96, 102–3, 104–9, 192–93, 198, 234 (*see also* individuation; state, the); as (pretender)-ruler-redeemer (Dostoevsky), 81–85; "surplus," 64, 69–70, 72, 74, 144–45; and triangulation, 105–27; in tragedy vs. novel, 192–93; and women/mediation, 115–27; "zone of," 195–96, 200–201, 208. *See also individual rulers*; family; patriarchalism; political theology; power; state, the; substance

state, Russian: authority of, in fiction, 6–7; and individual (Goncharov, Pisemsky, et al.), 7, 64–68, 69, 70, 74, 87, 90, 91, 95 (*see also* individuation); made visible, 85, 95, 133, 144, 193, 233, 234, 235–37; providential control by, 59, 149, 153–62; and realist hermeneutic, 4; represented as invisible, 110, 125, 135, 179, 205; sovereign's position in, 37–42, 54–55, 69–70 (*see also* sovereign/sovereignty); "well-regulated" 66–67, 68, 101, 125, 161; vs. Western, 35–36, 37, 235–36

state, the: Belinsky vs. Hegel on, 11–12; career in, stymied (*Who Is to Blame?*), 128–29; as charismatic locus, 38–44; civil society and, 26–28, 32–34, 53; contagion with culture, 38; control over literature, 47–50 (*see also* censorship); cultural production as service to, 50–51; "dominance without hegemony," 44; family and, 12–16, 21–22, 57–58, 97–145, 190; as "*fatum* of the ancients," 76, 135, 205; "integral" (Gramsci), 28; male gentry and, 3–4; modernity and (*Same Old Story*), 62, 69; and nation, 149–52; novel vs. tragedy and, 193; Russian (*see* state, Russian); Russian realism and, 4, 6–8; as seat of ambivalence, 3–4; "tragic harshness of" (Foucault), 193; and war, 11–12, 54–56. *See also* autocracy; civil society; monarchy; nation, the; sovereign/sovereignty; substance; war

state(s) of exception: conflates private and political, 60–61, 87, 104, 114, 189–90; defined (Schmitt), 56–57; intimate encounters within, 105–6; and lawlessness, 59–61; in mania, 218; in Pushkin, 57–59; sovereign's absence as, 102–3; sovereign power vs. individualism within, 57–61, 81–82, 95–96,

state(s) of exception (*continued*)
102–3, 104, 114, 144–45, 190, 195–96, 236–37

statues: of Peter I, 58, 59, 61, 65, 70, 112, 201, 216; as sovereign authority, 105–6, 112–13, 184–85, 216

Steinlight, Emily, 33

Strakhov, Nikolai, 232

substance
— in Belinsky, 14–17, 38, 54, 55, 190, 208, 228
— and belonging 14, 146, 152, 235; affect of, 214–16, 222; contradictions of, 200; defined, 8; as element of "reality effect," 95; in family (*On the Eve*), 138; in Gogol, 16, 60; melancholy, 228, 232; *peripeteia* of, 209; tableaux of, 226; as Russian realist motif, 52
— as charismatic center, 38, 171
— and family, 21, 22, 71, 101, 129, 137, 143, 184, 226
— and individuation, 46, 59, 60, 65, 77, 107, 224, 233–34; catastrophic, 127; dramatic scenarios of, 104, 146, 126–27, 131–33, 164, 186–87, 190–91; against familial authority, 123–24, 138, 143, 185; in mania, 218–20; paradoxes of, 213; *pathos* of, 216; as self-sacrifice, 150–52; in "state of exception," 54–57, 145; and symbolic center, 188; tragic, 131–33, 190–91, 196
— in Hegel, 12, 14, 17, 190, 208
— and nation, 146, 150–152, 156, 161–65, 170–71, 173–75, 181, 184, 188
— and *philia*, 190, 205, 208, 216
— and *pathos*, 214–234
— and "simplification" (Annenkov), 47, 55, 65, 210
— and sovereignty, 40, 70, 84, 104, 150, 152, 187, 205, 219
— and state, 15, 21, 22, 46, 50, 53, 55, 68, 95, 101, 129, 143
— and tragedy, 17, 182, 189–234

Susanin, Ivan, life sacrificed for czar, 150

Tanner, Tony, 98–99
Tennenhouse, Leonard, 192

Todd, William, III, 49–50

Tolstoy, Lev: *Anna Karenina*, 139–144, 226, 230–32; *War and Peace*, 150–52, 163, 164, 173, 219

tragedy: *Ajax*, 216; *Antigone*, 14, 15, 189–90, 207; *Anthony and Cleopatra*, 111–12, 261n35; bloodless modern, 133; chorus in, 214; *Cinna*, 204; in Goncharov, 67–68; hubris, 139, 212–13, 222; individual as threat within, 190–91; Jacobean, and Shakespeare, 192; miasma in Greek, 211–12; in narrative fiction (Belinsky), 15–17; *Oedipus*, 110, 209, 214, 216; Pentheus, 216; *peripeteia* in, 209–11; politics of (Moretti), 193; prose/novel and, 196–200; sovereignty and, 8, 189–94; *fatum*, 59, 76, 135, 157, 193–94, 205; and violence (Foucault), 193; Williams on action within, 200

"tragic realism," 192. *See also* tragedy

triangulation: in *Anna Karenina*, 139–140; in Chernyshevsky's rendezvous scenario, 110; and desire in the novel (Girard), 114–15; and homosociality (Sedgwick), 262n38; governmental in the family, 110–13, 116–44; in *Eugene Onegin*, 197; national, 175–81, 187; in *Oblomov*, 158, 161; Oedipal in *First Love*, 110–13; sovereign, 104–110, 113–15, 119, 121, 124, 126, 133, 135, 138, 139, 144–45, 194–95, 197; in *Spring Torrents*, 175; in *The Idiot*, 179–80; in *The Precipice*, 181, 186; in *Who Is to Blame?*, 132, 263–64n63

Turgenev, Ivan: *Asya*, 109; *On the Eve*, 135–9, 206, 218–19; *First Love*, 110–14, 160, 205–6, 212, 229–30; *Mumu* and censorship, 48; *Punin and Baburin*, 51; *Rudin*, 88–91, 198, 200, 221–22; serfdom in, 51, 175, 211; *A Sportsman's Sketches*, on Peter I, 165; *Spring Torrents*, 173–76, 201, 210–11

Tynianov, Yuri, 243–44n8; on "deformation," 4

Ukraine, war in, 235
Uvarov, Sergey, 148

Vernant, Jean-Pierre, 191, 211–12
violence: in absolutist state, 66, 69–70 (coup d'état); and domestic relations (Gogol, Sand, et al.), 16, 115–27; forms of "modern" (Elias), 66–67; and law in sovereignty, 59, 74–75, 193, 195; and mania, 218–24; and miasma, 213; vs. self-mastery (Dostoevsky), 83–84; sovereign's, 56–57; sovereign's, over women, 224–27; sovereign's, surplus of, 144–45. *See also* patriarchalism; power; state(s) of exception; war
Vogl, Joseph, 27

war: Belinsky vs. Hegel on, 11–12, 55; consolidation triggered by (Belinsky et al.), 54–55, 146, 232; in Gogol's *Taras Bulba* (Belinsky), 54; independence and, 150; individuation and, 54–55, 151–52, 231–32. *See also* nation, the; patriarchalism; power; state, the; state(s) of exception; violence
Watt, Ian, on family ties vs. freedom in Richardson/Defoe, 98
Weber, Max: on Protestant ethic, 155; types of authority, 183, 184
Williams, Raymond, on tragic action, 200
work/labor, as recoding of Protestant ethic (Goncharov), 155–56
Wortman, Richard, 201

Zhivov, Viktor: on monarch as God figure in imperial Russia, 37–38; on salvation vs. discipline in Petrine Russia, 36
Zhukovsky, Vasily: Belinsky on, 11; revision of Pushkin, 216–18; on autocracy vs. the people, 39, 41; on "dominance without hegemony," 40–41
Zola, Émile, 232

www.ingramcontent.com/pod-product-compliance
Lightning Source LLC
Chambersburg PA
CBHW022040290426
44109CB00014B/920